1000 RECIPES
FOR SIMPLE FAMILY FOOD

1000 RECIPES
FOR SIMPLE FAMILY FOOD

FIREFLY BOOKS

A FIREFLY BOOK

Published by Firefly Books Ltd. 2010

First printing

Publisher Cataloging-in-Publication Data (U.S.)
1000 recipes for simple family food / Eleanor Maxfield, editor.
[400] p. : col. photos. ; cm.
Includes index.
ISBN-13: 978-1-55407-733-5
ISBN-10: 1-55407-733-8
1. Cookery. I. Maxfield, Eleanor. II. One thousand recipes for simple family food. III. Title.
641.5 dc22   TX715.O54 2010

Library and Archives Canada Cataloguing in Publication
1000 recipes for simple family food.
Includes index.
ISBN-13: 978-1-55407-733-5
ISBN-10: 1-55407-733-8
1. Cookery. I. Title: One thousand recipes for simple family food.
TX714.O545 2010   641.5   C2010-901563-0

Published in the United States by
Firefly Books (U.S.) Inc.
P.O. Box 1338, Ellicott Station
Buffalo, New York 14205

Published in Canada by
Firefly Books Ltd.
66 Leek Crescent
Richmond Hill, Ontario L4B 1H1

Printed in China

PLEASE NOTE:
Both metric and imperial measurements have been given in all recipes. Use one set of measurements only, and not a mixture of both.

Standard level spoon measurements are used in all recipes.
1 tablespoon = one 15 ml spoon
1 teaspoon = one 5 ml spoon

Ovens should be preheated to the specified temperature.
If using a fan-assisted oven, follow the manufacturer's instructions for adjusting the time and temperature.

Fresh herbs should be used unless otherwise stated.

Eggs should be medium unless otherwise stated; choose free-range if possible and preferably organic. The Department of Health advises that eggs should not be consumed raw. This book contains some dishes made with raw or lightly cooked eggs. It is prudent for more vulnerable people, such as pregnant and nursing mothers, invalids, the elderly, babies and young children, to avoid uncooked or lightly cooked dishes made with eggs.

This book includes dishes made with nuts and nut derivatives. It is advisable for those with known allergic reactions to nuts and nut derivatives and those who may be potentially vulnerable to these allergies, such as pregnant and nursing mothers, invalids, the elderly, babies and children, to avoid dishes made with nuts and nut oils. It is also prudent to check the labels of pre-prepared ingredients for the possible inclusion of nut derivatives.

CONTENTS

INTRODUCTION

With today's hectic lifestyles, it is easy to see how family mealtimes are often forced to fit around many competing activities and our diets may not always be as nutritious as they could be. Time is often in such short supply that we barely have time to sit down to eat our meals, never mind plan, shop and cook them properly. Most of us would love to reduce the amount of stress in our lives, and this book aims not only to help make mealtimes more interesting and healthier, but also to get the whole family involved. With 1,000 recipes to choose from, you'll be able to create a variety of simple, nutritious meals whatever the occasion. Chapters are color-coded so it's easy to find the right recipe for any occasion. There are snacks for breakfasts, brunches and light dishes, a chapter on budget eats that won't break the bank, classic family favorites that are foolproof crowdpleasers, one-pot meals for a fuss-free life in the kitchen, quick meals that can be prepared and cooked in 30 minutes, inspiring vegetarian dishes, and sweets, desserts, cakes and bakes galore.

Thinking ahead

It's never been easier to shop for and prepare great food. Fresh herbs, high-quality ingredients and a good combination of flavors and textures mean that easy cooking does not mean boring eating. For example, a fantastic olive oil or organic wild salmon fillet can make the difference between a dish that is merely acceptable and one that tastes wonderful.

If you know you have a busy week ahead, try to find the time to sit down the week before to plan your meals and write a shopping list. The majority of the recipes in this book serve four as a main course, but many of the salads, soups and vegetarian options would also make great starters and will comfortably feed up to eight people. If you are cooking for two people, simply halve the quantities. If you are serving a dessert, choose one that will cook while you are eating your first course or something that can be made in advance, such as a sorbet. Using the recipes as a base, feel free to alter the quantities or experiment with the choice of ingredients.

Cooking should be fun, so make sure you follow your instincts and cook to fit your mood.

Pantry essentials

There are certain basics that you will always need; these include staple carbohydrates such as rice and pasta (ideally the brown varieties), couscous, noodles and rolled oats. You may not always have fresh meat, but keep a bag of cashew nuts and cans of tuna, salmon and beans in the cupboard, some eggs in the fridge and a supply of frozen shrimp in the freezer, and you'll have everything you need to create a nutritious, protein-rich dinner in a matter of minutes. To add flavor and to help the cooking process, ensure you have chicken and vegetable stock and soy sauce in the cupboard, along with olive, sesame and canola oils, salt and pepper, tomato and sun-dried tomato paste, and key herbs and spices such as mixed herbs, pumpkin pie spice, Chinese five-spice, ground cinnamon, coriander, cumin and nutmeg and hot pepper sauce or flakes.

Other ingredients that will enable you to whip up tasty sauces include flour, cornstarch, canned tomatoes, tomato sauce, olives, mature Cheddar and a dried milk powder. And for last-minute desserts, keep sugar, honey, maple syrup, a couple of cans of tinned fruit and some graham wafers in the cupboard, plus some vanilla ice cream, fruit sorbet and waffles in the freezer. Cartons of crème fraîche and plain yogurt never go amiss in the fridge for both savory and sweet dishes, but as these ingredients have a short shelf life, ideally they should be bought as part of your meal-planning process.

Don't feel guilty about making life a little easier for yourself by using ready-made items, so stock up on jars of pesto and tapenades, cooked rice, lentils and beans and deli-style roast vegetables. Look out too for jars of ready-minced garlic and ginger (widely available in supermarkets), which mean that you can add these wonderful flavors without having to spend time peeling, crushing and grating. Don't forget that you can also buy pre-cut strips of meat, such as beef or pork, which are perfect for stir-fries. Frozen pastry is essential for anyone wanting to cook easy pies or tarts: just remember to take it out of the freezer in good time to thaw before you start cooking.

Family food that's good food

Whether young or old, vegetarian or omnivore, we all need to get sufficient nutrients from our food intake to provide our bodies with energy and help to promote long-term good health. To get the complete range of nutrients our bodies need, we should be consuming carbohydrates, protein, fats, fiber and water, as well as a variety of vitamins and minerals. These nutrients not only fuel our bodies, but many of them actually help to improve our health and protect the body against disease. If we eat well, we feel well, our mood is improved and we cope better with stress, which can only be a good thing for anyone leading a busy life!

The secret is to mix up the recipes so that your family is eating as wide a variety of foods as possible – that way, they will get all the benefits of improved nutrition. You may not always be able to please the whole family in one sitting, but at least if you vary the recipes, everyone will have at least one meal a week that they really love and you will not find yourself in a "meal rut" where you eat the same foods day after day.

You will see throughout the book that recipes center on a range of carbohydrate-based meals. Although carbs have had a bad press in recent years, good carbohydrates (otherwise known as complex carbohydrates) are vital to our health and should form the basis of every healthy diet. Complex carbohydrates include grains, bread, rice and pasta, as well as fruits and vegetables, legumes and dairy products.

Choose brown versions of pasta, bread and rice where possible as these have not had all the nutrients processed out of them and retain their fiber content. Fiber is found only in plant-based foods and plays an important role in keeping our bodies healthy – firstly because fiber keeps the gut healthy and secondly because fibrous foods help maintain our blood sugar levels. They also take longer to digest, thereby keeping you fuller for longer and reducing the temptation to eat unhealthy snacks between meals.

Fruits and vegetables may not be every child's favorite food, but they should form the basis of most meals and should also, ideally, be your first choice for snacks. They are packed full of antioxidants that protect against disease, plus they are loaded with vitamins and minerals such as iron and calcium, which the body requires to function properly. For this reason, you will see that fruits and vegetables feature very highly in this book – in recipes such as French Toast with Blueberries on page 14, Greek Vegetable Casserole on page 233 and Minted Pea Soup on page 46. As well as providing important vitamins and minerals, they also add wonderful flavor, texture and color to your meals.

Legumes are also an excellent source of fiber and feature in a variety of tasty recipes within our "One Pot" meals and "Vegetarian" chapters. Introducing your family to legumes is a great idea. Not only are they good sources of protein, but they are also full of B vitamins, calcium and iron, are low in saturated fat and are cholesterol-free!

If your children are anything like the norm, getting them to eat protein should not be a problem. Many of the meaty treats such as Lamb Hotpot with Dumplings on page 103 are real family classics. And who could resist Fast Chicken Curry on page 189 or Meatballs with Tomato Sauce on page 141 – they are absolute winners with adults and children alike! Getting younger children to eat fish and seafood may be a little more tricky, but try the Tuna Melts on page 274 or the Salmon Pasta Bake on page 287, and watch the whole family wolf down their fish and come back for more.

Get cooking!

A successful meal takes a little planning and time, good ingredients, a dash of inspiration and some gentle encouragement. If cooking for your family has been a disappointing or time-consuming experience in the past, this book should provide you with plenty of inspiration to turn the tide on those mealtime blues.

SIMPLE SNACKS
& LIGHT BITES

CRUNCHY HONEY YOGURT

Serves 6
Preparation time 10 minutes
Cooking time 5 minutes

2 cups (500 ml) Greek yogurt
4 oz (125 g) strawberries, quartered

Topping
2 oz (60 g) flaked almonds
2 oz (60 g) pumpkin seeds
2 oz (60 g) sunflower seeds
3 tbsp (45 ml) sesame seeds
2 oz (60 g) rolled oats
6 tbsp (90 ml) light brown sugar
¼ cup (60 ml) liquid honey, plus extra to drizzle
   (optional)

Mix the almonds, seeds, oats and sugar in a large bowl. Line a large baking sheet with parchment paper, then pour the nut and seed mixture over. Lightly shake the baking sheet to level the ingredients.

Drizzle the honey in thin streams over the top, then place under a preheated medium broiler for 3 to 4 minutes, until the sugar begins to caramelize and the nuts and seeds turn golden brown. Remove from the oven and set aside to cool and harden. Place the hardened nuts and seeds in a plastic bag and bash with a rolling pin to crush into a crunchy topping.

Spoon the yogurt into a bowl and fold in the strawberries. Divide between 6 serving bowls and sprinkle with the topping. (Store any leftover topping in an airtight container for up to 2 weeks.) Drizzle with more honey, if desired.

For yogurt-coated cereal topping, melt 4 oz (125 g) white chocolate in a heatproof bowl set over a pan of gently simmering water. Remove from the heat and add 2 tbsp (30 ml) of natural yogurt. Crunch up 2 oz (60 g) cornflakes and 2 whole shredded wheat biscuits on to a baking parchment–lined baking sheet and scatter over 1 oz (25 g) rice puffs. Drizzle over the warm white chocolate and yogurt coating and refrigerate for 1 hour, until set. Once set, transfer the paper to a chopping board and roughly chop the cereals to form a rough and chunky topping.

LATE GREAT BREAKFAST

Serves 4
Preparation time 15 minutes
Cooking time 15–20 minutes

13 oz (400 g) package puff pastry
1 red bell pepper, cored, seeded and roughly chopped
2 tomatoes, cut into wedges
4 oz (125 g) button mushrooms, cut in half
2 tbsp (30 ml) olive oil
6 eggs
8 thin-cut strips bacon or back bacon
½ oz (15 g) butter, plus extra for greasing

Unroll the pastry and cut out four 5 x 4 inch (12 x 10 cm) rectangles. Using the tip of a small knife, make a shallow cut about ½ inch (1 cm) in from the edges of each rectangle, making sure you don't cut right through to the base. Place the pastry rectangles on a greased baking sheet.

Arrange the pepper, tomatoes and mushrooms on the pastry cases, keeping them away from the marked rims. Drizzle with 1 tbsp (15 ml) of the oil and bake in a preheated 425°F (220°C) oven for 15 to 20 minutes, until the pastry is well risen and golden.

While the pastry cases are baking, beat the eggs in a bowl. Heat the remaining oil in a frying pan and gently fry the bacon for about 2 minutes on each side until crisp, turning with a metal or wooden spatula. Melt the butter in a large saucepan. Tip in the beaten eggs and cook over a gentle heat, stirring continuously until scrambled.

Remove the baking sheet from the oven and transfer the pastries to serving plates. Spoon some scrambled eggs onto the center of each and top with the bacon. Serve while still hot.

For sausage & tomato pastries, place 8 good-quality chipolata sausages under a hot broiler and cook, turning, for 8 to 10 minutes until golden and cooked, adding 8 halved, small tomatoes to the broiler pan, cut side up, for the final 5 minutes of cooking. Halve the sausages and toss with the tomatoes and 1 tbsp (15 ml) chopped parsley and use to fill the pastries as above.

MORNING MUFFINS & TOMATO KETCHUP

Serves 4
Preparation time 15 minutes
Cooking time 20–25 minutes

1 lb (500 g) good-quality sausages
1 tbsp (15 ml) chopped fresh rosemary
3 tbsp (45 ml) chopped fresh parsley
1 tbsp (15 ml) thick honey
1 tsp (5 ml) vinegar
4 eggs
2 English muffins, halved

Ketchup
14-oz (398 ml) can chopped tomatoes
2 tbsp (30 ml) maple syrup
1 tbsp (15 ml) brown sugar
3 tbsp (45 ml) red wine vinegar

Place all the ketchup ingredients into a heavy-bottomed frying pan and bring to a boil. Reduce the heat and gently simmer for 5 to 7 minutes, uncovered, stirring occasionally, until the sauce is thick and pulpy. Mix in a food processor until smooth, then place in a jar and cool.

Cut along the length of each sausage, ease the skin off and discard it. Place the sausage meat in a bowl with the herbs and honey and mix well. Using damp hands, shape into 8 small patties, then cook under a preheated medium broiler for 10 to 12 minutes, turning once, until golden.

Meanwhile, bring a frying pan half-filled with water, with the vinegar added, to a boil. Reduce the heat to a simmer, then immediately break the eggs, well spaced apart, into the water and cook for 1 minute, until the white is opaque. Remove from the water using a slotted spoon and keep warm.

Toast the muffin halves until golden and lightly crisp. Place a warm muffin half onto each of 4 serving plates and top with 2 sausage patties, a poached egg and a spoonful of ketchup.

For tomato & mushroom muffins, heat 1 tbsp (15 ml) olive oil in a heavy-bottomed frying pan and cook 8 oz (250 g) halved cremini mushrooms and 4 halved plum tomatoes over a moderate heat for 4 to 5 minutes until soft and golden, turning occasionally. Poach the eggs and toast the muffins as above. Serve the muffins with the warm tomatoes, mushrooms and eggs on top with a drizzle of ketchup.

SIMPLE SNACKS & LIGHT BITES

PANCAKE STACK WITH MAPLE SYRUP

Serves 4
Preparation time 10 minutes
Cooking time 6 minutes

1 egg
¾ cup (175 ml) all-purpose or bread flour
½ cup (125 ml) milk
2½ tbsp (37 ml) vegetable oil
1 tbsp (15 ml) granulated or fruit sugar
Maple syrup, to drizzle
8 scoops of vanilla ice cream

Put the egg, flour, milk, oil and sugar in a food processor or blender and mix until smooth and creamy.

Heat a large frying pan over medium heat and put in 2 tbsp (30 ml) of the batter to make each pancake.

After about 1 minute, the tops of the pancakes will start to set and air bubbles will rise to the top and burst. Use a spatula to turn the pancakes over and cook on the other side for 1 minute.

Repeat twice more until you have used all the batter and made 12 small pancakes in all.

Bring the pancakes to the table as a stack, drizzled with maple syrup, and serve 3 pancakes to each person, with scoops of ice cream.

For orange-flavored pancakes, make a batter from 1 cup (250 ml) all-purpose flour, 2 tsp (10 ml) each granulated or fruit sugar and grated orange zest, 1 tsp (5 ml) each cream of tartar and corn syrup, ½ tsp (2 ml) each salt and baking soda, 1 egg, ½ cup (125 ml) warm milk and a few drops of orange essence. Cook the pancakes as above.

FRENCH TOAST WITH BLUEBERRIES

Serves 4
Preparation time 5 minutes
Cooking time 10 minutes

2 eggs
1 oz (25 g) granulated or fruit sugar
½ tsp (2ml) ground cinnamon
¼ cup (60 ml) milk
1 oz (25 g) butter
4 thick slices brioche
3½ oz (100 g) blueberries
½ cup (125 ml) thick Greek yogurt
4 tsp (20 ml) honey, to drizzle

Beat the eggs in a bowl with the sugar, cinnamon and milk. Heat the butter in a large, heavy-bottomed frying pan. Dip the brioche slices, 2 at a time, into the egg mixture on both sides, then lift into the hot pan and fry for 1 to 2 minutes on each side until golden.

Repeat with the remaining brioche slices. Mix half the blueberries into the yogurt.

Serve the warm French toasts with spoonfuls of the yogurt on top, the remaining blueberries scattered over and a thin drizzle of honey on top.

For sugar & cinnamon French toast, make the French toasts as above and place on serving plates once cooked and warm. Mix 2 oz (60 g) light brown sugar with ½ tsp (2 ml) ground cinnamon. Dredge each of the warm French toasts with the cinnamon sugar and serve.

BREAKFAST SMOOTHIES

Serves 2
Preparation time 5 minutes

2 bananas
1¼ cups (300 ml) milk
¼ cup (60 ml) natural fromage frais or low-fat
    cream cheese
3 tbsp (45 ml) maple syrup
2 oz (60 g) hot oatmeal

To serve
Banana slices
Malt or multigrain loaf, cut into chunks

Place the bananas in a food processor with the milk, fromage frais and maple syrup and blend until smooth. Add the oatmeal and mix again to thicken. Pour into 2 large glasses.

Arrange banana slices and chunks of malt loaf on 2 cocktail sticks and balance them across the top of the glasses, to serve.

For peanut butter smoothies, replace the banana slices with ¼ cup (60 ml) crunchy peanut butter, and substitute honey for the maple syrup. Make as above, mixing until smooth.

MELTING MUSHROOMS

Serves 4
Preparation time 10 minutes
Cooking time 9–12 minutes

2 tbsp (3 ml) olive oil
4 large flat mushrooms
4 small fresh tomatoes, roughly chopped
1 tbsp (15 ml) tomato sauce
¼ cup (60 ml) canned cannellini beans, drained
  and rinsed
1 tbsp (15 ml) liquid honey
1 tbsp (15 ml) chopped fresh parsley
2 oz (60 g) Gruyère or Edam cheese, thinly sliced
1 tbsp (15 ml) freshly grated Parmesan cheese
4 slices whole wheat toast, to serve

Heat the oil in a large, heavy-bottomed frying pan and cook the mushrooms over moderate heat for 2 to 3 minutes, turning once, until they are softened. Place the mushrooms, stalk side up, on a foil-lined broiler pan.

Add the tomatoes to the pan juices, and cook, stirring occasionally, for 4 to 5 minutes until the tomatoes are thick and pulpy. Add the tomato sauce, beans and honey and continue to cook for a further 1 minute. Remove from the heat and stir in the parsley.

Divide the mixture between the mushrooms and arrange the slices of Gruyère or Edam over the top. Sprinkle the mushrooms with the Parmesan and place under a preheated hot broiler for 2 to 3 minutes, until golden and bubbling. Serve with slices of hot buttered whole wheat toast.

For egg-topped melting mushrooms, follow the recipe as above. Towards the end, poach 4 eggs in a frying pan half-filled with boiling water with 1 tsp (5 ml) vinegar for 1 to 2 minutes, then remove from the water using a slotted spoon and place on the mushrooms.

SMOKED SALMON CONES

Serves 4
Preparation time 15 minutes

2 small cucumbers, halved lengthwise, seeded and cut
  into thin strips
1 tsp (5 ml) prepared English mustard
1 tbsp (15 ml) white wine vinegar
½ tsp (2 ml) granulated or fruit sugar
1 tbsp (15 ml) finely chopped fresh dill
Salt and pepper
2 flour tortillas
¼ cup (60 ml) crème fraîche
4 oz (125 g) smoked salmon trimmings, any larger
  pieces cut into wide strips

Put the cucumber strips in a shallow glass or ceramic bowl. In a small bowl, mix together the mustard, vinegar, sugar and dill. Season well with salt and pepper, then pour over the cucumbers. Leave to stand for 5 minutes.

Cut the tortillas in half and lay on a board or work surface. Spread 1 tbsp (15 ml) crème fraîche over each tortilla half.

Divide the smoked salmon pieces between the tortillas and top with the cucumber mixture. Add a little salt and pepper, if desired, and roll up each tortilla to form a cone around the filling. Secure each cone with a cocktail stick, if desired.

For chicken & mango cones, put 4 oz (125 g) diced, cooked chicken breast, 1 large peeled, pitted and diced mango and 1 tbsp (15 ml) chopped coriander leaves in a bowl. Add ¼ cup (60 ml) mayonnaise, a squeeze of lime juice, and salt and pepper to taste. Toss gently to combine, then divide between the tortilla halves and roll up as above.

CHICKEN CLUB SANDWICH

Serves 4
Preparation time 15 minutes
Cooking time 10 minutes

4 small boneless skinless chicken breasts,
    thinly sliced
8 strips smoked bacon
1 tbsp (15 ml) sunflower oil
12 slices bread
¼ cup (60 ml) light mayonnaise
4 oz (125 g) mild Gorgonzola or bleu d'Auvergne
    cheese, thinly sliced
4 tomatoes, thinly sliced
1½ oz (40 g) watercress

Fry the chicken and bacon in the oil for 6 to 8 minutes, turning once or twice, until golden and the chicken is cooked through.

Toast the bread, then spread with the mayonnaise. Divide the chicken and bacon between 4 slices of toast, then top with the sliced cheese. Cover the cheese with 4 more slices of toast, then add the tomato slices and watercress. Complete the sandwich stacks with the final slices of toast.

Press the sandwiches together, then cut each stack into 4 small triangles. Secure with cocktail sticks, if needed, and serve immediately.

For deli deluxe chicken sandwich, fry the chicken in the oil as above, omitting the bacon. Split and toast the cut sides of a ciabatta loaf, spread the lower half with 4 tsp (20 ml) of black olive tapenade, then top with 2 tbsp (30 ml) of mayonnaise. Add the chicken to the tapenade toast, cover with 4 oz (125 g) sliced Brie cheese, then 3 oz (75 g) sun-dried tomatoes and 1½ oz (40 g) arugula leaves. Top with the remaining toast, then cut into 4 thick slices. Serve warm.

EGGPLANT, TOMATO & FETA ROLLS

Serves 4
Preparation time 15 minutes
Cooking time about 6 minutes

2 eggplants
3 tbsp (45 ml) olive oil
4 oz (125 g) feta cheese, roughly diced
12 sun-dried tomatoes in oil, drained
15–20 basil leaves
Salt and pepper

Trim the ends of the eggplants, then cut a thin slice lengthwise from either side of each; discard these slices, which should be mainly skin. Cut each eggplant lengthwise into 4 slices. Heat the broiler on the hottest setting or heat a grill pan until very hot.

Brush both sides of the eggplant slices with the oil, then cook under the broiler or in the grill pan for 3 minutes on each side or until browned and softened.

Lay the eggplant slices on a board and divide the feta, tomatoes and basil leaves between them. Season well with salt and pepper. Roll up each slice from a short end and secure with a cocktail stick. Arrange on serving plates and serve immediately, or cover and set aside in a cool place, but not the refrigerator, and serve at room temperature when required.

For zucchini & mozzarella rolls, use 3 to 4 large zucchinis, then trim the ends and sides as for the eggplants. Cut each zucchini lengthwise into 3 slices, depending on their thickness, brush with oil and cook under the broiler or in a grill pan as for the eggplants until browned and softened. Spread the zucchini slices with sun-dried tomato pesto, then top with 4 oz (125 g) diced mozzarella cheese and the basil leaves. Roll up and serve as above.

SHRIMP TOASTS

Serves 4
Preparation time 15 minutes
Cooking time about 5 minutes

6 oz (175 g) shrimp
1-inch (2.5 cm) piece fresh ginger, peeled
  and finely grated
1 green onion, finely chopped
1 egg white, beaten
1 tbsp (15 ml) cornstarch
1 tsp (5 ml) toasted sesame oil
1 tsp (5 ml) dark soy sauce, plus extra to serve
4 medium-cut slices "best of both" or "smart" bread
¼ cup (60 ml) sesame seeds
6 tbsp (90 ml) vegetable oil

Place the shrimp in a food processor with the ginger, green onion, egg white, cornstarch, sesame oil and soy sauce and mix to form a thick paste.

Spread the mixture on each of the slices of bread. Place the sesame seeds on a large plate and press the shrimp toast, shrimp side down, in the seeds to lightly cover.

Heat 2 tbsp (30 ml) of the oil in a large, heavy-bottomed frying pan. Cook 2 of the shrimp toasts, shrimp side down first for 1 to 2 minutes, until golden; turn over and cook the other side for 1 minute until golden. Repeat the process, wiping out the pan with paper towels and heating the remaining oil first. Drain on paper towels, then cut into triangles.

Serve the toasts with plenty of cucumber and corn salsa (see below), if desired.

For cucumber & corn salsa to serve as an accompaniment, finely chop ¼ cucumber and place in a bowl with ¼ cup (60 ml) chopped fresh coriander and a 7 oz (200 g) can corn, drained. Finely chop ½ red bell pepper and add to the mix, then add 1 tbsp (15 ml) sweet chile sauce and mix together. Spoon on to the sesame shrimp toasts to serve.

SIMPLE SNACKS & LIGHT BITES

ITALIAN PESTO CHICKEN BURGERS

Serves 4
Preparation time 15 minutes, plus chilling
Cooking time 10–13 minutes

1 lb (500 g) ground chicken
2 cloves garlic, finely chopped
4 green onions, finely chopped
2 tsp (10 ml) pesto
1 egg yolk
Salt and pepper
1 tbsp (15 ml) sunflower oil
4 ciabatta rolls
2 tbsp (30 ml) mayonnaise
1½ oz (40 g) arugula, watercress and spinach salad
2 oz (60 g) sun-dried tomatoes in oil, drained, sliced

Put the chicken, garlic, green onions, pesto and egg yolk in a bowl, add seasoning, then mix together well. Divide into 4, then shape into thick burgers. Chill for 1 hour.

Heat the oil in a nonstick frying pan; add the burgers and fry for about 10 to 13 minutes, turning once or twice, until they are golden brown and cooked through.

Split the ciabatta rolls in half and lightly toast the cut sides. Spread with mayonnaise, then add the salad and tomatoes to the lower half of each roll. Top with the burgers and the other half of each roll, and serve with oven chips.

For curried chicken burgers, mix 2 tsp (10 ml) hot curry paste and 2 tbsp (30 ml) chopped coriander into the chicken mixture instead of the pesto. Fry as above, then serve in warmed naan breads with salad and mango chutney.

CHEESY TWISTS

Makes about 15
Preparation time 15 minutes
Cooking time 8–12 minutes

2 oz (60 g) Cheddar cheese, grated
⅔ cup (150 ml) self-raising flour, plus extra for dusting
½ tsp (1 ml) mustard powder
2 oz (60 g) chilled butter, cut into cubes
1 egg yolk

Put the Cheddar into a mixing bowl, then sift the flour and mustard powder into the bowl. Add the butter, then rub the cheese, butter and flour together until the butter is broken up and covered in flour and the mixture looks like fine breadcrumbs. Add the egg yolk to the mixture and stir with a wooden spoon until you have a stiff dough.

Roll out the dough on a well-floured surface until it is about ¼ inch (5 mm) thick. Take a sharp knife and cut the dough into about 15 long strips, about ½ inch (1 cm) thick. Pick up each strip carefully and twist it gently before laying it on a baking sheet lined with parchment paper.

Bake the twists in a preheated 425°F (220°C) oven for 8 to 2 minutes, until golden brown, then remove them from the oven and allow to cool on the baking sheet.

For spinach & Parmesan twists, place the flour in a food processor with a handful of spinach leaves and mix until fine and green in color. Add the remaining ingredients, replacing the Cheddar with freshly grated Parmesan, then continue as above.

CHOCOLATE-CARAMEL POPCORN

Makes about 6 oz (175 g)
Preparation time 15 minutes
Cooking time about 10 minutes

About 2 oz (60 g) milk chocolate, broken into pieces
2 oz (60 g) hard caramel candies
¼ cup (60 ml) milk
1 tbsp (15 ml) vegetable oil
3 oz (75 g) popcorn kernels

Place the chocolate pieces in a small heatproof bowl. Microwave on medium power for 1 minute. Leave to stand for 2 minutes, then microwave again for 30 seconds at a time until melted, stirring frequently to avoid lumps. (Alternatively, melt the chocolate carefully in a small heatproof bowl over a small saucepan of gently simmering water.)

Unwrap the candies and put them in a plastic bag. Place on a chopping board and tap firmly with a rolling pin until the caramels have broken into small pieces. Tip the pieces into a small saucepan and add the milk. Cook on the lowest possible heat until the candy has melted (this will take several minutes, depending on the firmness of the caramels). Remove from the heat.

Put the oil in a large saucepan with a tight-fitting lid and heat for 1 minute. Add the popcorn kernels and cover with the lid. Cook until the popping sound stops, then tip the corn out onto a large baking sheet or roasting pan and leave for 5 minutes.

Using a teaspoon, drizzle lines of the caramel sauce over the corn until lightly coated. Drizzle with lines of chocolate in the same way.

For golden nugget popcorn, cook the popcorn kernels as above, but replace the remaining ingredients with ¼ cup (60 ml) corn syrup heated in a small pan with 1 oz (25 g) butter until melted, then add 2 oz (60 g) roughly chopped roasted cashews. Cool slightly, then toss with the popcorn to coat lightly.

CHEESY RED DIP WITH BREADSTICKS

Serves 4
Preparation time 45 minutes, plus resting
Cooking time 30–40 minutes

3⅔ cups (800 ml) all-purpose flour
½ tsp (2 ml) salt
1 tsp (5 ml) granulated sugar
¼ oz (5 g) fast-acting dried yeast
1¼ cups (300 ml) warm water
6 tbsp (90 ml) olive oil
2 tbsp (30 ml) sesame seeds
1 tbsp (15 ml) poppy seeds

Dip
2 red bell peppers, cored, seeded and quartered
2 tomatoes
1 tbsp (15 ml) olive oil
1 tbsp (15 ml) balsamic vinegar
7 oz (200 g) soft cheese
1 tbsp (15 ml) chopped fresh thyme (optional)

Sift the flour and salt into a large bowl and add the sugar and yeast. Stir in the measured warm water and 3 tbsp (45 ml) of the oil. Mix well to form a smooth dough, then turn out onto a well-floured surface and knead for 10 minutes, until smooth and elastic. Cover and allow to rest for 15 minutes before kneading again for a further 10 minutes. Return to the bowl, cover with plastic wrap and allow to stand for 30 minutes.

Knead the dough again to knock out the air, then cut into 4 pieces. Cut each quarter into 4 pieces, then stretch and roll each piece to make a long breadstick shape. Brush a baking sheet with the remaining oil. Roll the breadsticks in the oil, then sprinkle half with the sesame seeds and half with the poppy seeds. Bake in a preheated 350°F (180°C) oven for 30 minutes, until golden and crisp. Remove from the oven and allow to cool.

Meanwhile, place the peppers on a baking sheet with the tomatoes and drizzle with the oil. Roast for 30 minutes in the oven with the breadsticks. Remove and place in a plastic bag and allow to cool. Remove from the bag and peel away the skins and discard. Place in a food processor with all the cooking juices, vinegar, cheese and thyme, if using, and mix until well blended and rough-textured. Transfer to a serving bowl and serve with the breadsticks.

For creamy avocado dip, place 1 large quartered avocado in a food processor with the finely grated rind and juice of 1 lime, 4 oz (100 g) soft cheese and 2 tbsp (30 ml) sweet chile sauce and mix until smooth. Serve with the breadsticks.

SALTED PRETZELS

Makes 35–40 pretzels
Time 1½–2½ hours, depending on the bread machine, plus shaping, proofing and baking

Dough
1 cup + 2 tbsp (275 ml) milk
1 tsp (5 ml) salt
2⅓ cups (575 ml) white bread flour
¾ cup (175 ml) rye flour
1 tbsp (15 ml) granulated or fruit sugar
1 tsp (5 ml) fast-acting dried yeast

To finish
4 tsp (20 ml) sea salt, divided
2 tsp (10 ml) granulate or fruit sugar

Lift the bread pan out of the machine and fit the blade. Put the dough ingredients in the pan, following the order specified in the manual. Fit the pan into the machine and close the lid. Set to the dough program.

Put 2 tsp (10 ml) sea salt in a small saucepan with the sugar and 3 tbsp (45 ml) water. Heat until the salt and sugar dissolve, then turn into a small bowl. Grease 2 baking sheets.

At the end of the program turn the dough out onto a floured surface and roll it out to a rectangle, about 14 x 10 inches (35 x 25 cm). Cover loosely with a clean, dry tea towel and leave to stand for 20 minutes. Cut the rectangle across at ½-inch (1 cm) intervals. Take a piece of dough and bend the ends around to meet, twisting the ends together. Press the ends down onto the curved side of the rope to shape the pretzel. Use the remaining dough to make more pretzels and place them on the greased baking sheets. Cover loosely with oiled plastic wrap and leave for a further 20 minutes.

Bake in a preheated 425°F (220°C) oven for 8 minutes, until golden. Brush with the salt glaze and sprinkle with more salt. Cool on a wire rack.

For garlic & rosemary twigs, make the dough as above, adding 1 crushed clove garlic and 1 tbsp (15 ml) finely chopped fresh rosemary with the milk. Roll out the dough and cut into 10-inch (25 cm) strips, then through the center into shorter sticks. Brush with 1 egg yolk, mixed with 2 tsp (10 ml) water and 1 tsp (5 ml) sugar. Place on greased baking sheets, sprinkle with salt and bake as above.

ONION & MUSHROOM QUESADILLAS

Serves 4
Preparation time 10 minutes
Cooking time about 30 minutes

3 tbsp (45 ml) olive oil
2 red onions, thinly sliced
1 tsp (5 ml) granulated or fruit sugar
8 flour tortillas
7 oz (200 g) button mushrooms, sliced
5 oz (150 g) Cheddar cheese, grated
A small handful of fresh parsley, chopped
Salt and pepper

Heat 2 tbsp (30 ml) of the oil in a large frying pan, add the onions and cook until soft. Add the sugar and cook for 3 minutes or until caramelized. Remove the onions with a slotted spoon and set aside. Heat the remaining oil in the pan; add the mushrooms and cook for 3 minutes or until golden brown. Set aside.

Heat a nonstick frying pan and add 1 tortilla. Scatter over a quarter of the red onions, mushrooms, Cheddar and parsley. Season to taste with salt and pepper. Cover with another tortilla and cook until browned on the underside. Turn over and cook until browned on the other side. Remove from the pan and keep warm.

Repeat with the remaining tortillas and ingredients. Cut into wedges and serve with a salad.

For spinach & Brie quesadillas, replace the mushrooms with 7 oz (200 g) cooked, chopped spinach leaves and use 5 oz (150 g) Brie, cut into slices, instead of the Cheddar. Cook and serve as above.

SMOKED TROUT BRUSCHETTA

Serves 4
Preparation time 5 minutes
Cooking time 5 minutes

12 thick slices of French bread
2 large cloves garlic, halved
2 tbsp (30 ml) extra virgin olive oil, plus extra
  for drizzling
8 oz (250 g) tzatziki
8 oz (250 g) hot-smoked trout, flaked
Chopped fresh dill, to garnish
Pepper

Toast the bread in a preheated grill pan or under a preheated broiler.

While still hot, rub the toast all over with the garlic halves and sprinkle with the oil. Top each piece with a large spoonful of tzatziki and pile on the trout. Season to taste with pepper and serve garnished with chopped dill and drizzled with extra oil.

For homemade tzatziki, coarsely grate 1 large cucumber and squeeze out all the liquid, then put the flesh in a bowl. Add 4 to 5 tbsp (60 to 75 ml) thick Greek yogurt, season well with salt and pepper and mix together.

SIMPLE SNACKS & LIGHT BITES

MIXED BEAN SALSA WITH TORTILLA CHIPS

Serves 4
Preparation time 10 minutes, plus standing

2 cans (14 oz/398 ml each) mixed beans, drained
   and rinsed
3 tomatoes, chopped
1 red bell pepper, cored, seeded and finely diced
6 green onions, sliced
1 tsp (5 ml) finely chopped red chile
2 tbsp (30 ml) olive oil
1 tbsp (15 ml) white wine vinegar
Chopped fresh coriander, to garnish
Salt and pepper

To serve
Tortilla chips
Sour cream

Put the beans, tomatoes, red bell pepper and green onions in a food processor and blend until fairly smooth.

In a small bowl, whisk together the chile, oil and vinegar. Pour over the bean mixture and toss to coat. Season to taste with salt and pepper and garnish with coriander. Cover and leave to stand at room temperature for about 30 minutes to allow the flavors to mingle.

Serve the salsa with tortilla chips and sour cream.

For mixed bean pilau, which will work as a substantial starter or side dish, add 1½ cups (375 ml) basmati rice to a pan, cover with 2½ cups (625 ml) water and bring to a boil. Reduce the heat, cover and simmer for 12 minutes without removing the lid. Remove from the heat, toss in the mixed bean salsa (see above) and stir in 3 tbsp (45 ml) chopped coriander leaves. Replace the lid and return to a very low heat for 5 minutes. Serve hot.

CAMEMBERT "FONDUE"

Serves 4
Preparation time 10 minutes
Cooking time 5–10 minutes

1 whole Camembert cheese, 8 oz (250 g) in weight
2 tbsp (30 ml) olive oil
Leaves stripped from 2 fresh rosemary sprigs
Crusty French bread
2 oz (60 g) walnuts, roughly chopped and toasted
2 tbsp (30 ml) liquid honey

Put the Camembert in an ovenproof dish. Make a few cuts in the top, then drizzle with the oil and sprinkle with the rosemary leaves.

Cover with foil and bake in a preheated 400°F (200°C) oven for 5 to 10 minutes, until gooey.

Cut the bread into chunky pieces and lightly toast until golden brown.

Sprinkle the walnuts over the cooked Camembert, drizzle with the honey and serve immediately with the toasted chunks of bread.

For Brie & hazelnut "fondue," use an 8 oz (250 g) round of Brie instead of the Camembert and sprinkle 2 oz (60 g) chopped, toasted hazelnuts over the baked cheese in place of the walnuts.

BEEF & ASPARAGUS BAGELS

Serves 2
Preparation time 5 minutes
Cooking time 2 minutes

4 asparagus spears, each cut into three
1½ oz (40 g) watercress
1 tbsp (15 ml) low-fat mayonnaise
1 tsp (5 ml) Dijon mustard (optional)
2 multigrain bagels
3½ oz (100 g) cooked beef, very thinly sliced

Bring a pan of lightly salted water to a boil. Boil the asparagus, if fresh, briefly, for 30 seconds or so, then drain well and set aside. (Asparagus in jars or cans does not need cooking.)

Remove the larger stalks from the watercress and chop it. Place the mayonnaise and mustard, if using, in a bowl and stir in the watercress.

Split the bagels in half and toast under a preheated broiler. Spread the halves with the flavored mayonnaise. Top with the beef and asparagus spears and wrap securely. The bagels can be refrigerated for 1 to 2 days.

For smoked salmon & asparagus bagels, replace the cooked beef with 4 oz (125 g) smoked salmon and replace the watercress used to flavor the mayonnaise with 1 tsp (5 ml) finely grated lemon zest. Toast the bagels as above and fill with the salmon, lemon mayonnaise and asparagus.

LIGHTLY SPICED CHICKEN NUGGETS

Serves 4
Preparation time 15 minutes
Cooking time 15–20 minutes

⅓ cup (75 ml) all-purpose flour
4 boneles skinless chicken breasts, each about 5 oz
   (150 g) cut into bite-sized chunks
1 egg, beaten
½ cup (125 ml) fine dry whole wheat breadcrumbs
1 tsp (5 ml) Cajun spices
2 tbsp (30 ml) chopped fresh parsley
Tomato ketchup (see page 12), to dip

Place the flour on a plate and toss the chicken in it.

Pour the beaten egg onto a plate. Mix the breadcrumbs with the Cajun spices and parsley on a separate plate. Dip each of the chicken pieces in the beaten egg, then toss in the seasoned breadcrumbs and place on a large baking sheet.

Bake the chicken nuggets in a preheated 400°F (200°C) oven for 15 to 20 minutes until golden and cooked through.

Serve hot with tomato ketchup to dip, if desired.

For salmon goujons, replace the chicken with salmon fillets. Cut the fillets into chunks or strips and toss in breadcrumbs seasoned with the finely grated zest of 1 lemon, instead of Cajun spice, and the parsley as above. Bake for 10 to 15 minutes and serve with mayonnaise flavored with the juice from the lemon.

MULTICOLORED ROOT CHIPS

Serves 4
Preparation time 15 minutes
Cooking time 25–30 minutes

2 sweet potatoes, cut into slim wedges with skin on
1 large baking potato, cut into slim wedges with
  skin on
2 parsnips, cut into long wedges
3 tbsp (45 ml) olive oil
1 tsp (5 ml) Cajun spices
3 tbsp (45 ml) chopped fresh parsley

Mayonnaise
1 egg
⅔ cup (150 ml) olive oil
½ tsp (2 ml) mustard powder
1 tbsp (15 ml) white wine vinegar
1 tbsp (15 ml) chopped fresh parsley

Put the sweet potato, baking potato and parsnip wedges in a bowl and drizzle with the olive oil, tossing well to coat lightly. Sprinkle with the Cajun spices and toss again to coat. Transfer to a large baking sheet and roast in a preheated 400°F (200°C) oven for 25 to 30 minutes, until the vegetables are crisp and golden.

Meanwhile, make the mayonnaise. Place all the ingredients except the parsley in a small measuring cup, and using a handheld blender, mix until a thick mayonnaise is formed. Stir in the parsley.

Serve the chips tossed with the 3 tbsp (45 ml) parsley, with a tub of the mayonnaise, to dip.

For cheese & chive mayonnaise to serve as an alternative accompaniment, make the mayonnaise as above and stir in 2 tbsp (30 ml) sour cream, 1 tbsp (15 ml) freshly grated Parmesan cheese and 2 tbsp (30 ml) snipped fresh chives. Serve with the root chips, to dip.

SIMPLE SNACKS & LIGHT BITES

PAN-FRIED CHICKEN WRAPS

Serves 4
Preparation time 15 minutes
Cooking time 5 minutes

2 tbsp (30 ml) olive oil
3 boneless skinless chicken breasts, about 5 oz
   (150 g) each, thinly sliced into strips
3 tbsp (45 ml) liquid honey
1 tsp (5 ml) whole-grain mustard
4 soft flour tortillas

Coleslaw
¼ small white cabbage, finely shredded
1 large carrot, grated
3 tbsp (45 ml) olive oil
2 tbsp (30 ml) red wine vinegar
1 tsp (5 ml) Dijon mustard
2 tbsp (30 ml) chopped fresh parsley

Make the coleslaw. Put the white cabbage in a large mixing bowl with the carrot and toss together well. In a small bowl, whisk together the oil, vinegar and mustard. Pour over the cabbage and carrot and toss well to coat. Add the parsley and toss again. Set aside.

Heat the oil in a large nonstick frying pan and cook the chicken strips over a high heat for 4 to 5 minutes, until golden and cooked through. Remove from the heat and add the honey and mustard. Toss well to coat.

Warm the tortillas in a microwave for 10 seconds on high (or in a warm oven), then spread each with the coleslaw and top with the chicken pieces. Wrap each tightly, then cut in half to serve.

For maple-glazed ham wraps, omit the chicken and cut 3 ham steaks about 6 oz (175 g) each, into strips. Heat the oil and cook the ham over high heat for 3 to 4 minutes, until golden and cooked through. Remove from the heat and toss with 3 tbsp (45 ml) maple syrup (instead of the honey) and the mustard. Assemble the wraps as above.

LIMA OR FAVA BEAN & ANCHOVY PÂTÉ

Serves 2–3
Preparation time 5 minutes

14-oz (398 ml) can lima or fava beans, drained and
   rinsed
2-oz (50 g) can anchovy fillets in oil
2 green onions, finely chopped
2 tbsp (30 ml) lemon juice
1 tbsp (15 ml) olive oil
¼ cup (60 ml) chopped fresh coriander
Salt and pepper

To serve
Lemon wedges
4–6 slices rye bread, toasted

Put all the ingredients except the coriander in a food processor or blender and process until well mixed but not smooth. Alternatively, mash the beans with a fork, finely chop the anchovies and mix the ingredients together by hand.

Stir in the coriander and season well. Serve with lemon wedges and accompanied with toasted rye bread.

For lima or fava bean & mushroom pâté, replace the anchovies with 8 oz (250 g) sliced mushrooms. Cook these in 2 tbsp (30 ml) olive oil with 1 finely chopped clove garlic until greatly reduced and all juices have evaporated. Cool. Purée the mushrooms in a food processor or blender, or mash with a fork, and add the lima or fava beans, processing or mixing as above.

30

THAI CHICKEN SHELLS WITH CORIANDER

Serves 4
Preparation time 10 minutes
Cooking time 15 minutes

1 tsp (5 ml) vegetable oil
2 boneless skinless chicken breasts, about
   5 oz (150 g) each, sliced
1 tbsp (15 ml) red or green Thai curry paste
14-oz (400 ml) can coconut milk
1 cup (250 ml) basmati rice
3 tbsp (45 ml) chopped fresh coriander
3 green onions, sliced
4 Little Gem lettuces or romaine hearts, separated into
   individual leaves
2 limes, cut into wedges

Heat the oil in a nonstick frying pan; add the chicken and fry for 2 minutes.

Add the curry paste and continue to fry for 1 minute, then add half the coconut milk, bring to a boil and simmer gently for 10 minutes.

Meanwhile, put the rice in a saucepan with the remaining coconut milk and 7 tbsp (105 ml) water. Bring to a boil, then reduce the heat, cover and simmer for 10 to 12 minutes until the liquid is absorbed, adding a little extra water if necessary. Turn the heat off and stir in the coriander.

Put chicken and green onion slices and some rice on a lettuce leaf and squeeze the lime wedges over the filled shells before eating.

For quick Chinese-style stir-fry, cook 10 oz (300 g) chicken strips for 1 minute in 2 tbsp (60 ml) vegetable oil with 1 tbsp (15 ml) chopped garlic. Add 1 cup (250 ml) sliced green bell pepper and 5 seeded and sliced red chiles and cook for a minute, then stir in ⅔ cup (150 ml) sliced onion, 1 tbsp (15 ml) oyster sauce, 1 tsp (5 ml) fish sauce, ½ tbsp (7½ ml) light soy sauce and ¼ tsp (1 ml) dark soy sauce. Stir-fry until the chicken is cooked through, then serve.

ORANGE & AVOCADO SALAD

Serves 4
Preparation time 15 minutes

4 large juicy oranges
2 small ripe avocados, peeled and pitted
2 tsp (10 ml) cardamom pods
3 tbsp (45 ml) light olive oil
1 tbsp (15 ml) liquid honey
Pinch ground allspice
2 tsp (10 ml) lemon juice
Salt and pepper
Sprigs of watercress,
    to garnish

Cut the skin and the white membrane off the oranges. Working over a bowl to catch the juice, cut between the membranes to remove the segments. Slice the avocados and toss gently with the orange segments. Pile onto serving plates.

Reserve a few whole cardamom pods for garnishing. Crush the remainder using a mortar and pestle to extract the seeds or place them in a small bowl and crush with the end of a rolling pin. Pick out and discard the pods.

Mix the seeds with the oil, honey, allspice and lemon juice. Season to taste and stir in the reserved orange juice. Garnish the salads with sprigs of watercress and the reserved cardamom pods and serve with the dressing spooned over the top.

For orange & walnut salad, separate the segments from 2 large oranges as above and mix them with 1 crushed clove garlic, 3 oz (75 g) chopped walnut halves and 4 thinly sliced heads of chicory. Stir in 3 tbsp (45 ml) walnut oil and 1/2 tsp (2 ml) granulated or fruit sugar. Decorate with whole walnuts and serve.

HALOUMI WITH CUCUMBER SALAD

Serves 4
Preparation time 10 minutes
Cooking time 5–6 minutes

1 cucumber, sliced into long, thin ribbons
20 Greek-style pitted black olives
2 tbsp (30 ml) chopped fresh parsley
2 tbsp (30 ml) chopped fresh mint
1 green bell pepper, cored, seeded and diced
8 radishes, sliced into thin sticks
2 green onions, thinly sliced (optional)
1/4 cup (60 ml) olive oil, divided
2 tbsp (30 ml) lemon juice
8 thick slices of country-style bread
8 oz (250 g) haloumi cheese, sliced
1 tbsp (15 ml) finely grated lemon zest
Pepper

Combine the cucumber, olives, herbs, green pepper, radishes and green onions (if used) with 3 tbsp (45 ml) of the oil and the lemon juice. Season with pepper and set aside.

Heat a frying pan or grill pan to medium-hot and toast the bread for 1 to 2 minutes on each side, until golden and slightly charred. Toss the cheese in the remaining oil and lemon zest and season with pepper, add to the pan and cook for 3 to 4 minutes, turning once, until golden.

Put a cheese slice on top of each piece of toast and serve with the salad.

For tomato, mint & avocado salad, roughly chop 4 ripe plum tomatoes, very finely slice 1/2 red onion and roughly dice 1 ripe but firm avocado. Gently toss all the ingredients in 2 tbsp (30 ml) olive oil, with 2 tbsp (30 ml) chopped fresh mint and the juice of 1/2 lemon.

THAI CHICKEN NOODLE SALAD

Serves 4
Preparation time 10 minutes
Cooking time 10 minutes

8 oz (250 g) thin rice noodles
6 tbsp (90 ml) Thai sweet chile sauce
2 tbsp (30 ml) Thai fish sauce
Juice of 2 limes
2 cooked boneless skinless chicken breasts
1 cucumber, cut into ribbons
1 red chile, finely chopped
1 small handful of fresh coriander leaves

Put the noodles in a large heatproof bowl and pour boiling water over to cover. Leave for 6 to 8 minutes, until tender, then drain and rinse well under cold running water.

Whisk together the sweet chile sauce, fish sauce and lime juice in a bowl. Shred the chicken and toss with the dressing to coat.

Add the noodles, cucumber and chile to the chicken mixture and toss gently to combine. Scatter the coriander leaves over the salad and serve immediately.

For seafood noodle salad, replace the chicken with 1 lb (500 g) cooked peeled shrimp and 7 oz (200 g) cooked shelled mussels, and top with a small handful of basil leaves instead of coriander leaves.

PAN-FRIED LIVER & BACON SALAD

Serves 4
Preparation time 10 minutes
Cooking time 8–12 minutes

6 tbsp (90 ml) olive oil
12 oz (375 g) calf's liver divided, dusted with
    seasoned flour
8 oz (250 g) cooked new potatoes, sliced
7 oz (200 g) bacon
3 shallots, sliced
2 tbsp (30 ml) raspberry vinegar
1 tbsp (15 ml) whole-grain mustard
1 head frisée, leaves separated
Salt and pepper

Heat 2 tbsp (30 ml) of the oil in a frying pan. Fry the floured liver for 1 to 2 minutes on each side. Lift onto paper towels and keep warm.

Add 1 tbsp (15 ml) of the oil to the pan and fry the potato slices, turning occasionally, for 4 to 5 minutes or until crisp and golden. Lift onto paper towels and keep warm with the liver.

Add 1 tbsp (15 ml) of the oil to the pan and fry the bacon for 2 to 3 minutes before adding the shallots. Cook until soft and golden.

Mix together the raspberry vinegar, mustard and remaining oil.

Arrange the salad leaves on serving plates and pile on the potatoes, bacon and shallots. Slice the liver thinly before arranging on each salad, drizzle on the dressing and serve.

For chicken liver, mushroom & bacon salad, omit the calf's liver and start by frying the potatoes, as above. When adding the shallots to the bacon, also add 3 1/2 oz (100 g) button mushrooms. Lastly, fry 12 oz (375 g) diced chicken livers. Arrange as above.

GREEK-STYLE FETA SALAD

Serves 4
Preparation time 15 minutes

4 tomatoes, cut into wedges
½ cucumber, cut into bite-size cubes
1 green bell pepper, cored, seeded and cut into rings
  or thinly sliced
1 red onion, thinly sliced
7 oz (200 g) feta cheese, cubed
3½ oz (100 g) pitted black olives
Salt and pepper
¼ cup (60 ml) olive oil
2 tbsp (30 ml) white wine vinegar
2 to 3 tsp (10 t0 15 ml) finely chopped fresh oregano

Arrange the tomatoes, cucumber, green bell pepper and red onion in a serving dish.

Top the salad ingredients with the feta and olives. Season well with salt and pepper and drizzle with the oil and vinegar. Serve sprinkled with the oregano.

For watermelon, feta & sunflower seed salad, add 1⅓ cup (325 ml) cubed watermelon to the salad ingredients used above. Toast 2 tbsp (30 ml) sunflower seeds and sprinkle over the salad before serving.

SIMPLE SNACKS & LIGHT BITES

CHORIZO, EGG & CIABATTA SALAD

Serves 4
Preparation time 10 minutes
Cooking time 10 minutes

½ ciabatta loaf, cut into chunks
6 tbsp (90 ml) olive oil, divided
2 tbsp (30 ml) red wine vinegar
2 tsp (10 ml) whole-grain mustard
4 eggs
7 oz (200 g) chorizo, thickly sliced
4 handfuls of young spinach leaves
Salt and pepper

Toss the ciabatta chunks in 2 tbsp (30 ml) of the oil, spread out on a baking sheet and bake in a preheated 400°F (200°C) oven for 10 minutes or until golden brown.

Meanwhile, in a small bowl, whisk together the remaining oil, the vinegar and whole-grain mustard to make the dressing.

Poach the eggs in a large saucepan of barely simmering water for 5 minutes. Fry the chorizo in a dry frying pan over medium heat for 3 to 4 minutes or until crisp and cooked through.

Toss the spinach and chorizo in a bowl with a little of the dressing. Divide between 4 plates, scatter over the ciabatta croutons and top each salad with a poached egg. Drizzle with the remaining dressing, season to taste with salt and pepper and serve immediately.

For fatoush pita salad, combine 2 cored, seeded and diced green bell peppers, ½ cucumber, diced, 4 ripe tomatoes, diced, 1 finely chopped red onion, 2 crushed cloves garlic, 2 tbsp (30 ml) chopped fresh parsley and 1 tbsp (15 ml) each of chopped fresh mint and fresh coriander in a large bowl. Toss with the lemon dressing on page 38. Toast 2 pita breads in a preheated grill pan or under a preheated broiler, then tear into bite-size pieces and stir into the salad. Cover and leave to stand at room temperature for about 30 minutes to allow the flavors to mingle.

CREAMY ZUCCHINI WITH WALNUTS

Serves 4
Preparation time 10 minutes
Cooking time 10–15 minutes

3 tbsp (45 ml) olive oil
1 onion, chopped
4 zucchini, cut into batons
2 stalks celery, cut into batons
8 oz (250 g) soft cream cheese with garlic
3½ oz (100 g) walnut pieces
Salt and pepper

Heat the oil in a large frying pan; add the onion and cook for 5 minutes until soft. Add the zucchini and celery and cook for 4 to 5 minutes, until soft and starting to brown.

Add the cheese and cook for 2 to 3 minutes, until melted. Stir in the walnuts, season to taste with salt and pepper and serve immediately.

For curried zucchini, cook the onion as above, then add 2 small, quartered potatoes and cook for 2 to 3 minutes. Stir in the zucchini, sliced, with ½ tsp (2 ml) chile powder, ½ tsp (2 ml) turmeric, 1 tsp (5 ml) ground coriander and ½ tsp (2 ml) salt. Add ⅔ cup (150 ml) water, cover and cook over a low heat for 8 to 10 minutes, until the potatoes are tender.

STRAWBERRY & CUCUMBER SALAD

Serves 4–6
Preparation time 10 minutes, plus chilling

1 large cucumber, halved lengthwise, seeded and thinly sliced
8 oz (250 g) strawberries, halved or quartered if large

For the balsamic dressing
1 tbsp (15 ml) balsamic vinegar
1 tsp (5 ml) whole-grain mustard
1 tsp (5 ml) liquid honey
3 tbsp (45 ml) olive oil
Salt and pepper

Put the cucumber slices and strawberry halves or quarters in a shallow bowl.

Put all the dressing ingredients in a screw-top jar, season to taste with salt and pepper, and shake well.

Pour the dressing over the cucumber and strawberries. Toss gently, then cover and chill for 5 to 10 minutes before serving.

For cucumber & dill salad, prepare the cucumber as specified above, then put the slices in a colander set over a plate or in the sink. Sprinkle with 2 tsp (10 ml) salt and leave to stand for 20 to 30 minutes, to allow the excess moisture to drain away. Rinse under cold running water, then drain thoroughly and transfer to a shallow serving dish. In a bowl, mix together ¼ cup (60 ml) thick Greek yogurt, 1 tsp (5 ml) white wine vinegar and 2 tbsp (30 ml) chopped fresh dill. Season well with pepper. Pour over the cucumber, toss gently to combine and serve garnished with dill sprigs.

CHICKPEA & CHILE SALAD

Serves 4
Preparation time 10 minutes, plus standing

2 cans (14 oz/398 ml each) chickpeas, drained and
 rinsed
2 plum tomatoes, roughly chopped
4 green onions, thinly sliced
1 red chile, seeded and thinly sliced
¼ cup (60 ml) roughly chopped fresh coriander leaves
Grilled pita bread, cut into thin fingers, to serve

For the lemon dressing
2 tbsp (30 ml) lemon juice
1 clove garlic, crushed
2 tbsp (30 ml) olive oil
Salt and pepper

Combine all the salad ingredients in a shallow bowl.

Put all the dressing ingredients in a screw-top jar, season to taste with salt and pepper, and shake well. Pour over the salad and toss well to coat all the ingredients.

Cover the salad and leave to stand at room temperature for about 10 minutes to allow the flavors to mingle. Serve with grilled pita bread fingers.

For white bean & sun-dried tomato salad, combine two 14-oz (398 ml) cans cannellini beans, drained and rinsed, 4 oz (125 g) sun-dried tomatoes in oil, drained and roughly chopped, 1 tbsp (15 ml) chopped and pitted black olives, 2 tsp (10 ml) drained and rinsed capers and 2 tsp (10 ml) chopped fresh thyme leaves. Toss in the lemon dressing and leave to stand as above, then serve with toasted slices of ciabatta bread.

38

EGGPLANT & ZUCCHINI SALAD

Serves 4
Preparation time 15 minutes
Cooking time 4–6 minutes

2 eggplants, thinly sliced
2 zucchini, thinly sliced
3 tbsp (45 ml) olive oil
4 oz (125 g) feta cheese

For the honey-mint dressing
2 oz (60 g) fresh mint leaves, roughly chopped, plus
 extra leaves to garnish
1 tbsp (15 ml) liquid honey
1 tsp (5 ml) prepared English mustard
2 tbsp (30 ml) lime juice
Salt and pepper

Brush the eggplant and zucchini slices with the oil. Heat the broiler on the hottest setting. Cook the vegetables under the broiler for 2 to 3 minutes on each side until lightly cooked.

Arrange the grilled vegetables in a shallow dish. Crumble the feta and sprinkle it over the vegetables.

Whisk all the dressing ingredients together in a small bowl, seasoning to taste with salt and pepper. Pour the dressing over the salad and toss to coat. Scatter with mint leaves to garnish and serve with toasted flatbreads or crusty baguette.

For tahini dressing, as an alternative to the honey-mint dressing, put 2 tbsp (30 ml) tahini paste in a bowl. Slowly beat in ¼ cup (60 ml) natural yogurt and 1 to 2 tbsp (15 to 30 ml) cold water as necessary to make a drizzling consistency. Stir in 2 tbsp (30 ml) chopped fresh parsley and 1 crushed clove garlic. Season to taste with salt and pepper. Pour over the salad and toss to coat.

CELERY, RED ONION & POTATO SALAD

Serves 4
Preparation time 10 minutes
Cooking time 10–15 minutes

1 lb (500 g) new potatoes, halved
1 small bulb fennel, halved, cored and finely sliced
2 stalks celery, thinly sliced
1 red onion, halved and thinly sliced
Celery leaves or fresh dill sprigs, to garnish (optional)

For the mayonnaise dressing
⅔ cup (150 ml) mayonnaise
2 tsp (10 ml) whole-grain mustard
2 tbsp (30 ml) finely chopped fresh dill
Salt and pepper

Cook the potatoes in a large saucepan of salted boiling water for 10 to 15 minutes or until tender.

Meanwhile, combine the fennel, celery and onion in a large, shallow bowl. To make the dressing, mix all the ingredients together in a small bowl and season to taste with salt and pepper.

Drain the potatoes, rinse under cold running water, then drain again. Add the potatoes to the salad. Add the dressing and toss until well coated. Garnish with celery leaves or dill sprigs, if desired, before serving.

For herbed vinaigrette dressing, as a fresh, fragrant alternative to the mayonnaise dressing above, put ¼ cup (60 ml) olive oil, 1 tbsp (15 ml) chopped fresh parsley, 1 tbsp (15 ml) chopped fresh basil, 1 tsp (5 ml) grated lemon zest and 1 tbsp (15 ml) white wine vinegar in a screw-top jar with salt and pepper to taste and shake well. Toss with the vegetables as directed above, and garnish with a few torn fresh basil leaves.

GADO GADO SALAD

Serves 4
Preparation time 15 minutes
Cooking time 10 minutes

For the salad
4 eggs
1 iceberg lettuce, finely shredded
2 carrots, peeled and cut into matchsticks
½ cucumber, peeled and cut into matchsticks
½ red bell pepper, cored, seeded and cut into batons

For the peanut dressing
¼ cup (60 ml) crunchy peanut butter
Juice of 1 lime
1 tbsp (15 ml) liquid honey
1 tbsp (15 ml) soy sauce
½ tsp (2 ml) finely chopped red chile

Put the eggs in a saucepan of cold water and bring to a boil. Cook for 10 minutes, then plunge into cold water to cool. Shell the eggs, then cut them in half lengthwise.

Combine all the remaining salad ingredients in a bowl, then add the egg halves.

Put all the dressing ingredients in a saucepan and heat gently, stirring, until combined. Drizzle the dressing over the salad and serve immediately or serve the dressing as a dipping sauce for the salad.

For gado gado with noodles & tofu to serve as an impressive main course, cook 10 oz (300 g) fine dry egg noodles in a saucepan of boiling water for 4 minutes or until just tender while the eggs are cooking as in step 1 above. Drain and refresh the noodles under cold running water. Spread over the base of a shallow serving platter. Pat 4 oz (125 g) firm tofu dry with paper towels, then cut into bite-size cubes. Heat a shallow depth of peanut oil in a frying pan; add the tofu cubes and cook over a high heat until crisp and browned all over. Remove with a slotted spoon and drain on paper towel. Assemble the salad as above, spoon on top of the noodles and scatter the tofu over top. Drizzle on the dressing and serve warm.

THAI BEEF SALAD

Serves 4
Preparation time 15 minutes, plus standing
Cooking time 6–8 minutes

2 lean rump or sirloin steaks, about 5 oz (150 g) each, trimmed
5 oz (150 g) whole baby corn
1 large cucumber
1 small red onion, finely chopped
3 tbsp (45 ml) chopped fresh coriander
¼ cup (60 ml) rice wine vinegar
¼ cup (60 ml) Asian sweet chile dipping sauce
2 tbsp (30 ml) sesame seeds, lightly toasted, to garnish

Put the steaks in a preheated hot grill or frying pan and cook for 3 to 4 minutes on each side. Allow to rest for 10 to 15 minutes, then slice the meat thinly.

Meanwhile, cook the baby corn in boiling water for 3 to 4 minutes or until tender. Refresh under cold water and drain well.

Slice the cucumber in half lengthwise, then scoop out and discard the seeds. Cut the cucumber into ¼-inch (5 mm) slices.

Put the beef, baby corn, cucumber, onion and chopped coriander in a large bowl. Stir in the vinegar and chile sauce and mix well. Garnish the salad with sesame seeds and serve.

For Thai tofu salad, omit the steaks and cube 1 lb (500 g) firm tofu. Fry for 2 to 3 minutes on each side until hot and golden. Mix with the other ingredients and garnish as above.

SIMPLE SNACKS & LIGHT BITES

SOFT−BOILED EGG & BACON SALAD

Serves 4
Preparation time 10 minutes
Cooking time 10 minutes

4 thick slices of day-old bread
6 tbsp (90 ml) olive oil, divided
4 eggs
1 tbsp (15 ml) Dijon mustard
Juice of ½ lemon
3½ oz (100 g) bacon, cut into bite-size pieces
3½ oz (100 g) baby arugula leaves
Salt and pepper

Cut the bread into small bite-size pieces and toss in 2 tbsp (30 ml) of the oil. Spread out on a baking sheet and bake in a preheated 400°F (200°C) oven for 10 minutes or until golden brown.

Meanwhile, cook the eggs in a saucepan of boiling water for 4 minutes. Drain, then cool under cold running water for 1 minute.

Whisk together the remaining oil, mustard and lemon juice in a small bowl.

Heat a nonstick frying pan; add the bacon and cook over medium heat for 5 minutes, until crisp and golden. Put into a bowl with the arugula.

Shell the eggs, then roughly break in half and add to the bacon and arugula. Scatter over the croutons, then drizzle on the dressing, season to taste with salt and pepper and serve immediately.

For creamy yogurt dressing, to drizzle over the salad instead of the mustard dressing, whisk together ¼ cup (60 ml) olive oil, the juice of 1 lemon, 6 tbsp (90 ml) natural yogurt, 1 crushed clove garlic, 1 tsp (5 ml) liquid honey and 1 tsp (5 ml) dried oregano.

MALAY BEEF WITH PEANUT SAUCE

Serves 4
Preparation time 10 minutes
Cooking time 15 minutes

1 lb (500 g) sirloin or rump steak, thinly sliced
1 tbsp (15 ml) vegetable oil

Marinade
½ tsp (2 ml) ground turmeric
1 tsp (5 ml) ground cumin
½ tsp (2 ml) fennel seeds
1 bay leaf, finely shredded
½ tsp (2 ml) ground cinnamon
⅓ cup (75 ml) coconut cream

Rice
1 cup (250 ml) Thai jasmine rice
¾ cup + 2 tbsp (200 ml) coconut milk
½ tsp (2 ml) salt

Peanut sauce
2 tbsp (30 ml) crunchy peanut butter
¼ tsp (1 ml) cayenne pepper
1 tbsp (15 ml) light soy sauce
½ cup (125 ml) coconut cream
½ tsp (2 ml) granulated or fruit sugar

Make the marinade by mixing together all the ingredients in a non-metallic bowl. Add the beef, mix thoroughly, then thread the beef onto skewers and set aside to marinate.

Put the rice, coconut milk, salt and 1 cup (250 ml) water in a rice cooker or a covered saucepan over low heat. Cook for about 15 minutes until the rice is cooked and the liquid has been absorbed.

Meanwhile, add the ingredients for the peanut sauce to a small saucepan with 3 tbsp (45 ml) water and heat gently, stirring.

Heat the oil in a large frying pan and cook the beef skewers for about 5 minutes, turning so that each side is browned evenly. Serve immediately with the rice and peanut sauce.

For bean sprout & carrot salad to serve as an accompaniment, coarsely grate 4 carrots, roughly chop 4 green onions and combine with 7 oz (200 g) bean sprouts.

42

HOT & SOUR SOUP

Serves 4
Preparation time 10 minutes
Cooking time 10 minutes

2⅓ cups (575 ml) fish stock
4 kaffir lime leaves
4 slices fresh ginger
1 red chile, seeded and sliced
1 stalk lemongrass
4 oz (125 g) mushrooms, sliced
3½ oz (100 g) dry rice noodles
3 oz (75 g) baby spinach
4 oz (125 g) cooked peeled tiger shrimp
2 tbsp (30 ml) lemon juice
Pepper

Put the stock, lime leaves, ginger, chile and lemongrass in a large saucepan. Cover and bring to a boil. Add the mushrooms, reduce the heat and simmer for 2 minutes.

Break the noodles into short lengths, drop into the soup and simmer for 3 minutes. Add the spinach and shrimp and simmer for 2 minutes, until the shrimp are heated through. Add the lemon juice. Remove and discard the lemongrass and season with pepper before serving.

For whole wheat soda bread to serve as an accompaniment, stir 2 cups (500 ml) all-purpose flour, 1 tsp (5 ml) baking soda, 2 tsp (10 ml) cream of tartar and 2 tsp (10 ml) salt into a large bowl. Stir in 3 cups (750 ml) whole wheat flour, 1¼ cups (300 ml) milk and ¼ cup (60 ml) water and mix to a soft dough. Turn out onto a floured surface, knead lightly, then shape into a large round about 5 cm (2 inches) thick. Put on a floured baking sheet, cut a deep cross in the top and sprinkle with flour. Bake in a preheated 425°F (220°C) oven for 25 to 30 minutes.

SEAFOOD HOTPOT

Serves 4
Preparation time 25 minutes
Cooking time 15 minutes

1 tsp (5 ml) toasted sesame oil
1 tbsp (15 ml) vegetable oil
3 shallots, chopped
3 cloves garlic, crushed
1 onion, sliced
⅔ cup (150 ml) coconut milk
⅔ cup (150 ml) water
3 tbsp (45 ml) rice wine vinegar
1 stalk lemongrass, chopped
4 kaffir lime leaves
1 red chile, chopped
1⅓ cups (325 ml) fish stock or water
1 tbsp (15 ml) granulated or fruit sugar
2 tomatoes, quartered
¼ cup (60 ml) fish sauce
1 tsp (5 ml) tomato paste
12 oz (375 g) straight-to-wok rice noodles
12 oz (375 g) tiger shrimp, heads removed and peeled
4 oz (125 g) squid, cleaned and cut into rings
6 oz (175 g) clams, scrubbed
14-oz (398 ml) can straw mushrooms, drained
20 fresh basil leaves

Heat the sesame and vegetable oils together in a large pan; add the shallots and garlic and fry gently for 2 minutes or until softened but not browned.

Add the onion, coconut milk, water, vinegar, lemongrass, lime leaves, chile, stock or water and sugar to the pan; bring to a boil and boil for 2 minutes. Reduce the heat and add the tomatoes, fish sauce and tomato paste and cook for 5 minutes. Stir in the rice noodles.

Add the shrimp, squid rings, clams and mushrooms to the hotpot and simmer gently for 5 to 6 minutes or until the seafood is cooked. Stir in the basil leaves. Serve the hotpot immediately.

For nuoc mam dipping sauce to serve as an accompaniment, mix the following ingredients together: 6 tbsp (90 ml) fish sauce, 2 tsp (10 ml) granulated or fruit sugar, 1 tbsp (15 ml) rice wine vinegar, 3 finely chopped hot red chiles, 2 finely chopped hot green chiles. Leave to stand for 1 hour.

THAI SHRIMP SOUP

Serves 4
Preparation time 20 minutes
Cooking time 20 minutes

Soup base
2-inch (5 cm) piece of galangal or fresh ginger, cut into
   very thin slices
2 cups (500 ml) coconut milk
1 cup (250 ml) chicken stock or vegetable stock
2 tbsp (30 ml) fish sauce
6 kaffir lime leaves
1 to 2 tbsp (15 to 30 ml) Thai green curry paste

Soup
½ bunch green onions, chopped
5 oz (150 g) cup mushrooms, sliced
8 oz (250 g) broccoli, finely chopped
10 oz (300 g) raw peeled shrimp
1 tbsp (15 ml) freshly squeezed lime juice
¼ cup (60 ml) roughly chopped fresh coriander

To make the soup base, combine the galangal or ginger, coconut milk, stock, fish sauce, lime leaves and curry paste in a saucepan and bring to a boil, then simmer for 10 minutes, stirring occasionally.

Add the green onions, mushrooms and broccoli to the hot soup base, then simmer for 5 to 6 minutes, until the vegetables are cooked but still crunchy.

Add the shrimp and simmer for 3 to 5 minutes, until they are pink and cooked through. Stir in the lime juice and fresh coriander and serve.

For homemade green curry paste, toast 1 tbsp (15 ml) coriander seeds and 2 tsp (10 ml) cumin seeds in a dry pan over medium heat for 2 to 3 minutes, shaking constantly. Grind the roasted seeds and 1 tsp (5 ml) black peppercorns using a pestle and mortar until finely ground. Put the ground spices in a food processor and blend for 5 minutes. Add 8 roughly chopped large green chiles, 20 chopped shallots, a 2-inch (5 cm) piece fresh ginger, chopped, 12 chopped small cloves garlic, 3 oz (75 g) chopped fresh coriander leaves, 6 shredded kaffir lime leaves, 3 finely chopped stalks lemongrass, 2 tsp (10 ml) grated lime zest, 2 tsp (10 ml) salt and 2 tbsp (30 ml) olive oil. Blend for 10 seconds at a time until you have a smooth paste. Store in the refrigerator for up to 2 weeks.

NOODLE SOUP WITH CHICKEN

Serves 4–6
Preparation time 20 minutes
Cooking time 30 minutes

10 oz (300 g) boneless skinless chicken breasts
1 tsp (5 ml) ground turmeric
2 tsp (10 ml) salt
2 stalks lemongrass
3 tbsp (45 ml) skinned roasted peanuts
3 tbsp (45 ml) long-grain white rice
2 tbsp (30 ml) vegetable oil
1 onion, chopped
3 cloves garlic, crushed
2-inch (5 cm) piece of fresh ginger, peeled and finely
    chopped
1/4 tsp (1 ml) ground paprika
1 hot red bird chile, chopped
2 tbsp (30 ml) fish sauce
3 1/4 cups (875 ml) water
8 oz (250 g) straight-to-wok wheat noodles (somen)

To garnish
3 hard-boiled eggs, halved
2 tbsp (30 ml) chopped fresh coriander
Handful green onions, shredded

Cut the chicken breasts into 3/4-inch (2 cm) cubes. Mix the turmeric with the salt, rub into the cubes of chicken and leave to stand for 30 minutes.

Bruise the lemongrass with the side of a rolling pin to release the flavor. Finely crush the roasted peanuts in a food processor or using a pestle and mortar. Heat a dry frying pan and toast the rice until golden brown, then finely crush to a powder in a food processor or spice grinder.

Heat the oil in a large pan and fry the onion until just softened. Add the chicken together with the garlic, ginger, lemongrass, paprika and chile. Add the fish sauce and water and bring to a boil.

Reduce the heat to a simmer. Mix together the crushed peanuts and ground rice and add to the pan. Simmer for about 10 to 15 minutes or until the chicken has cooked through and the broth has thickened slightly.

Stir the noodles into the pan and heat for 1 minute.

Ladle the chicken soup into bowls and serve garnished with the hard-boiled eggs, chopped coriander and shredded green onions. Add an extra splash of fish sauce, to taste.

For shrimp noodle soup, use 13 oz (400 g) raw peeled shrimp instead of the chicken and add to the pan with the noodles, cooking gently until they turn pink. Replace the wheat noodles with rice noodles and omit the hard-boiled eggs.

TOMATO RISONI SOUP

Serves 4
Preparation time 10 minutes
Cooking time 18 minutes

2 tbsp (30 ml) olive oil, plus extra for drizzling
1 large onion, finely chopped
2 stalks celery, finely chopped
4 large tomatoes
6 cups (1.5 L) vegetable stock
5 oz (150 g) risoni or orzo or any tiny dry pasta
6 tbsp (90 ml) finely chopped flat-leaf Italian parsley
Salt and pepper

Heat the oil in a large saucepan over medium heat; add the onion and celery and cook until soft.

Meanwhile, score a cross in the base of each tomato, then put in a heatproof bowl of boiling water for 1 minute. Plunge into cold water, then peel the skin away from the cross. Halve the tomatoes, then scoop out the seeds and discard. Roughly chop the flesh.

Add the tomatoes, stock, onions and celery to the pan and bring to a boil. Add the pasta and cook for 10 minutes or until al dente. Season to taste with salt and pepper and stir in the parsley.

Remove from the heat, ladle into warmed bowls and drizzle with oil before serving.

For homemade vegetable stock, put 1 1/4 lb (625 g) mixed vegetables (excluding potatoes, parsnips and other starchy root vegetables), 2 peeled cloves garlic, 8 peppercorns and 1 bouquet garni in a large saucepan, add 7 cups (1.8 L) water and bring to a boil. Reduce the heat and simmer gently for 40 minutes, skimming any scum that rises to the surface. Strain through a muslin-lined sieve. If not using straight away, leave to cool before covering and refrigerating.

LIMA OR FAVA BEAN & BACON SOUP

Serves 4
Preparation time 15 minutes
Cooking time 24 minutes

2 tbsp (30 ml) olive oil
6 oz (175 g) smoked bacon, chopped
2 tbsp (30 ml) butter
1 onion, chopped
2 cloves garlic, roughly chopped
2 stalks celery, chopped
1 leek, roughly chopped
3 cups (750 ml) hot ham or vegetable stock
14-oz (398 ml) can lima or fava beans, drained and
   rinsed
2 large sprigs of fresh parsley
3 sprigs of fresh thyme
2 bay leaves
Salt and pepper
7 tbsp (105 ml) whipping (35%) cream

Heat 1 tbsp (15 ml) of the oil in a large pan and fry the bacon until it is crisp and golden. Remove with a slotted spoon and set aside to drain on kitchen paper.

Melt the butter and remaining oil in the pan over medium heat and cook the onion, garlic, celery and leek, stirring frequently, for about 10 minutes or until soft and golden.

Add the stock and lima or fava beans with the herbs and season to taste. Bring to a boil, then turn the heat down and simmer gently for about 10 minutes before removing from the heat. Remove the herbs and blend until smooth.

Stir in the cream, season to taste and serve in large bowls, scattered with crispy bacon.

For smoked sausage & borlotti bean soup, replace the smoked bacon with 8 oz (250 g) smoked pork sausage and use a 14-oz (398 ml) can of borlotti beans instead of the lima or fava beans. Omit the cream.

MINTED PEA SOUP

Serves 4
Preparation time 10 minutes
Cooking time 20 minutes

1 tbsp (15 ml) butter
1 onion, finely chopped
1 potato, finely chopped
4 cups (1 L) vegetable stock
13 oz (400 g) frozen peas
6 tbsp (90 ml) finely chopped fresh mint leaves
Salt and pepper
Crème fraîche (optional)

Melt the butter in a saucepan; add the onion and potato and cook for 5 minutes. Add the stock and bring to a boil, then reduce heat and simmer gently for 10 minutes or until the potato is tender.

Add the peas to the pan and cook for a further 3 to 4 minutes. Season well with salt and pepper, remove from the heat and stir in the mint. Purée in a food processor or blender until smooth. Ladle into warmed bowls and top each with a dollop of crème fraîche, if desired.

For chunky pea & ham soup, cook 1 chopped carrot and 1 chopped turnip with the onion and potato, then add 4 cups (1 liter) ham or chicken stock. Once the root vegetables are tender, add 10 oz (300 g) chopped cooked ham, 4 finely chopped green onions and 2 tbsp (30 ml) chopped fresh parsley with the peas and cook for 3 to 4 minutes. Do not blend the soup, but ladle into warmed bowls and serve with crusty bread.

FRIED GOAT'S CHEESE

Serves 4
Preparation time 15 minutes
Cooking time 10 minutes

4 individual goat's cheeses, about 2½ oz (65 g) each
2 eggs, beaten
¼ cup (60 ml) fresh white breadcrumbs
about ¾ cup (175 ml) vegetable oil, for deep-frying
4 oz (125 g) arugula leaves
2 tbsp (30 ml) olive oil
Salt and pepper

For red onion marmalade
1 tbsp (15 ml) olive oil
2 red onions, thinly sliced
½ cup (125 ml) red wine
3 tbsp (45 ml) red wine vinegar
2 oz (60 g) granulated or fruit sugar

Dip the cheeses in the beaten egg and then coat evenly with the breadcrumbs. Cover and chill while you prepare the onion marmalade.

Heat the olive oil in a small saucepan; add the onions and cook for 2 minutes. Stir in the wine, vinegar and sugar, then cook for 5 minutes or until the onions are translucent. Remove with a slotted spoon and set aside, reserving the juices in the pan.

Heat the vegetable oil in a nonstick frying pan to 375°F (190°C) or until a cube of bread browns in 30 seconds. (Take care not to overfill the frying pan. If necessary, use a saucepan or deep frying pan.) Add the goat's cheeses and cook for 2 minutes or until golden. Remove with a slotted spoon and drain well on paper towels.

Divide the arugula between 4 plates and drizzle the olive oil and reserved juices from the onions over the top. Season to taste with salt and pepper. Place the goat's cheeses on the arugula and top with the onion marmalade. Serve immediately.

For fried Camembert & tomato-chile sauce, cut an 8-oz (250 g) Camembert into wedges, coat and chill as above. Bring a 14-oz (398 ml) can chopped tomatoes, 2 to 3 finely chopped red chiles, 2 crushed cloves garlic, ½ cup (125 ml) light brown sugar, ¼ cup (60 ml) white wine vinegar, 1 tbsp (15 ml) Worcestershire sauce and ½ tsp (2 ml) salt to a boil in a saucepan. Reduce the heat and simmer gently for 30 minutes or until thick. Cook the Camembert as above and serve with the sauce.

GOAT'S CHEESE & TOMATO TARTS

Serves 4
Preparation time 15 minutes
Cooking time 10–12 minutes

4 sheets of phyllo pastry, about 10 inches (25 cm)
   square each
1 tbsp (15 ml) olive oil
20 cherry tomatoes, halved
7 oz (200 g) firm goat's cheese, cut into ½-inch
   (1 cm) cubes
¾ oz (20 g) pine nuts
2 tsp (10 ml) fresh thyme leaves
Salt and pepper

Lightly oil 4 individual tartlet tins, each about 4 inches (10 cm) in diameter. Brush a sheet of phyllo pastry with a little of the oil. Cut in half, then across into 4 equal-sized squares and use to line one of the tins. Repeat with the remaining pastry sheets. Brush any remaining oil over the pastry in the tins.

Put 5 tomato halves in the bottom of each tartlet. Top with the goat's cheese, then add the remaining tomato halves and pine nuts. Sprinkle with the thyme leaves and season well with salt and pepper.

Bake the tartlets in a preheated 400°F (200°C) oven for 10 to 12 minutes or until the pastry is crisp and golden. Serve hot with a leafy green salad.

For feta & pepper tarts, roll out 6 oz (175 g) puff pastry on a lightly floured work surface and use to line the tartlet tins. Core and seed 1 yellow and 1 orange bell pepper, then slice into thin strips and toss in a little olive oil. Cut 7 oz (200 g) feta cheese into ½-inch (1 cm) cubes. Divide half the pepper strips between the tartlets, top with the cheese, then add the remaining pepper strips and scatter over the pine nuts as above. Sprinkle with 2 tsp (10 ml) dried oregano and season well with salt and pepper. Bake at the same temperature as specified above for about 15 minutes or until the pastry is golden.

CIABATTA

Makes 2 loaves

Time 2–3 hours, depending on bread machine, plus
standing, shaping, proofing and baking

Starter
²⁄₃ cup (150 ml) warm water
1 cup (250 ml) white bread flour
¼ tsp (1 ml) granulated or fruit sugar
¼ tsp (1 ml) fast-acting dried yeast

To finish
⅞ cup (225 ml) water
2 tbsp (30 ml) olive oil
1½ tsp (7 ml) salt
2¾ cups (675 ml) white bread flour, plus extra
   for dusting
1½ tsp (7 ml) granulated or fruit sugar
1 tsp (5 ml) fast-acting dried yeast

Lift the bread pan out of the machine and fit the blade. Put the starter ingredients in the pan, following the order specified in the manual.

Fit the pan into the machine and close the lid. Set to the dough program. Turn off the machine before the second kneading cycle and leave the dough to stand for at least 4 hours.

Lift the bread pan out of the machine and add the remaining ingredients. Return to the machine and set to the dough program.

At the end of the program, turn the dough out onto a floured surface and cut it in half. (The dough will be very sticky.) Using well-floured hands, gently pull the dough into 2 loaves, each about 11 inches (28 cm) long. Place them on a greased and floured baking sheet. Leave in a warm place, uncovered, for about 30 minutes or until it is about half as big again.

Bake in a preheated 425°F (220°C) oven for about 20 minutes, until golden and the loaves sound hollow when tapped with the fingertips. Transfer to a wire rack to cool. Dust with flour.

For sun-dried tomato & herb ciabatta, drain and thinly slice 3 oz (75 g) sun-dried tomatoes in olive oil. Roughly chop ½ cup (125 ml) fresh mixed herbs (such as basil, parsley, oregano and thyme). Make the dough in the machine as above using olive oil from the tomato jar and adding the sliced tomatoes and herbs when the machine beeps. Turn out on to a floured surface and finish as above.

48

PITA BREAD

Makes 8 breads
Time 1½–2½ hours, depending on bread machine, plus shaping, proofing and baking

1 cup (250 ml) water
1 tbsp (15 ml) olive oil
1 tsp (5 ml) salt
½ tsp (2 ml) ground cumin
2¾ cups (675 ml) white bread flour
1 tsp (5 ml) granulated or fruit sugar
1 tsp (5 ml) fast-acting dried yeast

Lift the bread pan out of the machine and fit the blade. Put the ingredients in the pan, following the order specified in the manual.

Fit the pan into the machine and close the lid. Set to the dough program.

At the end of the program, turn the dough out onto a floured surface and cut it into 8 equal-sized pieces. Roll out each piece to an oval about 6 inches (15 cm) long. Arrange in a single layer on a well-floured clean, dry tea towel. Cover loosely with a second clean, dry tea towel and leave to rise in a warm place for 30 minutes.

Put a floured baking sheet in a preheated 450°F (230°C) oven, and leave to heat up for 5 minutes. Transfer half the breads to the baking sheet and cook for 5 to 6 minutes, until just beginning to color. Remove from the oven and leave to cool on a wire rack while you cook the remainder. Wrap the still warm pitas in a clean, dry tea towel to keep them soft until ready to serve. If they are left to go cold, warm the pitas through in a hot oven before serving.

For olive & herb mini pitas, make the dough as above, but add 2 oz (60 g) pitted and chopped black olives and a large handful of chopped parsley and mint to the dough when the machine beeps. At the end of the program, turn the dough out onto a floured surface and cut it into 16 pieces. Thinly roll out each piece to an oval 4 to 5 inches (10 to 12 cm) long. Proof and bake as above.

CHORIZO & MANCHEGO BUNS

Makes 12 buns
Time 1½–2½ hours, depending on bread machine, plus
  shaping, proofing and baking

⅞ cup (225 ml) water
3 tbsp (45 ml) olive oil
3½ oz (100 g) Manchego cheese, grated
1 tsp (5 ml) salt
1 tsp (5 ml) hot paprika
3⅓ cups (825 ml) white bread flour
2 tsp (10 ml) granulated or fruit sugar
1¼ tsp (6 ml) fast-acting dried yeast
4 oz (125 g) chorizo sausage, diced

Lift the bread pan out of the machine and fit the blade. Put the ingredients, except the chorizo, in the pan, following the order specified in the manual.

Fit the pan into the machine and close the lid. Set to the dough program, adding the chorizo when the machine beeps.

At the end of the program, turn the dough out onto a floured surface and divide it into 12 equal pieces. Shape each piece into a ball. Cut 6-inch (15 cm) squares of baking parchment. Push a parchment square down into the section of a muffin or Yorkshire pudding tin and drop a ball of dough into it. Repeat with the remainder. Cover loosely with a clean, dry tea towel and leave in a warm place for 30 minutes, until risen.

Use a pair of kitchen scissors to snip across the top of each bun. Bake in a preheated 425°F (220°C) oven for 20 minutes, until risen and golden. Transfer to a wire rack to cool.

For prosciutto & Parmesan crown, fry 3½ oz (100 g) chopped prosciutto in 1 tbsp (15 ml) olive oil until lightly browned. Make the dough as above, using 3 oz (75 g) grated Parmesan cheese instead of the Manchego and adding the prosciutto when the machine beeps. Once the dough is shaped into balls, fit them into a greased 8-inch (20 cm) round cake tin. Leave to rise and bake as above, but increasing the cooking time to 25 to 30 minutes. After baking, transfer to a wire rack to cool, and serve torn into individual buns.

50

PROVENÇAL-STYLE PICNIC SLICE

Makes 10 thick slices
Time 1½–2½ hours, depending on bread machine, plus
  shaping, proofing and baking

Dough
2 tbsp (30 ml) olive oil
¼ cup (60 ml) chopped fresh herbs, such as thyme,
  oregano and rosemary
3 oz (75 g) Parmesan cheese, grated
1 cup (250 ml) milk
1 tsp (5 ml) salt
2⅔ cups (650 ml) white bread flour
1 tbsp (15 ml) granulated or fruit sugar
1 tsp (5 ml) fast-acting dried yeast

To finish
5 tbsp (75 ml) sun-dried tomato paste
11½ oz (350 g) mixed roasted vegetables, such as
  peppers, zucchini and red onions
2 tbsp (30 ml) olive oil
Milk, to brush
1 oz (25 g) Parmesan cheese, grated, for sprinkling
Salt and pepper

Lift the bread pan out of the machine and fit the blade. Put the dough ingredients in the pan, following the order specified in the manual. Add the herbs and cheese with the milk.

Fit the pan into the machine and close the lid. Set to the dough program.

At the end of the program, turn the dough out onto a floured surface and roll it out to a 11-inch (28 cm) square. Spread with the tomato paste and scatter with the roasted vegetables. Drizzle with the oil and a little salt and pepper.

Roll up the dough so the filling is enclosed and cut it into 10 thick slices. Arrange the slices in a staggered line on a large, greased baking sheet, resting each slice against the one behind so the filling is revealed. Cover with oiled plastic wrap and leave to rise in a warm place for about 40 minutes or until almost doubled in size.

Brush the dough with milk and sprinkle with cheese. Bake in a preheated 400°F (200°C) oven for 25 minutes, until risen and golden. Serve warm, broken into slices.

For leek & Stilton picnic loaf, make the dough as above but reducing the Parmesan to 1½ oz (40 g). Thinly slice 11½ oz (350 g) leeks and sauté them in 2 tbsp (30 ml) butter until soft. Leave to cool. Roll out the dough as above and scatter with the leeks, 5 oz (150 g) crumbled, creamy Stilton cheese and plenty of pepper. Roll up the dough and finish as above.

HOT CROSS BUNS

Makes 12 buns
Time 1½–2½ hours, depending on machine, plus
  shaping, proofing and baking

Dough
1 egg, beaten
1 cup + 2 tbsp (275 ml) milk
3 tbsp (45 ml) unsalted butter, softened
½ tsp (2 ml) salt
2 tsp (10 ml) pumpkin pie spice
3⅔ cups (900 ml) white bread flour
3 tbsp (45 ml) light muscovado sugar
1½ tsp (7 ml) fast-acting dried yeast
3½ oz (100 g) raisins

To finish
½ cup (125 ml) all-purpose flour
¼ cup (60 ml) milk
2 tbsp (30 ml) granulated or fruit sugar

Lift the bread pan out of the machine and fit the blade. Add the dough ingredients, except the raisins, to the pan, following the order specified in the manual.

Fit the pan into the machine and close the lid. Set to the dough program, adding the raisins when the machine beeps.

At the end of the program, turn the dough out onto a floured surface and divide it into 12 pieces. Shape each into a ball and space 2 inches (5 cm) apart on a greased baking sheet. Cover loosely with oiled plastic wrap and leave to rise in a warm place for 30 minutes.

Make the crosses. Beat ¼ cup (60 ml) water into the flour to make a paste. Put it in a greaseproof piping bag (or spoon it into the corner of a small plastic bag) and snip off the tip. Pipe crosses over the buns.

Bake in a preheated 425°F (220°C) oven for 15 minutes, until risen and golden. Heat the milk and sugar in a pan until the sugar dissolves. Bring to a boil and brush over the buns. Cool on a wire rack.

For hot cross bun loaf, put 1 cup + 2 tbsp (275 ml) milk, 1 oz (25 g) soft butter, ½ tsp (2 ml) salt, grated zest of 1 lemon, 2 tsp (10 ml) pumpkin pie spice, 3⅓ cups (825 ml) white bread flour, ¼ cup (60 ml) light muscovado sugar and 1½ tsp (7 ml) fast-acting dried yeast in the bread pan, following the order specified in the manual. Set to a 1½ lb (750 g) loaf size on the sweet program, adding 7½ oz (225 g) luxury mixed dried fruit when the machine beeps. Halfway through baking, pipe a cross on the surface using the mixture above. After baking brush with the glaze.

FRUITED TEACAKES

Makes 8 teacakes
Time 1½–2½ hours, depending on bread machine, plus
  shaping, proofing and baking

Dough
1¼ cups (300 ml) milk
¼ cup (60 ml) unsalted butter, softened
½ tsp (2 ml) salt
1 tsp (5 ml) pumpkin pie spice
2 tsp (10 ml) vanilla bean paste or vanilla extract
3⅓ cups (825 ml) white bread flour
⅓ cup (75 ml) light muscovado sugar
1¼ tsp (6 ml) fast-acting dried yeast
5 oz (150 g) mixed dried fruit, to glaze

To finish
Beaten egg, to glaze
Granulated or fruit sugar, for sprinkling

Lift the bread pan out of the machine and fit the blade. Put the dough ingredients, except the dried fruit, in the pan, following the order specified in the manual.

Fit the pan into the machine and close the lid. Set to the dough program, adding the dried fruit when the machine beeps.

At the end of the program, turn the dough out onto a floured surface and cut it into 8 equal pieces. Shape each piece into a ball and space them about 1¼ inches (3 cm) apart on a large, greased baking sheet. Cover loosely with oiled plastic wrap and leave to rise in a warm place for about 30 minutes or until almost doubled in size.

Brush with beaten egg to glaze and bake in a preheated 425°F (220°C) oven for 15 to 20 minutes, until risen and golden. Transfer to a wire rack to cool and sprinkle with the granulated or fruit sugar. Serve split and buttered.

For iced finger buns, beat 2 eggs and make up to 1¼ cups (300 ml) with milk. Continue to make the dough as above, omitting the mixed spices and dried fruit, and using the milk and egg mixture to replace the 1¼ cups (300 ml) milk. Turn the dough out onto a floured surface and cut it into 8 equal pieces. Shape each into finger roll shapes and place on a greased baking sheet, spacing them about 1½ inches (4 cm) apart. Leave the buns to rise and bake as above. Once cooled, spread the tops with glacé icing, made by mixing together ¾ cup (175 ml) icing sugar with 2 to 3 tsp (10 to 15 ml) lemon or orange juice.

QUICK
MIDWEEK
MEALS

MUSSELS IN TARRAGON CREAM SAUCE

Serves 4
Preparation time 20 minutes
Cooking time 15 minutes

2 lb (1 kg) fresh mussels
¼ cup (60 ml) butter
2 shallots, finely chopped
2 cloves garlic, crushed
1 tsp (5 ml) ground coriander
2 tsp (10 ml) chopped fresh lemon thyme
1 tbsp (15 ml) all-purpose flour
About ⅔ cup (150 ml) white wine
2 tbsp (30 ml) chopped fresh tarragon
⅔ cup (150 ml) whipping (35%) cream
Salt and pepper
Crusty bread (optional)

Scrub the mussels, scraping off any barnacles and pulling away the beards. Discard any damaged shells or any open ones that don't close when tapped firmly with a knife or against the edge of the sink.

Melt the butter in a large saucepan. Add the shallots, garlic, coriander and thyme and fry very gently for 2 minutes. Remove from the heat and stir in the flour to make a thin paste. Gradually beat in the wine, using a whisk or wooden spoon, until smooth.

Return to the heat and cook, stirring, until the sauce is thick and smooth. Stir in the tarragon. Tip in the mussels and cover with a lid. Cook for about 5 minutes, shaking the pan frequently, until the shells have opened.

Drain the mussels to warmed bowls, discarding any that remain closed.

Stir the cream into the sauce and bring to a boil. Season to taste and ladle the sauce over the mussels. Serve with warm, crusty bread, if desired.

For steamed mussels in white wine sauce, prepare the mussels as in the first step. Melt 2 tbsp (30 ml) butter in a large saucepan and fry 1 small onion chopped, 1 to 2 cloves garlic finely chopped, and 1 small leek, finely sliced, until soft. Add the mussels, 1¼ cups (300 ml) dry white wine and ⅔ cup (150 ml) water, cover and bring to a boil. Cook for 2 to 5 minutes, until the mussels open, then divide into serving bowls. Mix 2 tbsp (30 ml) butter with 2 tbsp (30 ml) all-purse flour to form a paste. Gradually add to the juices in the pan, stirring to thicken. Bring to a boil, stir in 2 tbsp (30 ml) chopped fresh parsley, season and pour over the mussels.

HADDOCK & SHELLFISH SOUP

Serves 4
Preparation time 15 minutes
Cooking time 20 minutes

1 lb (500 g) undyed smoked haddock
2 tbsp (30 ml) butter
1 large leek, chopped
2 tsp (10 ml) medium curry paste
4 cups (1 L) fish stock
2 oz (60 g) creamed coconut, chopped
3 bay leaves
5 oz (150 g) French beans, cut into ½-inch
  (1 cm) lengths
3 small zucchini, chopped
8 oz (250 g) cooked mixed seafood, e.g. shrimp,
  mussels, squid rings, thawed if frozen
7 tbsp (105 ml) table (18%) or half-and-half cream
¼ cup (60 ml) finely chopped fresh parsley
Salt and pepper

Cut the haddock into small pieces, discarding the skin and any bones.

Melt the butter in a large saucepan and gently fry the leek for 3 minutes to soften. Add the curry paste, stock and creamed coconut and bring almost to a boil. Reduce the heat and simmer gently, covered, for 10 minutes, until the leek is soft.

Stir in the bay leaves, beans and zucchini and cook for 2 minutes to soften slightly. Add the smoked haddock and mixed seafood, 3 tbsp (45 ml) of the cream and the parsley and cook very gently for 5 minutes, until the haddock flakes easily.

Season to taste and spoon into serving bowls. Serve swirled with the remaining cream.

For smoked salmon and snow pea or sugar snap pea soup, replace the haddock with 1 lb (500 g) lightly smoked salmon and cook as above. Replace the French beans with the same quantity of snow peas or sugar snap peas.

SALMON FILLETS WITH SAGE & QUINOA

Serves 4
Preparation time 5 minutes
Cooking time 15 minutes

1⅓ cups (325 ml) quinoa
7 tbsp (105 ml) butter, at room temperature
8 fresh sage leaves, chopped
Small bunch of fresh chives
Grated zest and juice of 1 lemon
4 pieces salmon fillet, about 4 oz (125 g) each
1 tbsp (15 ml) olive oil
Salt and pepper

Cook the quinoa in unsalted boiling water for about 15 minutes or until cooked but firm.

Meanwhile, mix the butter with the sage, chives and lemon zest and add salt and pepper to taste.

Rub the salmon with the oil, season with pepper and cook in a preheated hot grill pan for about 6 minutes, turning carefully once. Remove and set aside to rest.

Drain the quinoa, stir in the lemon juice and season to taste. Spoon onto serving plates and top with the salmon, topping each piece with a knob of sage butter.

For salmon with tarragon & couscous, replace the sage leaves with 4 sprigs of fresh tarragon and the quinoa with 1⅔ cups (400 ml) couscous. Soak the couscous in 1⅔ cups (400 ml) just-boiled water for 5 to 8 minutes, until the grains are soft. Fluff the couscous with a fork and season. Dress with a little lemon juice and olive oil and serve with the salmon as above.

BUTTERY LOBSTER TAILS WITH AÏOLI

Serves 4
Preparation time 20 minutes
Cooking time 7–8 minutes

4 raw lobster tails
¼ cup (60 ml) butter
2 tbsp (30 ml) garlic-infused oil
Finely grated zest of 1 lemon
2 tbsp (30 ml) chopped fresh chervil, plus extra sprigs
   to garnish
Cucumber ribbons, to serve

Aïoli
1 large egg yolk
3 to 4 cloves garlic, crushed
1 tbsp (15 ml) lemon juice
Salt and pepper
¾ cup (175 ml) olive oil
1 tbsp (15 ml) snipped fresh chives

Make the aïoli. With all the ingredients at room temperature, beat the egg yolk in a bowl with the garlic, lemon juice and a large pinch of salt and pepper, either by hand or with an electric mixer. Gradually add the oil, drop by drop, beating constantly until it is all completely incorporated and you have a thick, smooth emulsion. Stir in the chives.

Dot the lobster tails with the butter and drizzle with the garlic oil. Cook the lobster tails, flesh side up, under a preheated broiler for 7 to 8 minutes, until cooked through. Sprinkle with the lemon zest and chopped chervil and serve immediately with cucumber ribbons and the aïoli in small bowls.

For lobster tails with sun-dried tomato sauce, combine 2 tbsp (30 ml) each of sun-dried tomato paste, mascarpone and pesto with 2 tsp (10 ml) finely grated lemon zest and 2 tsp (10 ml) lemon juice. Season well.

SCALLOPS WITH PANCETTA

Serves 4

Preparation time 10 minutes, plus cooling time

Cooking time 15 minutes

8 small vine-ripened tomatoes, halved

2 cloves garlic, finely chopped

8 fresh basil leaves

2 tbsp (30 ml) olive oil, divided

2 tbsp (30 ml) balsamic vinegar, divided

8 thin slices of pancetta

16 to 20 king scallops, corals and muscles removed

8 canned artichoke hearts in oil, drained and halved

4 oz (125 g) lamb's lettuce or mâche, trimmed

Salt and pepper

Arrange the tomatoes close together, cut side up, in a roasting pan. Scatter over the chopped garlic and basil, drizzle with 1 tbsp (15 ml) each of the oil and balsamic vinegar and season well with salt and pepper. Cook in a preheated 425°F (220°C) oven for 15 minutes.

Meanwhile, cook the pancetta slices in a preheated hot grill pan for about 2 minutes, turning once, until crisp and golden. Transfer to a plate lined with paper towel until needed.

Quickly sear the scallops for 1 minute in the hot pan, then turn them over and cook for a further minute on the other side, until cooked and starting to caramelize. Remove, cover with foil and leave to rest for 2 minutes.

Meanwhile, cook the artichoke hearts for about 2 minutes, until hot and charred.

Toss the lamb's lettuce with the remaining oil and balsamic vinegar and arrange on serving plates. Top with the artichokes, tomatoes, crispy pancetta and scallops. Serve immediately.

For salmon & pancetta salad, omit the tomatoes and cook the pancetta as above. Instead of the scallops, use a chunky 14½ oz (450 g) fresh salmon fillet. Brush the salmon lightly with olive oil before searing on a hot grill for 2 to 3 minutes, until golden, turning once. Cook the artichoke hearts as above. Substitute the lamb's lettuce with arugula and shredded Little Gem or romaine hearts. Toss and arrange as above.

CRUNCHY SWORDFISH WITH PUY LENTILS

Serves 4

Preparation time 12 minutes

Cooking time 15 minutes

4 skinless swordfish fillets, about 6 oz (175 g) each

2 tbsp (30 ml) olive oil

1 lb (500 g) cooked Puy lentils, heated

8 sun-blushed tomatoes, roughly chopped

Small bunch of fresh basil, shredded

1 tbsp (15 ml) capers in brine, drained and rinsed

4 green onions, finely sliced

8 pitted black olives, roughly chopped

2 tbsp (30 ml) olive oil

Salt and pepper

2 lemons, halved, to serve

Crust

⅔ cup (150 ml) breadcrumbs

Grated zest of 1 lemon

1 tsp (5 ml) finely chopped fresh rosemary

2 tbsp (30 ml) finely chopped fresh parsley

Mix together the ingredients for the crust and add some salt and pepper. Rub the fish fillets with the oil and then press them into the crust mixture to coat.

Transfer the fish to a nonstick baking sheet and carefully tip over the remaining crust. Cook in a preheated 425°F (220°C) oven for 15 minutes, until the fish is flaky and the crust is golden and crunchy.

Put the hot lentils in a bowl and stir in the remaining ingredients. Serve immediately with the fish fillets and lemon halves.

For crunchy hake with Mediterranean potatoes, replace the swordfish with 4 hake steaks, each about 7 oz (200 g), and prepare as above. Instead of the lentils, peel and halve 1 lb 7 oz (700 g) red new potatoes, boil them for 10 to 15 minutes, drain, then toss with the other ingredients.

COCONUT & CORIANDER MUSSELS

Serves 4
Preparation time 10 minutes
Cooking time 15 minutes

1 tbsp (15 ml) vegetable oil
4 green onions, finely chopped
1-inch (2½ cm) length galangal or fresh ginger,
   shredded
1 green chile, finely chopped
¾ cup (175 ml) can coconut milk
Large bunch of fresh coriander, chopped, plus extra
   to garnish
1 tbsp (15 ml) chopped fresh Thai basil (optional)
¾ cup (175 ml) fish stock
2 tbsp (30 ml) Thai fish sauce
2 tbsp (30 ml) lime juice
1 tbsp (15 ml) soy sauce
1 tbsp (15 ml) brown sugar
3 to 4 kaffir lime leaves, shredded (optional)
2 lb (1 kg) mussels, scrubbed and debearded
Flaked or shredded coconut, toasted, to garnish
   (optional)

Heat the oil in a large saucepan and cook the green onions, galangal or ginger and chile for 2 minutes, until soft. Add the remaining ingredients except the mussels and warm gently until the sugar has dissolved. Turn up the heat and bring up to boiling point, then reduce the heat and simmer gently for 5 minutes to allow the flavors to develop.

Tip the mussels into the coconut sauce and cover with a tight-fitting lid. Cook for 3 to 4 minutes or until the mussels have opened – discard any that have not.

Spoon into serving bowls with plenty of the juices and sprinkle with extra coriander leaves and flaked coconut, if using. Serve immediately with steamed jasmine rice or butternut squash.

For coconut & coriander seafood with lime rice, replace the mussels with 1 lb (500 g) fresh or frozen prepared seafood mix and cook as above, but omitting the lime leaves. Cook 1 cup (250 ml) rice with the grated zest of 1 lime. Serve the rice in bowls and ladle over the seafood. Serve with shrimp crackers.

MUSSEL & LEMON CURRY

Serves 4
Preparation time 15 minutes
Cooking time 15 minutes

½ cup (125 ml) lager
½ cup (125 ml) unsalted butter
1 onion, chopped
1 clove garlic, crushed
1-inch (2.5 cm) fresh ginger, peeled and grated
1 tbsp (15 ml) medium curry powder
⅔ cup (150 ml) table (18%) or half-and-half (10%)
   cream
2 tbsp (30 ml) lemon juice
2 lb (1 kg) mussels, scrubbed and debearded
Salt and pepper
Chopped fresh parsley, to garnish

Discard any mussels that are broken or do not close immediately when sharply tapped with a knife. Put them in a large saucepan with the lager; cover and cook, shaking the pan frequently, for 4 minutes, until all the shells have opened. Discard any that remain closed. Strain; reserve the cooking liquid and keep it warm.

Meanwhile, melt the butter in a large saucepan and fry the onion, garlic, ginger and curry powder, stirring frequently, for 5 minutes. Strain in the reserved mussel liquid and bring to a boil. Boil until reduced by half. Whisk in the cream and lemon juice and simmer gently.

Stir in the mussels, warm through and season to taste. Garnish with chopped parsley and serve with crusty bread, if desired.

For shrimp & lemon curry with warm lemon naan, substitute the mussels with shelled raw shrimp. You will need about 10 shrimp per person, cut almost in half down the center to allow the flavors to penetrate the flesh. Cook in the same way as the mussels for 3 to 4 minutes, until the flesh turns pink. Serve with 4 warm naan breads brushed with lemon butter, made by mixing the zest of 1 lemon with ¼ cup (60 ml) melted butter.

SQUID WITH LEMON MAYONNAISE

Serves 4
Preparation time 30 minutes
Cooking time 9 minutes

1 lb (500 g) prepared squid
6 tbsp (90 ml) all-purpose flour
1 tbsp (15 ml) paprika
Pinch cayenne pepper
Olive oil, for deep-frying
Salt and pepper

Lemon and herb mayonnaise
2 egg yolks
½ tsp (2 ml) whole-grain mustard
1 tbsp (15 ml) lemon juice, plus extra to taste
¾ cup + 2 tbsp (200 ml) light olive oil
1 tbsp (15 ml) chopped flat-leaf (Italian) parsley, plus
    extra to garnish
1 tbsp (15 ml) chopped fresh chervil
1 tbsp (15 ml) chopped fresh chives
2 tbsp (30 ml) chopped watercress
Finely grated zest of 1 lemon
1 small clove garlic, crushed
Lemon wedges, to serve

Make the mayonnaise. Beat the egg yolks in a bowl with the mustard and lemon juice. Add the oil, drop by drop, beating constantly until it is incorporated and you have a thick, smooth emulsion. Season and stir in the herbs, watercress, lemon zest and garlic, adding extra lemon juice to taste. Cover and chill until required.

Wash the squid and pat dry with kitchen paper. Cut the bodies into rings about ¾-inch (2 cm) thick. Mix together the flour, paprika and cayenne and season well. Put the flour in a plastic bag, add the squid rings and tentacles and shake until they are coated.

Heat the oil in a large frying pan or deep-fat fryer to 350°F (180°C) or until a cube of bread browns in 20 seconds. Remove about one-third of the squid from the bag and shake off the excess flour. Carefully drop the squid into the oil and fry for 2 to 3 minutes, until golden and crispy, then remove with a slotted spoon. Drain on paper towel and keep them warm.

Transfer the squid to 4 serving plates, sprinkle with parsley and serve immediately with lemon wedges and lemon and herb mayonnaise.

For stir-fried squid, prepare and season the squid as above. Stir-fry in 6 tbsp (90 ml) olive oil. Remove, drain and keep warm while you cook 1 sliced onion, 1 sliced green pepper, 2 crushed cloves garlic, 1 bay leaf, 14½ oz (450 g) chopped tomatoes and 2 oz (60 g) pitted black olives. Return the squid to the pan, sprinkle over ¼ cup (60 ml) chopped parsley and serve.

BREAM WITH NEW POTATOES

Serves 4
Preparation time 5 minutes
Cooking time 20 minutes

1 lb (500 g) baby new potatoes
Sea salt and pepper
3 to 4 tbsp (45 to 60 ml) olive oil, divided
6 tbsp (90 ml) fresh mayonnaise
1 tbsp (15 ml) chopped fresh chervil
½ clove garlic, crushed
4 boned sea bream or tilapia fillets
2 tbsp (30 ml) lemon juice

Put the new potatoes in a large saucepan with 1 to 2 tbsp (15 to 30 ml) of the oil. Place over medium-low heat and cover with a tight-fitting lid. Cook for about 20 minutes, shaking the pan frequently to move the potatoes around. When done, the potatoes should be cooked and crispy golden. Remove from the pan and sprinkle with sea salt.

Meanwhile, mix the mayonnaise with the chervil and garlic.

Heat the remaining oil in a large frying pan over medium-high heat. Season the fish with salt and pepper and cook, flesh side down, for 1 minute before turning carefully and frying for a further 2 to 3 minutes, until the skin is crispy. Squeeze over the lemon juice and serve immediately with the crispy potatoes and garlicky mayonnaise.

For mackerel with horseradish sour cream, replace the chervil and garlic with 2 tbsp (30 ml) horseradish sauce and the mayonnaise with sour cream. Substitute the bream with 4 mackerel fillets, seasoned with salt and pepper and a pinch of chile powder. Cook in the same way as the bream and serve with new potatoes, as above.

SCALLOPS WITH CITRUS DRESSING

Serves 4
Preparation time 10 minutes
Cooking time 7–9 minutes

16 large raw shrimp, heads removed
24 fresh scallops, roe removed
1 large ripe but firm mango, peeled, pitted and
  cut into chunks
4 oz (125 g) mixed salad leaves

Citrus dressing
Juice of ½ pink grapefruit
Finely grated zest and juice of 1 lime
1 tsp (5 ml) liquid honey
1 tbsp (15 ml) raspberry vinegar
⅓ cup (75 ml) lemon oil

Make the citrus dressing by mixing together all the ingredients in a small bowl.

Poach the shrimp in simmering water for 2 minutes and drain.

Put the scallops, mango and shrimp in a bowl and pour over 3 tbsp (45 ml) of the dressing. Mix well to coat before threading them alternately on skewers.

Heat the oil in a large frying pan over medium heat and fry the skewers for about 5 to 7 minutes, turning and basting occasionally until golden brown and cooked.

Arrange the skewers on plates with salad leaves and serve with the remaining dressing.

For haloumi & mango kebabs with citrus dressing, replace the scallops and shrimp with 14½ oz to 1 lb (400 to 500 g) haloumi, cut into cubes. Coat with the dressing, skewer with the mango and fry, as above. Alternatively, cook on a barbecue for the same amount of time until slightly charred.

TERIYAKI SALMON WITH NOODLES

Serves 4
Preparation time 12 minutes
Cooking time 15 minutes

4 boneless skinless salmon fillets, about 5 oz
  (150 g) each
2 tsp (10 ml) toasted sesame oil
4 green onions, thinly sliced
1½ cups (375 ml) hot vegetable stock
2 tbsp (30 ml) light soy sauce
3 tbsp (45 ml) miso paste
1 tbsp (15 ml) mirin or 1 tsp (5 ml) brown sugar
10 oz (300 g) ready-cooked udon noodles
4 heads baby bok choy, halved lengthwise

Teriyaki sauce
3 tbsp (45 ml) sake
1 tsp (5 ml) dark soy sauce
3 tbsp (45 ml) light soy sauce
2 tbsp (30 ml) granulated or fruit sugar
1 tbsp (15 ml) liquid honey
2 tbsp (30 ml) mirin or extra sugar

Make the teriyaki sauce. Put all the ingredients in a small saucepan and stir over medium heat until the sugar has dissolved. Increase the heat a little and simmer for 5 minutes, until thickened. Set aside to cool.

Rub the teriyaki sauce over the salmon fillets and arrange them in an ovenproof dish. Cook under a preheated broiler for 4 to 5 minutes on each side, basting occasionally. Remove and set aside.

Heat the sesame oil in a frying pan and stir-fry the green onions for 2 minutes. Add the stock, soy sauce, miso paste and mirin or sugar, stirring to dissolve. Simmer gently and add the noodles and bok choy and cook for 2 minutes, until the leaves have wilted.

Serve immediately topped with the grilled salmon.

For herb-crusted salmon with grilled asparagus, cook 8 oz (250 g) trimmed asparagus spears in boiling water for 5 minutes. Brush one side of each salmon fillet with olive oil. Chop about ¾ cup (175 ml) parsley and use to coat the salmon, then grill or fry in olive oil for about 3 minutes on each side. Serve the salmon topped with the asparagus spears and with some crusty bread.

GARGANELLI WITH RED MULLET or SNAPPER

Serves 4
Preparation time 10 minutes
Cooking time 12 minutes

13 oz (400 g) dried garganelli or other tube-shaped
  pasta
½ cup (125 ml) unsalted butter
4 slices of Parma ham, cut into 1-inch (2.5 cm) strips
10 oz (300 g) red mullet or snapper fillets, cut into
  1-inch (2.5 cm) pieces
10 fresh sage leaves, roughly chopped
Salt and pepper

Cook the pasta in a large saucepan of salted boiling water according to the package instructions until al dente.

Meanwhile, melt the butter in a large skillet over medium heat. When the butter starts to foam, add the Parma ham and cook, stirring, for 2 to 3 minutes. Season the red mullet with salt and pepper and add to the pan, skin side down. Scatter with the sage and cook for 2 to 3 minutes, until the fish is opaque all the way through. If the butter begins to color too much, reduce the heat slightly.

Drain the pasta, reserving a ladleful of the cooking water, and toss into the pan with the fish. Stir gently to combine, then add the reserved pasta cooking water and stir over a medium heat until the pasta is well coated and looks silky. Serve immediately.

For lemon sole garganelli, use 10 oz (300 g) lemon sole instead of the mullet and replace the sage with 4 sprigs fresh tarragon. Toss 2 oz (60 g) roughly chopped pitted black olives into the pasta at the last minute.

JUMBO SHRIMP & ZUCCHINI LINGUINE

Serves 4
Preparation time 10 minutes
Cooking time 10–12 minutes

13 oz (400 g) dried linguine
3 tbsp (45 ml) olive oil
7 oz (200 g) peeled raw jumbo shrimp
2 cloves garlic, crushed
Finely grated zest of 1 unwaxed lemon
1 fresh red chile, seeded and finely chopped
13 oz (400 g) zucchini, coarsely grated
¼ cup (60 ml) unsalted butter, cut into cubes
Salt

Cook the pasta in a large saucepan of salted boiling water according to the package instructions until al dente. Drain.

Meanwhile, heat the oil in a large skillet over high heat until the surface of the oil seems to shimmer slightly. Add the shrimp, garlic, lemon zest and chile, season with salt and cook, stirring, for 2 minutes, until the shrimp turn pink. Add the zucchini and butter, season with a little more salt and stir well. Cook, stirring, for 30 seconds.

Toss in the pasta and stir until the butter has melted and all the ingredients are well combined. Serve immediately.

For squid & butternut squash sauce, replace the shrimp with 7 oz (200 g) prepared squid rings and the zucchini with 13 oz (400 g) coarsely grated butternut squash, and cook as described above.

SHRIMP WITH SESAME NOODLES

Serves 4
Preparation time 8 minutes
Cooking time 6 minutes

8 oz (250 g) egg noodles
1 tbsp (15 ml) toasted sesame oil, plus extra to serve
1 tbsp (15 ml) vegetable oil
1 yellow bell pepper, cored, seeded and sliced
1 red bell pepper, cored, seeded and sliced
3 oz (75 g) shiitake or chestnut mushrooms, trimmed and thinly sliced
1 large carrot, peeled and cut into thin sticks
2 green onions, thinly sliced lengthwise
1 red chile, finely chopped
10 oz (300 g) large cooked peeled shrimp
1 tbsp (15 ml) sesame seeds, lightly toasted

Cook the noodles in a large saucepan of unsalted water for 4 minutes or according to the instructions on the package.

Meanwhile, heat a large wok over high heat until smoking. Add the oils and stir-fry the peppers for 1 to 2 minutes. Add the mushrooms; cook for 1 minute, then add the carrot and cook for a further minute. Add the green onions, chile and shrimp and stir-fry for 2 minutes.

Drain the noodles and add them to the wok. Mix to combine, heat through, then scatter with the sesame seeds and serve immediately.

For teriyaki shrimp with vegetables on soba, substitute the egg noodles for soba noodles (made with buckwheat flour). Prepare the vegetables and noodles as above but cook the shrimp separately, adding 1 sliced clove garlic and 1/4 cup (60 ml) ready-made teriyaki sauce. Serve the shrimp on the soba noodles and sprinkle with fresh coriander instead of sesame seeds.

QUICK TUNA STEAK WITH GREEN SALSA

Serves 4
Preparation time 14 minutes, plus marinating
Cooking time 2–4 minutes

2 tbsp (30 ml) olive oil
Grated zest of 1 lemon
2 tsp (10 ml) chopped fresh parsley
1/2 tsp (2 ml) crushed coriander seeds
4 fresh tuna steaks, about 5 oz (150 g) each
Salt and pepper
Dressed lettuce salad, to serve

Salsa
2 tbsp (30 ml) capers, chopped
2 tbsp (30 ml) chopped cornichons
1 tbsp (15 ml) finely chopped fresh parsley
2 tsp (10 ml) chopped fresh chives
2 tsp (10 ml) finely chopped fresh chervil
1 1/2 oz (30 g) pitted green olives, chopped
1 shallot, finely chopped (optional)
2 tbsp (30 ml) lemon juice
2 tbsp (30 ml) olive oil

Mix together the oil, lemon zest, parsley and coriander seeds with plenty of pepper in a bowl. Rub the tuna steaks with the mixture.

Combine the ingredients for the salsa, season to taste and set aside.

Heat a grill pan or frying pan until hot and cook the tuna steaks for 1 to 2 minutes on each side to cook partially. The tuna should be well seared but rare. Remove and allow to rest for a couple of minutes.

Serve the tuna steaks with a spoonful of salsa, a dressed salad and plenty of fresh crusty bread.

For yellow pepper & mustard salsa, combine the following: 2 yellow bell peppers, finely chopped; 1 tbsp (15 ml) Dijon mustard; 2 tbsp (30 ml) each finely chopped fresh chives, parsley and dill; 1 tsp (5 ml) sugar; 1 tbsp (15 ml) cider vinegar; and 2 tbsp (30 ml) olive oil.

JUMBO SHRIMP WITH JAPANESE SALAD

Serves 4
Preparation time 10 minutes, plus cooling
Cooking time 3 minutes

13 oz (400 g) raw, peeled jumbo shrimp
7 oz (200 g) bean sprouts
4 oz (125 g) snow peas, shredded
3½ oz (100 g) water chestnuts, thinly sliced
½ iceberg lettuce, shredded
12 radishes, thinly sliced
1 tbsp (15 ml) sesame seeds, lightly toasted

Dressing
2 tbsp (30 ml) rice vinegar
½ cup (125 ml) sunflower oil
1 tsp (5 ml) five-spice powder (optional)
2 tbsp (30 ml) mirin

Set a steamer over a pan of simmering water and steam the shrimp for 2 to 3 minutes, until cooked and pink. Set aside and leave to cool.

Make the dressing by mixing together all the ingredients in a small bowl.

Toss together the bean sprouts, snow peas, water chestnuts, lettuce and radishes. Scatter the shrimp and sesame seeds overtop. Drizzle the dressing and serve immediately.

For chili sauce to serve as an accompaniment, combine 1 finely chopped clove garlic, ½ tsp (10 ml) finely grated fresh ginger, 2 tsp (10 ml) light soy sauce, 1 tbsp (15 ml) Asian sweet chili sauce and ½ tbsp (7 ml) ketchup. Mix well.

BROCCOLI & SAUSAGE ORECCHIETTE

Serves 4
Preparation time 5 minutes
Cooking time 15 minutes

2 tbsp (30 ml) olive oil
1 onion, finely chopped
7 oz (200 g) Italian pork sausage
Large pinch of hot pepper flakes
10 oz (300 g) dried orecchiette
7 oz (200 g) broccoli, broken into florets
1¼ oz (40 g) pecorino cheese, freshly grated, plus
   extra to serve
Salt

Heat the oil in a skillet over low heat; add the onion and cook, stirring occasionally, for 6 to 7 minutes, until softened. Split the sausage open and break up the meat with a fork. Add the sausage meat chunks and hot pepper flakes to the pan and increase the heat to medium. Cook, stirring, for 4 to 5 minutes, until the sausage meat is golden brown.

Meanwhile, cook the pasta and broccoli in a large saucepan of salted boiling water according to the pasta package instructions until the pasta is al dente. Don't be alarmed if the broccoli starts to break up – it needs to be very tender.

Drain the pasta and broccoli and toss into the pan with the sausage meat. Stir in the pecorino and serve immediately with a bowl of extra grated pecorino on the side.

For cauliflower & chorizo sauce, replace the Italian pork sausage with 7 oz (200 g) sliced chorizo. Cut 8 oz (250 g) cauliflower into small florets and cook with the pasta as above.

SWEET & SOUR PORK NOODLES

Serves 4
Preparation time 15 minutes
Cooking time 12–16 minutes

½ cup (125 ml) ketchup
3 tbsp (45 ml) brown sugar
2 tbsp (30 ml) white wine vinegar
6 oz (175 g) medium egg noodles
2 tbsp (30 ml) toasted sesame oil
12 oz (375 g) lean pork, cut into strips
1-inch (2.5 cm) piece fresh ginger, peeled
   and chopped
1 clove garlic, crushed
4 oz (125 g) snow peas, halved in length
1 large carrot, cut into strips
6 oz (175 g) bean sprouts
7-oz (200 g) can bamboo shoots, drained

Place the ketchup, sugar and vinegar in a small saucepan and heat gently for 2 to 3 minutes, until the sugar has dissolved, then set aside.

Cook the egg noodles for 3 to 5 minutes or according to package instructions until tender, then drain and set aside.

Heat the oil in a wok or large, heavy-bottomed frying pan and cook the pork strips over high heat for 2 to 3 minutes, until beginning to turn golden, then add the ginger, garlic, snow peas and carrot. Stir-fry for a further 2 minutes, then add the bean sprouts and bamboo shoots and stir-fry for 1 minute, until all the ingredients are piping hot.

Add the warm, drained noodles and sauce and toss over the heat, using 2 spoons to mix really well and heat through. Serve in warmed serving bowls.

For shrimp stir-fry with a thickened soy sauce, heat the oil and cook the ginger, garlic, snow peas and carrot for 2 to 3 minutes, then add the bean sprouts and bamboo shoots and 8 oz (250 g) shrimp and stir-fry for 1 to 2 minutes. Replace the sauce ingredients with ⅔ cup (150 ml) soy sauce, gently heated in a small pan. Add 1 tbsp (15 ml) cornstarch blended with 2 tbsp (30 ml) water and ½ tsp (10 ml) Chinese five-spice powder. Stir until warmed and thickened, then remove from the heat. Add to the stir-fry, toss and serve.

CHORIZO CARBONARA

Serves 4
Preparation time 5 minutes
Cooking time 18–20 minutes

4 oz (125 g) chorizo sausage, sliced
1 tbsp (15 ml) olive oil
12 oz (375 g) dried penne
4 eggs
2 oz (60 g) Parmesan cheese, freshly grated,
   plus extra to serve
Salt and pepper

Put the chorizo and oil in a frying pan over very low heat and cook, turning occasionally, until crisp. The melted fat released by the chorizo will be an essential part of your sauce.

Cook the pasta in a large saucepan of salted boiling water according to the package instructions until it is al dente.

Meanwhile, crack the eggs into a bowl, add the Parmesan and season with salt and a generous grinding of pepper. Mix together with a fork.

Just before the pasta is ready, increase the heat under the frying pan so that the oil and melted chorizo fat start to sizzle. Drain the pasta thoroughly, return to the pan and immediately stir in the egg mixture and the sizzling-hot contents of the frying pan. Stir vigorously so that the eggs cook evenly. Serve immediately with a scattering of grated Parmesan.

For spicy chorizo & leek carbonara, fry 1 finely sliced leek in 2 tbsp (30 ml) olive oil for 6 to 8 minutes, until soft, then add the chorizo and cook as above. Add ½ tsp (2 ml) hot paprika to the egg mixture and complete the recipe as above.

SPECK, SPINACH & TALEGGIO FUSILLI

Serves 4
Preparation time 5 minutes
Cooking time 15 minutes

12 oz (375 g) dried fusilli
3½ oz (100 g) speck or prosciutto slices
5 oz (150 g) Taleggio or fontina cheese, cut into small cubes
⅔ cup (150 ml) whipping (35%) cream
4 oz (125 g) baby spinach, roughly chopped
Salt and pepper
Freshly grated Parmesan cheese (optional)

Cook the pasta in a large saucepan of salted boiling water according to the package instructions until it is al dente.

Meanwhile, cut the speck into wide strips.

Drain the pasta, return to the pan and place over low heat. Add the speck, Taleggio, cream and spinach and stir until most of the cheese has melted. Season with a generous grinding of pepper and serve immediately with a scattering of grated Parmesan, if desired.

For mozzarella & ham fusilli, use 5 oz (150 g) mozzarella instead of the Taleggio and replace the speck or prociutto slices with 3½ oz (100 g) Black Forest ham. Mozzarella will give a milder flavor than Taleggio.

QUICK MIDWEEK MEALS

QUICK PASTA CARBONARA

Serves 4
Preparation time 10 minutes
Cooking time 10 minutes

13 oz (400 g) dried spaghetti or other long thin pasta
2 tbsp (30 ml) olive oil
7 oz (200 g) pancetta, cut into cubes
3 eggs
¼ cup (60 ml) freshly grated Parmesan cheese
3 tbsp (45 ml) chopped flat-leaf (Italian) parsley
3 tbsp (45 ml) table (18%) or half-and-half (10%) cream
Salt and pepper

Cook the pasta in a large saucepan of boiling salted water according to the package instructions until al dente.

Meanwhile, heat the oil in a large, nonstick frying pan over medium heat. Add the pancetta and cook, stirring frequently, for 4 to 5 minutes, until crisp.

Beat the eggs with the Parmesan, parsley and cream in a bowl. Season with salt and pepper and set aside.

Drain the pasta and add to the pancetta mixture. Stir over low heat until combined, then pour in the egg mixture. Stir and remove the pan from the heat. Continue stirring for a few seconds until the eggs are lightly cooked and creamy. Serve immediately.

For mushroom carbonara, add ½ to 1 cup (125 to 200 ml) sliced mushrooms with the pancetta and cook as above.

ASPARAGUS & BACON BOWTIES

Serves 4
Preparation time 10 minutes
Cooking time 15 minutes

13 oz (400 g) asparagus, trimmed
1 large clove garlic, crushed
¼ cup (60 ml) olive oil
Salt and pepper
2 oz (60 g) Parmesan cheese, freshly grated
8 slices bacon or pancetta
400 g (13 oz) dried bowtie pasta
Fresh Parmesan cheese shavings, to serve

Cut the tips off the asparagus and reserve. Cut the stalks into 1-inch (2.5 cm) pieces and blanch in a saucepan of boiling water for 3 to 4 minutes, until very tender. Drain and put in a food processor with the garlic, oil and Parmesan. Process to make a smooth paste. Season with salt and pepper.

Arrange the bacon slices in a single layer on a baking sheet and cook under a preheated hot broiler for 5 to 6 minutes, until crisp and golden. Break into 1-inch (2.5 cm) lengths.

Meanwhile, cook the pasta in a large saucepan of salted boiling water according to the package instructions until al dente, adding the reserved asparagus tips to the pan 3 minutes before the end of the cooking time.

Drain the pasta and stir into a bowl with the asparagus sauce. Scatter with the crispy bacon and Parmesan shavings and serve immediately.

For creamy zucchini & bacon bowties, omit the asparagus tips and instead pan-fry 8 oz (250 g) sliced small zucchini in 2 tbsp (30 ml) butter while the pasta is cooking and the bacon grilling. When cooked, toss the pasta with the zucchini and the bacon and ½ cup (60 ml) table (18%) or half-and-half (10%) cream.

TORTELLINI WITH CREAMY HAM & PEAS

Serves 4
Preparation time 2 minutes
Cooking time 8–12 minutes

1 tbsp (15 ml) unsalted butter
1 cup (250 ml) peas, defrosted if frozen
3 oz (75 g) ham, cut into strips
1¼ cups (300 ml) crème fraîche
Large pinch of freshly grated nutmeg
1 lb (500 g) fresh spinach and ricotta or meat tortellini
1½ oz (40 g) Parmesan cheese, freshly grated, plus extra to serve

Melt the butter in a large skillet over medium heat until it begins to sizzle. Add the peas and ham and cook, stirring, for 3 to 4 minutes if using fresh peas, or just 1 minute if using defrosted frozen peas.

Stir in the crème fraîche, add the nutmeg and season with salt and pepper. Bring to a boil and boil for 2 minutes, until slightly thickened.

Cook the tortellini in a large saucepan of salted boiling water according to the package instructions until it is al dente. Drain and toss into the creamy sauce with the Parmesan. Gently stir to combine and serve at once with a scattering of Parmesan.

For bacon & zucchini tortellini, replace the ham with the same quantity of bacon strips, frying them for 4 minutes. Then add 7 oz (200 g) chopped zucchini in place of the peas, and proceed as above.

PORK WITH EGGPLANT & NOODLES

Serves 4
Preparation time 15 minutes
Cooking time 15 minutes

8 oz (250 g) thick, flat rice noodles
About 3 tbsp (45 ml) vegetable or peanut oil
1 large eggplant, cut into ½-inch (1 cm) dice
1 lb (500 g) ground pork
2 tbsp (30 ml) fresh coriander leaves, plus extra to
   garnish

Marinade
1 tbsp (15 ml) dark soy sauce
3 tbsp (45 ml) light soy sauce, plus extra to serve
   (optional)
1 tbsp (15 ml) cornstarch
1 tsp (5 ml) liquid honey
1 tbsp (15 ml) Asian chili paste
2 tsp (10 ml) finely chopped garlic
1 tbsp (15 ml) finely chopped fresh ginger

Make the marinade by mixing together all the ingredients in a non-metallic bowl. Add the pork and combine thoroughly until the liquid has been absorbed. Set aside.

Cook the noodles in boiling water for 2 to 3 minutes or according to the instructions on the package. Drain.

Heat the oil until smoking in a large wok or frying pan. Carefully stir-fry the eggplant until golden and soft. Remove with a slotted spoon and leave to drain on paper towel.

Add more oil to the pan if necessary and stir-fry the pork until browned and cooked through. Pour in ⅓ cup (75 ml) water and allow to gently bubble. Return the eggplant to the wok and heat through, then add the coriander leaves.

Serve the pork and eggplant piled on top of the noodles and with a scattering of coriander leaves and some extra light soy sauce, if desired.

For ground steak with okra & rice, cook 8 oz (250 g) rice instead of noodles and substitute the ground pork with the same quantity of ground steak. Replace the eggplant with 7 oz (200 g) okra, sliced into ½-inch (1 cm) pieces and fry for 5 minutes. Serve as above.

74

PORK & PEPPERCORN TAGLIATELLE

Serves 4
Preparation time 10 minutes
Cooking time 20 minutes

11½ oz (350 g) dried tagliatelle verde or similar pasta
2 tbsp (30 ml) olive oil
1 lb (500 g) pork tenderloin, sliced
1 onion, finely chopped
1 large clove garlic, chopped
2 tbsp (30 ml) brandy
⅓ cup (75 ml) white wine
2 tbsp (30 ml) raisins soaked in ¼ cup (60 ml) warm
   apple juice
1 tsp (5 ml) chopped fresh rosemary
1½ tbsp (7 ml) green peppercorns in brine, drained and
   chopped
3 juniper berries (optional)
1 cup (250 ml) table (18%) or half-and-half (10%)
   cream
Salt and pepper

Cook the pasta in lightly salted boiling water according to the instructions on the package.

Meanwhile, heat the oil in a large frying pan and brown the pork slices for 2 minutes, turning once. Remove with a slotted spoon and set aside. Add the onion to the pan and cook for about 5 minutes before adding the garlic. Cook for a further minute, until softened.

Pour in the brandy, wine, raisins and apple juice, rosemary, green peppercorns and juniper berries (if used), bring to a boil and bubble over high heat for 1 to 2 minutes. Reduce the heat, stir in the cream and simmer gently for 5 minutes.

Return the pork to the pan and stir for 3 to 5 minutes, or until cooked through and tender. Turn the heat off. Toss through the prepared pasta and serve.

For pork & sun-dried tomato tagliatelle, replace the raisins with chopped sun-dried tomatoes. There is no need to soak them in the apple juice, but don't omit it altogether: just add it at the same time as the tomatoes.

PORK TENDERLOIN WITH MUSHROOMS

Serves 4
Preparation time 15 minutes
Cooking time 15–17 minutes

¼ cup (60 ml) olive oil
1 lb (500 g) pork tenderloin, sliced into ¼-inch
   (5 mm) discs
10 oz (300 g) mushrooms, trimmed and cut
   into chunks
1 lemon
1¼ cups (300 ml) crème fraîche
2 sprigs of fresh tarragon, leaves stripped
Salt and pepper

Heat 2 tbsp (30 ml) of the oil in a pan over medium-high heat and fry the pork slices for 3 to 4 minutes, turning once so that they are browned on both sides. Remove with a slotted spoon.

Add the remaining oil to the pan, tip in the mushrooms and cook for 3 to 4 minutes, stirring occasionally, until softened and golden.

Cut half of the lemon into slices and add to the pan to brown a little on each side, then remove and set aside.

Return the pork to the pan, add the crème fraîche and tarragon and pour in the juice from the remaining lemon. Season well, bring to a boil, then reduce the heat and leave to bubble gently for 5 minutes. Add the prepared lemon slices at the last minute and gently stir through.

Serve the pork with white rice or crispy potato wedges.

For couscous with petits pois to serve as an accompaniment, soak 1⅔ cups (400 ml) couscous in 1⅔ cups (400 ml) just-boiled water or vegetable stock and leave for 5 to 8 minutes, until soft. Fluff up the couscous with a fork and season. Boil 5 oz (150 g) frozen petits pois for 3 minutes, drain, then mix them with the couscous. Before serving, add a handful of chopped chives, a few knobs of butter and season with black pepper.

PORK IN CIDER WITH PAPPARDELLE

Serves 4
Preparation time 8 minutes
Cooking time 20 minutes

½ oz (15 g) dried wild mushrooms
3 tbsp (45 ml) olive oil
13 oz (400 g) boneless pork loin
5 oz (150 g) smoked bacon
8 shallots, quartered
1¼ cups (300 ml) unsweetened or dry cider
½ cup (125 ml) cider vinegar
2 sprigs of fresh thyme
1 bay leaf, torn
Salt and pepper
¾ cup + 2 tbsp (200 ml) crème fraîche
13 oz (400 g) fresh pappardelle or thick ribbon pasta

Soak the dried mushrooms for 5 to 10 minutes in 6 tbsp (90 ml) boiling water.

Meanwhile, heat the oil in a large frying pan over medium heat and fry the pork and bacon for approximately 3 minutes, until browned. Add the shallots and continue frying for a further 2 to 3 minutes, until golden and beginning to soften.

Pour in the cider and cider vinegar and add the mushrooms and soaking liquid. Stir in the herbs and season well. Bring to a boil, then reduce the heat, cover and leave to bubble gently for 10 to 12 minutes, until the shallots are soft.

Meanwhile, cook the pasta in lightly salted boiling water for 3 minutes or according to the instructions on the package. Drain and transfer to serving dishes.

Stir the crème fraîche into the pork, increase the heat briefly and then place the meat on the pasta and spoon the sauce over. Serve immediately.

For venison in red wine, substitute the pork with 4 venison steaks, cut into strips, and replace the cider with red wine. Omit the cider vinegar. Serve as above.

CRISPY PARMA HAM PARCELS

Serves 4
Preparation time 10 minutes
Cooking time 4 minutes

8 slices of Parma ham or prosciutto
3½ oz (100 g) creamy blue cheese, such as Roquefort,
 St Agur, dolcelatte or Gorgonzola, thinly sliced
1 tsp (5 ml) chopped fresh thyme leaves
1 pear, peeled, cored and diced
¼ cup (60 ml) walnuts, chopped

To serve
Watercress leaves tossed in olive oil and balsamic
 vinegar
1 pear, peeled, cored and sliced

Put a slice of Parma ham on a chopping board and then put a second slice across it to form a cross shape.

Arrange one-quarter of the cheese slices in the center, scatter over some thyme and top with one-quarter of the diced pear.

Add one-quarter of the walnuts, then fold over the sides of the ham to form a neat parcel. Repeat this process to make 4 parcels.

Transfer the parcels to a foil-lined broiler pan and cook under a pre-heated hot broiler for about 2 minutes on each side, until the ham is crisp and the cheese is beginning to ooze out of the sides.

Serve the parcels immediately with the dressed watercress leaves and slices of pear.

For figs with Parma ham, quarter 8 fresh figs, leaving them attached at the base. Mix 1 tsp (5 ml) Dijon mustard with 4 oz (125 g) ricotta cheese, season to taste and spoon over the figs. Divide 3¼ oz (85 g) Parma ham, cut into strips, among them and drizzle over 2 tbsp (30 ml) balsamic vinegar.

GREEN BEAN & BACON FRITTATA

Serves 4
Preparation time 10 minutes
Cooking time about 10 minutes

6 oz (175 g) slender green beans
6 slices back bacon
⅔ cup (150 ml) frozen peas, defrosted
6 eggs
1 tsp (5 ml) whole-grain mustard
½ tsp (2 ml) paprika
2 tbsp (30 ml) vegetable oil
¼ cup (60 ml) freshly grated Parmesan cheese

Cook the green beans in boiling water for 5 minutes. Drain and refresh with cold water to stop them from cooking further, then roughly chop and set aside. Meanwhile, place the bacon under a preheated medium broiler for 3 to 4 minutes, until golden and cooked. Cool slightly, then snip roughly with scissors. Toss the green beans and bacon with the peas.

Beat the eggs with the mustard and paprika. Heat the oil in a medium nonstick frying pan with a metal handle, then pour in the eggs. Working quickly, scatter over the beans, peas and bacon. Cook over a gentle heat until the base has set.

Sprinkle over the Parmesan and place the pan under the grill for 2 to 3 minutes, until the frittata is set and golden.

Cut the frittata into wedges. If not serving immediately, wrap it in foil to keep warm.

For mushroom & bacon frittata, omit the beans and peas. Heat 1 tbsp (15 ml) olive oil in a frying pan and cook 8 oz (250 g) quartered cremini mushrooms for 4 to 5 minutes, until soft and golden. Pour into the egg mixture in the pan and cook as above, with the Parmesan sprinkled over before grilling. Serve cut into wedges, either warm or cold.

PROSCIUTTO & PORCINI PAPPARDELLE

Serves 4
Preparation time 10 minutes
Cooking time 6–10 minutes

13 oz (400 g) dried pappardelle or homemade
  pappardelle
2 tbsp (30 ml) olive oil
1 clove garlic, crushed
8 oz (250 g) fresh porcini mushrooms, sliced
8 oz (250 g) prosciutto slices
⅔ cup (150 ml) whipping (35%) cream
Handful of flat-leaf (Italian) parsley, chopped
3 oz (75 g) Parmesan cheese, freshly grated
Salt and pepper

Cook the pasta in a large saucepan of salted boiling water until it is al dente: according to the package instructions for dried pasta or for 2 to 3 minutes if using fresh pasta.

Meanwhile, heat the oil in a saucepan over medium heat. Add the garlic and porcini and cook, stirring frequently, for 4 minutes. Cut the prosciutto into strips, trying to keep them separate. Add to the porcini mixture with the cream and parsley, and season with salt and pepper. Bring to a boil, then reduce the heat and simmer for 1 minute.

Drain the pasta, add to the sauce and toss well, using 2 spoons to mix evenly. Scatter with the Parmesan, toss well and serve immediately.

For spaghetti with dried porcini & pine nuts, soak 4 oz (125 g) dried porcini in enough hot water to cover them for 15 minutes, to rehydrate them. Drain, reserving the water, pat dry with paper towel and fry as above. Once the porcini have been fried, as above, add the reserved soaking water to the pan and boil until the liquid has almost evaporated. Stir in the prosciutto and cream as above. Briefly toast 2 tbsp (30 ml) pine nuts in the oven and add to the sauce before combining with the cooked spaghetti.

PASTA WITH PANCETTA & SCALLOPS

Serves 4
Preparation time 15 minutes
Cooking time 15–20 minutes

5 tbsp (75 ml) extra virgin olive oil
4 oz (125 g) pancetta, cut into cubes
1 red chile, seeded and finely chopped
2 cloves garlic, thinly sliced
8 oz (250 g) scallops
13 oz (400 g) dried linguine
7 tbsp (105 ml) dry white wine
2 tbsp (30 ml) roughly chopped flat-leaf (Italian)
  parsley
Salt

Heat the oil in a large frying pan over medium heat; add the pancetta and cook, stirring occasionally, for 4 to 5 minutes, until golden and crisp. Remove from the heat and stir in the chile and garlic. Leave the flavors to infuse while you prepare the scallops and start cooking the pasta.

If you have bought scallops with the orange roe, carefully separate the roe from the main body of the scallops. Using a small, sharp knife, slice once across the thickness of each scallop to make thinner disks. Set aside.

Cook the pasta in a large saucepan of salted boiling water according to the package instructions until al dente.

When the pasta is almost ready, heat the frying pan with the pancetta over high heat. When the oil starts to sizzle, season the scallops and roes with salt, add to the pan and cook, stirring gently, for 2 minutes. Pour in the wine and boil rapidly for 2 minutes.

Drain the pasta and stir into the frying pan with the parsley. Toss the pasta over the heat for 30 seconds to combine all the flavors. Serve immediately.

For pasta with asparagus, scallops & pancetta, simply add 1 cup (250 ml) asparagus tips to the pasta cooking water for the last 3 minutes of the cooking time and complete the recipe as above.

STIR-FRIED BEEF WITH VEGETABLES

Serves 4
Preparation time 15 minutes
Cooking time 5 minutes

3 tbsp (45 ml) rice wine vinegar
¼ cup (60 ml) liquid honey
¼ cup (60 ml) light soy sauce
3 tbsp (45 ml) mirin
½ cucumber
1 bulb fennel, quartered
1 bunch radishes, trimmed
1 lb (500 g) lean rump or sirloin steak
1 tbsp (15 ml) cornstarch
5 tbsp (75 ml) stir-fry or wok oil
1 medium red chile, seeded and thinly sliced
2-inch (5 cm) piece fresh ginger, chopped
1 bunch green onions, thinly sliced
10 oz (300 g) straight-to-wok noodles
1 oz (25 g) chopped fresh coriander

Mix together the vinegar, honey, soy sauce and mirin in a small bowl.

Halve the cucumber lengthwise and scoop out the seeds. Push the cucumber, fennel and radishes through a food processor fitted with a slicing attachment. (Alternatively, slice as thinly as possible by hand.)

Trim any fat from the beef and slice very thinly. Dust with the cornstarch.

Heat 2 tbsp (30 ml) of the oil in a wok or large frying pan. Add the chile, ginger and beef and stir-fry quickly for 1 minute. Drain to a large plate. Add the green onions to the pan and stir-fry quickly for a further minute. Drain to the plate.

Heat a little more oil and stir-fry half the shredded vegetables for about 30 seconds. Drain to the plate. Stir-fry the remainder and drain to the plate.

Pour the remaining oil into the pan and add the noodles and coriander. Cook, stirring, for a few seconds to heat through and break up the noodles, then tip the beef and vegetables back into the pan. Add the vinegar mixture and cook for about 30 seconds, until heated through. Serve immediately.

For stir-fried beef with Chinese vegetables, omit the cucumber, fennel and radishes. Thinly slice 7 oz (200 g) sugar snap peas, 2 zucchini and 2 sweet bell peppers and stir-fry in 2 batches with an 8-oz (200 g) can water chestnuts, halved, as in the fifth step.

INDIVIDUAL ITALIAN STEAK PARCELS

Serves 4
Preparation time 10 minutes
Cooking time 20 minutes

1 tbsp (15 ml) olive oil
4 filet mignon or beef tenderloin steaks, about 5 oz
    (150 g) each
8 large squares of phyllo pastry
⅔ cup (150 ml) butter, melted
4 oz (125 g) buffalo mozzarella cheese, cut into
    4 slices
2 tsp (10 ml) chopped fresh marjoram
2 tsp (10 ml) chopped fresh oregano
4 sun-blushed tomatoes, shredded
2 tbsp (30 ml) finely grated Parmesan cheese
Salt and pepper

Salad
5 oz (150 g) arugula
4 oz (125 g) buffalo mozzarella cheese, cubed
½ red onion, finely sliced (optional)
2 ripe plum tomatoes, sliced

Heat the oil in a hot frying pan and sear the steaks for 2 minutes on each side (they will continue cooking in the oven). Remove and set aside.

Brush each sheet of pastry with melted butter and arrange 2 sheets on a work surface. Place a steak in the center of the pastry, followed by a slice of mozzarella and one-quarter of the herbs and sun-blushed tomato shreds. Season and bring up the sides of the pastry. Scrunch it together at the top to seal the steak into a parcel. Sprinkle over one-quarter of the grated Parmesan. Repeat with the remaining steaks.

Cook in a preheated 425°F (220°C) oven for 15 minutes, until the pastry is crisp and golden brown. Remove and leave to rest for 2 to 3 minutes.

Toss the salad ingredients together, season and serve with the parcels.

For summertime chicken parcels, use 4 chicken breasts instead of the steaks – you will need to fry them for about 5 minutes on each side. For a stronger flavor, replace the toppings with either 4 oz (125 g) sliced Gorgonzola, ¼ cup (60 ml) roughly chopped walnuts and 2 tbsp (30 ml) roughly chopped fresh chives or 4 oz (125 g) sliced firm goat's cheese, ¼ cup (60 ml) black pitted olives and 2 tbsp (30 ml) shredded basil.

FETA & WATERMELON SALAD

Serves 4
Preparation time 10 minutes
Cooking time 2 minutes

1 tbsp (15 ml) black sesame seeds
1 lb (500 g) watermelon, peeled, seeded and diced
6 oz (175 g) feta cheese, diced
1¾ lb (875 g) arugula
Sprigs of fresh mint, parsley and coriander
6 tbsp (90 ml) olive oil
1 tbsp (15 ml) orange flower water
1½ tbsp (22 ml) lemon juice
1 tsp (5 ml) pomegranate syrup (optional)
½ tsp (2 ml) granulated or fruit sugar
Salt and pepper

Heat a frying pan and dry-fry the sesame seeds for 2 minutes, until aromatic, then set aside.

Arrange the watermelon and feta on a large plate with the arugula and herbs.

Whisk together the oil, orange flower water, lemon juice, pomegranate syrup (if used) and sugar. Season to taste with salt and pepper, then drizzle over the salad. Scatter over the sesame seeds and serve with toasted pita bread.

For quick feta & tomato salad, mix 1 lb (500 g) skinned and chopped tomatoes with 8 oz (250 g) cubed feta and 2 oz (60 g) pitted black olives. Drizzle over a mixture of 3 tbsp (45 ml) olive oil, 2 chopped cloves garlic and ½ tsp (2 ml) granulated or fruit sugar. Season with plenty of black pepper and serve.

QUICK ONE-POT RATATOUILLE

Serves 4
Preparation time 10 minutes
Cooking time 20 minutes

7 tbsp (105 ml) olive oil
2 onions, chopped
1 medium eggplant, cut into bite-size cubes
2 large zucchini, cut into bite-size pieces
1 red bell pepper, cored, seeded and cut into
    bite-size pieces
1 yellow bell pepper, cored, seeded and cut into
    bite-size pieces
2 cloves garlic, crushed
14-oz (398 ml) can chopped tomatoes
¼ cup (60 ml) chopped fresh parsley or basil
Salt and pepper

Heat the oil in a large saucepan until very hot. Add the onions, eggplant, zucchini, peppers and garlic and cook, stirring constantly, for a few minutes, until softened. Add the tomatoes, season to taste with salt and pepper and stir well.

Reduce the heat, cover the pan tightly and simmer for 15 minutes or until all the vegetables are cooked. Remove from the heat and stir in the chopped parsley or basil before serving.

For Mediterranean vegetable pie, spoon the cooked vegetable mixture into a medium-sized ovenproof dish. Cook 1 lb 10 oz (800 g) quartered potatoes in a large saucepan of salted boiling water for 12 to 15 minutes or until tender, then drain and roughly mash with 7 oz (200 g) finely grated Cheddar cheese. Spread over the vegetable mixture, then bake in a preheated 350°F (180°C) oven for 20 minutes, or until lightly golden on top.

FRAGRANT LAMB CUTLETS

Serves 4
Preparation time 5 minutes, plus marinating
Cooking time 15 minutes

12 lamb cutlets
4 sweet potatoes, baked in their skins
Salt and pepper
Arugula leaves, to serve

Marinade
Finely grated zest and juice of ½ lemon
2 cloves garlic, crushed
2 tbsp (30 ml) olive oil, plus extra for brushing
4 sprigs of fresh rosemary, finely chopped
4 anchovy fillets in olive oil, drained and finely chopped
2 tbsp (30 ml) lemon cordial or sweetened lemonade

Mix together all the marinade ingredients in a non-metallic bowl, then add the lamb cutlets. Season to taste with salt and pepper, turn the cutlets to coat and set aside for 15 minutes to marinate.

Cook the cutlets under a preheated hot broiler for 3 to 5 minutes on each side or until slightly charred and cooked through. Keep warm and allow to rest.

Meanwhile, cut the baked sweet potatoes into quarters, scoop out some of the flesh and brush the skins with oil. Season to taste with salt and pepper and cook for about 15 minutes under the broiler until crisp. Serve with the lamb cutlets and arugula leaves.

For pork patties with sweet potato slices, mix 1 lb (500 g) ground pork with the marinade ingredients, omitting the anchovies. Using your hands, form the ground mixture into little patties and cook under a hot broiler for 5 to 6 minutes on each side, until browned and cooked through. Serve with sweet potato skins and arugula leaves, as above.

CRISPY LAMB MOROCCAN ROLLS

Serves 2
Preparation time 15 minutes
Cooking time 10 minutes

8 oz (250 g) ground lamb
1 tsp (5 ml) ground cinnamon
3 tbsp (45 ml) pine nuts
2 naan breads, warmed
⅔ cup (150 ml) hummus
2 tbsp (30 ml) fresh mint leaves
1 Little Gem lettuce or romaine heart, finely shredded
   (optional)

Fry the ground lamb in a large, nonstick frying pan for 8 to 10 minutes, until it becomes golden brown. Add the cinnamon and pine nuts and cook again for 1 minute. Remove from the heat.

Place the warm naan breads on a chopping board and, using a rolling pin, firmly roll to flatten.

Mix the hummus with half the mint leaves, then spread in a thick layer over the warmed naans. Spoon over the crispy lamb, then scatter over the shredded lettuce, if using, and the remaining mint leaves. Tightly roll up and secure with cocktail sticks. Serve immediately, or wrap tightly in foil to transport.

For lamb kofta, mix the raw ground lamb with 4 finely chopped green onions, 1 tsp (5 ml) ground cinnamon, a very finely chopped tomato and 1 egg yolk until blended together. Form into a very large, thin patty shape, and grill or cook in a large, heavy-bottomed frying pan on one side for 3 minutes, then on the other side for 2 minutes, until golden. Spread 1 warm naan with 2 tbsp (30 ml) Greek yogurt, scatter with the mint leaves and shredded lettuce, if using, and slip the large flattened kofta on top. Roll tightly and secure with cocktail sticks. Cut the kofta in half to serve 2.

TAVERNA-STYLE GRILLED LAMB WITH FETA

Serves 4
Preparation time 8 minutes
Cooking time 6–8 minutes

1 lb (500 g) leg or shoulder of lamb, diced

Marinade
2 tbsp (30 ml) chopped fresh oregano
1 tbsp (15 ml) chopped fresh rosemary
Grated zest of 1 lemon
2 tbsp (30 ml) olive oil
Salt and pepper

Feta salad
7 oz (200 g) feta cheese, sliced
1 tbsp (15 ml) chopped fresh oregano
2 tbsp (30 ml) chopped fresh parsley
Grated zest and juice of 1 lemon
½ small red onion, finely sliced
3 tbsp (45 ml) olive oil

Mix together the marinade ingredients in a non-metallic bowl, add the lamb and mix to coat thoroughly. Thread the meat onto 4 skewers.

Arrange the sliced feta on a large serving dish and sprinkle over the herbs, lemon zest and sliced onion. Drizzle over the lemon juice and oil and season with salt and pepper.

Cook the lamb skewers under a preheated hot broiler or in a grill pan for about 6 to 8 minutes, turning frequently, until browned and almost cooked through. Remove from heat and leave to rest for 1 to 2 minutes.

Serve the lamb, with any pan juices poured over, with the salad and accompanied with plenty of crusty bread, if desired.

For pork with red cabbage, replace the lamb with the same quantity of lean boneless pork. Marinate and cook the pork as above. Replace the feta with 8 oz (250 g) finely chopped red cabbage. Omit the oregano and swap the lemon for an orange. Mix the ingredients together and marinate for 5 minutes before serving.

THAI SESAME CHICKEN PATTIES

Serves 4
Preparation time 15 minutes, plus chilling
Cooking time 10 minutes

4 green onions
½ oz (15 g) fresh coriander, plus extra to garnish
1 lb (500 g) ground chicken
3 tbsp (45 ml) sesame seeds, toasted
1 tbsp (15 ml) light soy sauce
1½-inch (3.5 cm) piece fresh ginger, finely grated
1 egg white
1 tbsp (15 ml) toasted sesame oil
1 tbsp (15 ml) sunflower oil
Thai sweet chili dipping sauce, to serve
Green onion curls (optional)

Finely chop the green onions and coriander in a food processor or with a knife. Mix with the chicken, sesame seeds, soy sauce, ginger and egg white.

Divide the mixture into 20 mounds on a chopping board, then shape into slightly flattened rounds with wet hands. Chill for 1 hour (or longer if you have time).

Heat the sesame and sunflower oils in a large frying pan; add the patties and fry for 10 minutes, turning once or twice, until golden and cooked through to the center. Arrange on a serving plate with a small bowl of chili dipping sauce in the center. Garnish with extra coriander leaves and green onion curls, if desired.

For baby leaf stir-fry with chili to serve as an accompaniment, heat 2 tsp (10 ml) toasted sesame oil in the finished patty pan, add an 8-oz (250 g) pack of prepared baby leaf and baby vegetable stir-fry ingredients and stir-fry for 2 to 3 minutes, until the vegetables are hot. Mix in 2 tbsp (30 ml) light soy sauce and 1 tbsp (15 ml) Thai sweet chili dipping sauce. Serve in a side bowl with the chicken patties.

CHICKEN & VEGETABLE SKEWERS

Serves 4
Preparation time 10 minutes
Cooking time 15 minutes

4 boneless skinless chicken thighs
2 tbsp (30 ml) liquid honey, plus extra for dipping
2 tbsp (30 ml) mild whole-grain mustard, plus extra for dipping
1 zucchini, cut into 8 large pieces
1 carrot, cut into 8 large pieces

Cut the chicken thighs into bite-size pieces and toss in the honey and mustard. Arrange the chicken pieces on a baking sheet and bake in a preheated 350°F (180°C) oven for 15 minutes, until cooked through and lightly golden. Set aside and leave to cool.

Take 8 bamboo skewers and thread with the cooked chicken pieces and the raw vegetables.

Serve with extra honey and mustard for dipping. The skewers can also be refrigerated for adding to the following day's lunchbox.

For sticky chicken with honey & garlic, mix together 2 tbsp (30 ml) tomato ketchup, 2 tsp (10 ml) runny honey, 2 finely chopped cloves garlic and 1 tbsp (15 ml) of sunflower oil. Dip the chicken into the ketchup mixture then cook as above. Thread on to skewers with 1 red bell pepper, seeded, cored and cut into chunks and 8 cherry tomatoes

CHICKEN WITH SPRING HERBS

Serves 4
Preparation time 15 minutes
Cooking time 20 minutes

8 oz (250 g) mascarpone cheese
1 handful of fresh chervil, finely chopped
½ bunch of fresh parsley, finely chopped
2 tbsp (30 ml) chopped fresh mint leaves
4 boneless chicken breasts, skin on
¾ cup + 2 tbsp (200 ml) white wine
2 tbsp (30 ml) butter
Salt and pepper

Mix together the mascarpone and herbs in a bowl and season well with salt and pepper.

Lift the skin away from each chicken breast and spread a quarter of the mascarpone mixture on each breast. Replace the skin and smooth carefully over the mascarpone mixture. Season to taste with salt and pepper.

Place the chicken in a baking dish and pour the wine around it. Dot the butter over the chicken.

Roast in a preheated 350°F (180°C) oven for 20 minutes, until the chicken is golden and crisp. Remove from the oven and serve with garlic bread.

For baby glazed carrots as an alternative accompaniment to garlic bread, melt 2 tbsp (30 ml) butter in a saucepan, add 1 lb (500 g) young carrots, quartered lengthwise, a pinch of sugar, and salt and pepper to taste. Pour over just enough water to cover and simmer gently for 15 to 20 minutes, until the carrots are tender and the liquid has evaporated, adding 2 tbsp (30 ml) orange juice toward the end of the cooking time. Serve with the chicken, garnished with chopped parsley.

CHICKEN WITH SPINACH & RICOTTA

Serves 4
Preparation time 5 minutes
Cooking time 25 minutes

4 boneless skinless chicken breasts, 4 oz
    (125 g) each
4 oz (125 g) ricotta cheese
4 oz (125 g) cooked spinach, squeezed dry
¼ tsp (1 ml) freshly grated nutmeg
8 slices Parma ham
2 tbsp (30 ml) olive oil, plus extra for drizzling
Salt and pepper

To serve
Lemon wedges
Arugula leaves

Make a long horizontal slit through the thickest part of each chicken breast without cutting right through.

Crumble the ricotta into a bowl. Chop the spinach and mix into the ricotta with the nutmeg. Season with salt and pepper.

Divide the stuffing between the slits in the chicken breasts and wrap each one in 2 pieces of Parma ham, winding it around the chicken to cover the meat totally.

Heat the oil in a shallow ovenproof pan; add the chicken breasts and sauté for 4 minutes on each side or until the ham starts to brown. Transfer to a preheated 400°F (200°C) oven and cook for 15 minutes. Serve with lemon wedges and arugula leaves drizzled with olive oil.

For chicken with mozzarella & sun-dried tomatoes, instead of the ricotta, spinach and nutmeg, stuff each chicken breast with a thick slice of mozzarella and a sun-dried tomato piece, drained of its olive oil. Season well with black pepper and continue as in the main recipe.

SZECHUAN CHICKEN

Serves 4
Preparation time 5 minutes, plus marinating
Cooking time 16–20 minutes

3 tbsp (45 ml) soy sauce
2 tbsp (30 ml) dry sherry
1 tsp (5 ml) rice vinegar
1¼-inch (3 cm) piece fresh ginger, peeled and finely
    chopped
1 clove garlic, crushed
1 tbsp (15 ml) Chinese chili paste
½ tsp (2 ml) Szechuan peppercorns, ground
1 tbsp (15 ml) toasted sesame oil
4 boneless skinless chicken breasts, 4 oz (125 g) each
Fresh coriander leaves, chopped, to garnish

Mix together all the ingredients except the chicken in a shallow dish to make the marinade. Add the chicken breasts, coat well with the marinade and leave to marinate at room temperature for 2 hours.

Heat a grill pan (or ordinary frying pan). Cook the chicken for 8 to 10 minutes on each side and garnish with coriander. Serve with soba noodles and stir-fried oyster mushrooms.

For sesame greens with black bean sauce to accompany the chicken, fry 2 tbsp (30 ml) sesame seeds in 1 tsp (5 ml) sunflower oil until lightly browned. Add 1 tbsp (15 ml) soy sauce, cover with a lid and take off the heat. When the bubbling subsides, scoop the seeds into a dish. Rinse 13 oz (400 g) spring greens and thickly slice. Stir-fry in 1 tbsp (15 ml) oil with 2 cloves garlic finely chopped until just wilted. Mix in 3 tbsp (45 ml) ready-made black bean sauce. Serve sprinkled with the seeds.

CHICKEN & SPINACH MASALA

Serves 4
Preparation time 15 minutes
Cooking time 13–16 minutes

2 tbsp (30 ml) oil
1 onion, thinly sliced
2 cloves garlic, crushed
1 green chile, seeded and thinly sliced
1 tsp (5 ml) finely grated fresh ginger
1 tsp (5 ml) ground coriander
1 tsp (5 ml) ground cumin
7-oz (200 ml) can tomatoes
1½ lb (750 g) chicken thighs, skinned, boned and cut
   into bite-size chunks
¾ cup + 2 tbsp (200 ml) crème fraîche
10 oz (300 g) spinach, roughly chopped
2 tbsp (30 ml) chopped fresh coriander
Salt and pepper
Flatbreads (optional)

Heat the oil in a large, heavy-bottomed saucepan. Add the onion, garlic, chile and ginger. Stir-fry for 2 to 3 minutes and then add the ground coriander and cumin. Stir and cook for a further 1 minute.

Pour in the tomatoes and cook gently for 3 minutes. Increase the heat and add the chicken. Cook, stirring, until the outside of the chicken is sealed. Stir in the crème fraîche and spinach.

Cover the pan and cook the chicken mixture gently for 6 to 8 minutes, stirring occasionally. Stir in the chopped coriander with seasoning to taste. Serve with toasted flatbreads, if desired.

For spiced lemon rice to serve as an accompaniment, place 1 cup (250 ml) basmati rice in a sieve and wash thoroughly under cold running water. Drain and set aside. Heat 1 tbsp (15 ml) olive oil in a nonstick saucepan and when hot add 12 to 14 curry leaves, 1 dried red chile, ½ cinnamon stick, 2 to 3 whole cloves, 4 to 6 cardamom pods, 2 tsp (10 ml) cumin seeds and ¼ tsp (1 ml) ground turmeric. Stir-fry for 20 to 30 seconds, then add the rice. Stir-fry for 2 minutes, then add the juice of 1 large lemon and 1¾ cups (425 ml) boiling water. Bring to a boil, cover the pan and reduce the heat to low. Cook for 10 to 12 minutes. Remove from heat and allow to stand for 10 minutes, then fluff up with a fork before serving.

NOODLES & SEVEN-SPICE CHICKEN

Serves 4
Preparation time 15 minutes
Cooking time 12 minutes

3 pieces of candied ginger from a jar, plus 3 tbsp
  (45 ml) of the syrup
2 tbsp (30 ml) rice wine vinegar
3 tbsp (45 ml) light soy sauce
4 boneless skinless chicken breasts, about 5 oz
  (150 g) to 16 oz (75 g) each
1 tbsp (15 ml) Thai seven-spice seasoning
3 tbsp (45 ml) stir-fry or wok oil
3 shallots, thinly sliced
4 oz (125 g) baby corn, halved
10 oz (300 g) straight-to-wok medium or thread
  noodles
10 oz (300 g) baby spinach
7 oz (200 g) bean sprouts

Finely shred the pieces of candied ginger. Mix the ginger syrup with the vinegar and soy sauce and reserve.

Halve each chicken breast horizontally and then cut widthwise into thin strips. Toss with the seven-spice seasoning.

Heat the oil in a large frying pan or wok and stir-fry the chicken pieces over a gentle heat for 5 minutes, until beginning to brown.

Add the shallots and fry for 2 minutes. Stir in the baby corn and fry for 1 minute. Add the noodles and spinach and scatter with the shredded ginger. Stir-fry, mixing the ingredients together, until the spinach starts to wilt.

Add the bean sprouts and soy sauce mixture and cook, stirring, for a further 1 minute or until heated through. Serve immediately.

For noodles with seven-spice shrimp, replace the chicken with 13 oz (400 g) peeled and deveined raw shrimp, toss with the seven-spice seasoning and cook as above. Replace the spinach with 7 oz (200 g) roughly chopped bok choy.

CHICKEN WITH PEANUT SAUCE

Serves 4
Preparation time 5 minutes
Cooking time 16–20 minutes

4 boneless skinless chicken breasts, 4 oz (125 g) each
1 tbsp (15 ml) soy sauce
2 tbsp (30 ml) crunchy or smooth peanut butter
1/4 cup (60 ml) lemon juice
1/4 cup (60 ml) water
Pepper

To garnish
Fresh coriander leaves
Peanuts, fried, chopped (optional)

Heat a grill pan (or ordinary frying pan). Place the chicken breasts in the pan and cook for 8 to 10 minutes on each side.

Meanwhile, place the soy sauce, peanut butter, lemon juice, water and a little pepper in a small saucepan. Mix well and heat gently, adjusting the consistency of the sauce with a little more water, if necessary, so that it is slightly runny but coats the back of a spoon.

When the chicken is cooked, serve with the peanut sauce drizzled over the top, garnished with coriander and chopped fried peanuts, if desired. Serve with mixed vegetable noodles.

For egg fried rice to serve as an alternative accompaniment, add 1 cup (250 ml) long-grain rice to a saucepan of boiling water. Simmer for 8 minutes, then add 1 cup (250 ml) frozen peas and cook for 2 minutes before draining. Heat 1 tsp (5 ml) sunflower oil in a frying pan, add 2 beaten eggs and make a thin omelette. Roll the omelette up, shred and mix with the cooked rice.

SPICED CHICKEN & MANGO SALAD

Serves 4
Preparation time 15 minutes
Cooking time 5–6 minutes

4 small boneless skinless chicken breasts
6 tsp (30 ml) mild curry paste, divided
Juice of 1 lemon
2/3 cup (150 ml) low-fat natural yogurt
1 mango
2 cups (250 ml) watercress
1/2 cucumber, diced
1/2 red onion, chopped
1/2 iceberg lettuce

Cut the chicken breasts into long, thin slices. Put 4 tsp (20 ml) of the curry paste in a plastic bag with the lemon juice and mix together by squeezing the bag. Add the chicken and toss together.

Half-fill the base of a steamer with water and bring to a boil. Place the chicken in the top of the steamer in a single layer, cover and steam for 5 to 6 minutes, until thoroughly cooked. Test the chicken.

Meanwhile, mix the remaining curry paste in a bowl with the yogurt.

Cut a thick slice off either side of the mango to reveal the large, flat pit. Trim the flesh away from the pit, then remove the peel and cut the flesh into bite-size chunks.

Rinse the watercress with cold water and tear it into bite-size pieces. Add to the yogurt dressing with the cucumber, red onion and mango and toss together gently.

Tear the lettuce into pieces, divide it among 4 plates, spoon the mango mixture on top and complete with the warm chicken strips.

For Coronation chicken, mix the curry paste and yogurt with 1/4 cup (60 ml) mayonnaise. Stir in 1 lb (500 g) cold cooked diced chicken and 1/4 cup (60 ml) sultanas. Sprinkle with 1/4 cup (60 ml) toasted flaked almonds and serve on a bed of mixed salad and herb leaves.

CHICKEN WITH SAGE & LEMON

Serves 4
Preparation time 15 minutes, plus marinating
Cooking time 20 minutes

4 boneless skinless chicken breasts, about 5 oz
   (150 g) each
5 tbsp (75 ml) olive oil, divided
3 tbsp (45 ml) lemon juice
28 small fresh sage leaves
3 tbsp (45 ml) unsalted butter
Cooked Puy lentils (optional)
Salt and pepper

Place the chicken breasts in a single layer in a non-metallic dish. Pour on 3 tbsp (45 ml) of the oil and the lemon juice. Scatter on the sage leaves, turn the chicken so that the breasts are evenly coated, then cover and leave to marinate for about 30 minutes.

Lift the chicken breasts from the marinade and reserve the sage leaves separately. Pat the breasts dry. Strain the marinade into a small bowl.

Heat the butter and the remaining oil in a frying pan; add the chicken, and cook for about 10 minutes over moderate heat until browned. Turn the chicken breasts over, season with salt and pepper, and tuck the sage leaves around them. Cook for a further 10 minutes, until the underside is brown and the chicken is cooked through. Transfer the chicken to a warmed serving plate, cover and keep warm.

Tilt the pan and pour off the fat. Place the pan back on the heat and stir in the reserved marinade, scraping up any brown bits from the bottom of the pan. Boil until reduced to a brown glaze. Serve the chicken in slices, on a bed of Puy lentils, if desired. Pour the remaining marinade over the chicken and garnish with the sage leaves.

For garlic & lemon mash, as an alternative to the lentil accompaniment, boil 1 ½ lb (750 g) potatoes until tender. Drain and mash with ¼ cup (60 ml) butter, the grated zest and juice of ½ lemon and 3 cloves garlic finely chopped.

ASIAN CITRUS CHICKEN SKEWERS

Serves 4
Preparation time 5 minutes, plus marinating
Cooking time 20 minutes

1 lb (500 g) boneless skinless chicken breasts, cubed
Grated zest and juice of 1 lemon
2 tsp (10 ml) Chinese five-spice powder
1 tbsp (15 ml) dark soy sauce
Mixed vegetables (carrots, green onions, radishes), cut
   into strips (optional)

Place the chicken, lemon zest and juice, five-spice powder and soy sauce in a bowl. Stir to combine, cover, then leave to marinate in the refrigerator for at least 1 hour or overnight.

Thread the chicken pieces onto 4 presoaked wooden skewers, pushing them tightly together. Grill for 10 minutes under a preheated moderate broiler. Turn the skewers, baste with any remaining marinade, and grill for a further 10 minutes. Serve on a bed of vegetables, if desired.

For piri piri chicken skewers, mix the grated lemon zest and juice with 2 tbsp (30 ml) olive oil, then add 2 tsp (10 ml) piri piri sauce, 2 tsp (10 ml) tomato paste and 2 cloves garlic finely chopped. Add the chicken, marinade then grill as above.

CHICKEN & AVOCADO SALAD

Serves 4
Preparation time 15 minutes

⅓ cup (75 ml) light mayonnaise
2 tbsp (30 ml) mango chutney
Grated zest and juice of 1 lime
2 avocados, halved, pitted, peeled, diced
4 green onions, thinly sliced
¼ cucumber, diced
4 to 5 oz (125 to 150 g) cooked chicken, diced
2 Little Gem lettuces or romaine hearts
1½ oz (40 g) mixed salad leaves
Small bunch fresh coriander, optional

Mix the mayonnaise, mango chutney and lime zest together in a large bowl. Toss the lime juice with the avocados, then add to the dressing. Add the green onions, cucumber and chicken and fold the mixture together lightly so that it is semi-mixed.

Divide the lettuce leaves between 4 serving plates and top with the other salad leaves. Spoon over the chicken salad and garnish with torn coriander leaves, if desired. Serve immediately.

For chicken Waldorf salad, mix the same quantity of mayonnaise with the grated zest of ½ lemon, tossing the juice with 2 cored and diced apples. Add the apples to the dressing along with ¼ cup (60 ml) sultanas, 4 stems celery, thickly sliced, and 4 to 5 oz (125 to 150 g) diced cooked chicken. Serve on salad leaves as above, omitting the coriander.

QUICK MIDWEEK MEALS

HOT DUCK & COCONUT NOODLES

Serves 4
Preparation time 10 minutes
Cooking time 15 minutes

4 duck confit legs
1 cup (250 ml) coconut milk
¾ cup + 2 tbsp (200 ml) chicken stock
2 tbsp (30 ml) Thai fish sauce
3 whole star anise
1 tsp (5 ml) hot pepper flakes
2-inch (5 cm) piece fresh ginger, thinly sliced
1 small bunch of fresh coriander, chopped
Juice of 2 limes
8 oz (250 g) flat rice noodles
¼ cup (60 ml) coconut shavings, toasted
2 oz (60 g) cashew nuts, toasted

Heat a large frying pan and put the duck legs and their fat, skin side down, in the pan. Cook over medium heat for 10 minutes, until the skins turn golden and crispy. Turn and cook for a further 2 to 3 minutes, until the legs are heated through. Drain on paper towel, then tear the meat into small pieces and discard the bones.

Meanwhile, pour the coconut milk into a pan with the stock, fish sauce, star anise, hot pepper flakes, ginger and half the chopped coriander and bring to simmering point. Leave to bubble gently for 10 minutes to allow the flavors to infuse. Stir in the lime juice.

Cook the noodles in unsalted boiling water for about 3 minutes or according to the instructions on the package, then drain and heap into serving bowls.

Scatter the duck meat over the noodles and pour in the hot coconut broth. Sprinkle with the coconut shavings, cashews and remaining coriander. Serve immediately.

For spiced shrimp stir-fry, omit the duck and instead mix 13 oz (400 g) raw shrimp with 2 tbsp (30 ml) freshly grated ginger, 1 crushed clove garlic, 1 freshly chopped red chile and 1 tbsp (15 ml) vegetable oil. Heat a wok until smoking, add another tbsp vegetable oil and stir-fry the shrimp for 2 to 3 minutes, until pink and cooked through. Serve with the noodles and a ladle of the hot coconut broth, finishing as before with cashews and coriander.

SMOKED DUCK SALAD

Serves 4
Preparation time 15 minutes

5 oz (150 g) lamb's lettuce or mâche
1½ oranges or blood oranges, cut into segments
3½ oz (100 g) smoked duck breast, thinly sliced
Seeds of 1 pomegranate
½ cup (125 ml) shelled pistachios

Dressing
Juice of ½ blood orange
1 small shallot, finely chopped
1 tbsp (15 ml) red wine vinegar
1 tsp (5 ml) whole-grain mustard
¼ cup (60 ml) olive oil

Arrange the lamb's lettuce on 4 large serving plates; add the orange segments and slices of duck. Scatter over the pomegranate seeds and pistachios.

Make the dressing by putting the ingredients in a screw-top jar and shaking well to combine. Drizzle the dressing over each salad, and serve immediately.

For duck & watercress salad with cranberries & pecans, replace the lamb's lettuce with watercress and the pomegranate seeds and pistachios with 4 tbsp dried cranberries and ½ cup (125 ml) chopped pecans.

CHICKEN ALLA MILANESE

Serves 4
Preparation time 12 minutes
Cooking time 20 minutes

2 lb (1 kg) baking or russet potatoes, peeled and cut in
   half
4 boneless skinless chicken breasts, about 5 oz
   (150 g) each
2 small eggs, beaten
3 tbsp (45 ml) olive oil
⅔ cup (150 ml) butter
4 ripe tomatoes, roughly chopped
2 tbsp (30 ml) capers in brine, drained and rinsed
¼ cup (60 ml) white wine
¼ cup (60 ml) lemon juice
3½ oz (100 g) arugula
Salt and pepper

Crust
2 tsp (10 ml) dried oregano
¾ cup (175 ml) breadcrumbs
½ tsp (2 ml) garlic powder
Finely grated zest of 1 lemon
2 oz (60 g) Parmesan cheese, finely grated

Cook the potatoes in lightly salted boiling water for about 20 minutes or until soft.

Meanwhile, mix together the ingredients for the crust and tip the mixture onto a plate. Put the chicken breasts between 2 sheets of plastic wrap or wax paper and batter with a rolling pin or mallet until flat. Dip the chicken into the beaten egg, then press into the crust mixture to coat.

Heat the oil in a large frying pan and cook the chicken for 3 minutes on each side or until cooked through and golden. Set aside and keep warm.

Add half the butter to the pan and stir in the tomatoes, capers and white wine. Season and allow to bubble for 2 to 3 minutes.

Drain and mash the potatoes with the lemon juice, the remaining butter and plenty of seasoning. Spoon onto serving plates with the crispy chicken. Quickly stir the arugula into the tomatoes and pile a little onto each piece of chicken. Serve immediately.

For spinach with raisins & pine nuts to serve as an accompaniment, put 1 chopped onion, ¼ cup (60 ml) raisins and ¼ cup (60 ml) butter in a large pan. Add 2 lb (1 kg) spinach and 3 tbsp (45 ml) water. Cover and cook for 3 to 5 minutes, shaking the pan occasionally, until the spinach has wilted. Mix well and serve.

ASIAN STEAMED-CHICKEN SALAD

Serves 4
Preparation time 10 minutes, plus cooling
Cooking time 8–10 minutes

4 boneless skinless chicken breasts, about 5 oz
  (150 g) each
½ small napa cabbage, finely shredded
1 large carrot, grated
7 oz (200 g) bean sprouts
Small bunch of fresh coriander, finely chopped
Small bunch of fresh mint, finely chopped
1 red chili, seeded and finely sliced (optional)

Dressing
½ cup (125 ml) sunflower oil
Juice of 2 limes
1½ tbsp (22 ml) Thai fish sauce
3 tbsp (45 ml) light soy sauce
1 tbsp (15 ml) finely chopped fresh ginger

Put the chicken breasts in a bamboo or other steamer set over a large pan of simmering water. Cover and leave to steam for about 8 minutes or until the chicken is cooked through. Alternatively, poach the chicken for 8 to 10 minutes, until the meat is cooked and tender.

Meanwhile, make the dressing by mixing together the ingredients in a bowl.

When the chicken is cool enough to handle, cut or tear it into strips and mix the pieces with 2 tbsp (30 ml) of the dressing. Leave to cool.

Toss all the vegetables and herbs together and arrange in serving dishes. Scatter over the cold chicken and serve immediately with the remaining dressing.

For Asian steamed-shrimp salad with peanuts, use 14½ oz (450 g) medium-sized raw, peeled shrimp steamed in the same way as the chicken for 2 to 3 minutes, until pink and firm. Finish 2 tbsp (30 ml) of crushed unsalted peanuts.

TURKEY & PUMPKIN SEED SALAD

Serves 4
Preparation time 12 minutes
Cooking time 6 minutes

3 tbsp (45 ml) sunflower oil
13 oz (400 g) ground turkey
1 tbsp (15 ml) pickled jalapeño peppers, sliced
7-oz (200 g) can corn, drained
1 ripe avocado, peeled, pitted and cut into chunks
2 ripe tomatoes, chopped
1 small red onion, finely diced
Small bunch of fresh coriander, chopped
Salt and pepper

Dressing
Juice of 2 limes
1 tsp (5 ml) liquid honey
¼ cup (60 ml) pumpkin seed oil

To serve
½ small red cabbage, shredded
8 oz (250 g) buffalo mozzarella cheese, cubed
4 taco shells
3 tbsp (45 ml) pumpkin seeds, to sprinkle

Make the dressing by mixing together the ingredients in a small bowl. Season to taste and set aside.

Heat the oil in a large frying pan and fry the turkey for 5 to 6 minutes, until cooked and beginning to color. Scrape into a bowl, mix with half the dressing and set aside to cool.

Make a chunky salsa by combining the peppers, corn, avocado, tomatoes, red onion and coriander. Mix with the remaining dressing.

When the turkey is cool, mix it with the salsa and serve with the cabbage, mozzarella and taco shells with the pumpkin seeds scattered over.

For turkey with white cabbage & sunflower seed salad, replace the pumpkin seed oil in the dressing with olive oil and the red cabbage with white cabbage. Substitute the mozzarella with finely diced Gruyère or Gouda and the pumpkin seeds with sunflower seeds. Omit the tacos, serving the salad as a base with the turkey mix on top.

FAST FAMILY FAVORITES

FISH & CHIPS IN PAPER CONES

Serves 4
Preparation time 20 minutes
Cooking time 30–40 minutes

1½ lbs (750 g) baking potatoes, cut into thick chips
2 tbsp (30 ml) olive oil
1 cup (250 ml) whole wheat breadcrumbs
Finely grated zest of 1 lemon
3 tbsp (45 ml) chopped fresh parsley
4 chunky white fish fillets, 5 oz (150 g) each, cut into
  4 chunky pieces or goujons
½ cup (125 ml) all-purpose flour
1 egg, beaten
Tomato ketchup (see page 12), to serve

Toss the potato chips with the oil, then roast in a preheated 400°F (200°C) oven for 30 to 40 minutes, turning occasionally, until golden and crisp.

Meanwhile, toss the breadcrumbs with the lemon zest and parsley on a plate. Lightly coat the fish goujons in the flour, then the beaten egg, and finally the breadcrumbs. Place on a baking sheet and roast in a preheated 400°F (200°C) oven for the final 20 minutes of the chips' cooking time, until the fish is opaque and cooked through.

Roll 4 sheets of heavy, notebook-sized paper into cones and seal with tape. Place in a bottle holder to help load each with chips, and place 4 goujons on top. Allow the kids to eat these healthy fish and chips with their fingers, dipping them into the ketchup for good measure!

For lemony mayonnaise dip to serve as an alternative accompaniment, place 1 egg, ⅔ cup (150 ml) olive oil and 1 tbsp (15 ml) white wine vinegar in a tall jar and mix with a handheld blender until a thick mayonnaise is formed. Fold in the grated zest of 1 small lemon and 2 tbsp (30 ml) of the juice, along with 2 tbsp (30 ml) chopped parsley.

FISH PIE

Serves 4
Preparation time 15 minutes
Cooking time 1 hour 10 minutes

10 oz (300 g) raw peeled shrimp
2 tsp (10 ml) cornstarch
10 oz (300 g) skinned white fish, e.g. haddock, cut into
  small pieces
2 tsp (10 ml) green peppercorns in brine, rinsed
  and drained
1 small bulb fennel, roughly chopped
1 small leek, roughly chopped
⅓ cup (75 ml) fresh dill
⅓ cup (75 ml) fresh parsley
½ cup (125 ml) fresh or frozen peas
1½ cups (375 ml) ready-made or homemade
  cheese sauce
1½ lbs (750 g) baking potatoes, thinly sliced
3 oz (75 g) Cheddar cheese, grated
Salt and pepper

Dry the shrimp, if frozen and thawed, by patting between sheets of paper towel. Season the cornstarch and use to coat the shrimp and white fish. Lightly crush the peppercorns using a pestle and mortar.

Put the peppercorns in a food processor with the fennel, leek, dill, parsley and a little salt and blend until very finely chopped, scraping the mixture down from the sides of the bowl if necessary. Tip into a shallow, ovenproof dish.

Scatter the shrimp and fish over the fennel mixture and mix together a little. Scatter the peas on top.

Spoon half the cheese sauce over the filling and spread roughly with the back of a spoon. Layer up the potatoes on top, seasoning each layer as you go. Spoon the remaining sauce over the top, spreading it in a thin layer. Sprinkle with the cheese.

Bake in a preheated 425°F (220°C) oven for 30 minutes, until the surface has turned pale golden. Reduce the oven temperature to 350°F (180°C), and cook for a further 30 to 40 minutes, until the potatoes are completely tender. Serve with a tomato salad.

For smoked fish and caper pie, use 1¼ lbs (625 g) smoked pollack, skinned and cut into small chunks, in place of the shrimp and white fish. Use 2 tbsp (30 ml) capers instead of the green peppercorns.

HERBY CHICKPEA CRAB CAKES

Serves 4
Preparation time 10 minutes
Cooking time 7 minutes

14-oz (398 ml) can chickpeas, rinsed and drained
2 green onions, thinly sliced
3 tbsp (45 ml) chopped fresh parsley
2 tbsp (30 ml) chopped fresh chives
1 egg yolk
1 tsp (5 ml) piri piri sauce
1 tsp (5 ml) Worcestershire sauce
2 tbsp (30 ml) mayonnaise
1¼ cups (300 ml) coarse dry breadcrumbs
10 oz (300 g) white crab meat
2 tbsp (30 ml) olive oil

To serve
4 oz (125 g) arugula leaves
¼ cup (60 ml) Aïoli (see page 57)

Put the chickpeas, green onions, herbs, egg yolk, piri piri sauce, Worcestershire sauce, mayonnaise and 2 oz (60 g) of the breadcrumbs in a food processor and process briefly. Add the crab meat and pulse quickly to combine, adding more breadcrumbs if the mixture is too wet.

Transfer the mixture to a bowl and form it into 4 large or 8 small patties. Press them into the remaining breadcrumbs until well coated.

Heat the oil in a large frying pan and fry the crab cakes for about 5 minutes, turning carefully once, until crisp and golden. Drain on paper towel and serve immediately with arugula leaves and a dollop of aïoli.

For avocado & watercress sauce to serve instead of the aïoli, chop 1 tbsp (15 ml) capers and 3½ oz (100 g) watercress and mash 1 avocado. Mix together with ¾ cup (175 ml) Greek yogurt.

COD FILLET WITH TOMATOES & ARUGULA

Serves 4
Preparation time 5 minutes
Cooking time 12–15 minutes

4 chunky cod fillets, about 5 oz (150 g) each
3 tbsp (45 ml) olive oil, divided
2 cloves garlic, chopped
10 oz (300 g) cherry tomatoes on the vine
2 tbsp (30 ml) balsamic vinegar
¼ cup (60 ml) shredded fresh basil
4 oz (125 g) arugula leaves
Salt and pepper

Rub the cod fillets all over with 1 tbsp (15 ml) of the oil and season well. Scatter the garlic over and put the fish in a roasting pan. Arrange the cherry tomatoes alongside and drizzle with the remaining oil, the balsamic vinegar and basil. Season to taste.

Transfer the tray to a preheated 425°F (220°C) oven and cook for 12 to15 minutes, until the fish is flaky and the tomatoes roasted.

Serve the cod with the tomatoes and arugula leaves.

For cod with Italian-style salsa, fry the cod fillets for 5 to 6 minutes, until cooked and golden brown. To make the salsa, combine 8 finely chopped sun-dried tomatoes, 2 tbsp (30 ml) roughly chopped fresh basil leaves, 1 tbsp (15 ml) drained capers, 1 tbsp (15 ml) lightly crushed toasted pine nuts and 2 tbsp (30 ml) olive oil. Serve with an arugula salad.

BLACKENED COD WITH CITRUS SALSA

Serves 4
Preparation time 15 minutes
Cooking time 15 minutes

1 large orange
1 clove garlic, crushed
2 large tomatoes, seeded and diced
2 tbsp (30 ml) chopped fresh basil, plus extra to garnish
3 oz (75 g) pitted black olives, chopped
5 tbsp (75 ml) olive oil, divided
Salt and pepper
4 cod fillets, about 6 oz (175 g) each
1 tbsp (15 ml) jerk seasoning

Cut the skin and the white membrane off the orange. Working over a bowl to catch the juice, cut between the membranes to remove the segments. Halve the segments and mix them with the reserved juice and the garlic, tomatoes, basil, olives and $\frac{1}{4}$ cup (60 ml) of the oil. Season to taste with salt and pepper and set aside to infuse.

Brush the cod with the remaining oil and coat with the jerk seasoning. Heat a large, heavy-bottomed frying pan and cook the cod, skin side down, for 5 minutes. Turn the fish over and cook for a further 3 minutes. Transfer to a preheated 300°F (150°C) oven to rest for about 5 minutes. Garnish the fish with basil and serve with the salsa and a green salad.

For quick crumbed cod, mix together 3 tbsp (45 ml) each breadcrumbs, torn basil leaves and grated Parmesan cheese, 2 pieces drained and chopped sun-dried tomato, 1 tbsp (15 ml) olive oil and the grated zest of 1 lemon. Press the mixture over 4 pieces of cod, each 6 oz (175 g), and cook in a preheated 375°F (190°C) oven for 20 minutes.

CREAMY SMOKED FISH GRATIN

Serves 4
Preparation time 10 minutes
Cooking time 20 minutes

4 plum tomatoes, chopped
8 oz (250 g) boneless smoked trout fillets, skin removed
13 oz (400 g) boneless smoked haddock fillets, skin removed
3 oz (75 g) grated Gruyère or Emmental cheese
2 tbsp (30 ml) freshly grated Parmesan cheese
2 tbsp (30 ml) chopped fresh chives
$\frac{3}{4}$ cup + 2 tbsp (200 ml) table (18%) or half-and-half (10%) cream
Salt and pepper
1 lb (500 g) new potatoes, steamed (optional)

Arrange the tomatoes over the bottom of 4 lightly buttered individual ovenproof dishes or 1 large ovenproof dish. Cut the fish into chunks and scatter them over the tomatoes. Top with the grated cheeses and chopped chives.

Pour in the cream, place on a baking sheet and cook in a preheated 425°F (220°C) oven for about 20 minutes, until the gratin is bubbling and golden and the fish is cooked.

Serve immediately with steamed new potatoes, if desired.

For creamy cod with shrimp, replace the trout and haddock with 14 $\frac{1}{2}$ oz (450 g) skinless boneless cod, cut into chunks, and 8 oz (250 g) peeled and cooked shrimp. Replace the chives with about $\frac{3}{4}$ cup (175 ml) chopped parsley. Finish as above and serve with mashed potatoes with chopped dill added.

PAN-FRIED HADDOCK FILLETS

Serves 4
Preparation time 15 minutes
Cooking time 20 minutes

2 lbs (1 kg) baking or russet potatoes, peeled
1/3 cup (75 ml) whole (homogenized) milk
2/3 cup (150 ml) butter, divided
4 haddock fillets, about 5 oz (150 g) each, skin on
2 tbsp (30 ml) capers in brine, drained and rinsed
1/4 cup (60 ml) lemon juice
Salt and pepper

Cook the potatoes in lightly salted boiling water for about 20 minutes. Mash until smooth with the milk and 1/4 cup (60 ml) of the butter. Season well.

Meanwhile, melt the remaining butter in a large frying pan; add the haddock fillets, skin side down, and cook for about 3 minutes, until golden and crispy. Carefully turn over the fillets and cook for a further 1 to 2 minutes.

Remove the fillets and transfer to serving plates with the mashed potato.

Return the pan to the stove. Increase the heat until the butter turns nut-brown in color, then add the capers and lemon juice. Bubble for a minute and then spoon over the fish and potatoes. Serve immediately.

For trout fillets with almonds, replace the haddock fillets with trout fillets and fry as above, finishing with almonds instead of capers.

102

SIMPLE SEAFOOD CURRY

Serves 4
Preparation time 20 minutes
Cooking time 35 minutes

3-inch (7.5 cm) piece fresh ginger, grated
1 tsp (5 ml) ground turmeric
2 cloves garlic, crushed
2 tsp (10 ml) medium curry paste
2/3 cup (150 ml) natural yogurt
1 1/4 lbs (625 g) white fish fillets, skinned
2 tbsp (30 ml) oil
1 large onion, sliced
1 cinnamon stick, halved
2 tsp (10 ml) dark muscovado sugar
2 bay leaves
14-oz (398 ml) can chopped tomatoes
1 1/4 cups (300 ml) fish stock or vegetable stock
1 lb (500 g) Yukon gold or red potatoes, cut into small chunks
1/2 cup (125 ml) chopped fresh coriander
Salt and pepper

Mix together the ginger, turmeric, garlic and curry paste in a bowl. Stir in the yogurt until combined. Cut the fish into large pieces and add to the bowl, stirring until coated in the spice mixture.

Heat the oil in a large saucepan and gently fry the onion, cinnamon, sugar and bay leaves until the onion is soft. Add the tomatoes, stock and potatoes and bring to a boil. Cook, uncovered, for about 20 minutes, until the potatoes are tender and the sauce has thickened.

Tip in the fish and spicy yogurt and reduce the heat to its lowest setting. Cook gently for about 10 minutes or until the fish is cooked through. Check the seasoning and stir in the coriander to serve.

For homemade fish stock, melt a knob of butter in a large saucepan and gently fry off 2 roughly chopped shallots, 1 small, roughly chopped leek and 1 roughly chopped celery stalk or bulb fennel. Add 2 lbs (1 kg) white fish or shellfish bones, heads and trimmings, several sprigs of parsley, 1/2 lemon and 1 tsp (5 ml) peppercorns. Cover with cold water and bring to a simmer. Cook, uncovered, on the lowest setting for 30 minutes. Strain through a sieve and leave to cool.

LAMB CHOPS WITH OLIVE COUSCOUS

Serves 4
Preparation time 25 minutes, plus marinating
Cooking time 10–12 minutes

6 anchovy fillets in olive oil, drained and chopped
2 tbsp (30 ml) black olive tapenade
2 to 3 sprigs of fresh thyme, leaves stripped and chopped
1 sprig of fresh rosemary, leaves stripped and chopped
2 bay leaves, torn
2 to 3 cloves garlic, crushed
Finely grated zest of 1 lemon
$\frac{1}{4}$ cup (60 ml) white wine
$\frac{1}{2}$ cup (125 ml) olive oil, divided
2 cups (500 ml) medium-grain couscous
4 lamb loin chops, about 5 oz (150 g) each
Salt and pepper
2 tbsp (30 ml) salted capers or capers in brine, drained and rinsed
3$\frac{1}{2}$ oz (100 g) spicy marinated green olives, chopped
3 oz (75 g) arugula leaves, plus extra for serving
$\frac{1}{4}$ cup (60 ml) lemon juice, plus extra for serving

Mash the anchovies with a fork and stir them into a bowl with the tapenade. Add the herbs, garlic and lemon zest, then pour in the wine and $\frac{1}{4}$ cup (60 ml) of the oil. Stir thoroughly, then rub the mixture into the lamb chops. Cover and leave at room temperature for about 1 hour.

Put the couscous into a heatproof bowl and stir in 2 tbsp (30 ml) of the oil so that the grains are covered. Season with salt and pour over 1$\frac{2}{3}$ cups (400 ml) boiling water. Leave to stand for 5 to 8 minutes, until the grains are soft.

Season the lamb chops with pepper and cook them for about 2 minutes in a preheated hot grill pan. Sprinkle with a little salt, then cook the other side for a further 2 minutes. Transfer to a warm dish, cover with foil and leave to rest for 5 minutes.

Fluff up the couscous with a fork and gently fold in the capers, olives and arugula. Sprinkle over the lemon juice, then heap the couscous onto warm plates. Arrange a lamb chop on each heap and spoon over the juices. Sprinkle with arugula leaves, drizzle with the remaining oil and an extra squeeze of lemon juice and serve immediately with lemon wedges.

For stir-fried lamb, heat 1$\frac{1}{2}$ tbsp (30 ml) vegetable oil in a wok and cook 8 oz (250 g) filet of lamb, thinly sliced, for a few minutes. Add 1 tbsp (15 ml) each oyster sauce and Thai fish sauce, 1 crushed clove garlic and 1 tbsp (15 ml) finely sliced red chile and cook for a further 2 minutes. Garnish with mint leaves.

LAMB HOTPOT WITH DUMPLINGS

Serves 4
Preparation time 30 minutes
Cooking time about 1 hour

1 tbsp (15 ml) vegetable oil
1 small onion, chopped
12 oz (375 g) boneless lamb, cubed
1 leek, chopped
3 oz (75 g) ready-to-eat dried apricots, chopped
12 oz (375 g) new potatoes, halved
1 tbsp (15 ml) fresh thyme leaves
2 tbsp (30 ml) all-purpose flour
2$\frac{1}{3}$ cups (575 ml) rich lamb stock

Dumplings
1 cup (250 ml) all-purpose flour
$\frac{1}{2}$ tsp (2 ml) salt
1 tsp (5 ml) fresh thyme leaves
$\frac{1}{4}$ cup (60 ml) vegetable suet or cold shortening or margarine
About $\frac{1}{4}$ cup (60 ml) cold water

Heat the oil in a large, heavy-bottomed saucepan and cook the onion and lamb over moderate heat for 4 to 5 minutes, until golden and soft. Add the leek, apricots and new potatoes and cook for 2 minutes, then add the thyme and flour and stir well to coat lightly. Pour in the stock, then bring to a boil and cover and simmer gently for 35 minutes, stirring occasionally.

Meanwhile, make the dumplings. Place the flour and salt in a bowl with the thyme leaves and suet and mix well. Mix in enough water to make an elastic dough. Divide into 12 and shape into small, walnut-sized balls using lightly floured hands. Stir the hotpot and top up with a little water if necessary, then drop the dumplings into the stock and cover and simmer for 15 minutes, until the dumplings have almost doubled in size.

Serve the hotpot ladled into warm serving bowls with the dumplings.

For vegetable hotpot with cheesy dumplings, omit the lamb and replace with 2 chopped carrots, 1 roughly chopped red pepper and 1 chopped zucchini. Also replace the lamb stock with vegetable stock, and cook as above. Add 3 tbsp (45 ml) raisins with the apricots. Add 1 oz (25 g) finely grated Cheddar cheese to the flour when making the dumplings and cook as above.

SPICED LAMB WITH BEAN PURÉE

Serves 2–3
Preparation time 20 minutes, plus resting
Cooking time 50 minutes

2 large baking potatoes, cut into ¾-inch (2 cm) pieces
¼ cup (60 ml) olive oil, divided
Salt and pepper
⅓ cup (75 ml) breadcrumbs
1 clove garlic, crushed
2 tbsp (30 ml) chopped fresh coriander
1 tsp (5 ml) ground coriander
1 tsp (5 ml) ground cumin
1 egg yolk
1 rack of lamb, chined and trimmed
4 portobello mushrooms
5 oz (150 g) frozen baby broad, lima or fava beans
1 tbsp (15 ml) chopped fresh mint
⅓ cup + 2 tbsp (100 ml) white wine

Toss the potatoes with 2 tbsp (30 ml) of the oil and salt and pepper in a small, sturdy roasting pan. Roast in a preheated 400°F (200°C) oven for 15 minutes.

Mix together the breadcrumbs, garlic, fresh coriander, spices and salt and pepper. Cut away any thick areas of fat from the skinned side of the lamb. Brush the lamb with the egg yolk and spoon the breadcrumb mixture over, pressing down gently with the back of the spoon. Brush the mushrooms with the remaining oil and a little salt and pepper.

Turn the potatoes in the pan and add the lamb, crusted side uppermost. Return to the oven for 30 minutes. (The cutlets will still be slightly pink in the middle after this time, so cook for a little longer if you prefer them well done.) After 15 minutes of the cooking time, turn the potatoes in the oil and add the mushrooms. Return to the oven for the remaining cooking time.

Drain the meat to a board. Cover with foil and leave to rest for 15 minutes. Transfer the potatoes and mushrooms to a warmed serving dish.

Add the beans, mint and wine to the roasting pan and cook over low heat for 5 minutes, until the beans are tender. Tip into a blender or food processor and blend until smooth. Check the seasoning and spoon onto warmed serving plates. Carve the lamb into chops and add to the plates with the mushrooms and potatoes.

TASTY LUNCH TURNOVERS

Makes 6
Preparation time 25 minutes, plus chilling
Cooking time 25 minutes

2¾ cups (675 ml) all-purpose flour
½ tsp (2 ml) salt
¾ cup (175 ml) butter, cubed
2 to 3 tbsp (30 to 45 ml) cold water
1 tbsp (15 ml) vegetable oil
½ small onion, chopped
6 oz (175 g) lean lamb, finely sliced
1 small potato or 2 baby new potatoes, peeled and diced
1¼ cups (300 ml) hot lamb stock
1 tsp (5 ml) Dijon mustard (optional)
2 tbsp (30 ml) finely chopped fresh mint
1 egg, beaten

Sift the flour and salt into a large mixing bowl and add the butter. Rub the butter into the flour until the mixture resembles fine breadcrumbs. Add the cold water and mix to form a rough dough. Turn onto a lightly floured work surface and knead until smooth. Place in a resealable bag and refrigerate for 30 minutes.

Meanwhile, heat the oil in a frying pan and cook the onion and lamb over medium heat for 5 minutes, stirring occasionally, until beginning to brown. Add the potato, reduce the heat and cook for a further 2 minutes, stirring occasionally, until beginning to brown.

Mix the lamb stock with the mustard (if using), and pour into the pan. Cover with a tight-fitting lid and simmer gently for 15 minutes, stirring occasionally, until the potatoes are soft yet still retain their shape and the meat is tender. Stir in the mint and set aside to cool.

Roll out the pastry to ¼ inch (5 mm) thick, and using a 6-inch (15 cm) saucer as a template, cut out 6 rounds. Lightly brush the edges of each of the circles with a little water and place 2 tbsp (30 ml) of the mixture in the center of each. Fold up to enclose the filling and pinch and gently twist the edges to seal. Place on a baking sheet and lightly glaze each one with the beaten egg. Bake in a preheated 400°F (200°C) oven for 20 to 25 minutes, until the pastry is golden and crisp. Wrap loosely in foil to keep warm.

ASIAN LAMB BURGERS

Serves 4
Preparation time 20 minutes
Cooking time 30 minutes

2 cloves garlic, crushed
1 stalk lemongrass, finely chopped
2-inch (5 cm) piece fresh ginger, grated
Large handful of fresh coriander, roughly chopped
1 hot red chile, seeded and thinly sliced
1 lb (500 g) lean ground lamb
2 tbsp (30 ml) oil
1 small cucumber
1 bunch green onions
7 oz (200 g) bok choy
3 tbsp (45 ml) light muscovado sugar
Finely grated zest of 2 limes, plus ¼ cup (60 ml) juice
2 tbsp (30 ml) fish sauce
⅓ cup (75 ml) roasted peanuts
Salt

Blend the garlic, lemongrass, ginger, coriander, chile and a little salt in a food processor to make a thick paste. Add the lamb and blend until mixed. Tip out onto the work surface and divide the mixture into 4 pieces. Roll each into a ball and flatten into a burger shape.

Heat the oil in a sturdy roasting pan and fry the burgers on both sides to sear. Transfer to a preheated 400°F (200°C) oven and cook, uncovered, for 25 minutes, until the burgers are cooked through.

Meanwhile, peel the cucumber and cut in half lengthwise. Scoop out the seeds with a spoon and discard. Cut the cucumber into thin, diagonal slices. Slice the green onions diagonally. Roughly shred the bok choy, keeping the white parts separate from the green.

Using a large metal spoon, drain off all but about 2 tbsp (30 ml) fat from the roasting pan. Arrange all the vegetables except the green parts of the bok choy around the meat and toss them gently in the pan juices. Return to the oven, uncovered, for 5 minutes.

Mix together the sugar, lime zest and juice and fish sauce. Scatter the bok choy greens and peanuts into the roasting pan and drizzle with half the dressing. Toss the salad ingredients together gently. Transfer the lamb and salad to serving plates and drizzle with the remaining dressing.

For chicken burgers, use ground chicken instead of the lamb. Replace the bok choy with shredded spring greens and peanuts with salted cashews.

LAMB WITH ROSEMARY OIL

Serves 4
Preparation time 10 minutes
Cooking time 10–20 minutes

About 1½ lb (750 g) lamb loin roast, trimmed of fat
4 cloves garlic, cut into slivers
A few small sprigs of fresh rosemary
2 red onions, quartered
¼ cup (60 ml) olive oil
1 tbsp (15 ml) chopped fresh rosemary
Salt and pepper

Make small incisions all over the lamb loin and insert the garlic slivers and rosemary sprigs.

Place the meat in a preheated hot grill pan and cook, turning occasionally, until seared all over, about 10 minutes for rare or about 20 minutes for well done.

Add the onions halfway through the cooking time and char on the outside. Let the lamb rest for 5 minutes, then carve into slices.

Meanwhile, put the oil and rosemary in a mortar and crush with a pestle to release the flavors. Season with salt and pepper.

Spoon the rosemary oil over the lamb slices and serve at once with the fried onions.

Serve with fresh pasta, lightly tossed in oil, and Parmesan shavings.

For lamb chops with garlic & herbs, cut 4 cloves garlic into slivers and insert into incisions in 8 lamb chops. Place each chop on a square of foil and divide ¼ cup (60 ml) butter, 3 tbsp (45 ml) lemon juice and 1 tbsp (15 ml) each dried oregano and dried mint among them. Season and fold the foil to encase the meat. Cook in a preheated 350°F (180°C) oven for 1½ to 2 hours.

SRI LANKAN–STYLE LAMB CURRY

Serves 4
Preparation time 10 minutes
Cooking time 28–33 minutes

1 lb (500 g) shoulder or leg of lamb, diced
2 potatoes, peeled and cut into large chunks
¼ cup (60 ml) olive oil
14-oz (398 ml) can chopped tomatoes
Salt and pepper

Curry paste
1 onion, grated
1 tbsp (15 ml) finely chopped fresh ginger
1 tsp (5 ml) finely chopped garlic
½ tsp (2 ml) ground turmeric
1 tsp (5 ml) ground coriander
½ tsp (2 ml) ground cumin
½ tsp (2 ml) fennel seeds
½ tsp (2 ml) cumin seeds
3 cardamom pods, lightly crushed
2 green chiles, finely chopped
2-inch (5 cm) cinnamon stick
2 stalks lemongrass, finely sliced

Make the curry paste by mixing together all the ingredients in a large bowl – for a milder curry, remove the seeds from the chiles before chopping them finely. Add the lamb and potatoes and combine well.

Heat the oil in a heavy-bottomed pan or casserole and tip in the meat and potatoes. Use a wooden spoon to stir-fry for 6 to 8 minutes. Pour in the chopped tomatoes and ⅔ cup (150 ml) water, bring to a boil and season well, then allow to bubble gently for 20 to 25 minutes, until the potatoes are cooked and the lamb is tender.

Serve accompanied with toasted naan bread and a bowl of Greek yogurt, if desired.

For beef & potato curry, use 1 lb (500 g) diced rump steak instead of the lamb. Prepare it in the same way as the lamb, then serve it with a generous sprinkling of chopped coriander.

108

MEDITERRANEAN ROAST LAMB

Serves 6
Preparation time 20 minutes, plus resting
Cooking time 1 hour 20 minutes to 1 hour
   40 minutes

1 tbsp (15 ml) chopped fresh rosemary
2 tsp (10 ml) mild paprika
Salt and pepper
3 lb (1.5 kg) leg of lamb
3 tbsp (45 ml) olive oil
2 tbsp (30 ml) sun-dried tomato paste
2 cloves garlic, crushed
2 red onions, cut into wedges
1 bulb fennel, cut into wedges
2 red bell peppers, seeded and cut into chunks
2 orange or yellow bell peppers, seeded and cut
   into chunks
3 zucchini, thickly sliced
¼ cup (60 ml) pine nuts
1¼ cups (300 ml) red or white wine

Mix the rosemary and paprika with a little salt and rub all over the surface of the lamb. Put in a large roasting pan and roast in a preheated 425°F (220°C) oven for 15 minutes.

Meanwhile, mix the oil with the tomato paste and garlic. Put all the vegetables in a bowl, add the oil mixture and toss the ingredients together until coated.

Reduce the oven temperature to 350°F (180°C). Tip the vegetables into the pan around the lamb and scatter with the pine nuts and a little salt. Return to the oven for a further 1 hour. (The lamb will still be pink in the center. If you prefer it well done, cook for an extra 20 minutes, draining the vegetables to a serving plate if they start to become too browned.)

Drain the lamb to a serving plate or board, ready to carve. Cover with foil and leave to rest for 15 minutes. Using a slotted spoon, drain the vegetables to a serving dish and keep warm.

Pour the wine into the roasting pan and bring to a boil on the stove, scraping up the residue from the base. Boil for a few minutes until slightly reduced and serve.

For fruited bulgur wheat to serve as an accompaniment, put 1⅔ cups (375 ml) bulgur wheat into a heatproof bowl with ¼ tsp (1 ml) each ground cinnamon and nutmeg. Add 1⅔ cups (375 ml) boiling water or stock, cover and leave to rest in a warm place for 20 minutes. Stir in 3 oz (75 g) each chopped dates and seedless sultanas and serve.

GREEK LAMB WITH TZATZIKI TOASTS

Serves 4
Preparation time 15 minutes
Cooking time 1½ hours

1½ lbs (750 g) lamb chops
2 tsp (10 ml) dried oregano
3 cloves garlic, crushed
Salt and pepper
¼ cup (60 ml) olive oil
1 medium eggplant, about 10 oz (300 g), diced
2 red onions, sliced
¾ cup + 2 tbsp (200 ml) white or red wine
14-oz (398 ml) can chopped tomatoes
2 tbsp (30 ml) liquid honey
8 kalamata olives
8 thin slices French bread
7 oz (200 g) tzatziki

Cut the lamb into large pieces, discarding any excess fat. Mix the oregano with the garlic and a little salt and pepper and rub into the lamb.

Heat half the oil in a large saucepan or sauté pan and fry the lamb in batches until browned. Drain to a plate.

Add the eggplant to the pan with the onions and remaining oil and cook very gently, stirring frequently, for about 10 minutes, until softened and lightly browned. Return the meat to the pan with the wine, tomatoes, honey, olives and salt and pepper to taste. Cover with a lid and cook on the lowest setting for about 1¼ hours or until the lamb is very tender. Lightly toast the bread and spoon the tzatziki on top.

Check the stew for seasoning and turn into shallow bowls. Serve with the toasts on the side.

For homemade tzatziki, coarsely grate a 2-inch (5 cm) piece peeled cucumber and pat dry between several sheets of paper towel. In a bowl, mix with ¾ cup + 2 tbsp (200 ml) natural yogurt, 1 tbsp (15 ml) finely chopped mint, 1 crushed clove garlic and salt and pepper.

110

BAKED TURKEY BURRITO

Serves 4
Preparation time 12 minutes
Cooking time 30–33 minutes

¼ cup (60 ml) vegetable oil
1 lb (500 g) turkey breast, thinly sliced
1 large onion, sliced
1 red bell pepper, cored, seeded and sliced
1 yellow bell pepper, cored, seeded and sliced
5-oz (150 g) can red kidney beans, rinsed and drained
1 cup (250 ml) cooked rice
Juice of 1 lime
8 medium-sized flour tortillas
6 tbsp (90 ml) medium-hot ready-made salsa
2 tbsp (30 ml) sliced, pickled jalapeño peppers
   (optional)
8 oz (250 g) Cheddar cheese, grated
Salt and pepper

To serve
Guacamole
½ iceberg lettuce, shredded

Heat 2 tbsp (30 ml) of the oil in a large frying pan and stir-fry the sliced turkey for 3 to 4 minutes, until it is beginning to color, then remove it with a slotted spoon. Increase the heat, add the remaining oil and fry the onion and peppers for 5 to 6 minutes, stirring only occasionally so that they color quickly without softening too much.

Reduce the heat, return the turkey to the pan and stir in the beans and cooked rice. Season well, squeeze over the lime juice and remove from the heat. Spoon the filling onto the tortillas, roll them up and arrange them in a rectangular ovenproof dish.

Pour the salsa over the tortillas and scatter over the jalapeño peppers (if used) and Cheddar. Cook in a preheated 400°F (200°C) oven for about 20 minutes, until hot and the cheese has melted. Serve immediately with guacamole and shredded lettuce on the side.

For hot tomato salsa to serve as an accompaniment, chop 1 lb (500 g) tomatoes, 1 hot red chile, 1 clove garlic and 1 small onion. Add 2 tbsp (30 ml) tomato purée, 2 tbsp (30 ml) red wine vinegar and 2 tbsp (30 ml) sugar. Mix well. Alternatively, blend all the ingredients in a food processor until finely chopped.

BIRYANI

Serves 4
Preparation time 25 minutes
Cooking time 40 minutes

3 onions
2 cloves garlic, chopped
2-inch (5 cm) piece fresh ginger, roughly chopped
2 tsp (10 ml) ground turmeric
¼ tsp (1 ml) ground cloves
½ tsp (2 ml) hot pepper flakes
¼ tsp (1 ml) ground cinnamon
2 tsp (10 ml) medium curry paste
1 tbsp (15 ml) lemon juice
2 tsp (10 ml) granulated or fruit sugar
Salt and pepper
10 oz (300 g) lean chicken, turkey breast or lamb, cut
  into small pieces
6 tbsp (90 ml) oil
1 small cauliflower, cut into small florets
2 bay leaves
1½ (375 ml) basmati rice
3 cups (750 ml) chicken or vegetable stock
1 tbsp (15 ml) black onion seeds
2 tbsp (30 ml) toasted flaked almonds, to garnish

Roughly chop 1 onion and put in a food processor with the garlic, ginger, turmeric, cloves, hot pepper flakes, cinnamon, curry paste, lemon juice, sugar and salt and pepper. Blend to a thick paste and turn into a bowl. Add the meat to the bowl and mix together well.

Thinly slice the second onion. Heat 5 tbsp (75 ml) of the oil in a large frying pan and fry the onion slices until deep golden and crisp. Drain on paper towel.

Chop the third onion. Add the cauliflower to the frying pan and fry gently for 5 minutes. Add the chopped onion and fry gently, stirring, for about 5 minutes, until the cauliflower is softened and golden. Drain.

Heat the remaining oil in the pan. Tip in the meat and marinade and fry gently for 5 minutes, stirring.

Stir in the bay leaves, rice and stock and bring to a boil. Reduce the heat and simmer very gently, stirring occasionally, for 10 to 12 minutes, until the rice is tender and the stock absorbed, adding a little water to the pan if the mixture is dry before the rice is cooked. Stir in the black onion seeds. Return the cauliflower to the pan and heat through.

Pile onto serving plates and serve scattered with the crisp onion and toasted almonds. Serve with a cucumber and mint raita (see below), if desired.

For cucumber and mint raita, gently mix together the following in a bowl: ¾ cup (175 ml) plain yogurt, ½ cup (125 ml) cucumber, seeded and coarsely grated, 2 tbsp (30 ml) chopped mint, 1 pinch ground cumin and lemon juice and salt to taste. Stand for 30 minutes.

THAI CHICKEN POT ROAST

Serves 3–4
Preparation time 15 minutes
Cooking time 1 hour 35 minutes

2½ lbs (1.25 kg) chicken
1 tbsp (15 ml) Thai seven-spice seasoning
2 tbsp (30 ml) oil
3 cloves garlic, crushed
1 hot red chili, seeded and sliced
3-inch (7.5 cm) piece fresh ginger, finely chopped
¾ cup + 2 tbsp (200 ml) chicken stock
2 stalks lemongrass, chopped
1 tbsp (15 ml) fish sauce
1 tbsp (15 ml) granulated or fruit sugar
2 tbsp (30 ml) lime juice
¼ cup (60 ml) fresh coriander, plus extra to sprinkle
1 bunch green onions
½ tsp (2 ml) ground turmeric
14-oz (398 ml) can coconut milk
7 oz (200 g) baby spinach
10 oz (300 g) straight-to-wok rice noodles

Rub the chicken skin with the seven-spice seasoning. Heat the oil in a flameproof casserole and fry the chicken on all sides until lightly browned. Scatter in the garlic, chile and ginger and fry for 1 minute.

Add the stock and bring to a boil. Cover and place in a preheated 350°F (180°C) oven for 45 minutes.

Put the lemongrass, fish sauce, sugar and lime juice in a food processor. Roughly chop the coriander and green onions and add to the processor with the turmeric. Blend until finely chopped. Add the coconut milk and blend until smooth.

Pour the spicy milk over the chicken and return to the oven for a further 45 minutes, until the chicken is very tender.

Remove from the oven and stir the spinach and rice noodles into the sauce around the chicken. Leave to rest for 10 minutes, then serve.

For homemade chicken stock, put a chicken carcass, trimmings such as the giblets and the scrapings left in the pan after a roast in a large saucepan. Add 1 large, unpeeled and halved onion, 1 chopped carrot, 1 celery stalk, roughly chopped, several bay leaves and 1 tsp (5 ml) of peppercorns. Cover with cold water and heat until simmering. Cook on the lowest setting, uncovered, for 1½ hours. Strain through a sieve and leave to cool.

ROAST CHICKEN WITH SPICE RUB

Serves 4
Preparation time 20 minutes
Cooking time 1 hour 20 minutes to 1 hour 30 minutes

3 lb (1.5 kg) whole chicken
3 tbsp (45 ml) olive oil, divided
1 tsp (5 ml) fennel seeds, roughly crushed
1 tsp (5 ml) cumin seeds, roughly crushed
1 tsp (5 ml) crushed dried red chiles
1 tsp (5 ml) dried oregano
½ tsp (2 ml) ground cinnamon
Salt and pepper
1¼ lbs (625 g) baby new potatoes
2 shallots, finely chopped
2 cloves garlic, finely chopped (optional)
5 oz (150 g) slender green beans
Juice of 1 lemon
¾ cup + 2 tbsp (200 ml) chicken stock
Small bunch fresh coriander or flat-leaf (Italian) parsley,
    or mix of the two, roughly chopped

Put the chicken into a large roasting tin and drizzle with 2 tbsp (30 ml) of the oil. Mix the crushed seeds, chiles, oregano and cinnamon with some salt and pepper, then sprinkle half over the chicken.

Cover the chicken loosely with foil, then roast in a preheated 375°F (190°C) oven for 40 minutes. Remove the foil and baste with the pan juices. Add the potatoes to the pan, toss in the juices, then cook uncovered for 40 to 50 minutes, basting and turning the potatoes once or twice until golden brown. Re-cover the chicken with foil if the spice rub begins to overbrown.

Meanwhile, heat the remaining oil in a small saucepan, add the shallots and garlic, if desired, and fry for 5 minutes, until softened. Stir in the remaining spice rub and cook for 1 minute. Cook the green beans in a saucepan of boiling water for 5 minutes, then drain and toss in the shallot mixture with the lemon juice.

When the chicken is cooked, add the green bean mixture to the potatoes. Mix together, then add the stock and bring to a boil on the stove. Sprinkle with the herbs, carve the chicken and serve.

For roast chicken with herbes de Provence, roughly chop the leaves from 3 stems of rosemary, 3 stems of thyme and 2 lavender flowers. Mix with 1 tsp (5 ml) coarse salt and ¼ tsp (1 ml) roughly crushed colored peppercorns. Sprinkle half over the chicken and the rest over the potatoes. Continue as above.

113

SWEET-GLAZED CHICKEN

Serves 4
Preparation time 10 minutes
Cooking time 45 minutes

2 tbsp (30 ml) olive oil
4 boneless skinless chicken breasts, about 5 oz
    (150 g) each
Salt and pepper
8 fresh apricots, halved and pitted
2 pears, peeled, quartered and cored
1 lb (500 g) new potatoes
1 onion, cut into wedges
Grated zest and juice of 2 oranges
A few fresh thyme sprigs, chopped
1 tbsp (15 ml) whole-grain mustard
1 tbsp (15 ml) liquid honey
¼ cup (60 ml) crème fraîche

Heat the oil in a flameproof casserole; season the chicken with salt and pepper and add to the pan. Fry for 2 to 3 minutes on each side until golden, then add the apricots, pears, potatoes and onion.

Mix together the orange zest and juice, thyme, mustard and honey and pour over the chicken. Cover the dish with foil and bake in a preheated 350°F (180°C) oven for 40 minutes, removing the foil halfway through the cooking time.

When the chicken is cooked, stir the crème fraîche into the sauce before serving.

For wilted spinach with pine nuts and raisins to serve as an accompaniment, place ½ cup (125 ml) raisins in a small heatproof bowl, cover with boiling water and leave for 5 minutes. Meanwhile, heat 3 tbsp (45 ml) olive oil in a frying pan and fry ¼ cup (60 ml) pine nuts until pale golden. Stir in 2 crushed cloves garlic. Drain the raisins and add to the pan with 1¼ lbs (625 g) baby spinach. Cook for 1 minute, turning until the spinach has wilted. Add grated lemon zest and salt and pepper to taste.

CLASSIC COQ AU VIN

Serves 4
Preparation time 25 minutes
Cooking time 1 hour 20 minutes

¼ cup (60 ml) all-purpose flour
Salt and pepper
8 mixed chicken thigh and drumstick pieces
2 tbsp (30 ml) olive oil
12 oz (375 g) shallots, halved if large
4 oz (125 g) smoked bacon
2 cloves garlic, finely chopped
¼ cup (60 ml) brandy or cognac
1¼ cups (300 ml) cheap red burgundy wine
¾ cup + 2 tbsp (200 ml) chicken stock
2 tsp (10 ml) tomato paste
Fresh or dried bouquet garni

For the garlic croutons
2 tbsp (30 ml) butter
1 tbsp (15 ml) olive oil
1 clove garlic, finely chopped
½ stick French bread, thinly sliced

Mix the flour on a plate with a little salt and pepper, then use to coat the chicken. Heat the oil in a large shallow flameproof casserole (or frying pan and transfer chicken to a casserole dish later), add the chicken and cook over high heat until golden on all sides. Lift out onto a plate.

Fry the shallots and bacon until golden, then stir in the garlic and return the chicken to the casserole. Pour over the brandy or cognac and, when bubbling, flame with a long match or barbeque lighter. As soon as the flames subside, pour in the red wine and stock, then mix in the tomato paste and bouquet garni. Season, then cover the casserole and transfer to a preheated 350°F (180°C) oven and cook for 1¼ hours, until tender.

When the chicken is cooked, pour the liquid from the casserole into a saucepan and boil for 5 minutes to reduce and thicken slightly, if desired. Return the liquid to the casserole.

Heat the butter and oil in a frying pan for the croutons; add the garlic and cook for 1 minute, then add the bread slices in a single layer. Fry on both sides until golden. Serve the coq au vin in shallow bowls topped with the croutons.

For flamed chicken with calvados & apple, fry the chicken as above, adding ¼ cup (60 ml) calvados instead of the brandy. Pour in 1¼ cups (300 ml) cider in place of the red wine and omit the tomato paste. Transfer to a casserole dish and add 1 cored and thickly sliced Granny Smith apple. Continue as above.

HONEY-SPICED CHICKEN BREASTS

Serves 4
Preparation time 8 minutes
Cooking time 20–25 minutes

4 boneless chicken breasts, with skins, about 5 oz
    (150 g) each

Spiced honey
2 tbsp (30 ml) mango chutney
1 tbsp (15 ml) liquid honey
2 tsp (10 ml) Worcestershire sauce
1 tsp (5 ml) garlic powder
1 tsp (5 ml) piri piri sauce
2 tbsp (30 ml) red wine vinegar
2 tsp (10 ml) whole-grain mustard
Salt and pepper

Slash the chicken breasts 3 to 4 times with a sharp knife, then place in a baking dish.

Mix together all the ingredients for the spiced honey and spoon over the chicken. Toss until well coated.

Put the chicken in a preheated 425°F (220°C) oven for 20 to 25 minutes or until the meat is cooked through and the skin is crispy.

Leave the chicken to rest for a few minutes before serving with chunky potato chips, if desired.

For herbed honey chicken with sweet potato fries, replace the spiced honey with a herbed honey sauce, as follows. Mix 2 tbsp (30 ml) of honey and 2 tbsp (30 ml) cider vinegar with 1 tbsp (15 ml) each of chopped fresh thyme, tarragon and sage. Spoon over the chicken as above and serve with chunky sweet potato fries, if desired.

CHICKEN KIEVS

Serves 4
Preparation time 40 minutes, plus freezing and chilling
Cooking time 20 minutes

½ cup (125 ml) butter, at room temperature
2 tbsp (30 ml) chopped fresh chives
1 tbsp (15 ml) chopped fresh parsley
2 tsp (10 ml) chopped fresh tarragon (optional)
1 clove garlic, finely chopped
2 tsp (10 ml) lemon juice
Pepper
4 boneless skinless chicken breasts, about 5 oz
  (150 g) each
2 tbsp (30 ml) all-purpose flour
2 cups (500 ml) fresh breadcrumbs
2 eggs
3 tbsp (45 ml) sunflower oil

Beat the butter with the herbs, garlic, lemon juice and a little pepper. Spoon into a line about 10 inches (25 cm) long on a sheet of plastic wrap or foil, then roll up into a neat log shape. Freeze for 15 minutes.

Meanwhile, put one of the chicken breasts between 2 large sheets of plastic wrap and beat with a rolling pin until it forms a rectangle about ⅛ inch (3 mm) thick, being careful not to make any holes in the chicken. Repeat with the other chicken breasts.

Cut the herb butter into 4 pieces and put one on each chicken breast. Fold in the sides, then the top and bottom, to make a tight parcel.

Put the flour on a plate and the breadcrumbs on a second plate, and beat the eggs in a shallow dish. Roll the kievs in the flour, then coat in the egg and roll in the breadcrumbs. Put back onto the empty flour plate and chill for 1 hour (longer if you have time).

Heat the oil in a large frying pan, add the kievs and cook over a medium heat for 5 minutes, turning until evenly browned. Transfer to a baking sheet, then complete cooking in a preheated 400°F (200°C) for 15 minutes, or until the chicken is cooked through. Serve with braised red cabbage.

For chicken, garlic & sun-dried tomato kievs, chop ¼ cup (60 ml) drained sun-dried tomatoes in oil and stir into 5 oz (150 g) garlic and herb cream cheese. Divide between the flattened chicken breasts, then shape, chill and cook as above.

STOVED CHICKEN WITH BLACK PUDDING

Serves 4

Preparation time 20 minutes

Cooking time 2 hours
  5 minutes

4 chicken legs, cut into drumsticks and thighs

2 tbsp (30 ml) all-purpose flour

Salt and pepper

1 tbsp (15 ml) sunflower oil

2 onions, thinly sliced

¼ cup (60 ml) butter, divided

2 lbs (1 kg) potatoes, thinly sliced

1 apple, cored, diced

4 oz (125 g) black pudding or other rich sausage, peeled, diced

1¾ cups (425 ml) chicken stock

Coat the chicken in the flour and salt and pepper.

Heat the oil in a large frying pan, add the onions and fry for 5 minutes, until pale golden. Mix in any remaining flour, then scoop the onions out of the pan and set aside.

Heat half the butter in the frying pan, add the chicken and fry on both sides until golden. Arrange a thin layer of potatoes in the base of an ovenproof casserole dish, top with half the onions, then the chicken pieces. Add the apple and black pudding, then spoon over the remaining onions. Arrange the remaining potatoes in an overlapping layer on the top. Pour the stock over the top, then season the potatoes.

Cover the dish tightly and cook in a preheated 350°F (180°C) oven for 1½ hours. Remove the lid, dot the potatoes with the remaining butter and cook for 30 minutes more, until golden brown. Serve in shallow bowls.

For stoved chicken with bacon & sage, omit the black pudding and apple and add 4 oz (125 g) diced smoked bacon when frying the onions. Add 2 to 3 stems sage, depending on size, to the casserole dish along with the fried chicken.

ROAST CHICKEN WITH LEMON BASTE

Serves 4–5
Preparation time 35 minutes
Cooking time 1 hour 30 minutes

3½ lb (1.75 kg) whole chicken
3½ oz (100 g) full-fat cream cheese
3 tbsp (45 ml) olive oil, divided
2 tbsp (30 ml) preserved lemon, well drained, seeded, finely chopped
2 tbsp (30 ml) mixed fresh basil and parsley, finely chopped
3 cloves garlic, finely chopped
Salt and cayenne pepper
1 lb 6 oz (675 g) small new potatoes, scrubbed
8 oz (250 g) Chantenay carrots, scrubbed
4 oz (125 g) baby corn
7 oz (200 g) fine asparagus, trimmed
¾ cup + 2 tbsp (200 ml) dry white wine
¾ cup + 2 tbsp (200 ml) chicken stock

Insert a small, sharp knife between the skin and the flesh at the top of one of the chicken breasts, then enlarge to make a small slit. Slide a finger into the slit and gently move the finger to lift the skin away from the chicken breast and make a pocket, being careful not to tear the skin. Do the same from the base of the breast until the skin is completely loosened, then continue over the top of the leg. Repeat on the other chicken breast and leg.

Mix the cream cheese with 1 tbsp (15 ml) of the oil and add the lemon, herbs, garlic, salt and cayenne pepper. Lift small amounts of the cheese mix at a time on to a round-bladed knife and insert into the pocket beneath the chicken skin until it has all been added. Ease it into an even layer by pressing the outside of the skin.

Transfer the chicken to a roasting tin and truss loosely. Cover with oiled foil and roast in a preheated 375°F (190°C) oven for 50 minutes. Baste the chicken with the pan juices, then re-cover. Add the potatoes, carrots and remaining oil (but do not cover these with foil) and roast for 30 minutes, turning once. Remove the foil from the chicken, baste and add the corn and asparagus. Roast for 10 minutes, until the asparagus is just tender and the chicken cooked when tested.

Transfer to a serving plate, add the wine and stock to the roasting pan and bring to a boil on the stove, scraping up the residue in the roasting pan and seasoning to taste. Strain into a gravy boat and serve with the chicken.

CHICKEN, LEMON & OLIVE STEW

Serves 4
Preparation time 20 minutes
Cooking time 1 hour

3 lbs (1.5 kg) chicken
About ¼ cup (60 ml) olive oil
12 baby onions, peeled but left whole
2 cloves garlic, crushed
1 tsp (5 ml) each ground cumin, ginger and turmeric
½ tsp (2 ml) ground cinnamon
1¾ cups (425 ml) chicken stock
4 oz (125 g) kalamata olives
1 preserved lemon, pulp and skin discarded, chopped
2 tbsp (30 ml) chopped fresh coriander
Salt and pepper

Cut the chicken into 8 pieces (or ask your butcher to do this for you). Heat the oil in a flameproof casserole and brown the chicken on all sides. Remove the pieces with a slotted spoon and set aside.

Add the onions, garlic and spices and sauté over low heat for 10 minutes, until just golden. Return the chicken to the pan, stir in the stock and bring to a boil. Cover and simmer gently for 30 minutes.

Add the olives, preserved lemon and coriander and cook for a further 15 to 20 minutes until the chicken is really tender. Taste and adjust the seasoning, if necessary.

For green couscous to serve as an accompaniment, shake together ²/₃ cup (150 ml) olive oil and ¼ cup (60 ml) lemon juice until well combined. Season with salt and pepper. Tip 2 cups (500 ml) cooked couscous into a warmed serving dish and stir in 1 bunch chopped green onions, ¼ cup (60 ml) chopped arugula and ½ cucumber, halved, seeded and chopped. Stir in the lemon juice dressing and serve.

ROAST POUSSINS WITH OREGANO

Serves 4
Preparation time 10 minutes, plus resting
Cooking time 55 minutes

¼ cup (60 ml) butter
Finely grated zest of 1 lemon
2 tbsp (30 ml) fresh oregano, chopped
Salt and pepper
1 large clove garlic, crushed
2 poussins, about 1 lb (500 g) each
5 oz (150 g) peppery mixed salad leaves

Mash together the butter, lemon zest, oregano, garlic and salt and pepper. Lift the skin from the poussins and slide the flavored butter between the flesh and skin, or, if you prefer, smear the butter over the skin.

Put the poussins side by side in a roasting pan and cook in a preheated 425°F (220°C) oven for about 55 minutes, basting occasionally, until golden and crispy and the juices run clear. Remove from the oven and leave to rest for 5 minutes.

Transfer the poussins to a chopping board and use a long, sharp knife to cut each one carefully in half lengthwise. Serve immediately with the salad leaves.

For classic potato gratin to serve as an accompaniment, and which can be cooked in the oven at the same time as the poussins, use 1½ lb (750 g) peeled and thinly sliced potatoes, blanched for a minute or two in boiling salted water. Drain the potatoes and tip them into a large ovenproof dish. Scatter over 2 finely chopped cloves garlic and season. Pour in 1⅓ cup + 2 tbsp (350 ml) table (18%) or half-and-half (10%) cream and sprinkle with a little grated nutmeg. Dot with ¼ cup (60 ml) butter, then put the dish in the oven for around 45 minutes or until soft when pierced with a knife.

SPICED TURKEY & PEPPER WRAPS

Serves 4
Preparation time 15 minutes
Cooking time 40 minutes

1 tsp (5 ml) mild chili powder
½ tsp (2 ml) ground cumin
1 tsp (5 ml) chopped fresh thyme
Salt
1¼ lbs (625 g) lean turkey breast, cut into
   small chunks
4 mixed bell peppers, seeded and cut into large chunks
2 red onions, sliced
¼ cup (60 ml) olive oil
2 large zucchini, cut into wedges
1 tsp (5 ml) cornstarch
2 tbsp (30 ml) red or white wine vinegar
2 tbsp (30 ml) liquid honey
2 tbsp (30 ml) sun-dried tomato paste
Few drops hot pepper sauce
¼ cup (60 ml) water
¼ cup (60 ml) dried pineapple, sliced
4 flour tortillas, warmed

Mix the chili powder with the cumin, thyme and a little salt and use to coat the turkey. Scatter in a large roasting pan with the peppers and onions.

Drizzle with the oil and toss the ingredients lightly together. Place the pan in a preheated 425°F (220°C) oven for 15 minutes. Add the zucchini to the pan, mixing them into the pan juices, and return to the oven for a further 20 minutes, until the turkey is cooked through and the vegetables are tender.

Mix together the cornstarch and vinegar to make a smooth paste. Add the honey, tomato paste, hot pepper sauce and a little salt and add to the roasting pan with the water. Stir together well. Scatter with the pineapple and return to the oven for a further 2 to 3 minutes, until the glaze has slightly thickened to coat the meat and vegetables. Divide between the warmed tortillas, roll up and serve.

For spiced sweet potato wraps, omit the turkey and use 1¼ lb (625 g) sweet potatoes, thinly sliced and coated in the chili mixture as above. Replace the onions with 2 bunches green onions, chopped, and the zucchini with 1 small eggplant, thinly sliced. Add the eggplant with the peppers and green onions after 15 minutes of the cooking time.

CHICKEN & SEAFOOD PAELLA

Serves 4
Preparation time 25 minutes
Cooking time 45 minutes

⅔ cup (150 ml) olive oil
5 oz (150 g) chorizo, cut into small pieces
4 boneless chicken thighs, cut into pieces
10 oz (300 g) squid rings
8 large raw shrimp
1 red bell pepper, seeded and chopped
4 cloves garlic, crushed
1 onion, chopped
1½ cups (375 ml) paella rice
1 tsp (5 ml) saffron threads
1¾ cups (425 ml) chicken stock or fish stock
⅔ cup (150 ml) peas or lima or fava beans
10 oz (300 g) fresh mussels
Salt and pepper
Lemon or lime wedges, to garnish

Heat half the oil in a large paella, sauté or frying pan and gently fry the chorizo for 5 minutes, turning it in the oil. Drain to a plate. Add the chicken thighs to the pan and fry for about 5 minutes, until cooked through. Drain to the plate. Cook the squid rings and shrimp in the oil, turning the shrimp once, until pink. Drain to the plate while cooking the rice.

Add the remaining oil, red bell pepper, garlic and onion to the pan and fry gently for 5 minutes, until softened. Stir in the rice, turning it in the oil for 1 minute. Add the saffron and stock to the pan and bring to a boil. Reduce the heat, cover with a lid or foil and cook gently for about 20 minutes, until the rice is cooked through.

Scrub the mussels, scraping off any barnacles and pulling away the beards. Discard any damaged shells or any open ones that don't close when tapped gently with a knife.

Return the chorizo, chicken, squid and shrimp to the pan with the peas or beans and mix thoroughly. Scatter the mussels over the top, pushing them down slightly into the rice. Cover and cook for a further 5 minutes or until the mussels have opened. Discard any shells that remain closed. Check the seasoning and serve garnished with lemon or lime wedges.

For pork paella, replace the chicken with 14 oz (400 g) lean pork, diced and cooked as above. Replace the squid with 8 fresh scallops with roes and the mussels with the same quantity of small clams.

SPICY BASQUE-STYLE CHICKEN

Serves 4
Preparation time 12 minutes
Cooking time 45–47 minutes

2 lbs (1 kg) chicken pieces (thighs, drumsticks, etc.)
1 heaped tbsp (20 ml) flour, seasoned with salt and pepper
3 tbsp (45 ml) olive oil
1 onion, sliced
1 red bell pepper, cored, seeded and sliced
1 green bell pepper, cored, seeded and sliced
2 cloves garlic, crushed
1 tsp (5 ml) paprika
1 tsp (5 ml) hot smoked paprika
3½ oz (100 g) prosciutto, torn into pieces
⅓ cup (75 ml) Marsala
⅔ cup (150 ml) white wine
14-oz (398 ml) can chopped tomatoes
1 tsp (5 ml) dried thyme
Salt and pepper

Dust the chicken in the seasoned flour. Heat the oil in a large, heavy-bottomed casserole over medium-high heat and fry the chicken until golden brown. Remove and set aside.

Reduce the heat, add the onion and peppers and cook, stirring frequently, for 4 to 5 minutes, until softened and golden. Stir in the garlic, paprikas and prosciutto and fry for a further 1 to 2 minutes.

Return the chicken to the pan, pour in the Marsala, wine, ½ cup (125 ml) water and the tomatoes. Stir in the thyme and season to taste. Bring to a boil, then reduce the heat to a simmer, cover the pan and leave for 30 to 35 minutes, until the chicken is cooked and the sauce is rich and thick.

Serve the chicken in bowls with lots of sauce.

For pan-fried polenta with olives to serve as an accompaniment, cut 2 packages, 1 lb (500 g) each, of ready-made polenta into 1-inch (2.5 cm) slices. Fry the slices in olive oil and sprinkle with 2 tbsp (30 ml) chopped black olives and 1 tsp (5 ml) chopped fresh parsley. Add 1 crushed clove garlic and fry quickly. Serve as above.

LEMON–CHILE CHICKEN

Serves 4
Preparation time 25 minutes, plus marinating
Cooking time 45 minutes

3½ lbs (1.75 kg) chicken, cut into 8 pieces
8 cloves garlic
4 juicy lemons, squeezed, skins reserved
1 small red chile, seeded and chopped
2 tbsp (30 ml) orange flower honey
¼ cup (60 ml) chopped fresh parsley, plus sprigs
   to garnish
Salt and pepper

Arrange the chicken pieces in a shallow flameproof dish. Peel and crush 2 of the cloves garlic and add them to the lemon juice with the chile and honey. Stir well, then pour this mixture over the chicken. Tuck the lemon skins around the meat, cover and leave to marinate in the refrigerator for at least 2 hours or overnight, turning once or twice.

Turn the chicken pieces so they are skin side up, scatter over the remaining whole cloves garlic and put the lemon skins, cut sides down, on top.

Cook the chicken in a preheated 400°F (200°C) oven for 45 minutes or until golden brown and tender. Stir in the parsley, season to taste and serve garnished with parsley sprigs.

For coriander rice & peas to serve as an accompaniment, boil 1⅓ cups (325 ml) frozen peas for about 3 minutes, drain them and toss them in ¼ cup (60 ml) melted butter with 2 chopped green onions and a handful of chopped fresh coriander. Fork the peas into the rice and serve.

LIME, GINGER & CORIANDER CHICKEN

Serves 4
Preparation time 5–10 minutes
Cooking time 50 minutes

3 limes
½-inch (1 cm) cube fresh ginger, peeled and finely
   grated
¼ cup (60 ml) finely chopped fresh coriander, plus extra
   leaves to serve
2 tsp (10 ml) vegetable oil, divided
4 chicken legs
1⅓ cup (325 ml) Thai jasmine rice
Salt

Finely grate the zest of 2 of the limes and halve these limes. Mix the zest with the ginger and coriander in a non-metallic bowl and stir in 1 tsp (5 ml) of the oil to make a rough paste.

Carefully lift the skin from the chicken legs and push in the ginger paste. Pull the skin back into place, then cut 3 or 4 slashes in the thickest parts of the legs and brush with the remaining oil.

Put the legs in a roasting pan, flesh side down, with the halved limes and cook in a preheated 425°F (220°C) oven for 45 to 50 minutes, basting occasionally. The legs are cooked when the meat comes away from the bone and the juices run clear.

Meanwhile, put the rice in a pan with 1⅔ cups (400 ml) cold water, cover with a tight-fitting lid and cook over medium-low heat for 10 minutes, until the water has been absorbed and the rice is almost cooked. Set aside somewhere warm until the chicken has finished cooking.

Spoon the rice into small bowls to mold, then turn it onto serving plates. Add the chicken legs, squeeze over the roasted lime and scatter with coriander leaves. Serve immediately with the remaining lime, cut into wedges.

For Mediterranean chicken, replace the ginger paste with a red pesto made by blending 6 sun-dried tomatoes, 1 tbsp (15 ml) pine nuts, ½ clove chopped garlic, 1 tbsp (15 ml) chopped basil, 1 tsp (5 ml) grated lemon zest, 1 tbsp (15 ml) lemon juice, 3 tbsp (45 ml) olive oil and 1 tbsp (15 ml) grated Parmesan cheese.

CRISPY DUCK WITH GINGER & ORANGE

Serves 4
Preparation time 10 minutes
Cooking time 24–26 minutes

1 tsp (5 ml) vegetable oil
4 duck breasts, skin slashed
11½ oz (350 g) spring greens, shredded
1 tbsp (15 ml) balsamic vinegar
1 piece preserved ginger in syrup, chopped
¼ cup (60 ml) strong orange and cinnamon tea
    infusion (or other citrus tea)
½ tsp (2 ml) mixed peppercorns, crushed
Salt

Heat the oil in a frying pan over medium heat and fry the duck breasts, skin side down, for about 15 minutes, until the skin is really crispy. Drain off the excess fat, turn the duck over and fry for a further 5 minutes. Remove and keep warm.

Put the spring greens in a steamer over a pan of boiling water and steam for 2 to 3 minutes or until wilted.

Add the remaining ingredients to the frying pan and season with salt to taste, then stir to mix and allow to bubble for 2 to 3 minutes.

Serve the duck breasts with the sauce poured over and with the steamed spring greens.

For duck with sherry-lime marmalade, omit the vinegar, ginger and tea and instead make a sauce with ¼ cup (60 ml) dry sherry and ¼ cup (60 ml) lime marmalade. Sprinkle a handful of chopped mint onto the spring greens before serving.

CHICKEN WITH SPRING VEGETABLES

Serves 4
Preparation time 10 minutes, plus resting
Cooking time about 1¼ hours

3 lbs (1.5 kg) chicken
About 6 cups (1.5 L) hot chicken stock
2 shallots, halved
2 cloves garlic
2 sprigs of fresh parsley
2 sprigs of fresh marjoram
2 sprigs of fresh lemon thyme
2 carrots, halved
1 leek, trimmed and sliced
7 oz (200 g) broccoli or broccoli rabe
8 oz (250 g) asparagus, trimmed
½ Savoy cabbage, shredded

Put the chicken in a large saucepan and pour in enough stock just to cover the chicken. Push the shallots, garlic, herbs, carrots and leek into the pan and place over medium-high heat. Bring to a boil, then reduce the heat and simmer gently for 1 hour or until the chicken is falling away from the bones.

Add the remaining vegetables to the pan and simmer for a further 6 to 8 minutes or until the vegetables are cooked.

Turn off the heat and leave to rest for 5 to 10 minutes before serving the chicken and vegetables in deep bowls with spoonfuls of the broth. Remove the skin, if preferred, and serve with plenty of crusty bread.

For Chinese chicken soup, use the same amount of stock, but omit all the vegetables and herbs. Instead, use a sliced 3-inch (7.5 cm) length of fresh ginger, 2 cloves garlic, sliced, 1 tsp (5 ml) Chinese five-spice powder, 4 to 5 whole star anise and ⅓ cup (75 ml) dark soy sauce. Add baby corn and snow peas instead of the spring vegetables and cook as above.

GARLIC BUTTER–STUFFED CHICKEN

Serves 4
Preparation time 25 minutes
Cooking time 40 minutes

1½ cups (375 ml) coarse fresh breadcrumbs
3 tbsp (45 ml) olive oil, divided
4 large boneless skinless chicken breasts
2 tbsp (30 ml) butter, softened
¼ cup (60 ml) cream cheese
2 cloves garlic, crushed
Finely grated zest of 1 lemon
¼ cup (60 ml) chopped fresh parsley
Salt and pepper
5 oz (150 g) young green beans, diagonally sliced into
   1½-inch (3.5 cm) lengths
14-oz (398 ml) can flageolet beans, drained
¾ cup + 2 tbsp (200 ml) white wine

Put the breadcrumbs in a flameproof casserole with 1 tbsp (15 ml) of the oil and heat gently until the breadcrumbs begin to brown and crisp. Drain to a plate.

Using a small knife, make a horizontal cut in each chicken breast to create a pocket for stuffing. Beat the butter with the cream cheese, garlic, lemon zest, 1 tbsp (15 ml) of the parsley and salt and pepper. Pack the stuffing into the chicken breasts and seal the openings with wooden cocktail sticks.

Heat the remaining oil in the casserole and fry the chicken on both sides until lightly browned. Drain. Scatter the green beans and flageolet beans into the casserole and add the wine and a little seasoning. Arrange the chicken on top.

Cover and place in a preheated 375°F (190°C) oven for 20 minutes. Remove the lid and sprinkle the chicken pieces with the breadcrumbs. Return to the oven, uncovered, for a further 10 minutes, until the chicken is cooked through. Transfer the chicken to plates. Stir the remaining parsley into the beans, then spoon around the chicken.

For roast potatoes with garlic to serve as an accompaniment, heat ¼ cup (60 ml) olive oil in a roasting pan in a preheated 450°F (230°C) oven. Quarter 1½ lbs (750 g) potatoes, then add with 2 tbsp (30 ml) chopped fresh rosemary to the hot oil, tossing to coat. Roast for 20 minutes. Remove, turn the potatoes, scatter with 4 sliced cloves garlic and return to the oven for a further 10 to 20 minutes.

124

FAST FAMILY FAVORITES

ALL-IN-ONE CHICKEN PIE

Serves 4

Preparation time 20 minutes

Cooking time 45–50 minutes

8 oz (250 g) broccoli florets

1 tbsp (15 ml) olive oil

12 oz (375 g) boneless skinless chicken
  breasts, cubed

6 slices bacon, chopped

2 small carrots, chopped

2 tbsp (30 ml) butter

¼ cup (60 ml) all-purpose flour

1 ¼ cups (300 ml) milk

1 tbsp (15 ml) white wine vinegar

1 tsp (5 ml) Dijon mustard

¾ cup + 2 tbsp (200 ml) crème fraîche

2 tbsp (30 ml) chopped fresh tarragon or parsley

1 lb (500 g) package pastry

1 beaten egg, for glazing

Cook the broccoli for 5 minutes, until tender. Drain and refresh with cold water, then set aside. Heat the oil in a nonstick frying pan and cook the chicken and bacon over moderate heat for 7 to 8 minutes. Add the carrots and cook for a further 3 to 4 minutes, until golden all over. Remove from the heat.

Heat the butter in a medium saucepan and add the flour. Cook over low heat for a few seconds, then remove from the heat and gradually add the milk until well mixed. Add the vinegar and mustard and mix well. Return to the heat and stir continuously until boiled and thickened. Add the crème fraîche and herbs. Add the chicken and vegetables and stir well to coat, then transfer to a round pie dish.

Roll out the pastry on a floured surface to just larger than the dish. Moisten the rim of the dish with a little water, then place the pastry over the top, trim the edges and decorate with any remaining pastry trimmings if desired. Glaze lightly with the beaten egg. Bake in a preheated 350°F (180°C) oven for 25 to 30 minutes, until crisp and golden.

For creamy chunky ham pie, replace the chicken and bacon with a 1 lb (500 g) ham. Half-fill a large pan with water, then add 3 peppercorns and a bay leaf. Lower the ham into the pan, then bring to a boil and cook for 1 ½ hours. Drain and set aside to cool. Cook the carrots with the broccoli, then cut the ham into chunks and add the vegetables and ham to the sauce. Continue as above.

GRILLED CHICKEN FAJITAS

Serves 4
Preparation time 20 minutes, plus marinating
Cooking time 16–20 minutes

4 boneless skinless chicken breasts, 4 oz (125 g) each
4 large soft flour tortillas
²/₃ cup (150 ml) sour cream
4 tomatoes, skinned and sliced
1 avocado, sliced
4 green onions, sliced
½ red onion, finely chopped
Salt and pepper
Tortilla chips (optional)

For the marinade
2 tbsp (30 ml) soy sauce
1¼-inch (3 cm) piece fresh ginger, finely chopped
2 cloves garlic, finely chopped
2 tbsp (30 ml) olive oil
1 bunch fresh coriander, chopped
1 chile, chopped
2 tbsp (30 ml) lime juice

Combine all the ingredients for the marinade in a shallow dish. Add the chicken breasts and leave to marinate at room temperature for 2 hours, or in the refrigerator for 24 hours.

Heat a grill pan (or ordinary frying pan). Place the marinated chicken breasts in the pan to cook for 8 to 10 minutes on each side. When cooked, remove the chicken from the pan and slice it into long strips.

Place the tortillas under a preheated broiler and cook for 30 seconds on each side. Spread over one side of each tortilla a spoonful of sour cream, a little tomato, avocado and a sprinkling of green onions and red onion.

Add the pieces of grilled chicken and season. Roll up each tortilla tightly and cut in half across each one. Serve with tortilla chips, if desired.

For guacamole to accompany the fajitas, halve and pit 2 ripe avocados. Scoop out the flesh, then mash with a fork. Mix with the juice of 1 lime, 3 tbsp (45 ml) chopped fresh coriander, 1 skinned and finely diced tomato, if desired, 1 finely chopped jalapeño pepper. Spoon onto the tortillas instead of sour cream.

126

CHICKEN THATCH

Serves 4
Preparation time 25 minutes
Cooking time 35 minutes

1 tbsp (15 ml) sunflower oil
4 boneless skinless chicken thighs, diced
1 onion, chopped
2 tbsp (30 ml) all-purpose flour
1¾ cups (425 ml) chicken stock
2 tsp (10 ml) Dijon mustard
1 large carrot, diced
Salt and pepper
1½ lbs (750 g) potatoes, quartered
5 oz (150 g) zucchini, diced
3 oz (75 g) sugar snap peas, halved
3 oz (75 g) frozen peas
3 tbsp (45 ml) butter
3 tbsp (45 ml) milk
3 oz (75 g) mature Cheddar cheese, grated

Heat the oil in a saucepan, add the chicken and onion and fry for 5 minutes, stirring, until browned. Stir in the flour, then gradually mix in the stock. Bring to a boil, then add the mustard, carrot and a little salt and pepper. Cover and simmer for 30 minutes.

Meanwhile, cook the potatoes in a saucepan of boiling water until tender. Add the zucchini, sugar snap peas and frozen peas to a smaller saucepan of boiling water and cook for 3 minutes. Drain and set aside.

Drain the potatoes and mash with two-thirds of the butter and all the milk. Season and stir in two-thirds of the cheese.

Spoon the chicken mixture into a 5-cup (1.3 L) pie dish or 4 individual dishes, add the just-cooked green vegetables, then spoon the mashed potatoes on top. Dot with the remaining butter and sprinkle with the remaining cheese. Grill until golden, then serve immediately. (For an oven-baked chicken thatch, chill the dish once the grated cheese has been sprinkled on top, then bake when needed, in a preheated 375°F (190°C) oven for 35 minutes, until piping hot, or 25 minutes for smaller dishes.)

For chicken & bacon thatch, add 4 chopped slices of smoked back bacon when frying the chicken and onion. Omit the zucchini, sugar snaps and peas and cook 4 oz (125 g) frozen corn instead. Drain and add to the chicken. Finish as above.

CHICKEN WITH PRESERVED LEMONS

Serves 4–5
Preparation time 20 minutes
Cooking time 1 hour 45 minutes

2 tbsp (30 ml) olive oil
1 onion, finely chopped
3 cloves garlic
1 tsp (5 ml) ground ginger
1½ tsp (7 ml) ground cinnamon
Large pinch saffron threads, toasted, crushed
3½ lbs (1.75 kg) whole chicken
3 cups (750 ml) chicken stock or water
5 oz (150 g) large black olives, rinsed, soaked
   (optional)
1 preserved lemon, chopped
Large bunch fresh coriander, finely chopped
Large bunch fresh parsley, finely chopped
Salt and pepper

Heat the oil in a frying pan; add the onion and fry gently, stirring frequently, until softened and golden.

Meanwhile, using a pestle and mortar, crush the garlic with a pinch of salt, then work in the ginger, cinnamon, saffron and a little pepper. Stir into the onions, cook until fragrant, then remove from the pan and spread over the chicken.

Put the chicken into a heavy saucepan or flameproof casserole that it just fits, heat gently and brown the chicken for about 2 to 3 minutes, turning often. Add the stock or water and bring to just simmering point. Cover and simmer gently for about 1¼ hours, turning the chicken over 2 to 3 times.

Add the olives, preserved lemon, coriander and parsley to the pan. Cover and cook for about 15 minutes, until the chicken is very tender. Taste the sauce – if the flavor needs to be more concentrated, transfer the chicken to a warmed serving dish, cover and keep warm, and boil the cooking juices to a rich sauce. Tilt the pan and skim off any surplus fat, then pour over the chicken. Serve with couscous, if desired.

For chicken & tomato tagine, reduce the stock or water to 1¾ cups (450 ml) and add a 14-oz (400 ml) can of chopped tomatoes. Cover and simmer as above. Omit the olives and lemon, instead adding 3 oz (75 g) thickly sliced okra and the coriander and parsley as above for the last 5 minutes of cooking. Serve with rice or warmed Arab flatbreads.

CHICKEN & MUSHROOM LASAGNA

Serves 4–6
Preparation time 45 minutes
Cooking time 1 hour 25 minutes

8 chicken thighs
⅔ cup (150 ml) dry white wine
1¼ cups (300 ml) chicken stock
Few stems fresh thyme
Salt and pepper
2 tbsp (30 ml) olive oil
2 onions, thinly sliced
2 cloves garlic, finely chopped
3½ oz (100 g) exotic mushrooms
4 oz (125 g) shiitake mushrooms, sliced
¼ cup (60 ml) butter
⅓ cup (75 ml) all-purpose flour
¾ cup + 2 tbsp (200 ml) whipping (35%) cream
8-oz (250 g) pack of 6 fresh lasagna sheets
1½ oz (40 g) Parmesan cheese, freshly grated

Pack the chicken thighs into the base of a saucepan; add the wine, stock, thyme and a little salt and pepper. Bring to a boil, then cover and simmer for 45 minutes, until tender.

Meanwhile, heat the oil in a frying pan; add the onions and fry for 5 minutes, until just turning golden. Mix in the garlic and cook for 2 to 3 minutes. Stir in the mushrooms and fry for 2 to 3 minutes, until golden.

Lift the chicken out of the pan, drain and set aside. Pour the stock into a measuring cup. Make up to 2⅓ cups (575 ml) with water if needed. Wash and dry the pan, then melt the butter in it. Stir in the flour, then gradually whisk in the stock and bring to a boil, stirring until thickened and smooth. Stir in the cream and adjust the seasoning, if needed.

Soak the lasagna sheets in boiling water for 5 minutes. Cut the skin and bones away from the chicken and dice the meat. Drain the lasagna sheets.

Pour a thin layer of sauce into the base of a 8 x 11 x 2 inch (20 x 28 x 5 cm) ovenproof dish or roasting pan, then cover with 2 sheets of the lasagna. Spoon over half the mushroom mixture and half the chicken, then cover with a thin layer of sauce. Repeat the layers, then cover with the remaining lasagna and sauce. Sprinkle with the Parmesan and set aside until required.

Cook in a preheated 375°F (190°C) oven for 40 minutes, until piping hot and the top is golden. Serve with salad and garlic bread.

TURKEY & WILD MUSHROOM TURNOVERS

Serves 4
Preparation time 8 minutes, plus soaking
Cooking time 29–32 minutes

1 oz (25 g) dried wild mushrooms
¼ cup (60 ml) olive oil
14½ oz (450 g) turkey breast, sliced
3½ oz (100 g) prosciutto, torn into pieces
7 oz (200 g) button or portobello mushrooms, trimmed
 and sliced
⅓ cup + 2 tbsp (100 ml) red wine
1 tsp (5 ml) chopped fresh thyme
8 oz (250 g) mascarpone cheese
1 lb (500 g) package puff pastry (thawed if frozen)
1 egg, beaten
Salt and pepper
Watercress, to garnish

Soak the mushrooms in ¼ cup (60 ml) boiling water for 5 to 10 minutes. Heat 2 tbsp (30 ml) of the oil in a frying pan and fry the turkey for 2 to 3 minutes, until golden. Add the prosciutto and cook for 2 minutes before adding the fresh and dried mushrooms. Fry for 3 to 4 minutes, until the mushrooms are soft and golden.

Pour the wine into the pan, then add the thyme. Allow the liquid to bubble for 2 to 3 minutes, until evaporated. Remove from the heat, stir in the mascarpone and season to taste.

Roll out the pastry into a rectangular shape until it forms a thin layer and cut into 4 pieces. Spoon one-quarter of the mixture on to the center of each quarter of pastry. Brush a little beaten egg around the edges, fold over the pastry and press firmly to seal.

Brush the remaining egg over the closed turnovers, score the tops with a knife, if desired, and cook in a preheated 400°F (200°C) oven for 20 minutes, until golden and crispy.

For turkey & mushroom pie, increase the wine to 1¼ cups (300 ml) and simmer for 5 minutes. Finish the filling as above. Replace the puff pastry with shortcrust. Roll it out into a thick layer to cover a 9-inch (22 cm) pie dish with an overlap of 2 inches (5 cm). Cut a strip of pastry ½ inch (1 cm) wide and put it round the rim of the dish. Add the filling and cover with the remaining pastry. Glaze with egg and bake in a preheated 400°F (200°C) oven for 20 minutes, then lower the heat to 350°F (180°C) for a further 10 to 15 minutes.

CHICKEN WITH SPINACH CHERMOULA

Serves 4
Preparation time 12 minutes
Cooking time 25 minutes

4 boneless skinless chicken breasts, about 6 oz
 (175 g) each, cut into large pieces
2 tbsp (30 ml) olive oil
1 large red onion, sliced
14-oz (398 ml) can chickpeas, rinsed and drained
8 ready-to-eat dried apricots, sliced
Pinch of saffron
7 oz (200 g) spinach leaves, stalks removed
½ small preserved lemon, finely diced (optional)
Small bunch of fresh coriander, roughly chopped
Small bunch of flat-leaf (Italian) parsley, roughly
 chopped

Chermoula
3 tbsp (45 ml) ready-made chermoula mix
1 tsp (5 ml) harissa paste
Juice of 1 lemon
⅓ cup + 2 tbsp (100 ml) olive oil

Make the chermoula by putting all the ingredients in a screw-top jar and shaking to combine. Mix half the paste with the chicken and set aside.

Heat the oil in a large frying pan over medium heat and fry the onion for about 8 minutes, until soft and golden. Increase the heat a little, tip in the coated chicken and cook for about 12 minutes, stirring frequently. Stir in the chickpeas, apricots, saffron and the remaining chermoula paste and cook for a further 3 to 4 minutes. The chicken and spices should be cooked through.

Stir in the spinach and cook until just wilted, then add the preserved lemon (if using) and herbs. Serve immediately on warm pita or flatbreads.

For homemade chermoula, instead of the ready-made chermoula mix, stir together 2 tsp (10 ml) ground cumin, 2 tsp (10 ml) ground coriander, 1 tsp (5 ml) ground turmeric, 1 tsp (5 ml) salt and 1 tsp (5 ml) ground black pepper.

SOUTHERN FRIED CHICKEN

Serves 4
Preparation time 25 minutes
Cooking time 35–40 minutes

1 lb (500 g) sweet potatoes, peeled
1 lb (500 g) baking potatoes, scrubbed
6 tbsp (90 ml) sunflower oil, divided
1½ tsp (7 ml) smoked paprika
1½ tsp (7 ml) dried oregano
Salt and pepper
1 tsp (5 ml) mustard powder
1 tsp (5 ml) hot pepper flakes
¼ cup (60 ml) all-purpose flour
2 eggs
2 tbsp (30 ml) water
2 cups (500 ml) fresh breadcrumbs
4 chicken legs, cut into drumsticks and thighs

Thickly slice the sweet and baking potatoes, then cut into thick wedges. Mix 3 tbsp (45 ml) of the oil with 1 tsp (5 ml) paprika, 1 tsp (5 ml) oregano, ½ tsp (2 ml) mustard, ½ tsp (2 ml) hot pepper flakes and some salt in a large plastic bag or bowl. Add the potatoes and toss in the oil mixture.

Mix the remaining paprika, oregano, mustard, hot pepper flakes and seasoning with the flour on a large plate. Beat the eggs and water in a shallow dish and put the breadcrumbs on a second large plate.

Coat the chicken pieces in the flour mixture, then the beaten egg, then the breadcrumbs, until completely covered.

Heat a large roasting pan in a 400°F (200°C) for 5 minutes. Meanwhile, heat the remaining oil in a large frying pan, add the chicken and fry until pale golden. Transfer the chicken to the hot roasting pan, add the potatoes and roast for 30 to 35 minutes, until the chicken is cooked through and the potatoes crisp and golden. Transfer to serving plates and serve with mayonnaise and salad.

For cheesy fried chicken scallops, make up the vegetables as above, then mix the remaining paprika, hot pepper flakes and a little salt and pepper with the flour. Coat 4 boneless skinless chicken breasts, each cut into thin, flat slices, in the flour mixture, then in the beaten egg, then in 2½ cups (625 ml) fresh breadcrumbs mixed with 2 tbsp (30 ml) grated Parmesan cheese. Fry in the oil for 10 to 12 minutes, until golden and cooked through.

CHEESE & BACON PASTRIES

Serves 6
Preparation time 15 minutes
Cooking time 20–25 minutes

1-lb (500 g) package puff pastry
Flour, for dusting
2 tsp (10 ml) Dijon mustard (optional)
2 oz (60 g) Gruyère cheese, thinly sliced
2 oz (60 g) Cheddar cheese, thinly sliced
3 tbsp (45 ml) chopped fresh parsley
6 slices back bacon, thinly sliced
1 egg, beaten

Roll out the pastry on a lightly floured surface to a rectangle measuring 12 x 18 inches (30 x 45 cm). Cut the pastry into 6-inch (15 cm) squares.

Spread the pastry all over with a thin layer of mustard. Arrange the Gruyère and Cheddar slices on each of the pastry squares in a diagonal line. Sprinkle with the parsley, then ruffle the bacon across the top. Lightly brush the pastry edges with a little warm water, then fold each of the opposite corners up and over the filling to meet; press to seal with a fork. Place on a baking sheet.

Lightly brush the pastries with beaten egg and bake in a preheated 400°F (200°C) oven for 20 to 25 minutes, until golden. Serve warm.

For haloumi & tomato pastries, replace the bacon and cheeses with 6 oz (175 g) haloumi cheese, thinly sliced, and 4 oz (125 g) halved cherry tomatoes. Arrange on top of the mustard-spread pastry and sprinkle with the parsley. Bake as above until golden.

SAUSAGE & SWEET POTATO HASH

Serves 4
Preparation time 15 minutes
Cooking time 45 minutes

3 tbsp (45 ml) olive oil
8 pork sausages
3 large red onions, thinly sliced
1 tsp (5 ml) granulated or fruit sugar
1 lb (500 g) sweet potatoes, scrubbed and cut
  into small chunks
8 fresh sage leaves
Salt and pepper
2 tbsp (30 ml) balsamic vinegar

Heat the oil in a large frying pan or flameproof casserole and fry the sausages, turning frequently, for about 10 minutes, until browned. Drain to a plate.

Add the onions and sugar to the pan and cook gently, stirring frequently, until lightly browned. Return the sausages to the pan with the sweet potatoes, sage leaves and a little salt and pepper.

Cover the pan with a lid or foil and cook over very low heat for about 25 minutes, until the potatoes are tender.

Drizzle with the vinegar and check the seasoning before serving.

For wilted watercress with garlic and nutmeg to serve as an accompaniment, heat ¼ cup (60 ml) olive oil in a large saucepan, add 1 crushed clove garlic and cook for 30 to 60 seconds, until soft. Add 1¼ lbs (750 g) watercress and stir-fry over high heat for 1 to 2 minutes, until wilted. Season with salt and pepper and add grated nutmeg to taste.

POT-ROASTED PORK WITH PRUNES

Serves 5–6
Preparation time 20 minutes, plus resting
Cooking time 2 hours

2 lbs (1 kg) skinned, boned and rolled loin of pork
Salt and pepper
2 tbsp (30 ml) butter
1 tbsp (15 ml) olive oil
3 tbsp (45 ml) mustard seeds
2 onions, sliced
4 cloves garlic, crushed
2 stalks celery, sliced
1 tbsp (15 ml) all-purpose flour
1 tbsp (15 ml) chopped fresh thyme
1¼ cups (300 ml) white wine
5 oz (150 g) pitted prunes, halved
1 lb (500 g) small new potatoes, e.g., fresh Jersey
  Royals
2 tbsp (30 ml) chopped fresh mint

Rub the pork with salt and pepper. Melt the butter with the oil in a large, flameproof casserole and sear the pork on all sides. Drain to a plate.

Add the mustard seeds and onions and fry for about 5 minutes, until beginning to color. Stir in the garlic and celery and cook for 2 minutes. Add the flour and cook, stirring for 1 minute.

Stir in the thyme, wine and salt and pepper and let the mixture bubble up. Return the pork to the pan and cover with a lid. Transfer to a preheated 325°F (160°C) oven for 45 minutes.

Stir the prunes, potatoes and mint into the cooking juices around the pork and return to the oven for a further 1 hour, until the potatoes are very tender. Leave to rest for 15 minutes before serving.

For pot-roasted pork with shallots and peaches, use 4 shallots instead of the onions in the second step. Omit the prunes and add 2 sliced fresh peaches and 1 tbsp (15 ml) liquid honey for the final 20 minutes of cooking time.

TARTIFLETTE-STYLE PIZZA

Serves 4
Preparation time 20 minutes, plus resting
Cooking time 23–25 minutes

9½ oz (290 g) pizza base mix
2 tbsp (30 ml) butter
1 tbsp (15 ml) olive oil
7 oz (200 g) smoked bacon, chopped
2 onions, sliced
1 clove garlic, chopped
¾ cup + 2 tbsp (200 ml) crème fraîche
8 oz (250 g) cooked potatoes, thinly sliced
8 oz (250 g) Reblochon cheese, sliced

Make the pizza base according to the instructions on the package. Form the dough into 4 balls and roll them out into ovals. Cover lightly with oiled plastic wrap and leave in a warm place.

Melt the butter and olive oil in a large frying pan and fry the bacon for 3 to 4 minutes or until cooked. Add the onions and garlic and fry gently for 5 to 6 minutes or until soft and golden.

Spread 1 tbsp (15 ml) of the crème fraîche over each pizza base. Top with slices of potato, some of the bacon and onion mixture and 2 to 3 slices of Reblochon. Cook in a preheated 425°F (220°C) oven for 15 minutes, until bubbling and golden.

Serve immediately with an extra dollop of the remaining crème fraîche on top, if desired.

For artichoke heart & dolcelatte pizza, replace the potatoes with two 15-oz (475 g) cans of artichoke hearts, drained and halved. Top with sliced dolcelatte or other creamy blue cheese.

POTATO & BACON CAKES

Serves 4
Preparation time 15 minutes, plus chilling
Cooking time about 45 minutes

2 lbs (1 kg) potatoes, cut into chunks
Vegetable oil, for shallow-frying
6 green onions, sliced
7 oz (200 g) back bacon, chopped
2 tbsp (30 ml) chopped flat-leaf (Italian) parsley
Salt and pepper
All-purpose flour, for coating
2 tbsp (30 ml) butter

For the tomato sauce
¾ cup + 2 tbsp (200 ml) crème fraîche
2 tbsp (30 ml) chopped fresh basil
2 tbsp (30 ml) chopped tomatoes
Salt and pepper

Cook the potatoes in a large saucepan of salted boiling water for 15 to 20 minutes until tender. Drain well, return to the pan and mash.

Heat a little oil in a frying pan, add the green onions and cook for 2 to 3 minutes, then add the bacon and cook until browned. Add to the mashed potatoes with the parsley. Season well with salt and pepper. Form the potato mixture into 8 cakes, then cover and chill in the refrigerator until firm.

Lightly coat the cakes in flour. Melt the butter in a nonstick frying pan; add the cakes, in batches, and cook over medium heat for 4 to 5 minutes on each side, until browned and heated through.

Meanwhile, to make the sauce, put the crème fraîche in a bowl and mix in the basil and tomatoes. Season well with salt and pepper.

Serve the cakes hot with the sauce.

For salmon fish cakes with sour cream & mushroom sauce, use a 7-oz (200 g) can red salmon instead of the bacon. Drain and flake the salmon into the mashed potato mixture. Form into cakes and cook as above. Meanwhile, melt 2 tbsp (30 ml) butter in a saucepan, add 3½ oz (100 g) sliced button mushrooms and cook for 1 minute. Stir in ¾ cup + 2 tbsp (200 ml) sour cream and ¼ tsp (1 ml) paprika and season to taste with salt and pepper. Heat through gently and serve with the fish cakes.

ONE-POT ROAST PORK

Serves 4
Preparation time 25 minutes
Cooking time 1½ hours

4 boneless pork steaks, e.g. leg or loin, each about
   1 inch (2.5 cm) thick
⅓ cup (75 ml) toasted hazelnuts
1 clove garlic, crushed
3 green onions, finely chopped
Salt and pepper
4 plump, ready-to-eat dried apricots, finely chopped
¼ cup (60 ml) oil
1¼ lbs (625 g) baking potatoes, cut into small chunks
1 red onion, cut into wedges
1 apple, peeled, cored and cut into wedges
2 red chicory hearts or radicchio, cut into wedges
2 tsp (10 ml) all-purpose flour
1¼ cups (300 ml) cider

Using a sharp knife, make deep horizontal cuts in each of the pork steaks to make cavities for the stuffing.

Mix the hazelnuts in a food processor. Add the garlic, green onions, apricots and a little seasoning and blend until combined. Pack the mixture into the pork steaks and flatten with the palms of your hands. Season the steaks with salt and pepper.

Heat 1 tbsp (15 ml) of the oil in a large, sturdy roasting pan and brown the pork on both sides. Drain.

Add the potatoes and onion to the roasting pan with the remaining oil and toss together until coated. Roast in a preheated 400°F (200°C) oven for 40 minutes, until pale golden, turning once. Add the pork to the pan and roast for 15 minutes. Add the apple and chicory wedges, brushing them with a little oil from the pan, and roast for a further 20 minutes or until the pork is cooked through. Drain the meat and vegetables to warmed serving plates.

Stir the flour into the pan juices, scraping up any residue around the edges of the pan. Gradually blend in the cider and cook, stirring, until thickened and bubbling. Season to taste and serve with the roast.

For roast pork with spicy prunes, mix ⅔ cup (150 ml) fresh breadcrumbs with 4 chopped plump prunes, 1 thin-cut slice bacon, finely chopped, 1 crushed clove garlic, 1 tsp (5 ml) grated fresh ginger and salt and pepper. Use to stuff the pork and continue as above.

CHORIZO & SMOKED PAPRIKA PENNE

Serves 4
Preparation time 15 minutes
Cooking time 26 minutes

1 tbsp (15 ml) olive oil
7 oz (200 g) chorizo sausage, diced
1 onion, chopped
2 cloves garlic, chopped
1 tsp (5 ml) hot smoked paprika
1 tbsp (15 ml) capers
1 tsp (5 ml) dried oregano
1 tsp (5 ml) finely grated lemon zest
Pinch of granulated or fruit sugar
5 oz (150 g) roasted red bell pepper, sliced
28-oz (796 ml) can chopped tomatoes
11½ oz (350 g) dried penne
Salt and pepper

To serve
Chile oil (optional)
¼ cup (60 ml) grated Parmesan cheese

Heat the oil in a large pan and fry the chorizo for 2 minutes, until golden. Add the onion and garlic and cook for about 5 minutes or until soft and golden.

Stir in the paprika and cook for a further minute, then add the capers, oregano, lemon zest, sugar, red bell pepper and tomatoes. Bring to a boil, then reduce the heat and simmer gently for 15 minutes.

Meanwhile, cook the penne in lightly salted boiling water according to the instructions on the package.

Drain the pasta and stir it into the chorizo sauce. Serve immediately with a drizzle of chile oil (if using) and the freshly grated Parmesan.

For garlic, oregano & Parmesan toasts to serve as an accompaniment, split a ciabatta loaf in half lengthwise and then cut each length in half. Mix 1 crushed clove garlic with 1 tsp (5 ml) dried oregano and 2 tbsp (30 ml) olive oil. Drizzle over the ciabatta and scatter each piece with 1 tsp (5 ml) finely grated Parmesan. Place under a hot broiler for 3 to 4 minutes, until toasted and golden.

PORK CHOPS WITH LEMON & THYME

Serves 4
Preparation time 20 minutes
Cooking time 28–30 minutes

Finely grated zest of 1 lemon
1 tbsp (15 ml) chopped fresh thyme
2 tbsp (30 ml) olive oil
2 cloves garlic, crushed
Salt and pepper
4 pork chops, about 7 oz (200 g) each
2 lbs (1 kg) russet or yukon gold potatoes, peeled and quartered
¾ cup + 2 tbsp (200 ml) whipping (35%) cream
2 tbsp (30 ml) butter
Fresh thyme, leaves or flowers, to garnish

Mix together the lemon zest, thyme, oil, garlic and plenty of pepper and rub the mixture over the pork chops. Set aside.

Meanwhile, cook the potatoes in lightly salted boiling water for about 20 minutes or until soft. Drain, return to the pan and mash. Add the cream, butter and salt and pepper and use a handheld beater to beat until smooth.

Heat a dry frying pan over medium-high heat and cook the pork chops for 4 to 5 minutes on each side, depending on their thickness, until cooked and golden.

Remove the pork from the heat and leave to rest for 1 to 2 minutes before serving garnished with a few thyme leaves or flowers and serve with the fluffy mashed potatoes.

For spinach & Parmesan mashed potatoes instead of plain mashed pototaoes, cook, drain and chop 1 lb (500 g) spinach. Mash the potatoes with butter and milk (omit the cream) and stir in the spinach and ¼ cup (60 ml) freshly grated Parmesan.

MEATY BOSTON BEANS

Serves 4–6
Preparation time 15 minutes, plus overnight soaking
Cooking time 2 hours

10 oz (300 g) dried navy beans
2 tbsp (30 ml) butter
7 oz (200 g) smoked bacon, chopped
12 oz (375 g) lean pork, diced
1 onion, chopped
1 tbsp (15 ml) chopped fresh thyme or fresh rosemary
14-oz (398 ml) can chopped tomatoes
3 tbsp (45 ml) molasses
2 tbsp (30 ml) tomato paste
2 tbsp (30 ml) grainy mustard
1 tbsp (15 ml) Worcestershire sauce
Salt and pepper

Put the beans in a bowl, cover with cold water and leave to soak overnight.

Drain the beans and put in a flameproof casserole. Cover with water and bring to a boil. Reduce the heat and simmer gently for 15 to 20 minutes or until the beans have softened slightly. Test by removing a few on a fork and squeezing them gently – they should give a little. Drain the beans.

Wipe out the dish and melt the butter. Add the bacon and pork and fry gently for 10 minutes, until beginning to brown. Add the onion and cook for a further 5 minutes.

Stir in the drained beans, thyme or rosemary and tomatoes. Add enough water to just cover the ingredients and bring to a boil. Cover with a lid and transfer to a preheated 300°F (150°C) oven. Cook for about 1 hour or until the beans are very tender.

Mix together the molasses, tomato paste, mustard, Worcestershire sauce and seasoning. Stir into the beans and return to the oven for a further 30 minutes.

For veggie Boston beans, replace the navy beans with the same quantity of dried butter, lima or fava, beans and soak and drain as above. Replace the bacon and pork with 12 vegetarian sausages and fry off before the onion in the third step until lightly browned. Remove from the pan and set aside. Add the onion and continue as above. Add the veggie sausages in the final stage before the sauce and cook for 30 minutes.

PORK & BEET GOULASH

Serves 4
Preparation time 30 minutes
Cooking time 2½ hours

2 tbsp (30 ml) olive oil
14½ oz (450 g) lean pork, diced
2 onions, sliced
1 tsp (5 ml) hot smoked paprika
1 tsp (5 ml) caraway seeds
1½-lb (750 g) piece of smoked bacon
3 bay leaves
4½ cups (1.2 L) water
10 oz (300 g) beets, diced
10 oz (300 g) red cabbage, finely sliced
3 tbsp (45 ml) tomato paste

Heat the oil in a large saucepan and fry the diced pork until browned. Add the onions, paprika and caraway and fry gently for a further 5 minutes, until the onions are browned.

Add the piece of bacon, the bay leaves and water. Bring to a boil, cover with a lid and reduce the heat to the lowest setting. Cook very gently for about 2 hours, until the bacon is very tender.

Drain the bacon to a plate and leave until cool enough to handle. Shred the meat back into the pan, discarding the skin and bone.

Add the beets, cabbage and tomato paste to the pan and cook gently, covered, for about 15 minutes, until the beets and cabbage are tender. Check the seasoning and serve.

For turnip (rutabaga) and carrot mash to serve as an accompaniment, cook 1 lb (500 g) carrots in boiling water for 10 minutes. Add 2 lbs (1 kg) turnip, peeled and cut into chunks. Cook until tender. Drain thoroughly and return to the pan. Mash with 1 tsp (5 ml) chopped thyme and 3 tbsp (45 ml) olive oil.

SPICY SAUSAGE CASSOULET

Serves 2
Preparation time 15 minutes
Cooking time 35 minutes

3 tbsp (45 ml) olive oil
1 red onion, finely chopped
1 clove garlic, crushed
1 red bell pepper, seeded and roughly chopped
2 stalks celery, roughly chopped
½ can (14 oz/398 ml) chopped tomatoes
½ cup (125 ml) chicken stock
2 tsp (10 ml) dark soy sauce
1 tsp (5 ml) Dijon mustard
14-oz (398 ml) can black-eyed peas, rinsed and drained
4 oz (125 g) smoked pork sausage, roughly chopped
1½ cups (375 ml) fresh breadcrumbs
2 tbsp (30 ml) freshly grated Parmesan cheese
2 tbsp (30 ml) chopped fresh parsley

Heat 1 tbsp (15 ml) of the oil in a frying pan or small sauté pan. Add the onion, garlic, red bell pepper and celery and cook over low heat, stirring occasionally, for 3 to 4 minutes.

Add the tomatoes, stock and soy sauce. Bring to a boil, then reduce the heat and simmer for about 15 minutes, or until the sauce begins to thicken. Add the mustard, peas and sausage and continue to cook for a further 10 minutes.

Mix the breadcrumbs, Parmesan and parsley together and sprinkle over the sausage mixture. Drizzle with the remaining oil. Place under a preheated moderate to hot broiler for 2 to 3 minutes or until golden brown.

For mixed leaf and pomegranate salad to serve as an accompaniment, put 1½ tbsp (22 ml) raspberry vinegar and 1 tbsp (15 ml) olive oil with a little salt and pepper in a salad bowl and mix lightly. Cut ½ pomegranate into large pieces and flex the skin so that the small seeds fall out. Add the seeds to the salad bowl. Break ¼ cup (60 ml) mixed salad leaves into bite-size pieces and add to the salad bowl, tossing all the ingredients in the salad dressing.

CORNED BEEF WITH SPRING VEGETABLES

Serves 6
Preparation time 10 minutes, plus resting
Cooking time 2½ hours

3½-lb (1.75 kg) piece of corned and rolled brisket beef
1 onion
15 whole cloves
10 oz (300 g) baby onions or shallots, peeled but left whole
3 bay leaves
Plenty of fresh thyme and fresh parsley sprigs
½ tsp (2 ml) ground allspice
Pepper
10 oz (300 g) small carrots
1 small rutabaga, cut into small chunks
1 lb (500 g) russet or yukon gold potatoes, cut into chunks
Chopped fresh parsley, to garnish

Put the beef in a flameproof casserole in which it fits quite snugly. Stud the onion with the cloves and add to the casserole with the baby onions or shallots, bay leaves, herbs, allspice and plenty of pepper.

Add just enough water to cover the beef and bring slowly to the boil. Cover with a lid and place in a preheated 250°F (120°C) oven for 2½ hours or until the meat is tender, adding the carrots, rutabaga and potatoes to the casserole after 1 hour of the cooking time. Leave to rest for 15 minutes before carving.

Drain the meat to a plate or board. Cut into thin slices and serve on warmed plates with the vegetables. Sprinkle with parsley and serve with a cup of the cooking juices for pouring over.

For herb dumplings to serve as an accompaniment, rub 2 tbsp (30 ml) diced butter into 1 cup (250 ml) self-raising flour until the mixture resembles fine breadcrumbs. Add 2 tbsp (30 ml) finely chopped flat-leaf (Italian) parsley and ½ tsp (2 ml) dried thyme; season with salt and pepper. Mix with 1 lightly beaten egg and add a little water to make a sticky dough. Using a tbsp, form into small balls and add to the casserole once cooked. Let the casserole bubble up on the stovetop, cover and cook for 15 to 20 minutes, until the dumplings have risen.

BEEF WITH WALNUT PESTO

Serves 6
Preparation time 20 minutes, plus resting
Cooking time 1 hour 40 minutes

1⅓ cups (325 ml) walnut pieces
2 cloves garlic, roughly chopped
2-oz (60 g) can anchovies
2 tbsp (30 ml) hot horseradish sauce
¾ cup (175 ml) chopped fresh parsley
2 tbsp (30 ml) olive oil, divided
Salt and pepper
3 lb (1.5 kg) rolled rump roast
1 large onion, finely chopped
2 stalks celery, chopped
1¼ cups (300 ml) red wine
⅔ cup (150 ml) beef stock
4 carrots, cut into chunky slices
10 oz (300 g) baby turnips
1 lb (500 g) new potatoes
7 oz (200 g) young green beans
Chopped fresh parsley, to garnish

Put the walnuts in a food processor or blender with the garlic, anchovies and their oil, horseradish, parsley, 1 tbsp (15 ml) of the oil and plenty of black pepper and blend to a thick paste, scraping the mixture down from the sides of the bowl.

Untie the beef and open it out slightly. If there is already a split through the flesh, make the cut deeper so that it will take the stuffing. If it is a perfectly rounded piece of beef, make a deep cut so that you can pack in the stuffing. Once the stuffing is in place, reshape the meat into a roll. Tie with string, securing at 1-inch (2.5 cm) intervals. Pat the meat dry with paper towel and season with salt and pepper.

Heat the remaining oil in a flameproof casserole and fry the meat on all sides to brown. Drain to a plate.

Add the onion and celery to the pan and fry gently for 5 minutes. Return the meat to the pan and pour the wine and stock over it. Add the carrots and turnips. Bring just to a boil, cover with a lid and place in preheated 325°F (160°C) oven. Cook for 30 minutes.

Tuck the potatoes around the beef and sprinkle with salt. Return to the oven for a further 40 minutes, until the potatoes are tender. Stir in the beans and return to the oven for 20 minutes, until the beans have softened. Leave to rest for 15 minutes before carving the meat.

For beef with hazelnut pesto, omit the walnuts and use the same quantity of hazelnuts. Replace the anchovies with ¼ cup (60 ml) capers and the turnips with the same quantity of rutabaga, cut into chunks.

CHILI CON CARNE

Serves 2
Preparation time 15 minutes
Cooking time 45 minutes

2 tbsp (30 ml) olive oil
1 red onion, finely chopped
3 cloves garlic, finely chopped
8 oz (250 g) lean ground beef
½ tsp (2 ml) ground cumin
1 small red bell pepper, seeded and diced
14-oz (398 ml) can chopped tomatoes
1 tbsp (15 ml) tomato paste
2 tsp (10 ml) mild chili powder
¾ cup + 2 tbsp (200 ml) beef stock
14-oz (398 ml) can red kidney beans, rinsed
   and drained
Salt and pepper

Heat the oil in a saucepan. Add the onion and garlic and cook for 5 minutes or until beginning to soften. Add the ground meat and cumin and cook for a further 5 to 6 minutes or until browned all over.

Stir in the red pepper, tomatoes, tomato paste, chili powder and stock and bring to a boil. Reduce the heat and simmer gently for 30 minutes.

Add the beans and cook for a further 5 minutes. Season to taste and serve with brown rice, cooked according to the package instructions.

For homemade beef stock, put 1½ lb (750 g) raw or cooked beef bones in a large, heavy-bottomed saucepan with a large, unpeeled and halved onion, 2 carrots and 2 stalks celery, roughly chopped, 1 tsp (5 ml) peppercorns and several bay leaves and thyme sprigs. Cover with cold water and heat until simmering. Reduce the heat to its lowest setting and cook very gently, uncovered, for 3 to 4 hours. Strain through a sieve and leave to cool. Store for up to a week in the refrigerator or freezer.

QUICK BEEF STROGANOFF

Serves 4
Preparation time 10 minutes
Cooking time 15 minutes

2 tbsp (30 ml) paprika
1 tbsp (15 ml) all-purpose flour
14½ oz (450 g) beef sirloin, sliced
1⅓ cups (325 ml) long-grain white rice
2 tbsp (30 ml) butter
¼ cup (60 ml) vegetable or sunflower oil
1 large onion, thinly sliced
8 oz (250 g) cremini mushrooms, trimmed and sliced
1¼ cups (300 ml) sour cream
Salt and pepper
1 tbsp (15 ml) chopped curly parsley, to garnish

Mix together the paprika and flour in a large bowl. Add the beef and turn to coat.

Cook the rice in lightly salted boiling water for 13 minutes, until cooked but firm. Drain, set aside and keep warm.

Meanwhile, melt the butter and 2 tbsp (30 ml) of the oil in a large frying pan and cook the onion for about 6 minutes or until soft. Add the mushrooms and cook for a further 5 minutes or until soft. Remove with a slotted spoon and set aside.

Add the remaining oil to the pan, increase the heat to high and add the beef. Fry until browned all over, then reduce the heat. Return the onion mixture to the pan along with the sour cream; bring to a boil, then reduce the heat and allow to bubble gently for 1 to 2 minutes. Season well.

Serve immediately with the cooked rice and a sprinkling of chopped parsley.

For mushroom & red pepper stroganoff, omit the beef, increase the quantity of cremini mushrooms to 1 lb (500 g) and add 2 thinly sliced red bell peppers. Cook the mushrooms with the onion until they have reduced and the onion is soft. Remove the mixture from the pan. Cook the peppers until tender. Return the onion mixture to the pan, as above. Sprinkle with pine nuts to serve.

MEATBALLS WITH TOMATO SAUCE

Serves 4
Preparation time 25 minutes
Cooking time 30 minutes

1 lb (500 g) lean ground beef
3 cloves garlic, crushed
2 small onions, finely chopped
¼ cup (60 ml) dry breadcrumbs
1½ oz (40 g) freshly grated Parmesan cheese
Salt and pepper
6 tbsp (90 ml) olive oil
7 tbsp (100 ml) red wine
2 cans (14 oz/398 ml) chopped tomatoes
1 tsp (5 ml) granulated or fruit sugar
3 tbsp (45 ml) sun-dried tomato paste
3 oz (75 g) pitted Italian black olives, roughly chopped
¼ cup (60 ml) roughly chopped fresh oregano
4 oz (125 g) mozzarella cheese, thinly sliced

Put the beef in a bowl with half the crushed garlic and half the onion, the breadcrumbs and 2 tbsp (30 ml) of the Parmesan. Season with salt and pepper and use your hands to thoroughly blend the ingredients together. Shape into small balls, about 1 inch (2.5 cm) in diameter.

Heat half the oil in a large frying pan or sauté pan and fry the meatballs, shaking the pan frequently, for about 10 minutes, until browned. Drain.

Add the remaining oil and onion to the pan and fry until softened. Add the wine and let the mixture bubble until the wine has almost evaporated. Stir in the remaining garlic, the tomatoes, sugar, tomato paste and a little seasoning. Bring to a boil and let the mixture bubble until slightly thickened.

Stir in the olives, all but 1 tbsp (15 ml) of the oregano and the meatballs. Cook gently for a further 5 minutes.

Arrange the mozzarella slices over the top and scatter with the remaining oregano and Parmesan. Season with black pepper and cook under the broiler until the cheese starts to melt. Serve in shallow bowls with warmed, crusty bread.

For Greek-style meatballs, use 1 lb (500 g) lean ground lamb instead of the beef. Replace the olives with ¼ cup (60 ml) pine nuts. Before adding them to the pan in the fourth step, dry-fry in a small frying pan over a medium heat for 3 to 5 minutes, until lightly browned, shaking constantly.

141

OXTAIL STEW

Serves 4
Preparation time 20 minutes
Cooking time 3¾ hours

2 tbsp (30 ml) all-purpose flour
1 tbsp (15 ml) mustard powder
1 tsp (5 ml) celery salt
4 lb (2 kg) oxtail pieces
¼ cup (60 ml) butter
2 tbsp (30 ml) oil
2 onions, sliced
3 large carrots, sliced
3 bay leaves
3½ oz (100 g) tomato purée
7 tbsp (100 ml) dry sherry
4 cups (1 L) beef stock or vegetable stock
Salt and pepper

Mix together the flour, mustard powder and celery salt on a large plate and use to coat the oxtail pieces. Melt half the butter with 1 tbsp (15 ml) of the oil in a large, flameproof casserole. Brown the oxtail, half at a time, and drain to a plate.

Add the onions and carrots to the pan with the remaining butter and oil. Fry until beginning to brown. Return the oxtail to the pan with the bay leaves and any remaining flour left on the plate.

Mix together the tomato purée, sherry and stock and add to the dish. Bring to a boil, then reduce the heat and cover with a lid.

Place in a preheated 300°F (150°C) oven for about 3½ hours or until the meat is meltingly tender and falling from the bone. Check the seasoning and serve with plenty of warmed bread.

For oxtail, herb and red wine stew, add 1 parsnip, cut into small chunks, with the onions and carrots in the second step. When returning the oxtail to the pan, add 1 tsp (5 ml) each finely chopped fresh rosemary and thyme with the bay leaves. Replace the sherry with the same quantity of red wine.

ONE POT,
FEED THE LOT

SEA BASS & SPICY POTATOES

Serves 2
Preparation time 15 minutes
Cooking time 1 hour

1 lb (500 g) baking potatoes
3 tbsp (45 ml) olive oil, divided
2 tbsp (30 ml) sun-dried tomato tapenade
½ tsp (2 ml) mild chili powder
Salt and pepper
2 small whole sea bass, scaled and gutted
2 tbsp (30 ml) mixed chopped fresh herbs, e.g. thyme,
    parsley, chervil, tarragon
1 clove garlic, crushed
2 bay leaves
½ lemon, sliced
Handful of pitted black olives

Cut the potatoes into ½-inch (1 cm) thick slices – you can peel them first if you wish to, but this isn't necessary. Cut into chunky french fries. Mix 2 tbsp (30 ml) of the oil with the tapenade, chili powder and plenty of salt. Toss in a bowl with the potatoes until evenly coated.

Tip the potatoes into a shallow ovenproof dish or roasting pan and bake in a preheated 400°F (200°C) oven for 30 minutes, until pale golden, turning the potatoes once or twice during cooking.

Meanwhile, score the fish several times on each side. Mix the remaining oil with 1 tbsp (15 ml) of the herbs, the garlic and a little salt and pepper. Pack the bay leaves, lemon slices and remaining herbs into the fish cavities and lay the fish over the potatoes in the dish, pushing the potatoes to the edges of the dish.

Brush the garlic-and-herb oil over the fish and scatter the olives over the potatoes. Return to the oven for a further 30 minutes, until the fish is cooked through. Test by piercing the thick end of the fish with a knife; the flesh should be cooked through to the bone.

For tomato salad to serve as an accompaniment, slice 2 large tomatoes and arrange on a platter. Slice ½ small red onion and place on top of the tomatoes. Mix the following dressing ingredients together thoroughly: 6 tbsp (90 ml) olive oil, 2 tbsp (30 ml) cider vinegar, 1 clove garlic, crushed, ½ tsp (2 ml) Dijon mustard and salt and pepper. Drizzle over the tomatoes and sprinkle on a little chopped parsley.

144

ONE POT, FEED THE LOT

POT-ROASTED TUNA WITH LENTILS

Serves 4
Preparation time 15 minutes
Cooking time 50 minutes–1 hour 5 minutes

½ tsp (2 ml) celery salt
Salt and pepper
1½ lb (750 g) tuna, in one slender piece
1 bulb fennel
3 tbsp (45 ml) olive oil
1 cup (250 ml) black lentils, rinsed
About ⅔ cup (150 ml) white wine
1 cup (250 ml) fish stock or vegetable stock
¼ cup (60 ml) chopped fennel fronds or fresh dill
2 tbsp (30 ml) capers, rinsed and drained
14-oz (398 ml) can chopped tomatoes

Mix the celery salt with a little pepper and rub all over the tuna. Cut the fennel bulb in half, then into thin slices.

Heat the oil in a flameproof casserole and fry the tuna on all sides until browned. Drain to a plate. Add the sliced fennel to the pan and fry gently until softened.

Add the lentils and wine and bring to a boil. Boil until the wine has reduced by about half. Stir in the stock, fennel fronds or dill, capers and tomatoes and return to a boil. Cover with a lid and transfer to a preheated 350°F (180°C) oven for 15 minutes.

Return the tuna to the casserole and cook gently for a further 20 minutes, until the lentils are completely tender. The tuna should still be slightly pink in the center. If you prefer it well done, return to the oven for a further 15 to 20 minutes. Check the seasoning and serve.

For pot-roasted lamb with lentils, replace the tuna with a 1¼-lb (625 g) piece of rolled loin of lamb. Fry the lamb as above in the second step. Omit the fennel bulb and use the same quantity of chicken stock instead of the fish or vegetable stock. Replace the fennel or dill with the same quantity of rosemary or oregano. Continue as above, cooking for 30 minutes instead of 20. If you prefer your lamb well done, return to the oven for a further 20 minutes.

PLAICE WITH SAMBAL

Serves 4
Preparation time 30 minutes
Cooking time 30 minutes

1 small stalk lemongrass
2 cloves garlic, crushed
6 tbsp (90 ml) grated fresh coconut
2 green chiles, seeded and finely chopped
4 small whole plaice or other flatfish, scaled and gutted
¼ cup (60 ml) oil

Coconut and tamarind sambal
1 onion, finely chopped
1 clove garlic, crushed
1 tbsp (15 ml) oil
2 tbsp (30 ml) grated fresh coconut
1 red chile, seeded and finely chopped
⅔ cup (150 ml) boiling water
2 tbsp (30 ml) dried tamarind pulp
2 tsp (10 ml) granulated or fruit sugar
1 tbsp (15 ml) white wine vinegar
1 tbsp (15 ml) chopped fresh coriander

Finely chop the lemongrass stalk and mix with the garlic, coconut and green chiles. Smear this dry mixture over each plaice, then cover and leave to marinate in the refrigerator for 2 hours or overnight.

Make the coconut and tamarind sambal by gently frying the onion and garlic in the oil in a large frying pan until softened. Add the coconut with the red chile, stir to coat in the oil and cook for 2 to 3 minutes. Pour the boiling water over the tamarind pulp in a heatproof bowl and let stand for 10 minutes to soften.

Strain the juice from the tamarind pulp, mashing as much of the pulp through the sieve as possible. Add this juice to the pan with the sugar and simmer gently for 5 minutes. Add the vinegar, remove from the heat and leave to cool. When cold, stir in the chopped coriander. Turn into a bowl and wipe the pan clean.

Heat the oil in the pan and gently fry the plaice 2 at a time in the hot oil, turning once. After 6 to 8 minutes, when they are golden brown and cooked, remove from the oil and drain on paper towels. Keep warm while cooking the remaining fish. Serve the fish piping hot with the coconut and tamarind sambal.

For perfumed rice to serve as an accompaniment, cook 1⅓ cups (325 ml) fragrant long-grain rice in boiling water until tender. Fry 1 bunch green onions, thinly sliced, in 2 tsp (10 ml) oil for 30 seconds. Add the finely grated zest of 1 lime and 4 to 6 shredded kaffir lime leaves. Stir in the drained rice and a little salt.

DILL & MUSTARD-BAKED SALMON

Serves 4
Preparation time 20 minutes
Cooking time 55 minutes

3 tbsp (45 ml) chopped fresh dill
2 tbsp (30 ml) grainy mustard
2 tbsp (30 ml) lime juice
1 tbsp (15 ml) granulated or fruit sugar
⅔ cup (150 ml) whipping (35%) cream
Salt and pepper
2 small bulbs fennel, thinly sliced
2 tbsp (30 ml) olive oil
1½ lb (750 g) salmon fillet, skinned
4 hard-boiled eggs, quartered
8 oz (250 g) puff pastry
Beaten egg yolk, to glaze

Mix together the dill, mustard, lime juice and sugar in a bowl. Stir in the cream and a little salt and pepper.

Put the fennel in an 8-cup (2 L) shallow ovenproof dish or pie dish. Drizzle with the oil and bake in a preheated 400°F (200°C) oven for 20 minutes, turning once or twice during cooking, until softened.

Cut the salmon into 8 chunky pieces and add to the dish with the egg quarters, tucking them between the fennel slices so that all the ingredients are evenly mixed. Spoon the cream mixture over and return to the oven for 15 minutes.

Roll out the pastry on a lightly floured surface and cut out eight 2½-inch (6 cm) squares. Brush the tops with egg yolk to glaze and make diagonal markings over the surface of the pastry with the tip of a sharp knife. Sprinkle with pepper.

Place a double thickness of wax or parchment paper over the dish of salmon and put the pastry squares on the paper. Bake for 10 to 15 minutes, until the pastry is risen and golden. Slide the pastry squares onto the salmon and serve with a herb salad.

For dill, mustard and salmon pie, replace the lime juice with lemon juice and scatter the salmon with 1 tbsp (15 ml) capers. Replace the puff pastry with 6 sheets of phyllo pastry. Place on top of the salmon dish in layers, brushing each layer with melted butter and crumpling slightly. Bake for 20 to 25 minutes.

SPICED FISH TAGINE

Serves 4
Preparation time 15 minutes
Cooking time 35 minutes

1 ¼ lb (625 g) halibut steaks
Salt and pepper
1 tsp (5 ml) cumin seeds
1 tsp (5 ml) coriander seeds
¼ cup (60 ml) olive oil
1 large onion, sliced
3 strips of orange zest, plus 2 tbsp (30 ml)
    juice
3 cloves garlic, sliced
½ tsp (2 ml) saffron threads
⅔ cup (150 ml) fish stock
2 oz (60 g) dates, sliced
1 oz (30 g) flaked almonds, lightly toasted

Cut the halibut into chunky pieces, discarding the skin and any bones. Season lightly. Crush the cumin and coriander seeds using a pestle and mortar.

Heat the oil in a large frying pan or sauté pan and gently fry the onion and orange zest for 5 minutes. Add the garlic and crushed spices and fry, stirring, for a further 2 to 3 minutes.

Add the fish, turning the pieces to coat in the spices. Crumble in the saffron and pour in the stock and orange juice. Scatter with the dates and almonds.

Cover with a lid or foil and cook very gently for 20 to 25 minutes or until the fish is cooked through. Check the seasoning and serve with steamed couscous.

For spicy swordfish tagine, replace the halibut with the same quantity of swordfish steaks, cut into chunks. Add a mild or medium red chile, seeded and chopped, with the crushed spices. Use 1 oz (25 g) dried figs and 1 oz (25 g) dried apricots instead of the dates.

RICH FISH STEW

Serves 4
Preparation time 25 minutes
Cooking time 40 minutes

¼ cup (60 ml) olive oil
1 onion, chopped
1 small leek, chopped
4 cloves garlic, crushed
1 tsp (5 ml) saffron threads
14-oz (398 ml) can chopped tomatoes
¼ cup (60 ml) sun-dried tomato paste
4 cups (1 L) fish stock
3 bay leaves
Several fresh thyme sprigs
1 ½ lb (750 g) mixed fish, e.g. haddock, bream, halibut,
    bass, skinned, boned and cut into chunky pieces
8 oz (250 g) raw peeled shrimp
Salt and pepper
½ cup (125 ml) aïoli (see opposite) and baguette slices,
    to garnish

Heat the oil in a large saucepan and gently fry the onion and leek for 5 minutes. Add the garlic and fry for a further 1 minute.

Stir in the saffron, tomatoes, tomato paste, stock, bay leaves and thyme. Bring to a boil, then reduce the heat and simmer gently for 25 minutes.

Gently stir in the mixed fish and cook very gently for 5 minutes. Stir in the shrimp and cook for a further 2 to 3 minutes, until the shrimp have turned pink and the fish flakes easily when pierced with a knife.

Check the seasoning and ladle the stew into shallow bowls. To garnish, spoon some aïoli onto baguette slices and rest them on top of the stew.

For homemade aïoli, combine the following ingredients in a food processor or blender and blend until creamy: 2 egg yolks, 1 crushed clove garlic, ½ tsp (2 ml) sea salt and 1 tbsp (15 ml) white wine vinegar. Season with pepper. With the motor running, gradually pour 1 ¼ cup (300 ml) olive oil through the funnel until the mixture is thick and glossy. Add a little boiling water if it becomes too thick. Transfer to a bowl, cover and refrigerate until required.

CLAM & POTATO CHOWDER

Serves 4
Preparation time 15 minutes
Cooking time 30 minutes

2 lb (1 kg) small fresh clams
2 tbsp (30 ml) butter
2 onions, chopped
⅔ cup (150 ml) white wine
4½ cups (1.2 L) fish stock or chicken stock
½ tsp (2 ml) medium curry paste
¼ tsp (1 ml) ground turmeric
1 lb (500 g) baking or russet potatoes, diced
5 oz (150 g) watercress, tough stalks removed
Plenty of freshly grated nutmeg
Squeeze of lemon juice
Salt and pepper

Rinse and check over the clams, discarding any damaged shells or any open ones that don't close when tapped with a knife. Transfer to a bowl.

Melt the butter in a large saucepan and gently fry the onions for 6 to 8 minutes, until soft. Add the wine and bring to a boil. Tip in the clams and cover with a lid. Cook for about 5 minutes, until the clams have opened, shaking the pan several times during cooking.

Once the shells are all opened, remove from the heat and tip into a colander set over a large bowl to catch the juices. When cool enough to handle, remove the clams from the shells and discard the shells. Reserve the clams and tip the cooking juices back into the pan.

Add the stock, curry paste, turmeric and potatoes to the saucepan and bring to a boil. Reduce the heat, cover and simmer for 10 to 15 minutes, until the potatoes are tender.

Return the clams to the pan with the watercress, nutmeg and lemon juice and heat through gently for 2 minutes. Use a handheld blender to lightly blend the chowder without completely puréeing it. Season with salt and pepper to taste.

For mussel, spinach and potato chowder, replace the clams with the same quantity of mussels and prepare as above. Replace the watercress with the same quantity of baby spinach.

148

ONE POT, FEED THE LOT

MEDITERRANEAN ROASTED FISH

Serves 4
Preparation time 15 minutes
Cooking time 40 minutes

5 tbsp (75 ml) olive oil, divided
2 shallots, thinly sliced
3 oz (90 g) pancetta, chopped
2 oz (60 g) pine nuts
2 tsp (10 ml) chopped fresh rosemary, plus several
    extra sprigs
Salt and pepper
1 thick slice white bread, made into breadcrumbs
2-oz (50 g) can anchovies, drained and chopped
2 red onions, thinly sliced
6 tomatoes, cut into wedges
2 haddock fillets, each about 10 oz (300 g), skinned

Heat 2 tbsp (30 ml) of the oil in a large roasting pan and fry the shallots and pancetta, stirring frequently, until beginning to color. Add the pine nuts and chopped rosemary with a little pepper and fry for a further 2 minutes. Drain to a bowl, add the breadcrumbs and anchovies and mix well.

Add the onions to the pan and fry for 5 minutes, until slightly softened. Stir in the tomato wedges and remove from the heat. Push to the edges of the pan to leave a space for the fish in the center.

Check the fish for any stray bones and place 1 fillet in the pan. Pack the stuffing mixture on top, pressing it firmly onto the fish with your hands. Lay the second fillet on top, skinned side down, and season with a little salt and pepper.

Drizzle with the remaining oil and place in a preheated 350°F (180°C) oven for 30 minutes, until the fish is cooked through. Test by piercing a thick area with a knife.

For spinach and walnut salad to serve as an accompaniment, heat 1 tbsp (15 ml) liquid honey in a small frying pan, add 4 oz (125 g) walnuts and stir-fry over medium heat for 2 to 3 minutes, until glazed. Meanwhile, blanch 8 oz (250 g) green beans in lightly salted boiling water for 3 minutes and drain. Place in a large bowl with 7 oz (200 g) baby spinach. Whisk the following dressing ingredients together and season with salt and pepper: ¼ cup (60 ml) walnut oil, 2 tbsp (30 ml) olive oil and 1 to 2 tbsp (15 to 30 ml) sherry vinegar. Pour over the leaves and scatter the walnuts overtop.

SPICY SHRIMP & POTATO SAUTÉ

Serves 2
Preparation time 15 minutes
Cooking time 25 minutes

3 tbsp (45 ml) smooth mango chutney
½ tsp (2 ml) hot smoked paprika
1 tbsp (15 ml) lemon or lime juice
¼ cup (60 ml) oil, divided
13 oz (400 g) raw peeled shrimp
1 lb (500 g) baking potatoes, cut into ¾-inch
   (1.5 cm) dice
2 cloves garlic, crushed
14-oz (398 ml) can chopped tomatoes
2 oz (60 g) creamed coconut, chopped into
   small pieces
Salt and pepper
Mustard and cress or snipped chives, to garnish

Mix together the mango chutney, paprika and lemon or lime juice in a small bowl.

Heat half the oil in a frying pan or sauté pan and fry the shrimp for about 3 minutes, turning once, until pink, then immediately drain them from the pan.

Add the potatoes to the pan with the remaining oil and fry very gently for about 10 minutes, turning frequently, until the potatoes are golden and cooked through. Add the garlic and cook for a further 1 minute.

Add the tomatoes and bring to a boil. Reduce the heat and cook gently until the sauce turns pulpy. Stir in the creamed coconut and the mango mixture and cook gently until the coconut has dissolved into the sauce.

Stir in the shrimp for a few seconds to heat through. Check the seasoning and serve scattered with mustard and cress or chives.

For curried shrimp and sweet potato sauté, replace the paprika with 1 to 2 tsp (5 to 10 ml) medium curry paste. Replace the potatoes with the same quantity of sweet potatoes, scrubbed or peeled.

MONKFISH WITH COCONUT RICE

Serves 4
Preparation time 20 minutes
Cooking time 25 minutes

1¼ lb (625 g) monkfish fillets
4 long, slender stalks lemongrass
1 bunch green onions
3 tbsp (45 ml) stir-fry or wok oil
½ tsp (2 ml) hot pepper flakes
2 cloves garlic, sliced
1¼ cups (300 ml) Thai fragrant rice
14-oz (398 ml) can coconut milk
2 oz (60 g) creamed coconut, chopped
¾ cup + 2 tbsp (200 ml) hot water
2 tbsp (30 ml) rice wine vinegar
5 oz (150 g) baby spinach
Salt and pepper

Cut the monkfish into 1¼-inch (3 cm) cubes. Using a large knife, slice each lemongrass stalk in half lengthwise. (If the stalks are very thick, pull off the outer layers, finely chop them and add to the oil with the hot pepper flakes.) Cut the ends of each stalk to a point and thread the monkfish onto the skewers. If it is difficult to thread the fish, pierce each piece with a small knife first to make threading easier.

Finely chop the green onions, keeping the white and green parts separate.

Heat the oil in a large frying pan with the hot pepper flakes, garlic and white parts of the green onions. Add the monkfish skewers and fry gently for about 5 minutes, turning once, until cooked through. Drain to a plate.

Add the rice, coconut milk and creamed coconut to the frying pan and bring to a boil. Reduce the heat, cover with a lid or foil and cook gently for 6 to 8 minutes, stirring frequently, until the rice is almost tender and the coconut milk absorbed. Add the hot water and cook, covered, for a further 10 minutes, until the rice is completely tender, adding a little more water if the mixture boils dry before the rice is tender.

Stir in the vinegar, remaining green onions and then the spinach, turning it in the rice until wilted. Arrange the skewers over the rice. Cover and cook gently for 3 minutes, then serve immediately.

FETA-STUFFED PLAICE

Serves 4
Preparation time 20 minutes
Cooking time 40 minutes

2 tbsp (30 ml) chopped fresh mint
2 tbsp (30 ml) chopped fresh oregano
1 oz (30 g) Parma ham, finely chopped
2 cloves garlic, crushed
4 green onions, finely chopped
7 oz (200 g) feta cheese
Salt and pepper
8 plaice or sole fillets, skinned
10 oz (300 g) zucchini, sliced
¼ cup (60 ml) garlic-infused olive oil, divided
8 portobello mushrooms
5 oz (150 g) baby plum tomatoes, halved
1 tbsp (15 ml) capers, rinsed and drained

Put the mint, oregano, ham, garlic and green onions in a bowl. Crumble in the feta cheese, season with plenty of pepper and mix together well.

Put the fish fillets, skinned side up, on the work surface and press the feta mixture down the centers. Roll up loosely and secure with wooden cocktail sticks.

Scatter the zucchini into a shallow ovenproof dish and drizzle with 1 tbsp (15 ml) of the oil. Place in a preheated 375°F (190°C) oven for 15 minutes. Remove from the oven and add the plaice fillets to the dish. Tuck the mushrooms, tomatoes and capers around the fish and season lightly. Drizzle with the remaining oil.

Return to the oven for a further 25 minutes, or until the fish is cooked through.

For tomato and garlic bread to serve as an accompaniment, mix together 6 tbsp (90 ml) softened butter, 2 crushed cloves garlic, 3 tbsp (45 ml) sun-dried tomato paste and a little salt and pepper. Make vertical cuts 1 inch (2.5 cm) apart through a ciabatta loaf, cutting not quite through the base. Push the garlic-and-tomato-paste mixture into the cuts. Wrap in foil and bake in the oven under the fish for 15 minutes. Unwrap the top of the bread and return to the oven for 10 minutes.

CRAYFISH RISOTTO

Serves 4
Preparation time 10 minutes
Cooking time 30 minutes

¼ cup (60 ml) butter, divided
2 shallots, finely chopped
1 mild red chile, thinly sliced
1 tsp (5 ml) mild paprika
1 clove garlic, crushed
1⅓ cups (325 ml) risotto rice
About ⅔ cup (150 ml) dry white wine
A few fresh lemon thyme sprigs
About 4½ cups (1.2 L) hot fish stock or chicken stock
3 tbsp (45 ml) roughly chopped fresh tarragon
10 oz (300 g) crayfish tails in brine, drained
Salt
Freshly grated Parmesan cheese, to garnish

Melt half the butter in a large saucepan or deep-sided sauté pan and gently fry the shallots until softened. Add the chile, paprika and garlic and fry gently for 30 seconds, without browning the garlic.

Sprinkle in the rice and fry gently for 1 minute, stirring. Add the wine and let it bubble until almost evaporated.

Add the thyme and a ladleful of the stock and cook, stirring, until the rice has almost absorbed the stock. Continue cooking, adding the stock a ladleful at a time and letting the rice absorb most of the stock before adding more. Once the rice is tender but retaining a little bite, the risotto is ready – this will take about 25 minutes. You may not need all the stock.

Stir in the tarragon, crayfish and remaining butter and heat through gently for 1 minute. Add a little extra salt if necessary and serve immediately, garnished with Parmesan and with a watercress salad, if desired.

For shrimp risotto, cook 11½ oz (350 g) raw peeled shrimp in the butter, as in the first step. Cook until pink, drain, then return to the pan in the fourth step. Omit the chile and replace the shallots with 1 bunch chopped green onions.

SPICY FISH

Serves 2
Preparation time 10 minutes, plus marinating
Cooking time 5 minutes

1 clove garlic, peeled
2 red shallots, chopped
1 stalk lemongrass
½ tsp (2 ml) ground turmeric
½ tsp (2 ml) ground ginger
1 mild red chile, seeded and roughly chopped
Salt and pepper
1 tbsp (15 ml) peanut oil
2 tsp (10 ml) fish sauce
10 oz (300 g) boneless white fish fillets, cut into bite-size pieces
1 tbsp (15 ml) chopped fresh coriander, to garnish

Put the garlic, shallots, lemongrass, turmeric, ginger, chile and salt and pepper into a food processor or blender and process until a paste is formed, adding the oil and fish sauce to help the grinding.

Place the fish in a bowl and toss with the spice paste. Cover and refrigerate for 15 minutes.

Thread the pieces of fish onto skewers and arrange on a foil-lined baking sheet. Cook under a preheated hot broiler for 4 to 5 minutes, turning once so that the pieces brown evenly. Serve sprinkled with the coriander.

For Chinese greens to serve as an accompaniment, put 10 oz (300 g) raw shredded Chinese greens in a saucepan of boiling water and cook for 1 to 2 minutes. Drain and place on warmed serving plates. Heat 1 tsp (5 ml) peanut oil in a small pan and cook ½ tsp (2 ml) finely chopped garlic briefly. Stir in 1 tsp (5 ml) oyster sauce, 1 tbsp (15 ml) water and ½ tbsp (7 ml) toasted sesame oil, then bring to a boil. Pour over the greens and toss together.

SEAFOOD LEMONGRASS CRUMBLE

Serves 4
Preparation time 20 minutes
Cooking time 40 minutes

1 lb (500 g) swordfish steaks
7 oz (200 g) raw peeled shrimp
Salt and pepper
8 oz (250 g) mascarpone cheese
¼ cup (60 ml) white wine
1 stalk lemongrass
1¼ cups (300 ml) all-purpose flour
6 tbsp (90 ml) butter, cut into pieces
¼ cup (60 ml) chopped fresh dill
¼ cup (60 ml) freshly grated Parmesan cheese

Cut the swordfish into large chunks, discarding any skin and bones, and scatter in a 6-cup (1.5 L) ovenproof dish or pie dish. Add the shrimp and season with salt and pepper.

Beat the mascarpone in a bowl to soften. Stir in the wine and spoon over the fish.

Chop the lemongrass as finely as possible and process in a blender or food processor with the flour and butter until the mixture resembles fine breadcrumbs. Add the dill and pulse very briefly to mix.

Tip the mixture over the fish and sprinkle with the Parmesan. Bake in a preheated 375°F (190°C) oven for about 35 to 40 minutes, until the topping is pale golden. Serve with a green salad.

For seafood puff pastry pie, omit the Parmesan cheese and replace the lemongrass crumble with 1 lb (500 g) puff pastry. Roll out the pastry on a lightly floured surface, then place on top of the fish in the dish. Brush the top with egg yolk to glaze, then sprinkle with pepper. Bake the pie in a preheated 425°F (220°C) oven for 15 minutes, then reduce the heat to 350°F (180°C) and bake for a further 15 to 20 minutes, until golden.

SALT COD WITH POTATOES

Serves 4
Preparation time 15 minutes, plus soaking
Cooking time 35 minutes

1 lb (500 g) salt cod
¼ cup (60 ml) olive oil
1 onion, finely chopped
3 cloves garlic, crushed
2½ cups (600 ml) fish stock
½ tsp (2 ml) saffron threads
1½ lb (750 g) baking or russet potatoes, cut into
    small chunks
1 lb (500 g) plum tomatoes, roughly
    chopped
¼ cup (60 ml) chopped fresh parsley
Salt and pepper

Put the salt cod in a bowl, cover with plenty of cold water and leave to soak for 1 to 2 days, changing the water twice daily. Drain the cod and cut into small chunks, discarding any skin and bones.

Heat the oil in a large saucepan and gently fry the onion for 5 minutes, until softened. Add the garlic and cook for 1 minute. Add the stock and crumble in the saffron. Bring to a boil, then reduce the heat to a gentle simmer.

Add the salt cod and potatoes and cover with a lid. Cook gently for about 20 minutes until the fish and potatoes are very tender.

Stir in the tomatoes and parsley and then cook for 5 minutes, until the tomatoes have softened. Season to taste (you might not need any salt, depending on the saltiness of the fish). Ladle into shallow bowls and serve with warm bread.

For smoked trout with potatoes, replace the salt cod with 10 oz (300 g) smoked trout. Cut into chunks, but don't soak in the first step. Add to the saucepan once the potatoes are cooked, along with 2 tbsp (30 ml) capers, rinsed and drained, and 2 tsp (10 ml) green peppercorns in brine, rinsed, drained and crushed.

MACKEREL & CIDER VICHYSSOISE

Serves 3–4 as a main course, 8 as a starter
Preparation time 15 minutes
Cooking time 30 minutes

1¼ lb (625 g) leeks
¼ cup (60 ml) butter
1¼ lb (625 g) new potatoes, diced
2½ cups (600 ml) strong (alcoholic) cider
2½ cups (600 ml) fish stock
2 tsp (10 ml) Dijon mustard
10 oz (300 g) smoked mackerel fillets
5 tbsp (75 ml) chopped fresh chives
Plenty of freshly grated nutmeg
¾ cup + 2 tbsp (200 g) crème fraîche, divided
Salt and pepper
Fresh chive sprigs, to garnish

Trim the leeks and chop, keeping the white and green parts separate. Melt the butter in a large saucepan and gently fry the white parts and half the green parts for 5 minutes. Add the potatoes, then stir in the cider, stock and mustard and bring almost to a boil. Reduce the heat and cook gently for 20 minutes, until the potatoes are soft but still holding their shape.

Flake the smoked mackerel into small pieces, discarding any skin and stray bones. Add to the pan with the chopped chives, nutmeg and remaining green leeks. Simmer gently for 5 minutes.

Stir in half the crème fraîche and season to taste with salt and pepper. Spoon into bowls, top with the remaining crème fraîche and garnish with chive sprigs.

For trout and white wine vichyssoise, replace the cider with 1¼ cups (300 ml) dry white wine and add an extra 1¼ cups (300 ml) fish stock. Instead of the mackerel, use 1 lb (500 g) fresh skinned and boned trout and flake and cook as above. Replace the crème fraîche with ⅔ cup (150 ml) table (18%) or half-and-half (10%) cream.

OVEN-STEAMED FISH WITH GREENS

Serves 2
Preparation time 15 minutes
Cooking time 25 minutes

1 ½-inch (4 cm) piece fresh ginger
¼ tsp (1 ml) red pepper flakes
1 clove garlic, thinly sliced
2 tbsp (30 ml) rice wine vinegar, divided
2 chunky cod fillets, each 5 to 7 oz (150 g to 200 g), skinned
⅔ cup (150 ml) hot fish stock
½ cucumber
2 tbsp (30 ml) light soy sauce
2 tbsp (30 ml) oyster sauce
1 tbsp (15 ml) granulated or fruit sugar
½ bunch green onions, cut into 1-inch (2.5 cm) lengths
¾ cup (175 ml) fresh coriander, roughly chopped
7 oz (200 g) ready-cooked rice

Peel and slice the ginger as finely as possible. Cut across into thin shreds and mix with the red pepper flakes, garlic and 1 tsp (5 ml) of the vinegar. Spoon over the pieces of cod, rubbing it in gently.

Lightly oil a wire rack and position over a small roasting pan. Pour the stock into the pan and place the cod fillets on the rack. Cover with foil and carefully transfer to a preheated 350°F (180°C) oven for 20 minutes or until cooked through.

Meanwhile, peel the cucumber, cut in half and scoop out the seeds. Cut the flesh into small pieces. Mix together the soy sauce, oyster sauce, sugar and remaining vinegar in a small bowl.

Remove the fish from the pan and keep warm. Drain off the juices from the pan and reserve. Add the cucumber, green onions, coriander and rice to the pan and heat through, stirring, for about 5 minutes, until hot, stirring in enough of the reserved juices to make the rice slightly moist.

Pile onto serving plates, top with the fish and serve with the sauce spooned over.

For oven-steamed chicken with greens, replace the fish with 4 small skinned chicken breasts. Use chicken stock instead of the fish stock. Make several deep scores in the chicken breasts, then cook as per the second step but for 30 to 40 minutes. Replace the oyster sauce with the same quantity of hoisin sauce.

CHILE & PANCETTA SUMMER SQUASH CUPS

Serves 4
Preparation time 20 minutes
Cooking time 45 minutes

5 oz (150 g) ciabatta
3½ oz (100 g) pine nuts
2½ lb (1.25 kg) marrow or other summer squash
2 tbsp (30 ml) butter
¼ cup (60 ml) olive oil, divided
75 g (3 oz) pancetta, cubed
3 cloves garlic, crushed
1 mild red chile, seeded and sliced
½ tsp (2 ml) hot smoked paprika
Salt
2 tsp (10 ml) chopped fresh thyme leaves
Small handful curly parsley, chopped

Crumble the ciabatta into small pieces and spread out on a foil-lined broiler pan. Scatter with the pine nuts and broil lightly until toasted.

Peel the marrow and cut across into 4 even-sized lengths, trimming off the ends. Using a large spoon, scoop out the seeds, leaving a small base in each, to make cups.

Melt the butter with 2 tbsp (30 ml) of the oil in a small roasting pan and gently fry the pancetta for about 5 minutes, until beginning to crisp and color. Add the garlic, chile and paprika and cook for a further 1 minute. Drain to a large bowl, leaving a little of the spicy oil in the pan.

Off the heat, put the marrow cups in the pan, turning them in the oil. Place upright and brush the centers with more of the spicy oil in the pan. Season with salt and bake in a preheated 400°F (200°C) oven for 25 minutes or until tender.

Toss the pine nuts and ciabatta with the pancetta mixture and herbs and divide between the cups. Drizzle with the remaining oil and return to the oven for a further 15 minutes.

For sun-dried tomato pumpkin cups, replace the pancetta with 2 oz (60 g) finely chopped sun-dried tomatoes and fry in the same way. Replace the marrow with small, single-portion-sized pumpkins. Slice off the tops and scoop out the seeds. Brush the spicy oil on the insides and bake for 50 minutes or until soft.

MAPLE PORK WITH ROASTED ROOTS

Serves 4
Preparation time 20 minutes
Cooking time 1½ hours

12 baby onions or shallots, peeled but left whole
1 lb (500 g) small Yukon Gold or red potatoes, cubed
10 oz (300 g) baby carrots
10 oz (300 g) small parsnips, cut into wedges
3 tbsp (45 ml) olive oil
Salt and pepper
2 zucchini, cut into chunky pieces
Several fresh rosemary sprigs
1 tbsp (15 ml) grainy mustard
3 tbsp (45 ml) maple syrup
4 large pork chops, trimmed of fat

Scatter the onions or shallots, potatoes, carrots and parsnips in a large, sturdy roasting pan. Drizzle with the oil and shake the pan so that the vegetables are coated in oil. Sprinkle with salt and pepper and roast in a preheated 375°F (190°C) oven for 30 minutes, until beginning to color.

Add the zucchini and rosemary sprigs to the pan and toss the vegetables together. Return to the oven for a further 10 minutes.

Mix together the mustard, maple syrup and a little salt. Tuck the pork chops among the vegetables and brush with about half the maple glaze. Return to the oven for 20 minutes.

Turn the pork chops over and brush with the remaining maple glaze. Return to the oven for a further 15 minutes or until the chops are cooked through.

For honey and lemon pork, replace the carrots and parsnips with 2 large zucchini and 3 red bell peppers, cut into chunky wedges, and roast as above. Instead of the mustard and maple syrup, mix together 3 tbsp (45 ml) liquid honey, 2 tbsp (30 ml) lemon juice and a 1-inch (2.5 cm) piece of fresh ginger, grated, in the third step and use in the same way as the maple glaze.

PUMPKIN & ROOT VEGETABLE STEW

Serves 8–10
Preparation time 20 minutes
Cooking time 1½–2 hours

1 pumpkin, about 3 lb (1.5 kg)
¼ cup (60 ml) sunflower or olive oil
1 large onion, finely chopped
3 to 4 cloves garlic, crushed
1 small red chile, seeded and chopped
4 stalks celery, cut into 1-inch (2.5 cm) lengths
1 lb (500 g) carrots, cut into 1-inch (2.5 cm) pieces
8 oz (250 g) parsnips, cut into 1-inch (2.5 cm) pieces
2 cans (14 oz/398 ml each) plum tomatoes
3 tbsp (45 ml) tomato purée
1 to 2 tbsp (15 to 30 ml) hot paprika
1 cup (250 ml) vegetable stock
1 bouquet garni
2 cans (14 oz/398 ml each) red kidney beans, drained
Salt and pepper
3 to 4 tbsp (45 to 60 ml) finely chopped fresh parsley, to garnish

Slice the pumpkin in half across its widest part and discard the seeds and fibers. Cut the flesh into cubes, removing the skin. You should have about 2 lb (1 kg) pumpkin flesh.

Heat the oil in a large saucepan and fry the onion, garlic and chile until soft but not colored. Add the pumpkin and celery and fry gently for 10 minutes. Stir in the carrots, parsnips, tomatoes, tomato purée, paprika, stock and bouquet garni. Bring to a boil, then reduce the heat, cover the pan and simmer for 1 to 1½ hours, until the vegetables are almost tender.

Add the beans and cook for 10 minutes. Season with salt and pepper and garnish with the parsley to serve. Serve with crusty bread or garlic mashed potatoes. This stew improves with reheating.

For pumpkin goulash, heat 2 tbsp (30 ml) oil in a flameproof casserole and fry 1 chopped onion until soft. Stir in 1 tbsp (15 ml) paprika and 1 tsp (5 ml) caraway seeds and cook for 1 minute. Add a 14-oz (398 ml) can chopped tomatoes and 2 tbsp (30 ml) dark muscovado sugar and bring to a boil. Add 12 oz (375 g) thickly sliced pumpkin, 8 oz (250 g) diced potatoes, a large sliced carrot and 1 chopped red bell pepper. Season, cover and bring to a boil, then simmer for 1 to 1½ hours. To serve, stir in ⅔ cup (150 ml) sour cream.

CREAMY PORK & CIDER HOTPOT

Serves 4
Preparation time 25 minutes
Cooking time 1½ hours

1¼ lb (625 g) piece lean, boneless leg of pork
2 tsp (10 ml) all-purpose flour
Salt
2 tbsp (30 ml) butter
1 tbsp (15 ml) oil
1 small onion, chopped
1 large leek, chopped
1¾ cups (425 ml) cider
1 tbsp (15 ml) chopped fresh sage
2 tbsp (30 ml) grainy mustard
7 tbsp (100 ml) crème fraîche
2 pears, peeled, cored and thickly sliced
14½ oz (450 g) sweet potatoes, scrubbed and
   thinly sliced
2 tbsp (30 ml) chile-infused oil
Chopped fresh parsley, to garnish

Cut the pork into small pieces, discarding any excess fat. Season the flour with a little salt and use to coat the meat.

Melt the butter with the oil in a shallow flameproof casserole and gently fry the pork in batches until lightly browned, draining each batch to a plate.

Add the onion and leek to the casserole and fry gently for 5 minutes. Return the meat to the pan, along with the cider, sage and mustard. Bring just to a boil, then cover with a lid, reduce the heat and cook on the lowest setting for 30 minutes.

Stir the crème fraîche into the sauce and scatter the pear slices on top. Arrange the sweet potato slices in overlapping layers on top, putting the end pieces underneath and keeping the best slices for the top layer. Brush with the chile oil and sprinkle with salt.

Place in a preheated 325°F (160°C) oven for 45 minutes or until the sweet potatoes are tender and lightly browned. Scatter the chopped parsley over.

For creamy pork and white wine hotpot, replace the cider with the same quantity of dry white wine in the third step. Use the same quantity of ordinary potatoes as the sweet potatoes and layer on top as above in the fourth step. Increase the cooking time in the oven to about 1 hour.

PORK & TOMATO LINGUINE

Serves 4
Preparation time 20 minutes
Cooking time 40 minutes

10 oz (300 g) leg of pork
2 tsp (10 ml) mild paprika
Salt and pepper
8 oz (250 g) dried linguine
5 tbsp (75 ml) olive oil, divided
2 oz (60 g) chorizo, diced
1 red onion, sliced
8 oz (250 g) tomato sauce or passata
3 tbsp (45 ml) sun-dried tomato paste
½ tsp (2 ml) saffron threads
3 cups (750 ml) chicken stock or vegetable stock
⅓ cup (75 ml) fresh or frozen peas
3 cloves garlic, crushed
¼ cup (60 ml) chopped fresh parsley
Finely grated zest of 1 lemon

Toss the pork in the paprika and salt and pepper. Roll up half the pasta in a dish towel. Run the dish towel firmly over the edge of a work surface so that you hear the pasta breaking into short lengths. Tip into a bowl and break the remainder in the same way.

Heat 3 tbsp (45 ml) of the oil in a large frying pan and fry the pork, chorizo and onion very gently for about 10 minutes, until browned.

Stir in the tomato sauce, tomato paste, saffron and stock and bring to a boil. Reduce the heat and cook very gently for 15 minutes, until the meat is tender.

Sprinkle in the pasta and stir well to mix. Cook gently, stirring frequently, for 10 minutes, until the pasta is tender, adding a little water to the pan if the mixture becomes dry before the pasta is cooked. Add the peas and cook for a further 3 minutes.

Stir in the garlic, parsley, lemon zest and remaining oil. Check the seasoning and serve.

For chicken and tomato linguine, omit the pork and use 4 skinned and boned chicken thighs, cut into chunks. Toss the chicken in the paprika and salt and pepper as in the first step. Follow the second step to fry the chicken, replacing the chorizo with the same quantity of smoked pork sausage. Cook as above, using chicken stock.

BEAN, PANCETTA & FONTINA RISOTTO

Serves 2
Preparation time 15 minutes
Cooking time 30 minutes

3 tbsp (45 ml) olive oil
1 onion, finely chopped
3 cloves garlic, crushed
3 oz (75 g) pancetta, chopped
1 cup (250 ml) risotto rice
½ tsp (2 ml) dried mixed herbs
3⅔ cups (900 ml) hot chicken stock or vegetable stock
Salt and pepper
4 oz (125 g) broad, lima or fava beans, defrosted if frozen
3 oz (90 g) peas
3 oz (90 g) fontina cheese, coarsely grated
¼ cup (60 ml) butter
2 tbsp (30 ml) freshly grated Parmesan cheese, plus extra shavings to garnish
1 tbsp (15 ml) chopped fresh mint leaves
6 to 8 fresh basil leaves, shredded, plus extra to garnish

Heat the oil in a large saucepan and fry the onion until softened. Add the garlic and pancetta to the pan and fry until the pancetta is golden brown. Add the rice and stir the grains into the onion mixture to coat in the oil.

With the pan still over medium heat, add the dried mixed herbs and the hot stock to the rice and bring the mixture to a boil, stirring constantly. Season with salt and pepper and reduce to a simmer. Simmer for 10 minutes, stirring frequently. Add the beans and peas and continue to cook for a further 10 minutes.

Remove the pan from the heat and stir the fontina through the risotto. Dot the butter on top together with the Parmesan. Cover the pan with a lid and set aside for 2 to 3 minutes to allow the cheese and butter to melt into the risotto.

Remove the lid and add the mint and basil and gently stir the cheese, butter and herbs through the risotto. Serve immediately, garnished with basil leaves and extra shavings of Parmesan.

For tomato and mushroom risotto, fry the onion, then 8 oz (250 g) sliced mushrooms, 2 crushed cloves garlic, 1 tsp (5 ml) dried oregano and 3 large, finely chopped tomatoes over low heat for 5 minutes. Stir in 1⅔ cups (400 ml) risotto rice, then a ladleful from 4 cups (1 L) of hot stock and cook over a low heat until absorbed. Add the remaining stock a ladleful at a time and cook for about 25 minutes, until absorbed. Stir in 2 tbsp (30 ml) butter and 1½ oz (45 g) Parmesan and season.

BRAISED LIVER & BACON WITH PRUNES

Serves 4
Preparation time 15 minutes
Cooking time 1 hour

13 oz (400 g) lamb's liver, sliced
2 tsp (10 ml) all-purpose flour
Salt and pepper
8 thin-cut slices smoked bacon
16 pitted prunes
3 tbsp (45 ml) olive oil, divided
2 large onions, thinly sliced
1½ lb (750 g) large potatoes, sliced
1¾ cups (425 ml) lamb stock or chicken stock
3 tbsp (45 ml) roughly chopped fresh parsley, to garnish

Cut the liver into thick strips, removing any tubes. Season the flour with salt and pepper and use to coat the liver. Cut the bacon slices in half and wrap a piece around each prune.

Heat half the oil in a flameproof casserole and fry the onions until lightly browned. Drain to a plate. Add the liver to the casserole and brown on both sides. Drain to the plate. Add the remaining oil to the pan with the bacon-wrapped prunes and fry on both sides until browned. Remove.

Arrange the potatoes in the casserole and put all the fried ingredients on top. Pour the stock over, season lightly and bring to a boil. Cover with a lid and transfer to a preheated 350°F (180°C) oven for 50 minutes, until the potatoes are very tender. Serve sprinkled with the parsley.

For lamb's liver with cranberries and bacon, fry 2 thinly sliced onions and 5 oz (150 g) diced smoked back bacon for 10 minutes in 2 tbsp (30 ml) oil. Set aside. Melt 2 tbsp (30 ml) butter and fry 1¼ lb (625 g) sliced lamb's liver for 3 minutes over high heat, turning once or twice, until browned on the outside and just pink in the center. Add 3 oz (90 g) frozen cranberries and 2 tbsp (30 ml) each cranberry sauce, red wine vinegar and water. Season and cook for 2 minutes, stirring. Stir in the onions and bacon and heat through, gently stirring to combine.

PORK & CABBAGE BAKE

Serves 4
Preparation time 15 minutes
Cooking time 40 minutes

2½ tbsp (37 ml) butter, divided
1 lb (500 g) pork and apple sausages, skinned
1 onion, chopped
2 tsp (10 ml) caraway seeds
Salt and pepper
1¼ lb (625 g) Savoy cabbage, shredded
13 oz (400 g) baking or russet potatoes, diced
¾ cup + 2 tbsp (200 ml) chicken stock or vegetable
    stock
1 tbsp (15 ml) cider vinegar

Melt half the butter in a shallow flameproof casserole and add the sausage meat. Fry quickly, breaking the meat up with a wooden spoon and stirring until browned.

Add the onion, caraway seeds and a little salt and pepper and fry for a further 5 minutes.

Stir in the cabbage and potatoes, mixing the ingredients together thoroughly. Pour the stock and cider vinegar over them and add a little more seasoning. Dot with the remaining butter and cover with a lid.

Bake in a preheated 325°F (160°C) oven for 30 minutes, until the cabbage and potatoes are very tender. Serve with chunks of whole-grain bread.

For chicken and cabbage bake, replace the sausages with 13 oz (400 g) skinned and boned chicken thighs, cut into chunks. Shallow-fry as above in the first step. Instead of the Savoy cabbage, use the same quantity of shredded red cabbage and replace the cider vinegar with 1 tbsp (15 ml) red wine vinegar along with 2 tbsp (30 ml) liquid honey. Cook as above.

LAMB WITH ORANGE & CHICKPEAS

Serves 8
Preparation time 25 minutes, plus overnight soaking
Cooking time 2½ hours

1¼ cups (300 ml) chickpeas, soaked in cold water
    overnight
¼ cup (60 ml) olive oil, divided
2 tsp (10 ml) ground cumin
1 tsp (5 ml) each ground cinnamon, ginger and turmeric
½ tsp (2 ml) saffron threads
Salt and pepper
3 lb (1.5 kg) shoulder of lamb, trimmed of all fat and cut
    into 1-inch (2.5 cm) cubes
2 onions, roughly chopped
3 cloves garlic, finely chopped
2 tomatoes, skinned, seeded and chopped
12 pitted black olives, sliced
Grated zest of 1 unwaxed lemon
Grated zest of 1 unwaxed orange
6 tbsp (90 ml) chopped fresh coriander

Drain the chickpeas and rinse under cold water. Put them in a flameproof casserole or large saucepan, cover with water and bring to a boil, then reduce the heat and simmer, covered, for about 1 to 1½ hours, until tender.

Meanwhile, combine half the olive oil with the cumin, cinnamon, ginger, turmeric and saffron in a large bowl, plus ½ tsp (2 ml) salt and ½ tsp (2 ml) pepper. Add the cubed lamb, toss and set aside in a cool place for 20 minutes.

Heat the remaining oil in a large pan. Fry the lamb in batches until well browned, draining to a plate.

Add the onions to the pan and cook, stirring constantly, until browned. Stir in the garlic and the tomatoes with 1 cup (250 ml) water, stirring and scraping the bottom of the pan. Return the lamb to the pan and add enough water to just cover. Bring to a boil over high heat and skim off any surface foam. Reduce the heat, cover and simmer for about 1 hour or until the meat is tender.

Drain the chickpeas and reserve the cooking liquid. Add the chickpeas with about 1 cup (250 ml) of the cooking liquid to the lamb. Simmer for 30 minutes.

Stir in the olives and lemon and orange zest and simmer for a final 30 minutes.

Mix in half the chopped coriander, then serve garnished with the remaining coriander. When cool, this dish may be frozen in a plastic container.

LAMB WITH ARTICHOKES & GREMOLATA

Serves 4
Preparation time 20 minutes
Cooking time 25 minutes

1 lb (500 g) lamb
2 tsp (10 ml) all-purpose flour
Salt and pepper
¼ cup (60 ml) olive oil, divided
1 onion, finely chopped
1 stalk celery, thinly sliced
⅔ cup (150 ml) chicken stock or vegetable stock
2 cloves garlic, finely chopped
Finely grated zest of 1 lemon
¼ cup (60 ml) chopped fresh parsley
5 oz (150 g) store-bought or homemade roasted artichokes, thinly sliced
¼ cup (60 ml) whipping (35%) cream

Trim any excess fat from the lamb and cut into thin slices. Season the flour with salt and pepper and use to coat the lamb. Heat half the oil in a large frying pan and fry the lamb, half at a time, until browned, draining each batch to a plate.

Gently fry the onion and celery in the remaining oil for 5 minutes, until softened. Return the lamb to the pan and stir in the stock. Bring to a boil, then reduce the heat and simmer very gently for about 8 minutes, until the lamb is cooked through.

Meanwhile, make the gremolata by mixing together the garlic, lemon zest and parsley.

Add the artichokes and cream to the pan and heat through for 2 minutes. Check the seasoning and serve sprinkled with the gremolata.

For home-roasted artichokes, thoroughly drain and slice a can of artichoke hearts. Drizzle with olive oil, sprinkle with dried oregano and salt and pepper and roast in a preheated 400°F (200°C) oven for 20 to 25 minutes.

LAMB & RED RICE PILAF

Serves 3–4
Preparation time 20 minutes
Cooking time 1 hour 10 minutes

2 tsp (10 ml) cumin seeds
2 tsp (10 ml) coriander seeds
10 cardamom pods
3 tbsp (45 ml) olive oil
1 lb (500 g) shoulder of lamb, diced
2 red onions, sliced
2-inch (5 cm) piece fresh ginger, grated
2 cloves garlic, crushed
½ tsp (2 ml) ground turmeric
1 cup (250 ml) red rice
2½ cups (600 ml) lamb stock or chicken stock
1½ oz (40 g) pine nuts
3 oz (75 g) ready-to-eat dried apricots, thinly sliced
60 g (2 oz) arugula
Salt and pepper

Grind the cumin, coriander and cardamom pods using a pestle and mortar until the cardamom pods have opened to release the seeds. Discard the shells.

Heat the oil in a small, sturdy roasting pan and fry the spices for 30 seconds. Add the lamb and onions and toss with the spices. Transfer to a preheated 350°F (180°C) oven and cook for 40 minutes, until the lamb and onions are browned.

Return to the stovetop and stir in the ginger, garlic, turmeric and rice. Add the stock and bring to a boil. Cover with a lid or foil and cook over the lowest setting for about 30 minutes, until the rice is tender and the stock has been absorbed.

Stir in the pine nuts and apricots and season to taste. Scatter with the arugula and fold in very lightly. Pile onto serving plates and serve immediately.

For homemade lamb stock, put 1½ lb (750 g) roasted lamb bones and meat scraps in a large, heavy-bottomed saucepan with 1 large onion, roughly chopped, 2 large carrots and 2 celery stalks, both roughly sliced, 1 tsp (5 ml) black peppercorns and several bay leaves and fresh thyme sprigs. Just cover with cold water and bring slowly to a boil. Reduce the heat and simmer for 3 hours, skimming the surface if necessary. Strain through a sieve and leave to cool. Store for up to a week in the refrigerator or freezer.

STEAK & ALE CASSEROLE

Serves 5–6
Preparation time 20 minutes
Cooking time 1¾ hours

2 tbsp (30 ml) all-purpose flour
Salt and pepper
2 lb (1 kg) braising steak, cut into chunks
2 tbsp (30 ml) butter
1 tbsp (15 ml) oil
2 onions, chopped
2 stalks celery, sliced
Several fresh thyme sprigs
2 bay leaves
1⅔ cups (400 ml) strong ale
1¼ cups (300 ml) beef stock
2 tbsp (30 ml) molasses
1 lb (500 g) parsnips, peeled and cut into wedges

Season the flour with salt and pepper and use to coat the beef. Melt the butter with the oil in a large flameproof casserole and fry the beef in batches until deep brown. Drain with a slotted spoon while cooking the remainder.

Add the onions and celery and fry gently for 5 minutes. Return the beef to the pan and add the herbs, ale, stock and molasses. Bring just to a boil, then reduce the heat and cover with a lid. Bake in a preheated 325°F (160°C) oven for 1 hour.

Add the parsnips to the dish and return to the oven for a further 30 minutes or until the beef and parsnips are tender. Check the seasoning and serve.

For potato champ to serve as an accompaniment, cook 3 lb (1.5 kg) scrubbed potatoes in a large saucepan of salted boiling water for 20 minutes. Peel away the skins, then return to the pan and mash. Beat in ⅔ cup (150 ml) milk, 3 to 4 finely chopped green onions and ¼ cup (60 ml) butter. Season with salt and pepper and then serve.

BEEF & FLAT NOODLE SOUP

Serves 4–6
Preparation time 30 minutes
Cooking time 2 hours

1 tbsp (15 ml) vegetable oil
1 lb (500 g) braising beef
7 cups (1.8 L) beef stock
4 whole star anise
1 cinnamon stick
1 tsp (5 ml) black peppercorns
4 shallots, thinly sliced, divided
4 cloves garlic, crushed
3-inch (7.5 cm) piece fresh ginger, finely sliced
10 oz (300 g) flat rice noodles
4 oz (125 g) bean sprouts
8 oz (250 g) beef tenderloin, sliced
6 green onions, thinly sliced
Handful of fresh coriander
Hot red chiles, to garnish

Nuoc cham sauce
2 red chiles, chopped
1 clove garlic, chopped
1½ tbsp (22 ml) granulated or fruit sugar
1 tbsp (15 ml) lime juice
1 tbsp (15 ml) rice wine vinegar
3 tbsp (45 ml) fish sauce

Heat the oil in a large saucepan or casserole and sear the beef on all sides, until thoroughly brown.

Add the stock, star anise, cinnamon, black peppercorns, half the shallots, the garlic and ginger. Bring to a boil, removing any scum. Reduce the heat, cover the pan with a lid and simmer very gently for about 1½ hours or until the beef is tender.

To make the nuoc cham sauce, pound the chiles, garlic and sugar until smooth, using a pestle and mortar. Add the lime juice, vinegar, fish sauce and ¼ cup (60 ml) water and blend together well.

When the beef in the broth is tender, lift it out and slice it thinly. Add the noodles to the broth and cook gently for 2 to 3 minutes to soften. Add the bean sprouts, along with the sliced beef and heat for 1 minute. Strain the broth, noodles and bean sprouts to warmed serving bowls. Scatter with the beef tenderloin, green onions, coriander and remaining shallots. Garnish with the chiles. Serve with the nuoc cham sauce.

For tofu and flat noodle soup, replace the beef with 8 oz (250 g) tofu, cut into small squares and drained on paper towels. Sear as above. Replace the beef stock with the same quantity of vegetable stock and replace the fish sauce with the same quantity of soy sauce throughout. Reduce the cooking time to 20 minutes. Add 5 oz (150 g) frozen soybeans with the noodles.

VENISON & CHESTNUT STEW

Serves 6
Preparation time 30 minutes
Cooking time 2½ hours

2 tbsp (30 ml) all-purpose flour
Salt and pepper
1¾ lbs (875 g) lean stewing venison, cut into
   small pieces
10 juniper berries
3 tbsp (45 ml) oil
5 oz (150 g) bacon, chopped
1 large onion, chopped
3 carrots, sliced
½ tsp (2 ml) ground cloves
1¼ cups (300 ml) red wine
¾ cup + 2 tbsp (200 ml) game stock or chicken stock
1 tbsp (15 ml) red wine vinegar
2 tbsp (30 ml) red currant jelly
12 oz (350 g) cooked chestnuts
2 lb (1 kg) large potatoes, thinly sliced
2 tsp (10 ml) chopped fresh rosemary
3 tbsp (45 ml) butter, softened

Season the flour with salt and pepper and use to coat the venison. Crush the juniper berries using a pestle and mortar.

Heat the oil in a large flameproof casserole and fry the meat in batches until browned, draining each batch to a plate. Add the bacon, onion and carrots to the casserole and fry gently for 5 minutes or until browned.

Stir in the crushed juniper berries, cloves, wine, stock, vinegar and red currant jelly and bring to a boil. Reduce the heat and stir in the chestnuts and venison.

Cover with a lid and place in a preheated 325°F (160°C) oven for 1 hour. Check the seasoning, then scatter with the potatoes and return to the oven, covered, for a further 30 minutes.

Blend the rosemary with the butter and a little salt and pepper and dot over the potatoes. Return to the oven, uncovered, for a further 45 minutes or until the potatoes are lightly browned.

For homemade game stock, brown 1 lb (500 g) game trimmings (for example, pheasant or pigeon bones) in a roasting pan in a preheated 400°F (200°C) oven for 15 minutes. Tip into a saucepan with 1 unpeeled, roughly chopped onion, 1 chopped carrot, 2 chopped celery stalks, ⅔ cup (150 ml) red wine, 1 tsp (5 ml) juniper berries and 3 bay leaves. Cover with water. Bring to a simmer and cook very gently for 1½ hours. Strain through a sieve and leave to cool.

STIFADO

Serves 3–4
Preparation time 20 minutes
Cooking time 2½ hours

½ tsp (2 ml) ground black pepper
½ tsp (2 ml) ground allspice
2 tsp (10 ml) finely chopped fresh rosemary
1 rabbit (about 1½ to 1¾ lb/750 to 875 g), cut into
    serving-size pieces
3 tbsp (45 ml) olive oil
3 large onions, sliced
2 tsp (10 ml) granulated or fruit sugar
3 cloves garlic, crushed
⅓ cup (75 ml) red wine vinegar
1¼ cups (300 ml) red wine
3 tbsp (45 ml) tomato purée
Salt
Flat-leaf (Italian) parsley, to sprinkle

Mix together the pepper, allspice and rosemary and rub over the rabbit.

Heat the oil in a large flameproof casserole and fry the meat in batches on all sides until thoroughly browned. Drain the meat to a plate.

Add the onions to the pan with the sugar and fry, stirring frequently, for about 15 minutes, until caramelized. Stir in the garlic and then cook for a further 1 minute.

Add the vinegar and wine to the pan. Bring to a boil and continue to boil until the mixture has reduced by about a third. Stir in the tomato purée and a little salt and return the meat to the pan.

Cover with a lid and place in a preheated 300°F (150°C) oven for about 2 hours, until the meat is very tender and the juices thick and glossy. Check the seasoning and sprinkle with the parsley.

For Greek salad to serve as an accompaniment, combine 6 roughly chopped tomatoes, 1 thickly sliced cucumber, ½ small, thinly sliced red onion and 4 oz (125 g) kalamata olives in a large bowl. Drizzle with olive oil and lemon juice to taste. Crumble 8 oz (250 g) feta cheese into pieces and scatter over the salad. Season with plenty of black pepper.

BEEF, SQASH & GINGER STEW

Serves 6
Preparation time 20 minutes
Cooking time 1½ hours

2 tbsp (30 ml) all-purpose flour
Salt and pepper
1½ lb (750 g) lean stewing beef, diced
1 tbsp (15 ml) butter
3 tbsp (45 ml) oil
1 onion, chopped
2 carrots, sliced
2 parsnips, sliced
3 bay leaves
Several fresh thyme sprigs
2 tbsp (30 ml) tomato purée
1¼ lbs (625 g) butternut or other orange winter squash,
    peeled, seeded and cut into small chunks
1 tbsp (15 ml) dark muscovado sugar
4-inch (10 cm) piece fresh ginger, finely chopped
Small handful of fresh parsley, chopped, plus extra
    to garnish

Season the flour with salt and pepper and use to coat the beef. Melt the butter with the oil in a large saucepan and fry the meat in 2 batches until browned, draining with a slotted spoon.

Add the onion, carrots and parsnips to the saucepan and fry gently for 5 minutes.

Return the meat to the pan and add the herbs and tomato purée. Add just enough water to cover the ingredients and bring slowly to a boil. Reduce the heat to its lowest setting, cover with a lid and simmer very gently for 45 minutes.

Add the squash, sugar, ginger and parsley and cook for a further 30 minutes, until the squash is soft and the meat is tender. Check the seasoning and serve scattered with extra parsley.

For beef, sweet potato and horseradish stew, replace the squash with 1 lb (500 g) sweet potato, cut into chunks and cooked as above. Replace the ginger with 3 tbsp (45 ml) hot horseradish sauce.

DAUBE OF BEEF

Serves 5–6
Preparation time 20 minutes
Cooking time 1½ hours

1 tbsp (15 ml) all-purpose flour
Salt and pepper
2 lb (1 kg) stewing beef, diced
¼ cup (60 ml) olive oil
3½ oz (100 g) bacon, chopped
1 large onion, chopped
4 cloves garlic, crushed
Several strips orange zest
2 to 3 medium carrots, sliced
Several fresh thyme sprigs
1¼ cups (300 ml) red wine
1¼ cups (300 ml) beef stock
3½ oz (100 g) pitted black olives
¼ cup (60 ml) sun-dried tomato paste

Season the flour with salt and pepper and use to coat the beef. Heat the oil in a large flameproof casserole and fry the meat in batches until browned, draining each batch to a plate. Add the bacon and onion to the casserole and fry for 5 minutes.

Return all the meat to the casserole with the garlic, orange zest, carrots, thyme sprigs, wine and stock. Bring almost to a boil, then cover with a lid and transfer to a preheated 325°F (160°C) oven for 1¼ hours or until the meat is very tender.

Put the olives and sun-dried tomato paste in a blender or food processor and blend very lightly until the olives are chopped but not puréed. Stir into the casserole and return to the oven for a further 15 minutes. Check the seasoning and serve with crusty bread, beans or mashed potatoes.

For beef bourguignon, place the same quantity of beef overnight in a marinade of sliced onion, parsley and thyme sprigs, crumbled bay leaf, 1⅔ cups (400 ml) red burgundy and 2 tbsp (30 ml) each brandy and olive oil. Cook 5 oz (150 g) diced bacon in ¼ cup (60 ml) butter in a flameproof casserole, then 24 small onions and 1 lb (500 g) button mushrooms and set aside. Remove the beef from the marinade. Brown the beef in the casserole, stir in 1 tbsp (15 ml) all-purpose flour, then the strained marinade, 1¼ cups (300 ml) beef stock, 1 crushed clove garlic, 1 bouquet garni and salt and pepper. Simmer, covered, for 2 hours. Return the bacon, onions and mushrooms, cover and simmer for 30 minutes.

VEAL WITH WINE & LEMON

Serves 5–6
Preparation time 20 minutes
Cooking time 40 minutes

2 tbsp (30 ml) olive oil
2 lbs (1 kg) veal, chopped into cubes
2 onions, sliced
4 cloves garlic, sliced
2 baby bulbs fennel, roughly chopped
1¼ cups (300 ml) white wine
1¼ cups (300 ml) chicken stock
Zest of ½ lemon, cut into julienne strips (matchsticks)
4 bay leaves
1 tbsp (15 ml) chopped fresh thyme
Salt and pepper

Heat the oil in a frying pan over high heat, then fry the meat in batches, draining to a plate with a slotted spoon.

Add the onions and garlic to the pan and cook over medium heat until golden. Add the fennel and fry for a further 3 to 4 minutes or until softened.

Return the veal to the pan and add the wine, stock, lemon zest, bay leaves and thyme. Bring to a boil.

Reduce the heat and simmer, covered, for a further 20 to 25 minutes. Season to taste and serve.

For fragrant brown rice to serve as an accompaniment, wash 2 cups (500 ml) brown basmati rice in a sieve until the water runs clear. Put crushed seeds from 4 cardamom pods, a large pinch of saffron threads, 1 cinnamon stick, ½ tsp (2 ml) cumin seeds and 2 bay leaves in a flameproof casserole and dry-fry over medium heat for 2 to 3 minutes. Add 1 tbsp (15 ml) olive oil and, when hot, stir in 1 chopped onion and cook for 10 minutes, stirring frequently. Add the rice, then stir in 2½ cups (600 ml) water, 2 tbsp (30 ml) lemon juice and salt and pepper. Bring to a boil, then cover and simmer for 15 minutes, until all the water has been absorbed, adding a little more water if the mixture dries out before it is cooked. Leave to stand for a few minutes before serving.

VEAL WITH TOMATOES & CAPERS

Serves 4
Preparation time 20 minutes
Cooking time 2¼ hours

1 tbsp (15 ml) all-purpose flour
Salt and pepper
4 thick slices veal shank
¼ cup (60 ml) olive oil
2 onions, finely chopped
2 cloves garlic, crushed
3 oz (75 g) prosciutto, torn into small pieces
Zest of 1 lemon, cut into strips
1¼ cups (300 ml) white wine
Several fresh thyme sprigs
4 tomatoes, peeled and cut into wedges
2 tbsp (30 ml) capers, rinsed and drained

Season the flour with salt and pepper and use to coat the meat. Heat the oil in a flameproof casserole and fry the pieces of meat on all sides until browned. Drain.

Add the onions to the pan and fry gently for 5 minutes. Add the garlic, prosciutto and strips of lemon zest and cook for 1 minute. Add the wine and thyme sprigs and bring to a boil.

Return the veal to the casserole and tuck the tomatoes around. Scatter with the capers and cover with a lid. Place in a preheated 325°F (160°C) oven for about 2 hours, until the meat is very tender. Check the seasoning and serve.

For spicy polenta with garlic to serve as an accompaniment, bring to a boil 3⅔ cups (900 ml) salted water in a large saucepan. Meanwhile, melt 2 tbsp (30 ml) butter and fry 1 crushed clove garlic with a pinch of hot pepper flakes for 1 minute. Remove from heat. Gradually whisk 1¼ cups (300 ml) cornmeal into boiling water, add the garlic butter and 2 tbsp (30 ml) chopped fresh mixed herbs. Stir over low heat for 8 to 10 minutes, until the polenta thickens. Remove from heat, beat in 2 tbsp (30 ml) butter and 2 oz (60 g) freshly grated Parmesan cheese and salt and pepper to taste.

CHICKEN & PICKLED WALNUT PILAF

Serves 4
Preparation time 20 minutes
Cooking time 35 minutes

13 oz (400 g) boneless skinless chicken thighs, cut into
    small pieces
2 tsp (10 ml) Moroccan spice blend (see opposite)
Salt and pepper
1/4 cup (60 ml) olive oil
2 oz (60 g) pine nuts
1 large onion, chopped
3 cloves garlic, sliced
1/2 tsp (2 ml) ground turmeric
1 cup (250 g) mixed long-grain and wild rice
1 1/4 cups (300 ml) chicken stock
3 pieces of preserved ginger in syrup, finely chopped
3 tbsp (45 ml) chopped fresh parsley
2 tbsp (30 ml) chopped fresh mint
2 oz (60 g) pickled walnuts, sliced

Toss the chicken pieces in the spice blend and a little salt.

Heat the oil in a large frying pan or sauté pan and fry the pine nuts until they begin to color. Drain with a slotted spoon.

Add the chicken to the pan and fry gently for 6 to 8 minutes, stirring, until lightly browned.

Stir in the onion and fry gently for 5 minutes. Add the garlic and turmeric and fry for a further 1 minute. Add the rice and stock and bring to a boil. Reduce the heat to its lowest setting and simmer very gently for about 15 minutes, until the rice is tender and the stock absorbed. Add a little water if the liquid has been absorbed before the rice is cooked through.

Stir in the ginger, parsley, mint, walnuts and pine nuts. Season to taste and heat through gently for 2 minutes before serving.

For homemade Moroccan spice blend, mix together 1/2 tsp (2 ml) each of crushed fennel, cumin, coriander and mustard seeds with 1/4 tsp (1 ml) each of ground cloves and cinnamon.

170

AROMATIC BRAISED DUCK

Serves 4
Preparation time 25 minutes
Cooking time 2 hours

4 duck portions
2 tsp (10 ml) Chinese five-spice powder
2 stalks lemongrass, bruised
5 cloves garlic, crushed
4 red shallots, chopped
4 oz (125 g) dried shiitake mushrooms, soaked for
    30 minutes
2-inch (5 cm) piece fresh ginger, peeled and cut into
    thick julienne strips
2 1/2 cups (600 ml) chicken stock
1 oz (30 g) dried medlar berries or Chinese
    red dates
1/2 oz (15 g) dried black fungus, broken into pieces
1 tbsp (15 ml) fish sauce
Salt and pepper
2 tsp (10 ml) cornstarch
4 green onions, quartered
Handful of fresh coriander, to garnish

Season the duck portions with the five-spice powder. Place them skin side down in a very hot frying pan or Dutch oven to brown the skin. Turn the pieces over. Add the lemongrass, garlic, shallots, mushrooms and ginger to the pan, then cover the duck with the stock. Cover the pan with a lid and simmer very gently for 1 1/2 hours.

Remove the duck from the pan and add the medlar berries or Chinese red dates, black fungus and fish sauce. Season with salt and pepper to taste. Mix the cornstarch to a smooth paste with a little water and add to the pan. Bring the sauce to a boil, stirring constantly, and cook until thickened. Return the duck to the pan and simmer gently for 30 minutes.

Add the green onions to the sauce and garnish the duck with the coriander.

For stir-fried bok choy to serve as an accompaniment, heat 1 tbsp (15 ml) olive oil in a nonstick sauté pan over high heat. Add 1 lb (500 g) bok choy, halved, a handful at a time, stirring occasionally. Cover the pan and cook for 2 to 3 minutes, until the bok choy leaves have wilted. Mix together 1 tsp (5 ml) tamari sauce, 1 tbsp (15 ml) Chinese rice wine and 3 tbsp (45 ml) vegetable stock in a small bowl. Add a cornstarch paste made from 1/2 tbsp (7 ml) cornstarch mixed with 1 tbsp (15 ml) water and pour over the bok choy, stirring constantly until the sauce thickens.

ONE POT, FEED THE LOT

171

CHICKEN, OKRA & RED LENTIL DHAL

Serves 4
Preparation time 15 minutes
Cooking time 45 minutes

2 tsp (10 ml) ground cumin
1 tsp (5 ml) ground coriander
½ tsp (2 ml) cayenne pepper
¼ tsp (1 ml) ground turmeric
1 lb (500 g) boneless skinless chicken thighs, cut into
    large pieces
3 tbsp (45 ml) oil
1 onion, sliced
2 cloves garlic, crushed
2-inch (5 cm) piece fresh ginger, finely chopped
3 cups (750 ml) water
1 cup (250 ml) red lentils, rinsed
7 oz (200 g) okra
Small handful of fresh coriander, chopped
Salt
Lime wedges, to garnish

Mix together the cumin, coriander, cayenne and turmeric and toss with the chicken pieces.

Heat the oil in a large saucepan. Fry the chicken pieces in batches until deep golden, draining each batch to a plate. Add the onion to the pan and fry for 5 minutes, until browned. Stir in the garlic and ginger and cook for a further 1 minute.

Return the chicken to the pan and add the water. Bring to a boil, then reduce the heat and simmer very gently, covered, for 20 minutes, until the chicken is cooked through. Add the lentils and cook for 5 minutes. Stir in the okra, coriander and a little salt and cook for a further 5 minutes, until the lentils are tender but not completely pulpy.

Check the seasoning and serve in shallow bowls with lime wedges, chutney and poppadums.

For chicken, zucchini and chile dhal, use 3 medium zucchini, thinly sliced, instead of the okra. For a hotter flavor, add a thinly sliced medium-strength red chile with the garlic and ginger.

CHICKEN & MUSHROOMS WITH POLENTA

Serves 4
Preparation time 20 minutes
Cooking time 55 minutes

1 tbsp (15 ml) butter
1 onion, chopped
1 lb (500 g) lean chicken, diced
8 oz (250 g) mushrooms, sliced
2 tsp (10 ml) all-purpose flour
⅔ cup (150 ml) chicken stock
1 tbsp (15 ml) grainy mustard
¼ cup (60 ml) chopped parsley
Salt and pepper
⅓ cup + 2 tbsp (100 ml) table (18%) or half-and-half
    (10%) cream
7 oz (200 g) fresh soybeans (edamame) or 14-oz
    (398 ml) can flageolet beans, drained
1-lb (500 g) pack ready-cooked polenta
2 oz (60 g) Gruyère cheese, grated

Melt the butter in a shallow, flameproof casserole. Add the onion and chicken and fry gently for 6 to 8 minutes, stirring frequently, until lightly browned.

Add the mushrooms and fry for a further 5 minutes. Sprinkle in the flour, then add the stock, mustard, parsley and a little salt and pepper. Bring to a boil, then reduce the heat and stir in the cream and beans.

Slice the polenta very thinly and arrange, overlapping the slices, on top of the chicken. Sprinkle with the cheese and a little black pepper.

Place in a preheated 375°F (190°C) oven for 30 to 40 minutes, until the cheese is melted and beginning to brown. Serve with a leafy salad.

For chicken and mushrooms with cheese toasts, replace the polenta with 8 thin slices of French bread. Arrange over the chicken, then sprinkle with the same quantity of Cheddar cheese instead of the Gruyère. Cook as above until the cheese has melted and the bread is turning golden.

TURKEY CHILE POBLANO

Serves 6
Preparation time 25 minutes
Cooking time 1 hour

1 cup (250 ml) flaked almonds
⅓ cup (75 ml) peanuts
½ tbsp (7 ml) coriander seeds
1 tsp (5 ml) ground cloves
3 tbsp (45 ml) sesame seeds
½ cinnamon stick
1 tsp (5 ml) fennel seeds or aniseed
4 large dried poblano or Anaheim chiles
1 green jalapeño pepper, chopped
14-oz (398 ml) can chopped tomatoes
½ cup (125 ml) raisins
6 tbsp (90 ml) vegetable oil
2 onions, finely chopped
3 cloves garlic, crushed
1¼ lb (625 g) turkey breast, finely sliced or cubed
1¼ cups (300 ml) vegetable stock
2 oz (60 g) unsweetened chocolate, roughly chopped

To garnish
Red and green chiles, finely chopped

Spread the almonds, peanuts, coriander seeds, cloves, sesame seeds, cinnamon, fennel or aniseed and dried chiles over a baking sheet and roast in a preheated 400°F (200°C) oven for 10 minutes, stirring once or twice.

Remove from the oven and put the nuts and spices in a food processor or blender and process until well combined. Add the chopped jalapeño and process once more until well mixed.

Spoon the spice mixture into a bowl and mix in the tomatoes and raisins.

Heat the oil in a large saucepan and fry the onions and garlic with the turkey on all sides until browned. Remove the turkey and set aside.

Add the spice mixture to the oil remaining in the saucepan and cook, stirring frequently, for 5 to 6 minutes or until the spice paste has heated through and is bubbling. Add the stock and chocolate and simmer gently until the chocolate has melted.

Reduce the heat, return the turkey to the pan and mix well. Cover the pan and simmer gently for 30 minutes, adding extra water if the sauce begins to dry out. Garnish with the chopped red and green chiles.

For Mexican-style rice to serve as an accompaniment, gently heat 2 tbsp (30 ml) vegetable oil in a saucepan and cook 11 oz (325 g) basmati rice for 5 minutes, stirring. Add 7 oz (200 g) chopped tomatoes, 1 crushed clove garlic, 2 oz (60 g) diced carrot and 1 chopped green chile. Bring to boil, then simmer for 10 minutes.

SPRING BRAISED DUCK

Serves 4
Preparation time 20 minutes
Cooking time 1¾ hours

4 duck legs
2 tsp (10 ml) all-purpose flour
Salt and pepper
1 tbsp (15 ml) butter
1 tbsp (15 ml) olive oil
2 onions, sliced
2 slices bacon, finely chopped
2 cloves garlic, crushed
About ⅔ cup (150 ml) white wine
1¼ cups (300 ml) chicken stock
3 bay leaves
1 lb (500 g) small new potatoes, e.g., Jersey Royals
7 oz (200 g) fresh peas
5 oz (150 g) asparagus tips
2 tbsp (30 ml) chopped fresh mint

Halve the duck legs through the joints. Mix the flour with a little salt and pepper and use to coat the duck pieces.

Melt the butter with the oil in a sturdy roasting pan or Dutch oven and gently fry the duck pieces for about 10 minutes, until browned. Drain to a plate and pour off all but 1 tbsp (15 ml) of the fat left in the pan.

Add the onions and bacon to the pan and fry gently for 5 minutes. Add the garlic and fry for a further 1 minute. Add the wine, stock and bay leaves and bring to a boil, stirring. Return the duck pieces and cover with a lid or foil. Place in a preheated 325°F (160°C) oven for 45 minutes.

Add the potatoes to the pan, stirring them into the juices. Sprinkle with salt and return to the oven for 30 minutes.

Add the peas, asparagus and mint to the pan and return to the oven for a further 15 minutes or until all the vegetables are tender. Check the seasoning and serve.

For spring braised chicken, replace the duck with 4 chicken thighs and omit the bacon. Add the following spring vegetables when adding the peas, asparagus and mint: 7 oz (200 g) baby turnips, 3½ oz (100 g) baby carrots and 2 small, sliced zucchini. Cook as above.

COQ AU VIN

Serves 6–8
Preparation time 20 minutes
Cooking time 1½ hours

3 tbsp (45 ml) oil, divided
3 to 4 slices of bread, crusts removed, diced
¼ cup (60 ml) butter
5 lbs (2.5 kg) chicken, cut into 12 serving pieces
24 small onions, peeled
4 oz (125 g) smoked bacon, diced
1 tbsp (15 ml) all-purpose flour
1 bottle (750 ml) red wine
1 bouquet garni
2 cloves garlic, peeled
Freshly grated nutmeg
24 button mushrooms, sliced
1 tbsp (15 ml) brandy
Salt and pepper

To garnish
Chopped fresh parsley
Strips of orange zest

Heat 1 tbsp (15 ml) of the oil in a large flameproof casserole and fry the bread until golden. Drain. Add the remaining oil, the butter and chicken pieces. Fry gently over low heat until golden on all sides, turning occasionally. Remove with a slotted spoon and keep warm. Pour off a little of the fat from the casserole, then add the onions and bacon. Sauté until lightly colored, then sprinkle in the flour and stir well.

Pour in the wine and bring to a boil, stirring. Add the bouquet garni, garlic cloves, nutmeg and salt and pepper to taste. Return the chicken to the casserole. Reduce the heat, cover and simmer for 15 minutes.

Add the mushrooms and continue cooking gently for a further 45 minutes or until the chicken is cooked and tender. Remove the chicken with a slotted spoon and arrange the pieces on a warmed serving plate. Keep hot. Pour the brandy into the sauce and boil, uncovered, for 5 minutes, until the sauce is thick and reduced. Remove the bouquet garni and garlic cloves.

Pour the sauce over the chicken and serve with the bread croutons. Garnish with the chopped parsley and orange zest.

For creamy mashed potatoes to serve as an accompaniment, cook 8 large potatoes, cut into chunks, in a saucepan of boiling salted water for 20 minutes. Mash, then beat until very smooth. Add ¼ cup (60 ml) butter, then gradually beat in ⅓ cup (75 ml) hot milk until fluffy. Season and add a pinch of nutmeg.

174

CHICKEN & TARRAGON RISOTTO

Serves 6
Preparation time 15 minutes
Cooking time 30 minutes

1 lb (500 g) boneless skinless chicken breasts or
   chicken tenders, cut into small chunks
Salt and pepper
1 tbsp (15 ml) butter
1 onion, finely chopped
2 cloves garlic, crushed
1¼ cups (300 ml) risotto rice
About ⅔ cup (150 ml) white wine
1⅔ cups (400 ml) chicken stock or vegetable stock
1 tsp (5 ml) saffron threads
8 oz (250 g) mascarpone cheese
3 tbsp (45 ml) roughly chopped fresh tarragon
3 tbsp (45 ml) chopped fresh parsley
⅓ cup (75 ml) snow peas or sugar snap peas, halved

Season the chicken with salt and pepper. Melt the butter in a flameproof casserole, then add the chicken and gently fry for 5 minutes, until lightly browned. Add the onion and cook for a further 5 minutes. Add the garlic and rice and cook for a further 1 minute, stirring.

Pour in the wine and let the mixture bubble until the wine has almost evaporated. Stir in the stock and saffron and bring to a boil.

Cover with a lid and bake in a preheated 350°F (180°C) oven for 10 minutes, until the stock is absorbed and the rice is almost tender.

Stir in the mascarpone, tarragon, parsley and peas. Mix well until the cheese has melted, then cover and return to the oven for a further 5 minutes. Stir in a little boiling water if the mixture has dried out. Check the seasoning and serve with a leafy salad.

For creamy swordfish and tarragon risotto, replace the chicken with 4 swordfish fillets, cut into chunks, and fry as above in the first step. Replace the mascarpone with ⅔ cup (150 ml) table (18%) or half-and-half (10%) cream.

CHICKEN WITH CORNMEAL DUMPLINGS

Serves 4
Preparation time 25 minutes
Cooking time 1½ hours

3 tbsp (45 ml) olive oil
8 boneless skinless chicken thighs, cut into small pieces
4 tsp (20 ml) Cajun spices
1 large onion, sliced
3½ oz (100 g) smoked bacon, chopped
2 each red and yellow bell peppers, seeded and roughly chopped
¾ cup + 2 tbsp (200 ml) chicken stock
Salt and pepper
1 cup (250 ml) self-raising flour
1 cup (250 ml) cornmeal
½ tsp (2 ml) hot pepper flakes
3 tbsp (45 ml) chopped fresh coriander
3 oz (75 g) Cheddar cheese, grated
1 tbsp (15 ml) butter, melted
1 egg
7 tbsp (100 ml) milk
4 small tomatoes, peeled and quartered
7 tbsp (100 ml) whipping (35%) cream

Heat the oil in a large, shallow flameproof casserole and fry the chicken pieces for about 5 minutes, until lightly browned. Stir in the spices and cook for a further 1 minute. Drain to a plate.

Add the onion, bacon and peppers and fry for 10 minutes, stirring frequently, until beginning to color.

Return the chicken to the casserole and stir in the stock and a little salt and pepper. Bring to a boil, then cover with a lid and bake in a pre-heated 350°F (180°C) oven for 45 minutes, until the chicken is tender.

While the chicken is cooking, prepare the dumplings: mix together the flour, cornmeal, hot pepper flakes, coriander and cheese in a bowl. Beat the butter with the egg and milk and add to the bowl. Mix together to make a thick paste that is fairly sticky but holds its shape.

Stir the tomatoes and cream into the chicken mixture and season to taste. Place spoonfuls of the dumpling mixture over the top. Return to the oven, uncovered, for a further 30 minutes or until the dumplings have slightly risen and form a firm crust.

For traditional dumplings, mix together 1½ cups (375 ml) self-raising flour, 2 tbsp (30 ml) shortening and ¼ cup (60 ml) chopped parsley in a bowl with a little salt and pepper. Add enough water to mix to a soft, slightly sticky dough. Spoon over the casserole and cook, covered, for 20 to 25 minutes, until the dumplings are light and fluffy.

GUINEA FOWL & BLACK-EYED PEA SOUP

Serves 4–6
Preparation time 20 minutes, plus overnight soaking
Cooking time 1½ hours

1 cup (250 ml) dried black-eyed peas
2-lb (1 kg) oven-ready guinea fowl or pheasant
1 onion, sliced
2 cloves garlic, crushed
6 cups (1.5 L) chicken stock
½ tsp (2 ml) ground cloves
2-oz (60 g) can anchovies, drained and finely chopped
3½ oz (100 g) watercress
5 oz (150 g) wild mushrooms
3 tbsp (45 ml) tomato purée
Salt and pepper

Put the peas in a bowl, cover with plenty of cold water and leave to soak overnight.

Drain the peas and put in a large saucepan. Cover with water and bring to a boil. Boil for 10 minutes, then drain in a colander.

Put the guinea fowl in the pan and add the drained peas, onion, garlic, stock and cloves. Bring just to a boil, then reduce the heat to its lowest setting and cover with a lid. Cook very gently for 1¼ hours, until the guinea fowl is very tender.

Drain the guinea fowl to a plate and leave until cool enough to handle. Flake all the meat from the bones, discarding the skin. Chop up any large pieces of meat and return all the meat to the pan.

Scoop a little of the stock into a small bowl with the anchovies and mix together so that the anchovies are blended with the stock. Discard the tough stalks from the watercress.

Add the anchovy mixture, mushrooms and tomato purée to the pan and season with salt and pepper. Reheat gently for a few minutes and stir in the watercress just before serving.

For chicken and navy bean soup, use the same quantity of navy beans rather than the black-eyed peas. Take 4 chicken legs, cook and flake the meat from the bones as above. Finally, replace the watercress with the same quantity of arugula, chopped.

GAME & CHESTNUT CASSEROLE

Serves 6
Preparation time 40 minutes
Cooking time 1 hour 40 minutes

1 lb (500 g) pork sausage meat
3 onions, finely chopped, divided
2 tbsp (30 ml) chopped fresh thyme, divided
Salt and pepper
13 oz (400 g) mixed game
12 oz (350 g) mixed poultry
2 tbsp (30 ml) all-purpose flour
½ cup (125 ml) butter, divided
2 stalks celery, chopped
2 cloves garlic, crushed
3 cups (750 ml) chicken or game stock
10 juniper berries, crushed
1¾ cups (425 ml) self-raising flour
1 tsp (5 ml) baking powder
About ⅔ cup (150 ml) milk, plus a little extra
    to glaze
7 oz (200 g) whole cooked chestnuts
3 tbsp (45 ml) Worcestershire sauce

Mix the sausage meat with one-third of the onions, half the thyme and plenty of salt and pepper. Shape into balls about ¾ inch (2 cm) in diameter.

Cut all the meat into small pieces. Season the all-purpose flour and use to coat the meat. Melt 1 tbsp (15 ml) of the butter in a large flameproof casserole and brown the meat in batches, draining each batch to a plate.

Melt another 1 tbsp (15 ml) of the butter and fry the remaining onions and the celery for 5 minutes. Add the garlic and fry for 1 minute. Stir in any remaining coating flour, then blend in the stock. Return the meat to the pan with the juniper berries. Cover and place in a preheated 325°F (160°C) oven for 1 hour, until the meat is tender.

Meanwhile, put the self-raising flour and baking powder in a food processor with a little salt, the remaining thyme and the remaining butter, cut into pieces. Blend to breadcrumb consistency. Add most of the milk to make a dough, adding the rest if it is very dry. Turn out onto a floured surface and roll out to ¾ inch (2 cm) thick. Cut out rounds using a 1¾-inch (4 cm) cutter.

Stir the chestnuts and the Worcestershire sauce into the casserole and check the seasoning. Arrange the biscuits around the edge and glaze with milk. Raise the oven temperature to 425°F (220°C) and cook for 20 minutes or until the biscuits are cooked through.

ITALIAN CHICKEN WITH TOMATO SAUCE

Serves 4
Preparation time 20 minutes
Cooking time 1¼ hours

4 chicken legs, cut into drumsticks and thighs
Salt and pepper
¼ cup (60 ml) olive oil
1 large onion, finely chopped
1 stalk celery, finely chopped
3 oz (75 g) pancetta, diced
2 cloves garlic, crushed
3 bay leaves
¼ cup (60 ml) dry vermouth or white wine
2 cans (14 oz/398 ml each) chopped tomatoes
1 tsp (5 ml) granulated or fruit sugar
3 tbsp (45 ml) sun-dried tomato paste
1 oz (30 g) fresh basil leaves, torn into pieces
8 black olives

Season the chicken pieces with salt and pepper. Heat the oil in a large saucepan or sauté pan and fry the chicken pieces on all sides to brown. Drain to a plate.

Add the onion, celery and pancetta to the pan and fry gently for 10 minutes. Add the garlic and bay leaves and fry for a further 1 minute.

Add the vermouth or wine, tomatoes, sugar, tomato paste and salt and pepper and bring to a boil. Return the chicken pieces to the pan and reduce the heat to its lowest setting. Cook very gently, uncovered, for about 1 hour or until the chicken is very tender.

Stir in the basil and olives and check the seasoning before serving.

For fennel, orange and olive salad to serve as an accompaniment, toss 1 large bulb fennel, thinly sliced, with 8 to 10 black olives, 1 tbsp (15 ml) olive oil and 2 tbsp (30 ml) lemon juice in a large bowl. Season with salt and pepper. Cut away the skin and pith of 2 oranges and slice thinly into rounds. Add the orange slices to the salad and toss gently to combine.

BEAN CHILI WITH AVOCADO SALSA

Serves 4–6
Preparation time 15 minutes
Cooking time 30 minutes

3 tbsp (45 ml) olive oil
2 tsp (10 ml) cumin seeds, crushed
1 tsp (5 ml) dried oregano
1 red onion, chopped
1 stalk celery, chopped
1 medium-hot red chile, seeded and sliced
2 cans (14 oz/398 ml each) chopped tomatoes
2 oz (60 g) sun-dried tomatoes, thinly sliced
2 tsp (10 ml) granulated sugar
1¼ cups (300 ml) vegetable stock
2 cans (14 oz/398 ml each) red kidney beans
Handful of fresh coriander, chopped
1 small avocado
2 tomatoes
2 tbsp (30 ml) sweet chili sauce
2 tsp (10 ml) lime juice
Salt and pepper
⅓ cup (75 ml) sour cream

Heat the oil in a large saucepan. Add the cumin seeds, oregano, onion, celery and chile and cook gently, stirring, for about 6 to 8 minutes, until the vegetables start to color.

Add the canned tomatoes, sun-dried tomatoes, sugar, stock, beans and coriander and bring to a boil. Reduce the heat and simmer for about 20 minutes, until the juices are thickened and pulpy.

To make the salsa, finely dice the avocado and put it in a small bowl. Halve the tomatoes, scoop out the seeds and finely dice the flesh. Add to the bowl with the chili sauce and lime juice. Mix well.

Season the bean mixture with salt and pepper and spoon into bowls. Top with spoonfuls of sour cream and the avocado salsa. Serve with toasted pita or flatbreads.

For bean stew, heat ¼ cup (60 ml) olive oil in a small saucepan and gently fry 2 crushed cloves garlic, 1 tbsp (15 ml) chopped rosemary and 2 tsp (10 ml) grated lemon zest for 3 minutes. Add 2 cans (14 oz/398 ml each) lima or fava beans with their liquid, 4 large skinned and chopped tomatoes and a little chili powder. Bring to a boil, then simmer over high heat for 8 to 10 minutes, until the sauce is thickened. Season and serve with the avocado salsa and sour cream.

PASTA IN CREAMY VEGETABLE BROTH

Serves 3–4
Preparation time 10 minutes
Cooking time 15 minutes

3 tbsp (45 ml) olive oil
1 large bulb fennel, finely chopped
5 oz (150 g) button mushrooms, halved
2 tbsp (30 ml) chopped fresh tarragon, parsley or
    fennel fronds
3 cups (750 ml) vegetable stock
7 oz (200 g) purple sprouting broccoli or broccoli rabe,
    halved lengthwise and cut into 2-inch (5 cm) lengths
10 oz (300 g) ready-made cheese or spinach tortellini
    or ravioli
6 tbsp (90 ml) whipping (35%) cream
Plenty of freshly grated nutmeg
Salt and pepper
Freshly grated Parmesan cheese, to garnish

Heat the oil in a large saucepan. Add the chopped fennel and cook gently, stirring frequently, for about 5 minutes, until soft. Add the mushrooms and cook for a further 5 minutes.

Add the herbs and stock and bring to a boil. Tip in the broccoli and return to a boil. Add the pasta and cook for about 3 minutes, until the pasta is tender.

Stir in the cream and nutmeg and salt and pepper to taste. Ladle into soup bowls and serve garnished with Parmesan.

For pasta in chickpea and spinach soup, heat 2 tbsp (30 ml) oil in a large saucepan and fry 2 crushed cloves garlic, 1 chopped onion and 1 tbsp (15 ml) chopped fresh rosemary for 5 minutes, until soft. Add 2 cans (14 oz/398 ml each) chickpeas with their liquid and 4¼ cups (1.2 L) vegetable stock and bring to a boil, then cover and simmer for 30 minutes. Add 3 oz (75 g) small pasta shapes and return to a boil, then simmer for 8 minutes. Stir in 4 oz (125 g) shredded spinach and cook for 5 minutes, until the pasta and spinach are tender. Season and serve topped with grated nutmeg, Parmesan and croutons.

TOMATO & BREAD SOUP

Serves 4
Preparation time 15 minutes
Cooking time 30 minutes

2 lb (1 kg) ripe vine tomatoes, peeled, seeded
  and chopped
1¼ cups (300 ml) vegetable stock
6 tbsp (90 ml) extra-virgin olive oil, divided
2 cloves garlic, crushed
1 tsp (5 ml) granulated sugar
2 tbsp (30 ml) chopped fresh basil
4 slices day-old good-quality bread, without crusts
1 tbsp (15 ml) balsamic vinegar
Salt and pepper

Put the tomatoes in a saucepan with the stock, 2 tbsp (30 ml) of the oil, the garlic, sugar and basil and bring gradually to a boil. Cover the pan, reduce the heat and simmer gently for 30 minutes.

Crumble the bread into the soup and stir over low heat until it has thickened. Stir in the vinegar and the remaining oil and season with salt and pepper to taste. Serve immediately or leave to cool to room temperature.

For tomato and almond soup, bring the tomatoes, oil, garlic and sugar to a boil as above, omitting the basil. Reduce the heat and simmer, uncovered, for 15 minutes. Meanwhile, blend ⅔ cup (150 ml) extra-virgin olive oil with ⅓ cup (75 ml) basil leaves and a pinch of salt, until really smooth. Set aside. Stir ⅔ cup (150 ml) toasted ground almonds into the soup and serve drizzled with the basil oil.

SPICY BEAN & YOGURT BAKE

Serves 4
Preparation time 15 minutes
Cooking time 1 hour

2 tsp (10 ml) cumin seeds
2 tsp (10 ml) fennel seeds
10 cardamom pods
2 cans (14 oz/398 ml each) red kidney beans, drained
¼ cup (60 ml) olive oil
1 large onion, chopped
1 medium-hot red chile, seeded and thinly sliced, divided
Finely grated zest of 1 lemon
2 cloves garlic, crushed
¼ cup (60 ml) dry breadcrumbs
⅔ cup (150 ml) blanched almonds, chopped
⅓ cup (75 ml) sultanas or raisins, chopped
2 eggs, divided
Salt and pepper
1¼ cups (300 ml) plain yogurt
2 tsp (10 ml) liquid honey
2 oz (60 g) Cheddar cheese, grated
3 bay leaves

Crush the cumin, fennel and cardamom using a pestle and mortar. Once the cardamom pods have opened, discard the shells and lightly crush the seeds. Mix with the beans in a bowl and crush the beans lightly by mashing them against the side of the bowl with a fork.

Heat the oil in a 6-cup (1.5 L) roasting pan or flameproof casserole and gently fry the onion for 5 minutes. Add two-thirds of the chile, reserving a few slices for a garnish, the lemon zest and the garlic and remove from the heat.

Add to the bowl with the breadcrumbs, almonds, sultanas or raisins, 1 egg and a little salt. Mix well and tip back into the pan. Spread the mixture in an even layer and pack down gently.

Beat the remaining egg in a bowl with the yogurt, honey and a little salt and pepper. Pour it over the bean mixture, spreading in an even layer. Scatter with the cheese, bay leaves and remaining chile slices. Bake in a preheated 325°F (160°C) oven for about 50 minutes, until the topping is very lightly set. Serve the bake hot.

For shredded iceberg salad to serve as an accompaniment, shred a small iceberg lettuce into a bowl and add ¼ cucumber, peeled and thinly sliced, and ½ bunch green onions, finely chopped. Mix the grated zest and juice of 1 lime with 3 tbsp (45 ml) peanut oil and 1 tbsp (15 ml) liquid honey and season with salt and pepper. Toss together and serve.

BEANS WITH COCONUT & CASHEWS

Serves 4
Preparation time 8 minutes
Cooking time 25 minutes

3 tbsp (45 ml) peanut or vegetable oil
2 onions, chopped
2 small carrots, thinly sliced
3 cloves garlic, crushed
1 red bell pepper, seeded and chopped
2 bay leaves
1 tbsp (15 ml) paprika
3 tbsp (45 ml) tomato purée
14-oz (400 ml) can coconut milk
7-oz (200 ml) can chopped tomatoes
⅔ cup (150 ml) vegetable stock
14-oz (398 ml) can red kidney beans, rinsed and
    drained
⅔ cup (150 ml) unsalted cashew nuts, toasted
Small handful of fresh coriander, roughly chopped
Salt and pepper

Heat the oil in a large saucepan. Add the onions and carrots and fry for 3 minutes. Add the garlic, red pepper and bay leaves and fry for 5 minutes, until the vegetables are soft and well browned.

Stir in the paprika, tomato purée, coconut milk, tomatoes, stock and beans and bring to a boil. Reduce the heat and simmer, uncovered, for 15 minutes, until the vegetables are tender.

Stir in the cashew nuts and coriander, season to taste with salt and pepper and heat through for 2 minutes. Serve with warmed grainy bread or boiled rice.

For red rice pilaf to serve as an accompaniment, place 1⅓ cups (325 ml) Camargue or other red rice in a saucepan with 3⅔ cups (900 ml) hot vegetable stock and 1 crushed clove garlic. Bring to a boil, then reduce the heat and simmer gently for 20 to 25 minutes or until the rice is tender, adding a little water if the mixture boils dry. Stir in 2 tbsp (30 ml) chopped parsley, the finely grated zest and juice of 1 lemon, 2 tbsp (30 ml) olive oil and 1 tsp (5 ml) granulated or fruit sugar, then season to taste with salt and pepper.

GREEN RISOTTO

Serves 4
Preparation time 10 minutes
Cooking time 30 minutes

½ cup (125 ml) butter, divided
1 tbsp (15 ml) olive oil
1 clove garlic, crushed or chopped
1 onion, finely diced
1¼ cups (300 ml) risotto rice
4 cups (1 L) hot vegetable stock
4 oz (125 g) green beans, cut into short lengths
4 oz (125 g) peas
4 oz (125 g) broad, lima or fava beans
4 oz (125 g) asparagus, cut into short lengths
4 oz (125 g) baby spinach, chopped
⅓ cup (75 ml) dry vermouth or white wine
Salt and pepper
2 tbsp (30 ml) chopped fresh parsley
4 oz (125 g) Parmesan cheese, freshly grated

Melt half the butter with the oil in a large saucepan; add the garlic and onion and fry gently for 5 minutes.

Add the rice and stir well to coat each grain with the butter and oil. Add enough stock to just cover the rice and stir well. Simmer gently, stirring frequently.

When most of the liquid is absorbed, add more stock and stir well. Continue adding the stock a little at a time, stirring until it is absorbed and the rice is tender but retaining a little bite – this will take about 25 minutes. You may not need all the stock. Add the vegetables and vermouth or wine, mix well and cook for 2 minutes.

Remove the pan from the heat, season and add the remaining butter, the parsley and the Parmesan. Mix well and serve.

For saffron and tomato risotto, omit the peas, asparagus and spinach from the above recipe. Add 3 oz (75 g) pine nuts to the pan when melting the butter. Fry until golden, then remove before adding the garlic and onions. Crumble in 1 tsp (5 ml) saffron threads with the rice. Add 10 oz (300 g) halved cherry tomatoes at the end of the third step, cooking for 2 to 3 minutes, until heated through, then stir in the pine nuts and a handful of shredded basil leaves.

BUDGET MEALS

JERK CHICKEN WINGS

Serves 4
Preparation time 5 minutes, plus marinating
Cooking time 12 minutes

12 large chicken wings
2 tbsp (30 ml) olive oil
1 tbsp (15 ml) jerk seasoning
Juice of ½ lemon
1 tsp (5 ml) salt
Chopped flat-leaf (Italian) parsley, to garnish
Lemon wedges, to serve

Put the chicken wings in a glass or ceramic dish. In a small bowl, whisk together the oil, jerk seasoning, lemon juice and salt, pour over the wings and stir well until evenly coated. Cover and leave to marinate in the refrigerator for at least 30 minutes or overnight.

Arrange the chicken wings on a broiler rack and cook under a preheated broiler, basting halfway through cooking with any remaining marinade, for 6 minutes on each side or until cooked through, tender and lightly charred at the edges. Increase or reduce the temperature setting of the broiler, if necessary, to ensure that the wings cook through. Garnish with the chopped parsley and serve immediately with lemon wedges for squeezing over.

For jerk lamb kebabs, coat 1 ½ lb (750 g) boneless lamb, cut into bite-size pieces, in the jerk marinade as above, leaving to marinate overnight if time allows. Thread the meat onto 8 metal skewers and cook under a preheated broiler or on a barbecue for 6 to 8 minutes on each side or until cooked to your liking.

DUCK BREASTS WITH FRUITY SALSA

Serves 4
Preparation time 15 minutes
Cooking time about 15 minutes

2 large boneless duck breasts, skin on, halved length-wise
2 tbsp (30 ml) dark soy sauce
1 tbsp (15 ml) liquid honey
1 tsp (5 ml) grated fresh ginger
1 tsp (5 ml) chili powder

For the fruity salsa
1 large ripe mango, peeled, pitted and finely diced
6 to 8 plums, pitted and finely diced
Grated zest and juice of 1 lime
1 small red onion, finely chopped
1 tbsp (15 ml) olive oil
1 tbsp (15 ml) roughly chopped fresh mint leaves
1 tbsp (15 ml) roughly chopped fresh coriander leaves
Salt and pepper

Use a sharp knife to score the skin on the duck breasts lightly, cutting down into the fat but not through to the meat.

Heat a frying pan until very hot, then add the duck breasts, skin side down, and cook for 3 minutes or until sealed and browned. Turn over and cook for 2 minutes. Use a slotted spoon to transfer the duck breasts to a baking sheet, skin side up.

In a small bowl, mix together the soy sauce, honey, ginger and chili powder. Spoon over the duck. Cook in a preheated 400°F (200°C) oven for 6 to 9 minutes, until cooked to your liking. The duck may be served pink in the center or more well cooked.

Meanwhile, in a bowl, mix together all the ingredients for the salsa and season well with salt and pepper.

Thinly slice the cooked duck and fan out the slices slightly on individual plates. Spoon some of the salsa over the duck and serve immediately, offering the remaining salsa separately.

For apricot & lime salsa as an alternative to the plum and mango salsa, in a bowl mix together 6 to 8 whole drained and finely chopped canned apricots in natural juice, the grated zest and juice of 1 lime, 1 finely chopped shallot, 1 tbsp (15 ml) finely chopped fresh ginger, 1 tbsp (15 ml) olive oil and 2 tsp (10 ml) liquid honey.

COCONUT CHICKEN

Serves 4
Preparation time 10 minutes
Cooking time 20 minutes

1 tbsp (15 ml) vegetable oil
1 onion, diced
1 red bell pepper, cored, seeded and diced
8 chicken thighs, boned, skinned and cut into
  bite-size pieces
7 oz (200 g) snow peas
2 tbsp (30 ml) medium curry paste
1 tsp (5 ml) finely chopped lemongrass
1 tsp (5 ml) finely chopped fresh ginger
2 cloves garlic, crushed
1 tbsp (15 ml) soy sauce
1⅔ cups (400 ml) coconut milk
Handful of fresh basil leaves
Salt and pepper (optional)

Heat the oil in a saucepan; add the onion and red bell pepper and cook for 5 minutes, until soft and just starting to brown. Add the chicken and cook for 5 minutes, until browned all over.

Add the snow peas, curry paste, lemongrass, ginger, garlic and soy sauce and cook, stirring, for 2 to 3 minutes. Add the coconut milk and stir well. Cover and simmer gently for 5 to 8 minutes.

Remove from the heat, check and adjust the seasoning, if necessary, and stir in the basil just before serving with boiled basmati rice.

For spicy fried rice to serve as an alternative accompaniment, heat 2 tbsp (30 ml) vegetable oil in a wok or large frying pan and crack 2 eggs into it, breaking the yolks and stirring them around. Add 2 cups (500 ml) cold cooked long-grain rice, 3 tsp (15 ml) granulated or fruit sugar, 1½ tbsp (22 ml) soy sauce, 2 tsp (10 ml) hot pepper flakes and 1 tsp (5 ml) Thai fish sauce and stir-fry over high heat for 2 minutes. Serve immediately with the coconut chicken and garnished with coriander leaves.

RICE NOODLES WITH LEMON CHICKEN

Serves 4
Preparation time 10 minutes
Cooking time 10 minutes

4 boneless chicken breasts, skin on
Juice of 2 lemons, divided
¼ cup (60 ml) sweet chili sauce
Salt and pepper
8 oz (250 g) dried rice noodles
1 small bunch of flat-leaf (Italian) parsley, chopped
1 small bunch of fresh coriander, chopped
½ cucumber, peeled into ribbons with a vegetable peeler
Finely chopped red chile, to garnish

Mix the chicken with half the lemon juice and the sweet chili sauce in a large bowl and season to taste with salt and pepper.

Lay a chicken breast between 2 sheets of plastic wrap and lightly pound with a mallet to flatten. Repeat with the remaining chicken breasts.

Arrange the chicken on a broiler rack in a single layer. Cook under a preheated broiler for 4 to 5 minutes on each side or until cooked through. Finish on the skin side so that it is crisp.

Meanwhile, put the noodles in a heatproof bowl, pour over boiling water to cover and leave for 10 minutes, until just tender, then drain. Add the remaining lemon juice, herbs and cucumber to the noodles and toss well to mix. Season to taste with salt and pepper.

Top the noodles with the cooked chicken and serve immediately, garnished with the chopped red chile.

For stir-fried ginger broccoli to serve as an accompaniment, trim the stalks from 1 lb (500 g) broccoli. Divide the heads into florets, then diagonally slice the stalks. Blanch the broccoli in a saucepan of salted boiling water for 30 seconds. Drain, refresh under cold running water and drain thoroughly. Heat 2 tbsp (30 ml) vegetable oil in a large frying pan, add 1 thinly sliced clove garlic and a 1-inch (2.5 cm) piece of fresh ginger, peeled and finely chopped, and stir-fry for a few seconds. Add the broccoli and stir-fry over high heat for 2 minutes. Sprinkle in 1 tsp (5 ml) toasted sesame oil and stir-fry for a further 30 seconds.

PESTO TURKEY KEBABS

Serves 4
Preparation time 15 minutes
Cooking time about 12 minutes

4 pieces turkey breast, about 1 lb (500 g) in total
2 tbsp (30 ml) pesto (see opposite)
4 slices Parma ham
4 oz (125 g) sun-dried tomatoes, finely chopped
4 oz (125 g) mozzarella cheese, finely diced
Salt and pepper
1 tbsp (15 ml) olive oil
Chopped fresh parsley, to garnish
Lemon wedges, to serve

Lay a piece of turkey between 2 sheets of plastic wrap and pound lightly with a mallet until about ½ inch (1 cm) thick. Repeat with the remaining turkey.

Spread the pesto over the beaten turkey and lay 1 slice of Parma ham on top of each. Sprinkle the tomatoes and mozzarella evenly over the turkey, then season to taste with salt and pepper and roll up each one from the long side.

Cut the turkey rolls into 1-inch (2.5 cm) slices. Carefully thread the slices of roll evenly onto 4 metal skewers.

Brush the turkey rolls lightly with the oil and grill under a preheated broiler for 6 minutes on each side or until cooked through. Increase or reduce the temperature setting of the broiler, if necessary, to ensure that the rolls cook through and brown on the outside. Garnish with chopped parsley and serve hot with lemon wedges for squeezing over.

For homemade pesto, put ¼ cup (60 ml) pine nuts and 2 crushed cloves garlic in a food processor or blender and process to a thick paste. Alternatively, put in a mortar and pound with a pestle. Tear 1½ cups (375 ml) basil leaves into shreds and process or pound to a thick paste. Transfer both pastes to a bowl. Stir in 5 oz (150 g) finely grated Parmesan cheese and 2 tbsp (30 ml) lemon juice. Add ⅔ cup (150 ml) olive oil a little at a time, beating well. Season to taste with salt and pepper.

CHICKEN RATATOUILLE

Serves 2
Preparation time 15 minutes
Cooking time 25 minutes

2 tbsp (30 ml) olive oil
2 boneless skinless chicken breasts, cut into
  bite-size pieces
½ medium zucchini, thinly sliced
⅔ cup (150 ml) eggplant, cubed
1 onion, thinly sliced
½ cup (125 ml) cored, seeded green bell pepper, thinly
  sliced
3 oz (75 g) mushrooms, sliced
14-oz (398 ml) can plum tomatoes
2 cloves garlic, finely chopped
1 tsp (5 ml) organic vegetable bouillon powder
1 tsp (5 ml) dried basil
1 tsp (5 ml) dried parsley
½ tsp (2 ml) ground black pepper

Heat the oil in a large frying pan; add the chicken and cook, stirring, for 3 to 4 minutes, until browned all over. Add the zucchini, eggplant, onion, green pepper and mushrooms and cook, stirring occasionally, for 15 minutes or until tender.

Add the tomatoes to the pan and gently stir. Stir in the garlic, bouillon powder, herbs and pepper and simmer, uncovered, for 5 minutes or until the chicken is tender. Serve immediately.

For roasted potatoes with rosemary and garlic to serve as an accompaniment, heat 2 tbsp (30 ml) olive oil in a large roasting pan in a preheated 450°F (230°C) oven. Meanwhile, cut 1½ lb (750 g) scrubbed, unpeeled potatoes into quarters lengthwise and pat dry with paper towels. Mix together 2 tbsp (30 ml) olive oil and 2 tbsp (30 ml) chopped rosemary in a bowl, add the potatoes and toss to coat. Add to the roasting pan, shake carefully to form an even layer, then roast at the top of the oven for 20 minutes. Meanwhile, peel and thinly slice 4 cloves garlic. Remove the pan and move the potatoes around so that they cook evenly. Scatter the garlic slices among the potatoes, then return to the oven and cook for a further 5 minutes. Season to taste with salt and pepper and serve immediately with the chicken ratatouille.

CHICKEN THIGHS WITH FRESH PESTO

Serves 4
Preparation time 15 minutes
Cooking time 25 minutes

1 tbsp (15 ml) olive oil
8 chicken thighs
Chopped fresh basil leaves, to garnish

For the pesto
6 tbsp (90 ml) olive oil
2 oz (60 g) pine nuts, toasted
2 oz (60 g) freshly grated Parmesan cheese
1½ cups (375 ml) fresh basil leaves
⅓ cup (75 ml) parsley
2 cloves garlic, chopped
Salt and pepper

Heat the oil in a nonstick frying pan over medium heat. Add the chicken thighs and cook gently, turning frequently, until the chicken is cooked through (about 20 minutes).

Meanwhile, make the pesto by placing all the ingredients in a food processor or blender and whizzing until smooth and well combined.

Remove the chicken from the pan and keep hot. Reduce the heat and add the pesto to the pan. Heat through for 2 to 3 minutes.

Pour the warmed pesto over the chicken thighs, garnish with basil and serve with zucchini ribbons and grilled tomatoes.

For tomato rice as an accompaniment, cut 13 oz (400 g) cherry tomatoes in half and place on a nonstick baking sheet. Sprinkle with 2 tbsp (30 ml) finely chopped garlic and sea salt and pepper to taste. Place in a hot oven for 12 to 15 minutes, then transfer to a mixing bowl with 2 cups (500 ml) cooked basmati or long-grain rice. Toss well to mix and serve with the chicken cooked as above.

FAST CHICKEN CURRY

Serves 4
Preparation time 5 minutes
Cooking time 20–25 minutes

3 tbsp (45 ml) olive oil
1 onion, finely chopped
¼ cup (60 ml) medium curry paste
8 chicken thighs, boned, skinned and cut into
  thin strips
14-oz (398 ml) can chopped tomatoes
½ bunch broccoli, broken into small florets, and stalks,
  peeled and sliced
⅓ cup + 2 tbsp (100 ml) coconut milk
Salt and pepper

Heat the oil in a deep nonstick saucepan, add the onion and cook for 3 minutes, until soft. Add the curry paste and cook, stirring, for 1 minute.

Add the chicken, tomatoes, broccoli and coconut milk to the pan. Bring to a boil, then reduce the heat, cover and cook over low heat for 15 to 20 minutes.

Remove from the heat, season well with salt and pepper and serve immediately.

For seafood patties with curry sauce, follow the first stage of the recipe above, then add the tomatoes, 7 oz (200 g) young spinach leaves and the coconut milk and cook as directed. Meanwhile, put 12 oz (375 g) roughly chopped white fish fillets and 6 oz (175 g) frozen cooked peeled shrimp, defrosted and roughly chopped, in a food processor and process until well combined. Alternatively, finely chop and mix together by hand. Transfer to a bowl, add 4 finely chopped green onions, 2 tbsp (30 ml) chopped coriander leaves, 1½ cups (375 ml) fresh white breadcrumbs, a squeeze of lemon juice, 1 beaten egg and salt and pepper to taste. Mix well, then form into 16 patties. Roll in 1 cup (250 ml) fresh white breadcrumbs to coat. Heat a shallow depth of vegetable oil in a large frying pan, add the patties, in batches, and cook for 5 minutes on each side or until crisp and golden brown. Serve hot with the curry sauce.

MINI CHICKEN & BROCCOLI FRITTATAS

Makes 12
Preparation time 15 minutes
Cooking time 15 minutes

½ bunch broccoli, cut into small florets
Oil, for greasing
4 to 5 oz (125 to 150 g) cooked chicken, diced
6 eggs
½ cup (125 ml) milk
1½ oz (40 g) Parmesan cheese, freshly grated
Salt and pepper

Add the broccoli to a saucepan of boiling water and cook for 3 minutes, then drain into a colander. Brush the insides of a 12-cup nonstick muffin pan with a little oil, then divide both the broccoli and the chicken between the cups.

Beat the eggs, milk and Parmesan together in a jug, season generously, then pour the mixture over the broccoli and chicken.

Bake in a preheated 375°F (190°C) oven for 15 minutes, until well risen and golden. Loosen the edges of the frittatas, then turn out and serve with a tomato salad or baked beans.

For chicken, bacon & red onion frittata, heat 1 tbsp (15 ml) olive oil in a medium frying pan; add 4 oz (125 g) diced bacon and 1 sliced red onion and fry for 5 minutes, until golden. Add 4 to 5 oz (125 to 150 g) diced cooked chicken and fry until piping hot. Beat the eggs and milk together, then season. Add an extra 1 tbsp (15 ml) oil to the pan, then pour in the egg mixture. Fry until the underside is golden, then finish off under a hot broiler until set and golden. Cut into wedges to serve.

TERIYAKI CHICKEN

Serves 4
Preparation time 10 minutes, plus marinating
Cooking time 8 minutes

2 boneless skinless chicken breasts, cut into thin strips
2 tbsp (30 ml) soy sauce
1 tbsp (15 ml) olive oil
2 large carrots, peeled and cut into small matchsticks
2 red bell peppers, cored, seeded and cut into small matchsticks
7-oz (200 g) jar teriyaki stir-fry sauce
6 green onions, chopped

Put the chicken in a glass or ceramic bowl, add the soy sauce and toss well to coat. Cover and leave to marinate in a cool place for 10 minutes.

Heat the oil in a wok or large frying pan; add the chicken and marinade and stir-fry for 2 minutes. Add the carrots and peppers and stir-fry for 4 minutes. Add the sauce and green onions and cook briefly, stirring, to heat through. Serve immediately over egg noodles.

For pork teriyaki with crispy garlic, substitute the chicken with 1¼ lb (625 g) boneless pork chops. Place the pork between sheets of plastic wrap and flatten with a wooden mallet. Cut into thin strips and cook as above. To make the crispy garlic, thinly slice 4 cloves garlic. Heat a 2-inch (5 cm) depth of oil in a deep, heavy-bottomed saucepan to 350° to 375°F (180° to 190°C) or until a cube of bread browns in 30 seconds. Add the garlic slices and cook until golden and crispy. Remove with a slotted spoon and drain on paper towels. Sprinkle over the finished dish.

TANDOORI CHICKEN

Serves 4
Preparation time 5 minutes, plus marinating
Cooking time 25–30 minutes

8 chicken drumsticks
8 chicken thighs
2 tbsp (30 ml) tikka or tandoori spice mix or paste
2 cloves garlic, crushed
1 tbsp (15 ml) tomato purée
Juice of 1 lemon
⅓ cup (75 ml) natural yogurt

To garnish
Grated lime zest
Chopped fresh coriander

Make deep slashes all over the chicken pieces. In a large glass or ceramic bowl, mix together all the remaining ingredients, then add the chicken and turn to coat thoroughly with the marinade. Cover and leave to marinate in the refrigerator for at least 30 minutes or overnight.

Transfer the chicken to an ovenproof dish and cook in a preheated 475°F (240°C) oven for 25 to 30 minutes, until cooked through, tender and lightly charred at the edges. Serve garnished with lime zest and chopped coriander.

For blackened tandoori salmon, use the marinade above to coat 4 thick skinless salmon fillets, then cover and leave to marinate in the refrigerator for 30 minutes to 1 hour. Transfer to a nonstick baking sheet and bake at 350°F (180°C) for 20 minutes or until cooked through. Serve with plain rice or couscous.

GRILLED SALSA CHICKEN

Serves 4
Preparation time 10 minutes
Cooking time 6 minutes

4 boneless chicken breasts, skin on
3 tbsp (45 ml) olive oil
Salt and pepper

For the cucumber and tomato salsa
1 red onion, finely chopped
2 tomatoes, seeded and diced
1 cucumber, finely diced
1 red chile, finely chopped
1 small handful of fresh coriander leaves, chopped
Juice of 1 lime
Salt and pepper

Remove the skin from the chicken breasts. Using kitchen scissors, cut each breast in half lengthwise but without cutting the whole way through. Open each breast out flat. Brush with the oil and season well with salt and pepper. Heat a grill pan until very hot. Add the chicken breasts and cook for 3 minutes on each side or until cooked through and grill-marked.

Meanwhile, to make the salsa, mix together the onion, tomatoes, cucumber, red chile, coriander and lime juice. Season well with salt and pepper.

Serve the chicken hot with the spicy salsa spooned over and around.

For grilled tuna with pineapple salsa, prepare and cook 4 thick fresh tuna steaks, about 6 oz (175 g) each, as for the butterflied chicken breasts above. Meanwhile, in a bowl, mix together 6 tbsp (90 ml) drained and roughly diced canned pineapple, 1 finely chopped red onion, 1 tbsp (15 ml) finely chopped fresh ginger, 1 finely chopped red chile, the grated zest and juice of 1 lime, 2 tsp (10 ml) liquid honey and salt and pepper to taste. Serve the pineapple salsa with the grilled tuna.

PEA & LAMB KORMA

Serves 4
Preparation time 10 minutes
Cooking time 30 minutes

2 tbsp (30 ml) olive oil
1 onion, chopped
2 cloves garlic, crushed
8 oz (250 g) potatoes, cut into ¾-inch (1.5 cm) dice
1 lb (500 g) ground lamb
1 tbsp (15 ml) korma curry powder
1½ cups (375 ml) frozen peas
¾ cup + 2 tbsp (200 ml) vegetable stock
2 tbsp (30 ml) mango chutney
Salt and pepper
Chopped fresh coriander leaves, to garnish

Heat the oil in a saucepan; add the onion and garlic and cook for 5 minutes, until the onion is soft and starting to brown. Add the potatoes and ground lamb and cook, stirring and breaking up the meat with a wooden spoon, for 5 minutes or until the meat has browned.

Add the curry powder and cook, stirring, for 1 minute. Add the remaining ingredients and season to taste with salt and pepper. Bring to a boil, then reduce the heat, cover tightly and simmer for 20 minutes.

Remove from the heat, garnish with chopped coriander and serve with natural yogurt and steamed rice.

For spicy Indian wraps, finely shred ½ iceberg lettuce and place in a bowl with 1 coarsely grated carrot. Heat 8 large flour wraps (or tortillas) on a grill pan for 1 to 2 minutes on each side and then add the lettuce mixture to the center of each one. Divide the korma mixture (cooked as above) between the wraps and roll each one to enclose the filling. Serve accompanied with a dollop of yogurt if desired.

MINTED LAMB SKEWERS

Serves 4
Preparation time 10 minutes
Cooking time 10 minutes

1 lb (500 g) ground lamb
2 tsp (10 ml) curry powder
6 tbsp (90 ml) finely chopped fresh mint leaves
Salt and pepper

Mix together the ground lamb, curry powder and mint in a bowl and season to taste with salt and pepper. Using your hands, knead to combine the mixture evenly.

Divide the mixture into small sausages and thread evenly onto metal skewers. Cook under a preheated broiler for 10 minutes, turning once. Serve hot with warmed naan bread, sour cream and a lime wedge. Sprinkle with chopped mint leaves and a little curry powder.

For cucumber raita to serve as an accompaniment, cut ½ large cucumber in half lengthwise, scoop out and discard the seeds, then thinly slice each half. In a bowl, mix together with 1 cup (250 ml) plain yogurt, 1 tbsp (15 ml) chopped fresh mint leaves and 1 tbsp (15 ml) chopped fresh coriander leaves. Season to taste with salt and pepper. Toast 2 tsp (10 ml) cumin seeds in a dry frying pan until fragrant. Sprinkle over the raita just before serving.

MEXICAN PIE

Serves 4
Preparation time 10 minutes
Cooking time 30 minutes

2 tbsp (30 ml) olive oil
1 onion, finely chopped
2 cloves garlic, crushed
2 carrots, diced
8 oz (250 g) ground beef
1 red chile, finely chopped
14-oz (398 ml) can chopped tomatoes
14-oz (398 ml) can red kidney beans, drained
   and rinsed
Salt and pepper
2 oz (60 g) tortilla chips
3½ oz (100 g) Cheddar cheese, grated
Chopped fresh parsley or coriander, to garnish

Heat the oil in a saucepan; add the onion, garlic and carrots and cook until softened. Add the ground beef and chile and cook, stirring and breaking up with a wooden spoon, for 5 minutes or until the meat has browned. Add the tomatoes and beans, mix well and season to taste with salt and pepper.

Transfer to an ovenproof dish, cover with the tortilla chips and sprinkle the Cheddar. Bake in a preheated 400°F (200°C) oven for 20 minutes or until golden brown. Garnish with chopped parsley or coriander before serving.

For tortilla-wrapped chili with guacamole, follow the first stage of the recipe above, but then cover and simmer on the stove for 20 minutes. Meanwhile, halve 2 large, ripe avocados lengthwise and remove the pits. Scoop the flesh into a bowl, add 3 tbsp (45 ml) lime juice and roughly mash. Add 4 oz (125 g) tomatoes, peeled, seeded and chopped, 2 crushed cloves garlic, 2 chopped green onions, 1 tbsp (15 ml) finely chopped green chiles and 2 tbsp (30 ml) chopped coriander leaves. Mix well and season to taste with salt and pepper. Divide the chili between 4 warmed flour tortillas and wrap up. Serve with the guacamole, and sour cream, if desired.

194

BEEF MEATBALLS WITH RIBBON PASTA

Serves 4
Preparation time 20 minutes
Cooking time 1 hour 20 minutes

2 slices of stale bread, crusts removed, broken into
   small pieces
⅓ cup (75 ml) milk
¼ cup (60 ml) olive oil, divided
6 green onions or 1 small onion, finely chopped
1 clove garlic, chopped
1½ lb (750 g) ground beef
2 tbsp (30 ml) freshly grated Parmesan cheese, plus
   extra to serve
Freshly grated nutmeg, to taste
Salt and pepper
1¼ cups (300 ml) dry white wine
14-oz (398 ml) can chopped tomatoes
2 bay leaves
13 oz (400 g) dried tagliatelle or fettuccine
fresh basil leaves, to garnish

For the meatballs, soak the bread in the milk in a large bowl. Meanwhile, heat half the oil in a frying pan over medium heat; add the green onions or onion and garlic and cook, stirring frequently, for 5 minutes, until soft and just beginning to brown.

Add the ground meat to the bread and mix well. Add the cooked onion and garlic, the Parmesan and nutmeg and season with salt and pepper. Work together with your hands until well combined and smooth. Shape into 28 even-sized balls. Heat the remaining oil in a large nonstick frying pan, add the meatballs, in batches, and cook over high heat, turning frequently, until golden brown. Transfer to a shallow ovenproof dish.

Pour the wine and tomatoes into the frying pan and bring to a boil, scraping up any sediment from the bottom. Add the bay leaves, season with salt and pepper and boil rapidly for 5 minutes. Pour the sauce over the meatballs, cover with foil and bake in a preheated 350°F (180°C) oven for 1 hour, or until tender.

When the meatballs and sauce are almost ready, cook the pasta in a large saucepan of salted boiling water according to the package instructions, until al dente. Drain thoroughly and serve with the meatballs and sauce. Garnish with basil leaves and a scattering of Parmesan cheese.

For pork meatballs with walnuts, replace the beef with 1½ lb (750 g) ground pork. Grind ¾ cup (175 ml) walnuts and add to the meat mixture, omitting the Parmesan, then cook as above.

BEEF WITH BLACK BEAN SAUCE

Serves 4
Preparation time 15 minutes
Cooking time 15 minutes

1½ lb (750 g) minute steak
2 tbsp (30 ml) peanut oil, divided
1 onion, thinly sliced
3½ oz (100 g) snow peas, halved lengthwise
1 clove garlic, finely chopped
1-inch (2.5 cm) piece fresh ginger, peeled and finely chopped
1 small red chile, finely chopped
7-oz (200 g) jar Asian black bean sauce
Salt and pepper

Trim the steak of all fat and then cut the meat into thin slices across the grain. Heat half the oil in a wok or large frying pan; add the beef, in 2 batches, and cook, stirring, until well browned all over. Transfer to a bowl.

Heat the remaining oil in the pan; add the onion and snow peas and stir-fry for 2 minutes. Add the garlic, ginger and chile and stir-fry for 1 minute. Add the black bean sauce and cook, stirring, for 5 minutes or until the sauce begins to thicken. Season to taste with salt and pepper and serve immediately with steamed rice or egg-fried rice.

For seafood with black bean sauce, stir-fry 1 lb (500 g) raw tiger shrimp and 7 oz (200 g) squid rings in a hot wok for 2 to 3 minutes. Add 8 roughly sliced green onions and 2 sliced red bell peppers and stir-fry for a further 2 to 3 minutes. Add the black bean sauce and cook for 5 minutes, stirring often. Serve hot with egg noodles.

PORK & RED PEPPER CHILI

Serves 4
Preparation time 10 minutes
Cooking time 30 minutes

2 tbsp (30 ml) olive oil
1 large onion, chopped
2 cloves garlic, crushed
1 red bell pepper, cored, seeded and diced
14½ oz (450 g) ground pork
1 red chile, finely chopped
1 tsp (5 ml) dried oregano
1 lb (500 g) passata (sieved tomatoes)
14-oz (398 ml) can red kidney beans, drained
  and rinsed
Salt and pepper
Sour cream, to serve

Heat the oil in a saucepan; add the onion, garlic and red bell pepper and cook for 5 minutes, until soft and starting to brown. Add the ground pork and cook, stirring and breaking up with a wooden spoon, for 5 minutes or until browned.

Add all the remaining ingredients and bring to a boil. Reduce the heat and simmer gently for 20 minutes. Remove from the heat, season well with salt and pepper and serve immediately with a dollop of sour cream and boiled rice or crusty bread.

For lamb & eggplant chili, substitute the ground pork and red bell pepper with 1 medium eggplant and 14¼ oz (450 g) ground lamb. Cut the eggplant into small cubes and fry as above with the ground lamb. Garnish the finished dish with 2 tbsp (30 ml) finely chopped fresh mint leaves and serve with rice or pasta.

MOROCCAN MEATBALL TAGINE

Serves 4
Preparation time 15 minutes
Cooking time 40 minutes

2 small onions, finely chopped, divided
2 tbsp (30 ml) raisins
1½ lb (750 g) ground beef
1 tbsp (15 ml) tomato purée
3 tsp (15 ml) curry powder
3 tbsp (45 ml) olive oil, divided
½ tsp (2 ml) ground cinnamon
20-oz (590 ml) can chopped tomatoes
Juice of ½ lemon
2 stalks celery, thickly sliced
1 large or 2 medium zucchini, roughly chopped
1 cup (250 ml) frozen peas

Mix together half the onions, the raisins, ground beef, tomato purée and curry powder in a bowl. Using your hands, knead to combine the mixture evenly. Form the mixture into 24 meatballs.

Heat 1 tbsp (15 ml) of the oil in a saucepan, add the meatballs, in small batches, and cook until browned all over. Tip out the excess fat and put all the meatballs in the pan. Add the cinnamon, tomatoes and lemon juice, cover and simmer gently for 25 minutes, until the meatballs are cooked.

Meanwhile, heat the remaining oil in a large frying pan, add the celery and zucchini and cook until soft and starting to brown. Add the peas and cook for a further 5 minutes, until the peas are tender.

Just before serving, stir the zucchini mixture into the meatball mixture.

For coriander & apricot couscous to serve as an accompaniment, put 7 oz (200 g) instant couscous in a large, heatproof bowl with 2 oz (60 g) chopped ready-to-eat dried apricots. Pour in boiling hot vegetable stock to just cover the couscous. Cover and leave to stand for 10 to 12 minutes, until all the stock has been absorbed. Meanwhile, chop 2 large, ripe tomatoes and finely chop 2 tbsp (30 ml) coriander leaves. Fluff up the couscous grains with a fork and tip into a warmed serving dish. Stir in the tomatoes and coriander with 2 tbsp (30 ml) olive oil and season to taste with salt and pepper. Toss well to mix and serve with the tagine.

BOBOTIE

Serves 4
Preparation time 10 minutes, plus cooling
Cooking time 40 minutes

2 tbsp (30 ml) olive oil
1 onion, chopped
2 cloves garlic, chopped
2 tbsp (30 ml) medium curry paste
1 lb (500 g) ground beef
2 tbsp (30 ml) tomato purée
1 tbsp (15 ml) white wine vinegar
½ cup (125 ml) sultanas
1 slice of white bread, soaked in 3 tbsp (45 ml) milk and mashed
4 eggs, beaten
⅓ cup + 2 tbsp (100 ml) whipping (35%) cream
Salt and pepper

Heat the oil in a saucepan; add the onion and garlic and cook until soft and starting to brown. Add the curry paste and ground beef and cook, stirring and breaking up with a wooden spoon, for 5 minutes or until browned.

Add the tomato purée, vinegar, sultanas and mashed bread. Season to taste with salt and pepper and transfer to a deep, medium-sized oven-proof dish or an 8-inch (20 cm) heavy cake pan.

Mix together the eggs and cream in a bowl, season to taste with salt and pepper and pour over the meat mixture.

Bake in a preheated 350°F (180°C) oven for 30 minutes or until the egg is set and golden brown. Remove from the oven and leave to cool for 10 to 15 minutes before serving.

For individual boboties to serve as a stylish starter for an elegant dinner, divide the meat mixture between 4 individual ramekin dishes and pour the egg mixture over each one. Bake in a preheated 350°F (180°C) oven for 20 to 25 minutes or until the tops are just set. Meanwhile, toast thin slices of bread in a preheated grill pan or under a preheated broiler. Serve with the boboties.

MUSTARD & HAM MACARONI & CHEESE

Serves 4
Preparation time 5 minutes
Cooking time 15 minutes

11½ oz (350 g) dried quick-cook macaroni

8 oz (250 g) mascarpone cheese

3½ oz (100 g) Cheddar cheese, grated

⅓ cup + 2 tbsp (100 ml) milk

2 tsp (10 ml) Dijon mustard

14-oz (398 ml) can premium cured ham, cut into
  small cubes

Salt and pepper

Chopped flat-leaf (Italian) parsley, to garnish

Cook the macaroni in a large saucepan of salted boiling water according to the package instructions, until al dente, then drain and put in a warmed serving bowl. Cover and keep warm.

Gently heat the mascarpone, Cheddar, milk and mustard in a saucepan until melted into a sauce. Stir in the ham and cook gently for 1 to 2 minutes. Season to taste with salt and pepper.

Serve the macaroni with the cheese sauce spooned over, garnished with chopped parsley.

For spinach with olive oil & lemon dressing, an ideal accompaniment to the above dish, rinse 1¼ lb (625 g) spinach leaves in cold water, then put in a large saucepan with just the water that is clinging to the leaves, sprinkling with salt to taste. Cover and cook over medium heat for 5 to 7 minutes, until wilted and tender, shaking the pan vigorously from time to time. Drain thoroughly in a colander, then return to the rinsed-out pan and toss over high heat until any remaining water has evaporated. Add 2 tbsp (30 ml) butter and 2 finely chopped cloves garlic, and continue tossing until combined with the spinach. Transfer to a warmed serving dish, drizzle in ¼ cup (60 ml) olive oil and 2 tbsp (30 ml) lemon juice, season to taste with salt and pepper and serve immediately with the macaroni dish.

200

THAI GREEN PORK CURRY

Serves 4
Preparation time 10 minutes
Cooking time 20 minutes

2 tbsp (30 ml) olive oil
4 boneless pork chops, cut into bite-size pieces
2 tbsp (30 ml) Thai green curry paste
14-oz (400 ml) can coconut milk
¾ cup (175 ml) green beans
7-oz (200 g) can water chestnuts, drained, rinsed and
    cut in half
Juice of 1 lime, or to taste
Handful of fresh coriander leaves

Heat the oil in a large saucepan; add the pork and cook, stirring, for 3 to 4 minutes, until browned all over. Add the curry paste and cook, stirring, for 1 minute, until fragrant.

Add the coconut milk, stir and reduce the heat to a gentle simmer. Cook for 10 minutes, then add the beans and water chestnuts. Cook for a further 3 minutes.

Remove from the heat, add lime juice to taste and stir the coriander through. Serve immediately with boiled rice.

For Thai red pork curry, replace the Thai green curry paste with Thai red curry paste. To prepare your own Thai red curry paste, put 10 large red chiles, 2 tsp (10 ml) coriander seeds, a 2-inch (5 cm) piece of fresh ginger, peeled and finely chopped, 1 finely chopped stalk lemongrass, 4 halved cloves garlic, 1 roughly chopped shallot, 1 tsp (5 ml) lime juice and 2 tbsp (30 ml) peanut oil in a food processor or blender and process to a thick paste. Alternatively, pound the ingredients together using a pestle and mortar. Transfer the paste to an airtight container; it can be stored in the refrigerator for up to 3 weeks.

RISI E BISI

Serves 4
Preparation time 5 minutes
Cooking time about 25 minutes

1 tbsp (15 ml) butter
1 tbsp (15 ml) olive oil
1 onion, finely chopped
2 cloves garlic, crushed
1 cup (250 ml) risotto rice
3⅔ cups (900 ml) hot chicken stock, made with
  1 chicken stock cube and boiling water, heated
  to simmering
14½ oz (450 g) frozen peas
1 oz (25 g) Parmesan cheese, grated
3½ oz (100 g) cooked ham, finely chopped
1 bunch fresh parsley, finely chopped
Salt and pepper

Melt the butter with the oil in a saucepan; add the onion and garlic and cook until the onion is soft and starting to brown. Add the rice and stir until coated with the butter mixture.

Add the hot stock, a ladleful at a time, and cook, stirring constantly, until each addition has been absorbed before adding the next. Continue until all the stock has been absorbed and the rice is creamy and cooked but still retains a little bite – this will take around 15 minutes.

Add the peas and heat through for 3 to 5 minutes. Remove from the heat and stir in the Parmesan, ham and parsley. Season to taste with salt and pepper and serve immediately.

For tuna & tomato risotto, after cooking the onion and garlic, add 3 tbsp (45 ml) white wine and cook, stirring, until it has evaporated. Then follow the recipe above, but use fish stock instead of chicken stock and add 2 chopped tomatoes in place of the peas, along with a 6½-oz (170 ml) can tuna, drained and flaked, and heat through for 3 to 5 minutes. Remove from the heat and stir in 2 tbsp (30 ml) chopped fresh basil with the Parmesan cheese and salt and pepper to taste. Serve immediately.

TOMATO & BACON RICE

Serves 4
Preparation time 10 minutes, plus standing
Cooking time about 20 minutes

2 tbsp (30 ml) olive oil
2 large leeks, sliced
1 clove garlic, crushed
7 oz (200 g) back bacon, chopped
14-oz (398 ml) can chopped tomatoes
1 cup (250 ml) long-grain rice
3 cups (750 ml) chicken stock
Salt and pepper
Chopped flat-leaf (Italian) parsley, to garnish

Heat the oil in a saucepan; add the leeks, garlic and bacon and cook over medium heat for a few minutes, until soft and starting to brown. Add the tomatoes and rice and cook, stirring, for 1 minute.

Add the stock and season to taste with salt and pepper. Reduce the heat, cover tightly and cook for 12 to 15 minutes or until all the stock has been absorbed and the rice is tender.

Remove from the heat and leave to stand, covered, for 10 minutes. Stir, then garnish with parsley and serve immediately.

For homemade chicken stock, chop a cooked chicken carcass into 3 or 4 pieces and put in a large saucepan with 1 chopped onion, 2 or 3 chopped carrots, 1 chopped stalk celery, 1 bay leaf, 3 to 4 parsley stalks and 1 thyme sprig. Add 7 cups (1.8 L) cold water and bring to a boil, skimming any scum that rises to the surface. Reduce the heat and simmer gently for 2 to 2½ hours. Strain through a muslin-lined sieve. If not using straight away, leave to cool before covering and refrigerating.

QUICK SAUSAGE & BEAN CASSEROLE

Serves 4

Preparation time 5 minutes

Cooking time 25 minutes

2 tbsp (30 ml) olive oil

16 cocktail sausages

2 cloves garlic, crushed

14-oz (398 ml) can chopped tomatoes

14-oz (398 ml) can baked beans

7-oz (200 g) can mixed beans, drained and rinsed

½ tsp (2 ml) dried thyme

Salt and pepper

3 tbsp (45 ml) chopped flat-leaf (Italian) parsley, to garnish

Heat the oil in a frying pan, add the sausages and cook until browned all over.

Transfer the sausages to a large saucepan and add all the remaining ingredients. Bring to a boil, then reduce the heat, cover tightly and simmer for 20 minutes. Season to taste with salt and pepper and serve hot, garnished with the chopped parsley.

For mustard mashed potatoes to serve as an accompaniment, cook 2 lb (1 kg) chopped potatoes in a large saucepan of salted boiling water until tender. Drain well and return to the pan. Mash with 6 tbsp (90 ml) butter, 1 tbsp (15 ml) whole-grain mustard, 3 tsp (15 ml) prepared English mustard and 1 crushed clove garlic. Season to taste with salt and pepper, then beat in 2 tbsp (30 ml) chopped fresh parsley and a dash of olive oil. Serve hot with the casserole.

SPICY PORK ROLLS WITH MINTED YOGURT

Serves 4

Preparation time 15 minutes

Cooking time 10–12 minutes

4 pork scallops, about 4 to 5 oz (125 to 150 g) each

1 small onion, roughly chopped

1 red chile, seeded and roughly chopped

¼ cup (60 ml) roughly chopped fresh coriander leaves

Grated zest and juice of 1 lime

1 tbsp (15 ml) Thai fish sauce

2 cloves garlic, crushed

1 tsp (5 ml) grated fresh ginger

1 tsp (5 ml) ground cumin

½ tsp (2 ml) ground coriander

¼ cup (60 ml) coconut milk

Fresh mint leaves (optional)

For the minted yogurt

¾ cup + 2 tbsp (200 ml) Greek yogurt

¼ cup (60 ml) roughly chopped fresh mint leaves

Salt and pepper

Lay a pork scallop between 2 sheets of plastic wrap and pound lightly with a mallet until about ¼ inch (5 mm) thick. Repeat with the remaining pork.

Process the remaining ingredients in a food processor or blender to a coarse paste. Spread a quarter of the paste over a pork cutlet and roll up to enclose the filling. Secure the roll with a wooden cocktail stick. Repeat with the remaining paste and pork.

Put the rolls on a baking sheet and cook in a preheated 400°F (200°C) oven for 10 to 12 minutes or until cooked through.

Meanwhile, to make the minted yogurt, put the yogurt in a small bowl, stir in the mint and season to taste with salt and pepper. Serve the rolls hot, with a dollop of the minted yogurt on the side and garnished with mint leaves, if desired.

For satay sauce to serve with the pork rolls instead of the minted yogurt, heat 1 tbsp (15 ml) peanut oil in a small frying pan, add 1 crushed clove garlic and cook, stirring, over low heat for 2 to 3 minutes, until softened. Stir in ¼ cup (60 ml) crunchy peanut butter, ¼ tsp (1 ml) hot pepper flakes, 1 tbsp (15 ml) dark soy sauce, 1 tbsp (15 ml) lime juice, 1 tsp (5 ml) liquid honey and 2 tbsp (30 ml) coconut cream and heat gently, stirring, until boiling. Serve warm with the pork rolls.

PASTA PIE

Serves 4
Preparation time 10 minutes
Cooking time 30 minutes

1 tbsp (15 ml) olive oil
14½ oz (450 g) leeks, sliced
2 cloves garlic, crushed
4 eggs, beaten
⅔ cup (150 ml) table (18%) or half-and-half (10%)
   cream
4 oz (125 g) Gruyère cheese, grated
1 cup (250 ml) cooked fusilli
Salt and pepper

Heat the oil in a frying pan; add the leeks and garlic and cook until soft.

Mix the leek mixture with all the remaining ingredients, season to taste with salt and pepper and transfer to a greased ovenproof dish or medium-sized cake pan.

Bake in a preheated 350°F (180°C) oven for 25 minutes or until the eggs have set and the pie is golden brown. Serve with a crisp green salad.

For chicken & mozzarella macaroni pie, follow the first stage of the recipe, then add 7 oz (200 g) cooked chicken, cut into small, bite-size pieces, and 2 tbsp (30 ml) finely chopped fresh tarragon with the eggs and cream, together with 4 oz (125 g) grated mozzarella cheese and 1 cup (250 ml) cooked macaroni. Bake in the oven as above.

SUMMER SHRIMP & FISH PHYLLO PIE

Serves 4
Preparation time 10 minutes
Cooking time 20–25 minutes

1½ lb (750 g) skinless white fish fillets
3½ oz (100 g) frozen cooked peeled shrimp, defrosted
½ cup (125 ml) frozen peas, defrosted
Grated zest and juice of 1 lemon
2⅓ cups (575 ml) bottled or prepared white sauce
1 bunch fresh dill, chopped
Salt and pepper
8 sheets phyllo pastry
Melted butter, for brushing

Cut the fish into large, bite-size pieces and put in a bowl with the shrimp and peas. Add the lemon zest and juice, stir in the white sauce and dill and season well with salt and pepper.

Tip the fish mixture into 4 individual gratin or pie dishes. Cover the surface of each pie with 2 sheets of phyllo pastry, scrunching up each sheet into a loosely crumpled ball. Brush the pastry with melted butter.

Bake in a preheated 400°F (200°C) oven for 20 to 25 minutes, until the pastry is golden brown and the fish is cooked through.

For seafood & potato pie, prepare the fish mixture as above, but use 2 tbsp (30 ml) chopped parsley in place of the dill. Put into a medium-sized ovenproof dish. Cook 1½ lbs (750 g) chopped potatoes in a large saucepan of salted boiling water until tender. Meanwhile, put 2 large eggs in a separate saucepan and bring to a boil. Cook for 10 minutes, then plunge into cold water to cool. Shell the eggs and cut in half lengthwise. Drain the potatoes and mash with 2 tbsp (30 ml) butter. Season well with salt and pepper. Gently press the egg halves, at evenly spaced intervals, into the fish mixture, then spoon or pipe the potatoes over the fish mixture. Bake in a preheated 400°F (200°C) oven for 20 to 25 minutes or until the top is lightly golden.

MACKEREL WITH AVOCADO SALSA

Serves 4
Preparation time 10 minutes
Cooking time 6–8 minutes

8 mackerel fillets
Salt and pepper
2 lemons, plus extra wedges to serve

For the avocado salsa
2 avocados, peeled, pitted and finely diced
Juice and zest of 1 lime
1 red onion, finely chopped
½ cucumber, finely diced
Handful of fresh coriander leaves, finely chopped
Salt and pepper

Make 3 diagonal slashes across each mackerel fillet on the skin side and season well with salt and pepper. Cut the lemons in half, then squeeze the juice over the fish.

Lay on a broiler rack, skin side up, and cook under a preheated broiler for 6 to 8 minutes or until the skin is lightly charred and the flesh is just cooked through.

Meanwhile, to make the salsa, mix together the avocados and lime juice and zest, then add the onion, cucumber and coriander. Toss well to mix and season to taste with salt and pepper.

Serve the mackerel hot with the avocado salsa and lemon wedges for squeezing over.

For grilled sardines with tomato relish, replace the mackerel fillets with 12 whole cleaned and gutted sardines and broil for 4 to 5 minutes on each side. Meanwhile, put the chopped white parts of 4 green onions, 2 tbsp (30 ml) lime juice, 8 oz (250 g) ripe tomatoes, peeled, seeded and chopped, ½ chopped sun-dried tomato, 1 seeded and chopped red chile and 3 tbsp (45 ml) chopped coriander leaves in a food processor or blender and process until well combined. Serve the sardines hot with the relish.

FISH KEBABS & GREEN ONION MASH

Serves 4
Preparation time 15 minutes, plus marinating
Cooking time 18–20 minutes

1 lb 3 oz (600 g) skinless haddock, cod or coley fillets, cut into 1-inch (2.5 cm) cubes
½ cup (125 ml) natural yogurt
1 tsp (5 ml) crushed garlic
1 tsp (5 ml) grated fresh ginger
1 tsp (5 ml) cayenne pepper
1 tbsp (15 ml) ground coriander
1 tbsp (15 ml) ground cumin
Salt and pepper

For the green onion mash
6 large Desirée or King Edward potatoes, diced
⅔ cup (150 ml) crème fraîche
¼ cup (60 ml) finely chopped fresh coriander leaves
1 red chile, seeded and thinly sliced
4 green onions, thinly sliced
Salt and pepper

Lay the fish cubes in a large, shallow glass or ceramic dish. In a small bowl, mix together the yogurt, garlic, ginger, cayenne, ground coriander and cumin. Season the mixture with salt and pepper to taste and pour over the fish. Cover and leave to marinate in a cool place while you make the mash.

Cook the potatoes in a large saucepan of salted boiling water for 10 minutes or until tender. Drain in a colander and return to the pan. Mash the potatoes and add the crème fraîche. Continue mashing until smooth, then stir in the chopped coriander, chile and green onions. Season to taste with salt and pepper, cover and set aside.

Heat the broiler or barbecue on the hottest setting. Thread the cubes of fish evenly onto 4 metal skewers and cook under the broiler or on the barbecue grill for 8 to 10 minutes, turning once. Serve immediately with the mash and a green salad.

For spinach mash, to serve as an alternative accompaniment, while the potatoes are cooking, heat 2 tbsp (30 ml) oil in a saucepan, add 1 finely chopped onion and 1 finely chopped clove garlic and cook for 5 minutes. Add 1 lb (500 g) chopped spinach leaves and cook, stirring, for 2 minutes or until the spinach just starts to wilt. Stir in 1 tsp (5 ml) ground ginger. Mash the potatoes with the spinach mixture and ¼ cup (60 ml) milk. Season to taste with salt and pepper.

MOROCCAN GRILLED SARDINES

Serves 4
Preparation time 10 minutes
Cooking time 6–8 minutes

12 sardines, cleaned and gutted
2 tbsp (30 ml) harissa
2 tbsp (30 ml) olive oil
Juice of 1 lemon
Salt and pepper
Chopped fresh coriander, to garnish
Lemon wedges, to serve

Heat the broiler on the hottest setting. Rinse the sardines and pat dry with paper towels. Make 3 deep slashes on both sides of each fish with a sharp knife.

Mix the harissa with the oil and lemon juice to make a thin paste. Rub into the sardines on both sides. Put the sardines on a lightly oiled baking sheet. Cook under preheated broiler for 3 to 4 minutes on each side, depending on their size, or until cooked through. Season to taste with salt and pepper and serve immediately, garnished with coriander and with lemon wedges for squeezing over.

For baked sardines with pesto, line a medium ovenproof dish with 2 sliced tomatoes and 2 sliced onions. Prepare the sardines as above, then rub ¼ cup (60 ml) pesto over the fish and arrange in a single layer on top of the tomatoes and onions. Cover with foil and bake in a preheated 400°F (200°C) oven for 20 to 25 minutes or until the fish is cooked through.

RED SALMON & ROASTED VEGETABLES

Serves 4
Preparation time 10 minutes
Cooking time 25 minutes

1 eggplant, cut into bite-size pieces
2 red bell peppers, cored, seeded and cut into bite-size
    pieces
2 red onions, quartered
1 clove garlic, crushed
¼ cup (60 ml) olive oil
Pinch of dried oregano
Salt and pepper
7-oz (200 g) can red salmon, drained and flaked
3½ oz (100 g) pitted black olives
Fresh basil leaves, to garnish

In a bowl, mix together the eggplant, red bell peppers, onions and garlic with the oil and oregano and season well with salt and pepper.

Spread the vegetables out in a single layer in a nonstick roasting pan and roast in a preheated 425°F (220°C) oven for 25 minutes or until the vegetables are just cooked.

Transfer the vegetables to a warmed serving dish and gently toss in the salmon and olives. Serve warm or at room temperature, garnished with basil leaves.

For arugula & cucumber couscous to serve with the salmon and vegetables, put 1 cup (250 ml) instant couscous in a large, heatproof bowl. Season well with salt and pepper and pour in boiling water to just cover the couscous. Cover and leave to stand for 10 to 12 minutes, until all the water has been absorbed. Meanwhile, finely chop 4 green onions, halve, seed and chop ½ cucumber and chop 3 oz (75 g) arugula leaves. Fluff up the couscous grains with a fork and tip into a warmed serving dish. Stir in the prepared ingredients with 2 tbsp (30 ml) olive oil and 1 tbsp (15 ml) lemon juice. Toss well to mix and serve with the salmon and vegetables.

209

CREAMY SHRIMP CURRY

Serves 4
Preparation time 10 minutes
Cooking time about 10 minutes

2 tbsp (30 ml) vegetable oil
1 onion, halved and finely sliced
2 cloves garlic, finely sliced
1-inch (2.5 cm) piece fresh ginger, peeled and finely
  chopped
1 tbsp (15 ml) ground coriander
1 tbsp (15 ml) ground cumin
$\frac{1}{2}$ tsp (2 ml) ground turmeric
$\frac{3}{4}$ cup + 2 tbsp (200 ml) coconut milk
$\frac{1}{2}$ cup (125 ml) vegetable stock
1 lb 3 oz (600 g) frozen large cooked, peeled shrimp,
  defrosted
Grated zest and juice of 1 lime
$\frac{1}{4}$ cup (60 ml) finely chopped fresh coriander leaves
Salt and pepper

Heat the oil in a large saucepan; add the onion, garlic and ginger and cook for 4 to 5 minutes. Add the ground coriander, cumin and turmeric and cook, stirring, for 1 minute.

Pour in the coconut milk and stock and bring to a boil. Reduce the heat and simmer for 2 to 3 minutes. Stir in the shrimp and lime zest and juice, then simmer for 2 minutes or until the shrimp are heated through.

Stir in the chopped coriander and season well with salt and pepper. Serve immediately with boiled basmati or jasmine rice.

For spiced coconut rice to serve with the curry, rinse 1 $\frac{1}{2}$ cups (375 ml) basmati rice in cold water until the water runs clear. Drain and put in a large, heavy-bottomed saucepan. Dissolve 4 oz (125 g) chopped creamed coconut in 3 cups (750 ml) boiling water and add to the rice with a 3-inch (7 cm) piece of lemongrass, halved lengthwise, 2 pieces (each 1 inch/2.5 cm) of cinnamon stick, 1 tsp (5 ml) salt, and pepper to taste. Bring the rice to a boil, then cover and cook for 10 minutes, until almost all the liquid has been absorbed. Turn off the heat and leave to stand for 10 minutes, until the rice is tender. Fluff up with a fork before serving with the curry.

THAI-STYLE COCONUT MUSSELS

Serves 4
Preparation time 20 minutes
Cooking time about 10 minutes

4 lb (2 kg) fresh, live mussels
2$\frac{1}{3}$ cups (575 ml) vegetable stock
14-oz (400 ml) can coconut milk
Grated zest and juice of 2 limes
2 stalks lemongrass, lightly bruised, plus extra stalks to
  garnish (optional)
1 tbsp (15 ml) Thai green curry paste
3 red chiles, seeded and finely sliced
$\frac{1}{4}$ cup (60 ml) chopped fresh coriander leaves, plus
  extra to garnish (optional)
2 green onions, shredded
Salt and pepper
1 red chile, seeded and chopped (optional)

Scrub the mussels in cold water, scrape off any barnacles and pull away the hairy beards that protrude from the shells. Discard any mussels with broken shells or any open mussels that do not close when tapped sharply.

Pour the stock and coconut milk into a large saucepan and bring to a boil. Stir in the lime zest and juice, lemongrass, curry paste, chiles, coriander and green onions. Season to taste with salt and pepper.

Add the mussels, cover and return to a boil. Cook for 3 to 4 minutes or until all the mussels have opened. Discard any shells that remain closed. Use a slotted spoon to divide the mussels between 4 serving bowls and keep warm until ready to serve.

Bring the liquid to a vigorous boil and boil rapidly for 5 minutes or until reduced. Strain through a fine sieve, then ladle over the mussels. Garnish with chopped red chile, chopped coriander leaves and lemongrass stalks.

For homemade Thai green curry paste, put 15 small green chiles, 4 halved cloves garlic, 2 finely chopped lemongrass stalks, 2 torn lime leaves, 2 chopped shallots, $\frac{3}{4}$ cup (175 ml) coriander leaves, stalks and roots, a 1-inch (2.5 cm) piece of fresh ginger, peeled and finely chopped, 2 tsp (10 ml) black peppercorns, 1 tsp (5 ml) pared lime zest, $\frac{1}{2}$ tsp (2 ml) salt and 1 tbsp (15 ml) peanut oil into a food processor or blender and process to a thick paste. Alternatively, use a pestle and mortar to crush the ingredients, working in the oil at the end. Transfer the paste to an airtight container; it can be stored in a refrigerator for up to 3 weeks.

TROUT WITH CUCUMBER RELISH

Serves 4
Preparation time 10 minutes
Cooking time 10–12 minutes

4 rainbow trout, cleaned and gutted
1 tbsp (15 ml) toasted sesame oil
Crushed Szechuan pepper, to taste
Salt

For the cucumber relish
1 cucumber, about 8 inches (20 cm) long
2 tsp (10 ml) salt
¼ cup (60 ml) rice vinegar
3 tbsp (45 ml) granulated or fruit sugar
1 red chile, seeded and sliced
1¼-inch (3 cm) piece fresh ginger, peeled and grated
¼ cup (60 ml) cold water

To garnish
Chopped fresh chives
Lemon wedges

For the cucumber relish, cut the cucumber in half lengthwise, scoop out and discard the seeds and cut the flesh into ½-inch (1 cm) slices. Put in a glass or ceramic bowl. In a small bowl, put the salt, vinegar, sugar, chile and ginger. Add the water and mix well. Pour mixture over the cucumber, cover and leave to marinate at room temperature while you cook the trout.

Brush the trout with the oil and season to taste with crushed Szechuan pepper and salt. Place the trout in a single layer on a broiler rack and grill or broil for 5 to 6 minutes on each side or until cooked through. Leave to rest for a few moments, then garnish with chopped chives and serve with the cucumber relish and lemon wedges.

For trout with ground almond dressing, brush the trout with 1 tbsp (15 ml) olive oil and season to taste with salt and pepper. While the trout is cooking as above, put ⅔ cup (150 ml) ground almonds in a small saucepan over medium heat and cook, stirring constantly, until lightly browned. Remove from the heat, add 6 tbsp (90 ml) olive oil, ¼ cup (60 ml) lemon juice and 2 tbsp (30 ml) chopped parsley, and season to taste with salt and pepper. Stir well, then return to the heat for 2 minutes. Pour the dressing over the cooked trout, garnish with parsley sprigs and serve immediately.

TUNA NIÇOISE SPAGHETTI

Serves 4
Preparation time 10 minutes
Cooking time 10 minutes

4 eggs
11½ oz (350 g) dried spaghetti
3 cans (6½ oz/170 ml each) tuna in brine, drained
1 cup (250 ml) green beans, trimmed and blanched
2 oz (60 g) kalamata olives, pitted
3½ oz (100 g) semi-dried tomatoes
1 tsp (5 ml) grated lemon zest
2 tbsp (30 ml) lemon juice
3 tbsp (45 ml) capers
Salt and pepper

Put the eggs in a saucepan of cold water and bring to a boil. Cook for 10 minutes, then plunge into cold water to cool. Shell the eggs, then roughly chop and set aside.

Meanwhile, cook the pasta in a large saucepan of salted boiling water according to the package instructions, until al dente.

Mix together the tuna, beans, olives, semi-dried tomatoes, lemon zest and juice and capers in a bowl. Season to taste with pepper.

Drain the pasta and return to the pan. Add the tuna mixture and gently toss to combine. Serve immediately, garnished with the eggs.

For tuna, pea & corn rice, cook 1 cup (250 ml) easy-cook basmati rice in a large saucepan of lightly salted boiling water for 12 to 15 minutes or until tender. Drain, refresh under cold running water and drain again. Meanwhile, cook the eggs as above, then shell and cut into quarters. In a separate saucepan, cook ½ cup (125 ml) frozen corn and ½ cup (125 ml) frozen peas in salted boiling water for 5 minutes or until tender. Drain, refresh under cold running water and drain again. In a large bowl, mix together the rice, corn and peas, together with the tuna and olives, as above, and 2 tbsp (30 ml) chopped fresh basil. Whisk together 2 tbsp (30 ml) lemon juice, 1 tbsp (15 ml) olive oil and 1 crushed clove garlic, add to the rice and toss well to coat. Serve garnished with the egg quarters.

TUNA & CORN PILAF

Serves 4
Preparation time 10 minutes
Cooking time 15–20 minutes

2 tbsp (30 ml) olive oil
1 onion, chopped
1 red bell pepper, cored, seeded and diced
1 clove garlic, crushed
1½ cups (375 ml) easy-cook long-grain rice
3 cups (750 ml) chicken stock
Salt and pepper
10-oz (284 ml) can corn niblets, drained
6½-oz (170 ml) can tuna in spring water, drained
6 chopped green onions, to garnish

Heat the oil in a saucepan; add the onion, red bell pepper and garlic and cook until soft. Stir in the rice, then add the stock and season to taste with salt and pepper.

Bring to a boil, then reduce the heat and simmer, stirring occasionally, for 10 to 15 minutes, until all the stock has been absorbed and the rice is tender.

Stir in the corn and tuna and cook briefly over low heat to heat through. Serve immediately, garnished with the green onions.

For picnic pilaf cake, put the cooked rice mixture in a 9-inch (23 cm) square nonstick cake pan. In a bowl, beat 4 eggs with ¼ cup (60 ml) finely chopped parsley, season well with salt and pepper and pour over the rice mixture. Bake in a preheated 350°F (180°C) oven for 25 to 30 minutes or until set. Leave to cool, then remove from the pan and serve cut into thick wedges.

LEMON, CHILE & SHRIMP LINGUINE

Serves 4
Preparation time 15 minutes
Cooking time about 10 minutes

12 oz (375 g) dried linguine or spaghetti
1 tbsp (15 ml) butter
1 tbsp (15 ml) olive oil
1 clove garlic, finely chopped
2 green onions, thinly sliced
2 red chiles, seeded and thinly sliced
14½ oz (450 g) frozen large peeled shrimp, defrosted
2 tbsp (30 ml) lemon juice
2 tbsp (30 ml) finely chopped fresh coriander leaves
Salt and pepper

Cook the pasta in a large saucepan of salted boiling water according to the package instructions, until al dente. When the pasta is about half cooked, melt the butter with the oil in a large nonstick frying pan. Add the garlic, green onions and chiles and cook, stirring, for 2 to 3 minutes.

Add the shrimp and cook briefly until heated through. Pour in the lemon juice and stir in the coriander until well mixed, then remove from the heat and set aside.

Drain the pasta and toss it with the shrimp mixture, either in the frying pan (if large enough) or in a large warmed serving bowl. Season well with salt and pepper and serve immediately.

For lime & chile squid noodles, slit the bodies of 14½ oz (450 g) small squid down one side and lay flat on a board, insides up. Using a sharp knife, score the flesh with a criss-cross pattern. Cut any tentacles into small pieces. Cook 12 oz (375 g) dried medium egg noodles in a saucepan of boiling water according to the package instructions, until just tender. Meanwhile, heat 2 tbsp (30 ml) peanut oil in a large nonstick frying pan or wok, add 2 thinly sliced cloves garlic and a 1-inch (2.5 cm) piece fresh ginger, peeled and chopped, together with the green onions and chiles as above, and stir-fry over high heat for 2 minutes. Add the squid and stir-fry for 2 to 3 minutes. Add the juice of 1 lime, 2 tbsp (30 ml) dark soy sauce, 1 tbsp (15 ml) Thai fish sauce and 2 tbsp (30 ml) finely chopped coriander leaves, stir briefly, then remove from the heat. Drain the noodles, toss with the squid mixture and serve immediately.

SPICED CALAMARI WITH PARSLEY SALAD

Serves 4

Preparation time 15 minutes, plus standing

Cooking time about 5 minutes

1 cup (250 ml) chickpea flour

1½ tsp (7 ml) paprika

1½ tsp (7 ml) ground cumin

½ tsp (2 ml) baking powder

¼ tsp (1 ml) pepper

1 cup (250 ml) soda water

Salt

Vegetable oil, for deep-frying

6 whole squid, cleaned and cut into ½-inch (1 cm) thick
  rings

For the parsley salad

¼ cup (60 ml) lemon juice

¼ cup (60 ml) olive oil

2 cloves garlic, finely chopped

½ cup (125 ml) flat-leaf (Italian) parsley

1 red onion, halved and thinly sliced

2 tomatoes, roughly chopped

Sift the chickpea flour, paprika, cumin and baking powder into a bowl, add the pepper and mix together. Make a well in the center. Gradually add the soda water and whisk until it is a smooth batter. Season to taste with salt. Cover and leave to stand for 30 minutes.

Meanwhile, for the salad dressing, in a bowl, whisk together the lemon juice, olive oil and garlic.

Fill a deep, heavy-bottomed saucepan one-third full with vegetable oil and heat until a cube of bread browns in 15 seconds. Dip the squid rings in the batter, add to the oil, in batches, and cook for 30 to 60 seconds, until golden brown. Remove with a slotted spoon and drain on paper towels.

Add the parsley, red onion and tomatoes to the dressing and toss well to mix. Top with the battered squid and serve immediately.

For pan-fried squid with chile, slit the bodies of the squid down one side and lay flat, insides up. Using a sharp knife, score the flesh with a criss-cross pattern. Cut any tentacles into small pieces. In a bowl, mix together 2 tbsp (30 ml) olive oil, 3 crushed cloves garlic, 1 finely chopped red chile and ¼ cup (60 ml) lemon juice. Add the squid, cover and leave to marinate in a cool place for 15 minutes. Remove the squid from the marinade. Heat 2 tbsp (30 ml) olive oil in a frying pan until just smoking. Add the squid and season to taste with salt and pepper. Cook, stirring, over high heat for 2 to 3 minutes, until browned. Strain the marinade and stir into the pan with 2 tbsp (30 ml) finely chopped flat-leaf (Italian) parsley.

EGG POTS WITH SMOKED SALMON

Serves 4
Preparation time 5 minutes
Cooking time 10–15 minutes

7 oz (200 g) smoked salmon trimmings
2 tbsp (30 ml) chopped fresh chives
4 eggs
Pepper
¼ cup (60 ml) whipping (35%) cream
Toasted bread, to serve

Divide the smoked salmon and chives between 4 buttered ramekins. Make a small indent in the salmon with the back of a spoon and break an egg into the hollow, sprinkle with a little pepper and spoon the cream over the top.

Put the ramekins in a roasting pan and half-fill the pan with boiling water. Bake in a preheated 350°F (180°C) oven for 10 to 15 minutes or until the eggs have just set.

Remove from the oven and leave to cool for a few minutes, then serve with the toasted bread.

For homemade Melba toast to serve with the baked egg pots, toast 4 slices of bread lightly on both sides. While hot, trim off the crusts, then split the toast in half widthwise. Lay the toast, cut side up, on a baking sheet and bake in the bottom of the oven with the egg pots, until dry.

SESAME SHRIMP WITH BOK CHOY

Serves 4
Preparation time 10 minutes, plus marinating
Cooking time about 3 minutes

1 lb 3 oz (600 g) large frozen peeled shrimp, defrosted
1 tsp (5 ml) toasted sesame oil
2 tbsp (30 ml) light soy sauce
1 tbsp (15 ml) liquid honey
1 tsp (5 ml) grated fresh ginger
1 tsp (5 ml) crushed garlic
1 tbsp (15 ml) lemon juice
Salt and pepper
1 lb (500 g) bok choy
2 tbsp (30 ml) vegetable oil

Put the shrimp in a glass or ceramic bowl. Add the toasted sesame oil, soy sauce, honey, ginger, garlic and lemon juice. Season to taste with salt and pepper and mix well, then cover and leave to marinate in a cool place for 5 to 10 minutes.

Cut the heads of bok choy in half lengthwise, then blanch in a large saucepan of boiling water for 40 to 50 seconds. Drain well, cover and keep warm.

Heat the vegetable oil in a wok or large frying pan. Add the shrimp and marinade and stir-fry over high heat for 2 minutes, until thoroughly hot.

Divide the bok choy between 4 serving plates, then top with the shrimp and any juices from the pan. Serve immediately.

For sesame chicken with broccoli & red bell pepper, use 1 lb 3 oz (600 g) boneless skinless chicken breasts, cut into thin strips, in place of the shrimp. Coat with the marinade as above, then cover and leave to marinate in the refrigerator for 1 to 2 hours. Meanwhile, trim the stalks from 1 bunch of broccoli. Divide the heads into small florets, then peel and diagonally slice the stalks. Blanch the florets and stalks in a large saucepan of salted boiling water for 30 seconds. Drain well, refresh under cold running water and drain again thoroughly. Core, seed and thinly slice 1 large red bell pepper. Heat the oil in the wok or large frying pan as above, add the chicken and marinade and stir-fry over high heat for 2 minutes. Add the broccoli and red bell pepper and stir-fry for a further 2 minutes. Serve immediately.

SHRIMP & CRAB CAKES WITH CHILE JAM

Serves 4
Preparation time 15 minutes, plus cooling and chilling
Cooking time 15 minutes

2 cans (6 oz/175 g) white crab meat
Grated zest and juice of 1 lime
4 green onions, chopped
1 red chile, seeded and finely chopped
1 tsp (5 ml) grated fresh ginger
1 tsp (5 ml) crushed garlic
3 tbsp (45 ml) chopped fresh coriander leaves, plus
    extra leaves to garnish
3 tbsp (45 ml) mayonnaise
2 cups (500 ml) fresh white breadcrumbs
7 oz (200 g) frozen cooked, peeled shrimp, defrosted
Salt and pepper
Vegetable oil, for shallow-frying

For the chile jam
2 red chiles, seeded and finely diced
6 tbsp (90 ml) granulated or fruit sugar
2 tbsp (30 ml) water

Put the crab meat, lime zest and juice, green onions, chile, ginger, garlic, coriander, mayonnaise and breadcrumbs in a food processor and process until well combined. Transfer the mixture to a bowl. Chop the shrimp and fold into the mixture with salt and pepper to taste. Alternatively, the ingredients can be mixed together by hand. Cover and chill while making and cooling the chile jam.

Put all the chile jam ingredients in a small saucepan and heat gently until simmering. Cook for 4 to 5 minutes, until the sugar has dissolved and the mixture has thickened slightly. Leave to cool.

Form the shrimp mixture into 12 cakes.

Heat the oil in a large nonstick frying pan, add the cakes and cook for 3 to 4 minutes on each side or until golden. Drain on paper towels and serve immediately, garnished with coriander leaves. Serve the chile jam spooned over the cakes or separately. A crisp arugula salad or green salad is a good accompaniment.

For coconut coriander sauce to serve as an alternative to the chile jam, put 1 cup (250 ml) coconut milk, 2 tbsp (30 ml) smooth peanut butter, 2 finely chopped green onions, white parts only, 1 crushed clove garlic, 1 finely chopped green chile, 2 tbsp (30 ml) chopped coriander leaves, 1 tbsp (15 ml) lime juice and 1 tsp (5 ml) sugar in a food processor or blender and process until smooth.

SALMON WITH LIME ZUCCHINI

Serves 4
Preparation time 10 minutes
Cooking time 10–15 minutes

4 salmon fillet portions, about 7 oz (200 g) each
1 tbsp (15 ml) prepared English mustard
1 tsp (5 ml) grated fresh ginger
1 tsp (5 ml) crushed garlic
2 tsp (10 ml) liquid honey
1 tbsp (15 ml) light soy sauce or tamari
Salt and pepper

For the lime zucchini
2 tbsp (30 ml) olive oil
1 lb (500 g) zucchini, thinly sliced lengthwise
Grated zest and juice of 1 lime
2 tbsp (30 ml) chopped fresh mint

Lay the salmon fillet portions, skin side down, in a shallow flameproof dish, to fit snugly in a single layer. In a small bowl, mix together the mustard, ginger, garlic, honey and soy sauce or tamari, then spoon evenly over the fillets. Season to taste with salt and pepper.

Heat the broiler on the hottest setting. Cook the salmon fillets under the broiler for 10 to 15 minutes, until lightly charred on top and cooked through.

Meanwhile, to prepare the lime zucchini, heat the oil in a large nonstick frying pan; add the zucchini and cook, stirring frequently, for 5 to 6 minutes or until lightly browned and tender. Stir in the lime zest and juice and mint and season to taste with salt and pepper.

Serve the salmon hot with the zucchini.

For stir-fried green beans to serve in place of the lime zucchini, cut 1 lb (500 g) green beans into 2-inch (5 cm) lengths. Heat 2 tbsp (30 ml) vegetable oil in a wok or large frying pan, add 2 crushed cloves garlic, 1 tsp (5 ml) grated fresh ginger and 2 thinly sliced shallots and stir-fry over medium heat for 1 minute. Add the beans and ½ tsp (2 ml) salt and stir-fry over high heat for 1 minute. Add 1 tbsp (15 ml) light soy sauce and ⅔ cup (150 ml) chicken or vegetable stock and bring to a boil. Reduce the heat and cook, stirring frequently, for a further 4 minutes or until the beans are tender and the liquid has thickened. Season with pepper and serve immediately with the salmon.

CREAMY GARLIC MUSSELS

Serves 4
Preparation time 15 minutes
Cooking time about 8 minutes

3 lb (1.5 kg) fresh, live mussels
1 tbsp (15 ml) butter
1 onion, finely chopped
6 cloves garlic, finely chopped
⅓ cup + 2 tbsp (100 ml) white wine
⅔ cup (150 ml) table (18%) or half-and-half (10%)
  cream
Large handful of flat-leaf (Italian) parsley, roughly
  chopped
Salt and pepper

Scrub the mussels in cold water, scrape off any barnacles and pull away the dark, hairy beards that protrude from the shells. Discard any mussels with broken shells or any open mussels that do not close when tapped sharply.

Melt the butter in a large saucepan; add the onion and garlic and cook for 2 to 3 minutes, until transparent and softened.

Increase the heat and tip in the mussels with the wine, then cover and cook for 3 minutes or until all the shells have opened. Discard any that remain closed.

Pour in the cream and heat through briefly, stirring well. Add the parsley, season well with salt and pepper and serve immediately in large bowls, with crusty bread to mop up the juices.

For mussels in spicy tomato sauce, cook the onion and garlic in 1 tbsp (15 ml) olive oil instead of the butter, together with 1 seeded and finely chopped red chile. Add 1 tsp (5 ml) paprika and cook, stirring, for 1 minute, then add a 14-oz (398 ml) can chopped tomatoes. Season to taste with salt and pepper, cover and simmer gently for 15 minutes. Meanwhile, clean the mussels as in the first stage above. Stir the mussels into the tomato sauce and increase the heat. Cover and cook for 3 minutes or until all the shells have opened. Discard any that remain closed. Add the parsley and serve as above.

CARROT, PEA & BROAD BEAN RISOTTO

Serves 4
Preparation time 15 minutes
Cooking time about 25 minutes

¼ cup (60 ml) butter
2 tbsp (30 ml) olive oil
1 large onion, finely chopped
2 carrots, finely chopped
2 cloves garlic, finely chopped
1½ cups (375 ml) risotto rice
¾ cup + 2 tbsp (200 ml) white wine
6 cups (1.5 L) vegetable stock, heated to simmering
7 oz (200 g) frozen peas, defrosted
3½ oz (100 g) frozen broad or fava beans, defrosted and peeled
2 oz (60 g) Parmesan cheese, finely grated
Handful of flat-leaf (Italian) parsley, roughly chopped
Salt and pepper

Melt the butter with the oil in a saucepan; add the onion, carrots and garlic and cook for about 3 minutes, until soft. Add the rice and stir until coated with the butter mixture. Add the wine and cook rapidly, stirring, until it has evaporated.

Add the hot stock, a ladleful at a time, and cook, stirring constantly, until each addition has been absorbed before adding the next. Continue until all the stock has been absorbed and the rice is creamy and cooked but still retains a little bite – this will take around 15 minutes.

Add the peas and beans and heat through for 3 to 5 minutes. Remove from the heat and stir in the Parmesan and parsley. Season to taste with salt and pepper and serve immediately.

For Italian-style risotto balls, leave the risotto to cool, then chill overnight in the refrigerator. Form the chilled mixture into walnut-sized balls. Beat 2 eggs together in a shallow bowl. Roll the rice balls through the egg, then in ¾ cup (175 ml) dried breadcrumbs to coat. Fill a deep, heavy-bottomed saucepan one-third full with vegetable oil and heat to 350° to 375°F (180° to 190°C) or until a cube of bread browns in 30 seconds. Add the rice balls, in batches, and cook for 2 to 3 minutes, until golden. Remove with a slotted spoon, drain on paper towels and serve.

PASTA WITH TOMATO & BASIL SAUCE

Serves 4
Preparation time 10 minutes
Cooking time 10 minutes

13 oz (400 g) dried spaghetti
5 tbsp (75 ml) olive oil
5 cloves garlic, finely chopped
6 vine-ripened tomatoes, seeded and chopped
¾ cup (175 ml) fresh basil leaves
Salt and pepper

Cook the pasta in a large saucepan of salted boiling water according to the package instructions.

Meanwhile, heat the oil in a frying pan, add the garlic and cook over low heat for 1 minute. As soon as the garlic begins to change color, remove the pan from the heat.

Drain the pasta and return to the pan. Add the garlic oil with the chopped tomatoes and basil leaves. Season to taste with salt and pepper and toss well to mix. Serve immediately.

For quick tomato & basil pizza, prepare the garlic oil as above, but use ¼ cup (60 ml) oil and 4 cloves garlic. Meanwhile, peel the tomatoes and seed and chop them as above. Pour off half the oil and reserve, add the tomatoes and half the basil to the pan, season well and leave to simmer while you make the dough. Sift 2 cups (500 ml) self-raising flour and 1 tsp (5 ml) salt into a large bowl, then gradually add ⅔ cup (150 ml) warm water, mixing well to form a soft dough. Work the dough into a ball with your hands. Knead on a lightly floured surface until smooth and soft. Roll out the dough to a 12-inch (30 cm) round, making the edge slightly thicker than the center, and lay on a warmed baking sheet. Spread the tomato mixture over the dough base, top with 4 oz (125 g) sliced mozzarella cheese and drizzle with the remaining garlic oil. Bake in a preheated 475°F (240°C) oven for 15 minutes or until the bottom is golden. Scatter with the remaining basil leaves and serve immediately.

SUMMER VEGETABLE FETTUCCINE

Serves 4
Preparation time 10 minutes
Cooking time 15 minutes

8 oz (250 g) asparagus, trimmed and cut into 2-inch
   (5 cm) lengths
4 oz (125 g) sugar snap peas
13 oz (400 g) dried fettuccine or pappardelle
7 oz (200 g) baby zucchini
5 oz (150 g) button mushrooms
1 tbsp (15 ml) olive oil
1 small onion, finely chopped
1 clove garlic, finely chopped
¼ cup (60 ml) lemon juice
2 tsp (10 ml) chopped fresh tarragon
2 tsp (10 ml) chopped fresh parsley
3½ oz (100 g) smoked mozzarella cheese, diced
Salt and pepper

Cook the asparagus and sugar snap peas in a saucepan of boiling water for 3 to 4 minutes, then drain and refresh under cold running water. Drain well and set aside.

Cook the pasta in a large saucepan of salted boiling water according to the package instructions, until al dente.

Meanwhile, halve the zucchini lengthwise and cut the mushrooms in half. Heat the oil in a large frying pan; add the onion and garlic and cook for 2 to 3 minutes. Add the zucchini and mushrooms and cook, stirring, for 3 to 4 minutes. Stir in the asparagus and sugar snap peas and cook for 1 to 2 minutes before adding the lemon juice and herbs.

Drain the pasta and return to the pan. Add the vegetable mixture and mozzarella and season to taste with salt and pepper. Toss gently to mix, and serve.

For cheesy garlic bread to serve with the pasta, cut a baguette into 1-inch (2.5 cm) thick slices, cutting almost through to the bottom crust but keeping the slices together at the bottom. In a bowl, beat ½ cup (125 ml) softened butter with 1 crushed clove garlic, 1½ tbsp (22 ml) finely chopped fresh parsley and 1 cup (250 ml) finely grated Parmesan cheese. Spread the butter on either side of the bread slices and over the top of the loaf. Wrap tightly in foil, place on a baking sheet and bake in a preheated 375°F (190°C) oven for 15 minutes. Carefully open up the foil and fold back, then bake for a further 5 minutes. Cut into slices and serve hot.

RED PEPPER & CHEESE TORTELLINI

Serves 4
Preparation time 10 minutes, plus cooling
Cooking time 15 minutes

2 red bell peppers
2 cloves garlic, chopped
8 green onions, finely sliced
1 lb (500 g) fresh cheese-stuffed tortellini or any other
   fresh stuffed tortellini
¾ cup (175 ml) olive oil
1 oz (30 g) Parmesan cheese, finely grated
Salt and pepper

Cut the peppers into large pieces, removing the cores and seeds. Lay, skin side up, under a preheated broiler and cook until the skin blackens and blisters. Transfer to a plastic bag, tie the top to enclose and leave to cool, then peel away the skin.

Place the peppers and garlic in a food processor and blend until fairly smooth. Stir in the green onions and set aside.

Cook the tortellini in a large saucepan of boiling water according to the package instructions, until al dente. Drain and return to the pan.

Toss the pepper mixture into the pasta and add the oil and Parmesan. Season to taste with salt and pepper and serve immediately.

For warm ham & red bell pepper tortellini salad, broil and peel the red bell peppers as above, then thinly slice. While the tortellini are cooking, thinly slice 1 red onion. Drain the pasta and toss with 4 oz (125 g) chopped cooked ham, 7 oz (200 g) arugula leaves and the onion and red bell peppers. Serve immediately.

ZUCCHINI & HERB RISOTTO

Serves 4
Preparation time 10 minutes
Cooking time about 20 minutes

¼ cup (60 ml) butter
2 tbsp (30 ml) olive oil
1 large onion, finely chopped
2 cloves garlic, finely chopped
1½ cups (375 ml) risotto rice
¾ cup + 2 tbsp (200 ml) white wine
6 cups (1.5 L) vegetable stock, heated to simmering
7 oz (200 g) baby spinach, chopped
3½ oz (100 g) zucchini, finely diced
2 oz (60 g) Parmesan cheese, finely grated
Small handful of fresh dill, mint and chives, roughly
   chopped
Salt and pepper

Melt the butter with the oil in a saucepan; add the onion and garlic and cook for about 3 minutes, until soft. Add the rice and stir until coated with the butter mixture. Add the wine and cook rapidly, stirring, until it has evaporated.

Add the hot stock, a ladleful at a time, and cook, stirring constantly, until each addition has been absorbed before adding the next. Continue until all the stock has been absorbed and the rice is creamy and cooked but still retains a little bite – this will take around 15 minutes.

Stir in the spinach and zucchini and heat through for 3 to 5 minutes. Remove from the heat and stir in the Parmesan and herbs. Season to taste with salt and pepper and serve immediately.

For zucchini & carrot risotto, cook the onion and garlic in the butter and oil as above, but add 2 finely chopped celery stalks and 3 small diced carrots. Continue with the recipe above until the end of the second stage. Meanwhile, cut 3 zucchini into ½-inch (1 cm) cubes. Add the zucchini to the risotto and heat through for 3 to 5 minutes. Remove from the heat and stir in 1 tbsp (15 ml) chopped fresh basil with the Parmesan. Season to taste with salt and pepper and serve immediately.

MIXED BEAN KEDGEREE

Serves 4
Preparation time 10 minutes
Cooking time 15–20 minutes

2 tbsp (30 ml) olive oil
1 onion, chopped
2 tbsp (30 ml) mild curry powder
1 cup (250 ml) long-grain rice
3 cups (750 ml) vegetable stock
4 eggs
2 cans (14 oz/398 ml) mixed beans, drained
   and rinsed
⅔ cup (150 ml) sour cream
Salt and pepper
2 tomatoes, finely chopped, to garnish
Flat-leaf (Italian) parsley, to garnish

Heat the oil in a saucepan, add the onion and cook until soft. Stir in the curry powder and rice. Add the stock and season to taste with salt and pepper. Bring to a boil, then reduce the heat, cover and simmer, stirring occasionally, for 10 to 15 minutes, until all the stock has been absorbed and the rice is tender.

Meanwhile, put the eggs in a saucepan of cold water and bring to a boil. Cook for 10 minutes, then plunge into cold water to cool. Shell the eggs, then cut them into wedges.

Stir the beans and sour cream through the rice and cook briefly over low heat to heat through. Serve garnished with the eggs, tomatoes and parsley.

For chicken & pineapple pilaf, follow the first stage of the recipe above, but stir in 2 tsp (10 ml) ground turmeric with the curry powder and use chicken stock in place of the vegetable stock. Stir 13 oz (400 g) chopped cooked chicken breast and an 8-oz (250 g) can pineapple pieces in natural juice, drained, into the rice with the sour cream and cook briefly over low heat to heat through. Serve garnished with 3 tbsp (45 ml) chopped coriander leaves.

PAPPARDELLE PUTTANESCA

Serves 4
Preparation time 10 minutes
Cooking time 15 minutes

2 tbsp (30 ml) olive oil
1 onion, chopped
2 red chiles, seeded and finely chopped
2 cloves garlic, crushed
1 tbsp (15 ml) capers
2 cans (14 oz/398 ml) chopped tomatoes
3½ oz (100 g) pitted black olives
2-oz (60 g) can anchovy fillets in oil, drained
13 oz (400 g) dried pappardelle or fettuccine
1 oz (30 g) Parmesan cheese, finely grated
Salt and pepper

Heat the oil in a saucepan; add the onion, chiles and garlic and cook until soft. Add the capers, tomatoes, olives and anchovies, cover tightly and simmer for 10 minutes. Season to taste with salt and pepper.

Meanwhile, cook the pasta in a large saucepan of salted boiling water according to the package instructions, until al dente.

Drain the pasta. Serve immediately topped with the sauce and the Parmesan.

For tuna & olive pasta sauce, cook the onion and garlic as above but with ½ tsp (2 ml) hot pepper flakes instead of the chiles. Then, in place of the anchovies, add a 6-oz (175 g) can tuna in oil, drained and flaked, to the pan with the capers, tomatoes and olives. Simmer for 10 minutes, then stir in ¾ cup + 2 tbsp (200 ml) half-fat crème fraîche and season to taste with salt and pepper just before serving on top of the drained pasta. Scatter with the Parmesan and 1 tbsp (15 ml) finely chopped parsley.

CREAMY BLUE CHEESE PASTA

Serves 4
Preparation time 10 minutes
Cooking time 10 minutes

12 oz (375 g) dried pasta shells
2 tbsp (30 ml) olive oil
6 green onions, thinly sliced
5 oz (150 g) dolcelatte or other creamy blue cheese, diced
7 oz (200 g) cream cheese
Salt and pepper
3 tbsp (45 ml) chopped fresh chives, to garnish

Cook the pasta shells in a large saucepan of salted boiling water according to the package instructions, until al dente.

Meanwhile, heat the oil in a large frying pan, add the green onions and cook over medium heat for 2 to 3 minutes. Add the cheeses and stir while they blend into a smooth sauce.

Drain the pasta shells and transfer to a warmed serving bowl. Stir in the sauce and season to taste with salt and pepper. Sprinkle with the chives and serve immediately.

For cheese & leek phyllo parcels, fry 3 leeks, thinly sliced, until soft and starting to brown, then leave to cool. Mix with the cheeses as above and 3 tbsp (45 ml) chives. Melt ⅓ cup (75 ml) butter in a saucepan. Put 8 sheets of phyllo pastry on a plate and cover with a damp dish towel. Working with 1 pastry sheet at a time, cut into 3 equal strips and brush well with melted butter. Put 1 tsp (5 ml) of the cheese mixture at one end of each strip. Fold one corner diagonally over to enclose and continue folding to the end of the strip to make a triangular parcel. Brush with melted butter and lay on a baking sheet. Repeat with the remaining cheese mixture and pastry to make about 24 small parcels. Bake in a preheated 425°F (220°C) oven for 8 to 10 minutes, until golden brown. Serve hot.

PASTA WITH EGGPLANT & PINE NUTS

Serves 4
Preparation time 10 minutes
Cooking time 15 minutes

8 tbsp (120 ml) olive oil
2 eggplants, diced
2 red onions, sliced
3 oz (75 g) pine nuts
3 cloves garlic, crushed
5 tbsp (75 ml) sun-dried tomato paste
⅔ cup (150 ml) vegetable stock
10 oz (300 g) cracked pepper-, tomato- or mushroom-
    flavoured fresh ribbon pasta
3½ oz (100 g) pitted black olives
Salt and pepper
3 tbsp (45 ml) roughly chopped flat-leaf (Italian) parsley,
    to garnish

Heat the oil in a large frying pan; add the eggplant and onions and cook for 8 to 10 minutes, until tender and golden. Add the pine nuts and garlic and cook, stirring, for 2 minutes. Stir in the sun-dried tomato paste and stock and simmer for 2 minutes.

Meanwhile, cook the pasta in a large saucepan of salted boiling water for 2 minutes or until al dente.

Drain the pasta and return to the pan. Add the vegetable mixture and olives, season to taste with salt and pepper and toss together over medium heat for 1 minute, until combined. Serve scattered with the chopped parsley.

For potato-topped eggplant & tomato casserole, cook 4 potatoes in a large saucepan of salted boiling water until just tender. Meanwhile, follow the first stage of the recipe above, but omit the pine nuts and add just 2 tbsp (30 ml) sun-dried tomato paste together with 3 large peeled and chopped tomatoes and the stock. Simmer for 5 minutes, then slice the olives and stir into the mixture. Transfer to a shallow ovenproof dish. Drain the potatoes, cut into slices and arrange, overlapping, on top of the vegetable mixture. Sprinkle with ¼ cup (60 ml) finely grated Parmesan cheese and bake in a preheated 400°F (200°C) oven for 35 to 40 minutes, until golden brown on top.

LEBANESE LENTIL & BULGUR SALAD

Serves 4
Preparation time 10 minutes
Cooking time 30 minutes

½ cup (125 ml) Puy lentils
1 tbsp (15 ml) tomato purée
3 cups (750 ml) vegetable stock
½ cup (125 ml) bulgur wheat
Juice of 1 lemon
Salt and pepper
1 tbsp (15 ml) olive oil
2 onions, sliced
1 tsp (5 ml) granulated sugar
1 bunch fresh mint, chopped
3 tomatoes, finely chopped

Put the lentils, tomato purée and stock in a saucepan and bring to a boil. Reduce the heat, cover tightly and simmer for 20 minutes. Add the bulgur wheat and lemon juice and season to taste with salt and pepper. Cook for 10 minutes, until all the stock has been absorbed.

Meanwhile, heat the oil in a frying pan; add the onions and sugar and cook over low heat until deep brown and caramelized.

Stir the mint into the lentil and bulgur wheat mixture, then serve warm, topped with the fried onions and chopped tomato.

For Lebanese-style chicken salad, season 3 chicken breasts with salt and pepper. Brush each one with a little olive oil and place on a very hot grill pan. Cook for 4 to 5 minutes on each side or until cooked through and lightly charred on the edges. Cut the breasts into thin slices and stir into the lentil salad above with 1 finely chopped cucumber and 10 to 12 sliced radishes.

GOLDEN MUSHROOM & LEEK PIES

Serves 4
Preparation time 15 minutes
Cooking time 25–30 minutes

2 tbsp (30 ml) butter
2 leeks, thinly sliced
10 oz (300 g) cremini mushrooms, quartered
10 oz (300 g) button mushrooms, quartered
1 tbsp (15 ml) all-purpose flour
1 cup (250 ml) milk
2/3 cup (150 ml) whipping (35%) cream
3 1/2 oz (100 g) strong Cheddar cheese, grated
1/4 cup (60 ml) finely chopped fresh parsley
2 sheets of ready-rolled puff pastry, defrosted
   if frozen
1 egg, beaten

Melt the butter in a large saucepan; add the leeks and cook for 1 to 2 minutes. Add the mushrooms and cook for 2 minutes. Stir in the flour and cook, stirring, for 1 minute, then gradually add the milk and cream and cook, stirring constantly, until the mixture thickens. Add the Cheddar and the parsley and cook, stirring, for 1 to 2 minutes. Remove from the heat.

Cut 4 rounds from the pastry sheets to cover 4 individual pie dishes. Divide the mushroom mixture between the pie dishes. Brush the rims with the beaten egg, then place the pastry rounds on top. Press down around the rims and crimp the edges with a fork. Cut a couple of slits in the top of each pie to let the steam out. Brush the pastry with the remaining egg.

Bake in a preheated 425°F (220°C) oven for 15 to 20 minutes, until the pastry is golden brown. Serve immediately.

For curried ham & mushroom pies, follow the first stage above, but after cooking the mushrooms add 1 tsp (5 ml) medium curry powder and 1/2 tsp (2 ml) ground turmeric to the pan and cook, stirring, for 1 minute, before adding the flour and continuing with the recipe. Once the sauce has thickened, stir in 7 oz (200 g) cooked ham, cut into small, bite-size pieces, in place of the Cheddar and 1/4 cup (60 ml) chopped coriander leaves instead of the parsley. Make and bake the pies as above.

GRILLED CHICORY WITH SALSA VERDE

Serves 4
Preparation time 15 minutes
Cooking time 10 minutes

4 heads of chicory or Belgian endive, about 5 oz
   (150 g) each, trimmed and halved lengthwise
2 tbsp (30 ml) olive oil
4 oz (125 g) Parmesan cheese, coarsely grated
Chopped fresh parsley, to garnish

For the salsa verde
2 bunches flat-leaf (Italian) parsley
2 oz (60 g) pine nuts, toasted
2 gherkin pickles
8 pitted green olives
1 clove garlic, chopped
1 tbsp (15 ml) lemon juice
2/3 cup (150 ml) olive oil
Salt and pepper

Coarsely purée all the ingredients for the salsa verde, except the oil, in a food processor or blender. With the motor still running, gradually trickle in the oil to make a creamy paste. Transfer to a serving dish, cover and set aside. (The salsa will keep for up to 1 week in the refrigerator.)

Heat the broiler on the hottest setting. Arrange the chicory halves on a grill rack, cut sides down, brush with some of the oil and cook under the broiler for 5 minutes. Turn the chicory halves over, brush with the remaining oil and sprinkle the Parmesan over the top. Cook for a further 4 minutes or until the cheese has melted and the edges of the chicory begin to char.

Transfer the chicory to plates and garnish with chopped parsley. Add a little salsa verde to each plate and serve immediately, offering the remaining salsa verde separately. Toasted ciabatta bread is a good accompaniment.

For grilled sardines with salsa verde, arrange 1 1/2 lbs (750 g) whole, cleaned and gutted sardines in a large, shallow glass or ceramic dish. Whisk together 3 tbsp (45 ml) olive oil, 2 chopped cloves garlic, the grated zest and juice of 1 lemon and 2 tsp (10 ml) dried oregano. Pour over the fish and turn them in the marinade to coat, then cover and leave to marinate in the refrigerator for about 1 hour. Meanwhile, prepare the salsa verde as above. Cook the sardines under a preheated broiler or on a barbecue for 4 to 5 minutes on each side, basting with the marinade. Serve with the salsa verde.

VEGETARIAN

GOAT'S CHEESE & CHIVE SOUFFLÉS

Serves 4
Preparation time 10 minutes
Cooking time 20–25 minutes

2 tbsp (30 ml) unsalted butter
2 tbsp (30 ml) all-purpose flour
1 cup (250 ml) milk
3½ oz (100 g) soft goat's cheese
3 eggs, separated
2 tbsp (30 ml) chopped fresh chives
Salt and pepper

Melt the butter in a saucepan; add the flour and cook over low heat, stirring, for 30 seconds. Remove the pan from the heat and gradually stir in the milk until smooth. Return to the heat and cook, stirring constantly, until the mixture thickens. Cook for 1 minute more.

Leave to cool slightly, then beat in the goat's cheese, egg yolks, chives and salt and pepper to taste.

Whisk the egg whites in a large, perfectly clean bowl, until soft peaks form. Fold the egg whites into the cheese mixture. Spoon the mixture into 4 greased individual soufflé ramekins and set on a baking sheet. Bake in a preheated 400°F (200°C) oven for 15 to 18 minutes, until risen and golden. Serve immediately.

For Cheddar & chile soufflés, use 3½ oz (100 g) grated Cheddar cheese instead of soft goat's cheese and 2 tbsp (30 ml) finely chopped coriander leaves in place of the chives, and also beat 2 finely chopped red chiles, seeded, according to taste, into the egg yolk mixture.

TOMATO & MOZZARELLA TARTLETS

Serves 6
Preparation time 20 minutes
Cooking time 20 minutes

8 oz (250 g) puff pastry, defrosted if frozen
6 tbsp (90 ml) sun-dried tomato paste
3 plum tomatoes, seeded and roughly chopped
4 oz (125 g) mozzarella cheese, roughly diced
8 pitted black olives, roughly chopped
1 clove garlic, finely chopped
2 tbsp (30 ml) roughly chopped fresh oregano
1 tbsp (15 ml) pine nuts
Salt and pepper
Olive oil, for drizzling

Line a large baking sheet with parchment paper. Roll out the pastry on a lightly floured work surface to ⅛-inch (3 mm) thick. Use a 5-inch (12 cm) round cutter to stamp out 6 rounds, and lay them on the prepared baking sheet.

Spread 1 tbsp (15 ml) sun-dried tomato paste over each pastry round. In a small bowl, mix together the tomatoes, mozzarella, olives, garlic, oregano and pine nuts and season well with salt and pepper. Divide the mixture between the pastry rounds.

Drizzle a little olive oil over the tartlets and bake in a preheated 400°F (200°C) oven for 20 minutes or until the pastry is golden. Serve immediately with mixed salad leaves.

For tomato & anchovy tartlets, follow the first stage of the recipe, then spread 1 tbsp (15 ml) pesto over each pastry round instead of the sun-dried tomato paste. In a bowl, mix the tomatoes, olives and garlic, as above, with a 2-oz (60 g) can anchovy fillets in oil, drained and snipped into small pieces, 2 oz (60 g) drained and chopped bottled roasted red peppers in oil and 2 tbsp (30 ml) chopped basil and season well with salt and pepper. Divide between the pastry rounds, drizzle with olive oil and bake as above.

MUSHROOM STROGANOFF

Serves 4
Preparation time 10 minutes
Cooking time 10 minutes

1 tbsp (15 ml) butter
2 tbsp (30 ml) olive oil
1 onion, thinly sliced
4 cloves garlic, finely chopped
1 lb (500 g) cremini mushrooms, sliced
2 tbsp (30 ml) whole-grain mustard
1 cup (250 ml) sour cream
Salt and pepper
3 tbsp (45 ml) chopped fresh parsley, to garnish

Melt the butter with the oil in a large frying pan; add the onion and garlic and cook until soft and starting to brown.

Add the mushrooms to the pan and cook until soft and starting to brown. Stir in the mustard and sour cream and just heat through. Season to taste with salt and pepper, then serve immediately, garnished with the chopped parsley.

For mushroom soup with garlic croutons, while the mushrooms are cooking, remove the crusts from 2 thick slices of day-old white bread and rub with 2 halved cloves garlic. Cut the bread into cubes. Fry the cubes of bread in a shallow depth of vegetable oil in a frying pan, turning constantly, for 5 minutes or until browned all over and crisp. Drain on paper towels. After adding the mustard and sour cream to the mushroom mixture as above, add 1 ^{2}/$_3$ cups (400 ml) boiling hot vegetable stock, then purée the mixture in a food processor or blender until smooth. Serve in warmed bowls, topped with the croutons and garnished with the chopped parsley.

MUSHROOMS À LA GRECQUE

Serves 4
Preparation time 10 minutes, plus standing
Cooking time 10 minutes

8 tbsp (120 ml) olive oil, divided
2 large onions, sliced
3 cloves garlic, finely chopped
1 lb 3½ oz (600 g) button mushrooms, halved
8 plum tomatoes, roughly chopped, or 14-oz (398 ml)
  can chopped tomatoes
3½ oz (100 g) pitted black olives
2 tbsp (30 ml) white wine vinegar
Salt and pepper
Chopped fresh parsley, to garnish

Heat 2 tbsp (30 ml) of the oil in a large frying pan; add the onions and garlic and cook until soft and starting to brown. Add the mushrooms and tomatoes and cook, stirring gently, for 4 to 5 minutes. Remove from the heat.

Transfer the mushroom mixture to a serving dish and garnish with the olives.

Whisk the remaining oil with the vinegar in a small bowl, season to taste with salt and pepper and drizzle over the salad. Garnish with the chopped parsley, cover and leave to stand at room temperature for 30 minutes to allow the flavors to mingle before serving.

For mushroom pasta salad, prepare the mushroom mixture as above. Cook 7 oz (200 g) dried pennette or bowties in a large saucepan of salted boiling water according to the package instructions, until al dente. Meanwhile, cook 1 cup (250 ml) green beans in a saucepan of salted boiling water until just tender. Drain the beans, refresh under cold running water and drain again. Drain the pasta thoroughly and toss with the mushroom mixture, the beans and 2 tbsp (30 ml) torn fresh basil leaves. Serve at room temperature.

SPINACH & POTATO GRATIN

Serves 4
Preparation time 10 minutes
Cooking time 35 minutes

1¼ lb (625 g) potatoes, thinly sliced
1 lb (500 g) spinach leaves
7 oz (200 g) mozzarella cheese, grated
Salt and pepper
4 tomatoes, sliced
3 eggs, beaten
1¼ cups (300 ml) whipping (35%) cream

Cook the potato slices in a large saucepan of salted boiling water for 5 minutes, then drain well.

Meanwhile, cook the spinach in a separate saucepan of boiling water for 1 to 2 minutes. Drain and squeeze out the excess water.

Grease a large ovenproof dish and line the bottom with half the potato slices. Cover with the spinach and half the mozzarella, seasoning each layer well with salt and pepper. Cover with the remaining potato slices and arrange the tomato slices on top. Sprinkle with the remaining mozzarella.

Whisk the eggs and cream together in a bowl and season well with salt and pepper. Pour over the ingredients in the dish.

Bake in a preheated 350°F (180°C) oven for about 30 minutes. Serve immediately with a salad and crusty bread.

For tomato, lime & basil salad to serve as an accompaniment, slice or quarter 2 lb (1 kg) tomatoes while the gratin is baking, and arrange in a large serving bowl. Scatter on ½ red onion, thinly sliced, and a handful of fresh basil leaves. Whisk together ¼ cup (60 ml) olive oil, 2 tbsp (30 ml) chopped basil, 1 tbsp (15 ml) lime juice, 1 tsp (5 ml) grated lime zest, ½ tsp (2 ml) liquid honey, 1 crushed clove garlic, a pinch of cayenne pepper and salt and pepper to taste. Pour over the salad. Cover and leave to stand at room temperature for about 30 minutes to allow the flavors to mingle, then serve with the gratin.

VEGETARIAN

CORN & PEPPER FRITTATA

Serves 4
Preparation time 10 minutes
Cooking time about 10 minutes

2 tbsp (30 ml) olive oil
4 green onions, thinly sliced
7-oz (200 g) can corn niblets, drained
5 oz (150 g) bottled roasted red peppers in oil, drained and cut into strips
4 eggs, lightly beaten
4 oz (125 g) strong Cheddar cheese, grated
Small handful of fresh chives, finely chopped
Salt and pepper

Heat the oil in a frying pan; add the green onions, corn and red peppers and cook for 30 seconds.

Add the eggs, Cheddar, chives and salt and pepper to taste and cook over medium heat for 4 to 5 minutes, until the underside is set. Remove from the stove, place under a preheated broiler and cook for 3 to 4 minutes or until golden and set. Cut into wedges and serve immediately with a green salad and crusty bread.

For zucchini, pepper & Gruyère frittata, use 1⅓ cups (325 ml) finely chopped zucchini instead of the corn and 4 oz (125 g) grated Gruyère cheese in place of the Cheddar and substitute ¼ cup (60 ml) chopped mint leaves for the chives.

STUFFED MUSHROOMS WITH TOFU

Serves 1
Preparation time 15 minutes
Cooking time 20 minutes

1 1/4 cups (300 ml) boiling water
1 tsp (5 ml) organic vegetable bouillon powder
2 large portobello mushrooms, stalks removed
1 tbsp (15 ml) olive oil, divided
1/4 red onion, finely chopped
4 oz (125 g) firm tofu, diced
1 tbsp (15 ml) pine nuts, toasted
1/4 tsp (1 ml) cayenne pepper
1 tbsp (15 ml) chopped fresh basil
Salt and pepper
1 oz (30 g) Parmesan cheese, finely grated
3 oz (90 g) baby spinach leaves

Pour the boiling water into a wide pan, then stir in the bouillon powder. Add the mushrooms and poach for 2 to 3 minutes, then remove with a slotted spoon and drain on paper towels.

Heat a little of the oil in a pan; add the onion and cook until soft. Remove from the heat and leave to cool.

Mix together the onion, tofu, pine nuts, cayenne pepper, basil and the remaining oil. Season well with salt and pepper.

Sprinkle some Parmesan over each mushroom, then stuff the mushrooms with the onion mixture. Arrange in a flameproof dish and cook about 6 inches (15 cm) below a preheated medium broiler for 10 minutes or until heated through and the cheese has melted.

To serve, scatter the spinach leaves on a plate and arrange the hot mushrooms on top.

For baba ghanoush, a Middle Eastern eggplant dip that makes a great accompaniment to this dish, prick 1 eggplant all over with a fork, cut lengthwise in half, then lay, cut side down, on a greased baking sheet. Bake in a preheated 375°F (190°C) oven for 30 to 40 minutes, until softened. When cool enough to handle, peel, then purée in a food processor or blender with 1/2 crushed clove garlic and 1 tsp (5 ml) lemon juice. With the motor still running, gradually trickle in 1 tbsp (15 ml) olive oil to make a creamy paste. Stir in 1 tbsp (15 ml) chopped fresh parsley and season to taste with salt and pepper. Add a generous dollop beside the mushrooms.

GREEK VEGETABLE CASSEROLE

Serves 4
Preparation time 10 minutes
Cooking time 25 minutes

1/4 cup (60 ml) olive oil, divided
1 onion, thinly sliced
3 bell peppers, mixed colors, cored, seeded and sliced
  into rings
4 cloves garlic, crushed
4 tomatoes, chopped
7 oz (200 g) feta cheese, cubed
1 tsp (5 ml) dried oregano
Salt and pepper
Chopped flat-leaf (Italian) parsley, to garnish

Heat 3 tbsp (45 ml) of the oil in a flameproof casserole; add the onion, bell peppers and garlic and cook until soft and starting to brown. Add the tomatoes and cook for a few minutes, until softened. Mix in the feta and oregano, season to taste with salt and pepper and drizzle with the remaining oil.

Cover and cook in a preheated 400°F (200°C) oven for 15 minutes. Garnish with the parsley and serve with warmed crusty bread.

For Middle Eastern vegetable casserole, heat 1 tbsp (15 ml) olive oil in a flameproof casserole; add 1 red onion, cut into wedges, 3 sliced celery stalks and 3 thinly sliced carrots and cook until soft and starting to brown. Add 2 tsp (10 ml) harissa and cook, stirring, for 1 minute. Add about 1 1/4 lb (625 g) eggplant, trimmed and chopped, 2 large chopped tomatoes and 1 cup (250 ml) water. Bring to a boil, then cover and cook in a preheated 350°F (180°C) oven for about 25 minutes. Stir in 2 large potatoes, peeled and thickly sliced, and cook for a further 15 minutes or until tender but still firm. Serve hot, garnished with chopped fresh coriander.

MUSHROOM & BROCCOLI PIE

Serves 4
Preparation time 8 minutes
Cooking time 30 minutes

2½ cups (625 ml) broccoli florets
3 tbsp (45 ml) olive oil
2½ cups (625 ml) trimmed and thickly sliced
mushrooms
5 oz (150 g) Gorgonzola cheese
3 tbsp (45 ml) mascarpone cheese
¼ cup (60 ml) crème fraîche
2 tbsp (30 ml) chopped fresh chives
Salt and pepper
1 large sheet ready-rolled puff pastry, thawed if frozen
1 egg, lightly beaten

Cook the broccoli in lightly salted boiling water for about 2 minutes or until the florets are just beginning to soften.

Meanwhile, heat the oil in a large frying pan and cook the mushrooms over medium heat, stirring occasionally, for about 5 minutes. Stir in the Gorgonzola, mascarpone and crème fraîche. Add the drained broccoli florets and the chives, season with salt and pepper and tip into 4 individual ovenproof dishes or 1 large rectangular ovenproof dish.

Lay the pastry over the filling, pressing it against the sides of the dish to seal. Brush the top with beaten egg and cut two slits. Cook in a preheated 425°F (220°C) oven for about 25 minutes, until the pastry is crisp and golden. Serve immediately.

For puff-crust cauliflower cheese pie, use 2 cups (500 g) cauliflower florets instead of the broccoli and 7 oz (200 g) grated strong Cheddar cheese instead of the Gorgonzola. Omit the mushrooms.

CUMIN LENTILS WITH YOGURT DRESSING

Serves 4
Preparation time 10 minutes
Cooking time 13 minutes

¼ cup (60 ml) olive oil
2 red onions, thinly sliced
2 cloves garlic, chopped
2 tsp (10 ml) cumin seeds
4 cups (1 L) cooked Puy lentils
4 oz (125 g) peppery leaves such as beet or arugula
1 large raw beet, peeled and coarsely grated
1 Granny Smith apple, peeled and coarsely grated (optional)
Lemon juice, to serve
Salt and pepper

Yogurt dressing
1¼ cups (300 ml) Greek yogurt
2 tbsp (30 ml) lemon juice
½ tsp (2 ml) ground cumin
½ cup (125 ml) fresh mint leaves, chopped

Heat the oil in a frying pan and fry the red onions over medium heat for about 8 minutes, until soft and golden. Add the garlic and cumin seeds and cook for a further 5 minutes.

Mix the onion mixture into the lentils, season well and leave to cool.

Make the dressing by mixing together the ingredients in a small bowl.

Serve the cooled lentils on a bed of leaves, with the grated beet and apple (if used), a couple of spoonfuls of minty yogurt and a generous squeeze of lemon juice.

For cumin chickpeas with apricots, use 2 cans (14 oz/398 ml each) chickpeas instead of the lentils. Chop and add 3½ oz (100 g) ready-to-eat dried apricots to replace the beet and apple.

CURRIED DHAL WITH SPINACH

Serves 4
Preparation time 5 minutes
Cooking time 15 minutes

2 cups (500 ml) red lentils
7 tbsp (105 ml) butter
1 onion, sliced
1 clove garlic, crushed
2 tbsp (30 ml) cider vinegar
1 tbsp (15 ml) ground coriander
1 tsp (5 ml) ground turmeric
1 tsp (5 ml) ground cumin
2 tbsp (30 ml) medium curry powder
½ tsp (2 ml) cayenne pepper
7 oz (200 g) spinach, chopped
1 tsp (5 ml) garam masala
Salt and pepper

To serve
8 chapatis
Mango chutney

Cook the lentils in plenty of unsalted boiling water for about 12 minutes or until they are soft but holding their shape.

Meanwhile, melt the butter in a saucepan and gently cook the onion for about 8 minutes, until it is softened but not colored. Add the garlic and cook for 1 minute, then stir in the vinegar and all the spices except the garam masala and fry gently for 2 minutes.

Drain the lentils and stir them into the spice mix with the chopped spinach. Heat until the spinach has wilted and the lentils are hot. Season to taste, stir in the garam masala and serve immediately with plenty of chapatis and mango chutney.

For potato & spinach curry, dice 1 lb (500 g) potatoes and cook them for 10 minutes, until just tender, and substitute for the lentils. Increase the quantity of spinach to 1 lb (500 g). Serve sprinkled with toasted, chopped cashew nuts.

VEGETARIAN

HERBY CHICKPEA FATOUSH

Serves 4
Preparation time 15 minutes
Cooking time 4 minutes

3 pita breads
1 clove garlic, peeled and halved
1 green bell pepper, cored, seeded and thinly sliced
10 to 12 radishes, thinly sliced
14-oz (398 ml) can chickpeas, rinsed and drained
½ cup (125 ml) fresh parsley, chopped
½ cup (125 ml) fresh mint, chopped
2 ripe tomatoes, seeded and sliced
½ red onion, finely chopped, or 4 green onions, finely sliced
½ cucumber, seeded and diced
⅓ cup (75 ml) olive oil
3 tbsp (45 ml) lemon juice
1 tbsp (15 ml) tahini (optional)
1 tsp (5 ml) sumac (optional)
8 romaine lettuce leaves, to serve

Heat a grill pan and toast the pita breads for 2 minutes on each side, until crisp and slightly charred. Remove from the pan and rub immediately with the cut garlic. Cut the breads into small squares.

Combine the pita cubes with the green bell pepper, radishes, chickpeas, parsley, mint, tomatoes, onion and cucumber. Pour in the oil and lemon juice and stir in the tahini (if used). Mix until the salad is well coated. Tip into a serving dish and scatter on the sumac (if used).

Put 2 lettuce leaves on each serving plate and let people help themselves to the fatoush.

For cannellini & French bread salad, replace the pita bread with French bread cubes baked in a preheated 350°F (180°C) oven for about 15 minutes, until crisp and browning. Use cannellini beans instead of chickpeas and replace the tahini with 2 tbsp (30 ml) pesto. Omit the sumac and garlic.

BALSAMIC BRAISED LEEKS & PEPPERS

Serves 4
Preparation time 5 minutes
Cooking time 20 minutes

2 tbsp (30 ml) olive oil
2 leeks, cut into ½-inch (1 cm) pieces
1 orange bell pepper, seeded and cut into ½-inch
(1 cm) chunks
1 red bell pepper, seeded and cut into ½-inch
(1 cm) chunks
3 tbsp (45 ml) balsamic vinegar
Salt and pepper
Handful of flat-leaf (Italian) parsley, chopped

Heat the oil in a saucepan; add the leeks and orange and red bell peppers and stir well. Cover the pan and cook very gently for 10 minutes.

Add the balsamic vinegar and cook for a further 10 minutes without a lid. The vegetables should be brown from the vinegar and all the liquid should have evaporated.

Season well with salt and pepper, then stir in the chopped parsley just before serving.

For balsamic braised onions, place 1 lb (500 g) peeled baby onions in a saucepan with 3 tbsp (45 ml) balsamic vinegar, 3 tbsp (45 ml) olive oil, 3 tbsp (45 ml) light muscovado sugar, 2 tbsp (30 ml) sun-dried tomato paste, several fresh thyme spigs, a handful of sultanas and 1¼ cups (300 ml) water. Bring to a boil, then reduce the heat and simmer gently for about 40 minutes, until the onions are tender and the sauce syrupy. Serve warm or cold.

ASPARAGUS & SNOW PEA STIR-FRY

Serves 4
Preparation time 10 minutes
Cooking time 7–9 minutes

2 tbsp (30 ml) vegetable oil
5-inch (12 cm) piece fresh ginger, peeled and thinly
shredded
2 large cloves garlic, thinly sliced
4 green onions, diagonally sliced
8 oz (250 g) thin asparagus spears, cut into 1¼-inch
(3 cm) lengths
5 oz (150 g) snow peas, cut in half diagonally
5 oz (150 g) bean sprouts
3 tbsp (45 ml) light soy sauce

To serve
Steamed rice
Extra soy sauce (optional)

Heat a large wok until it is smoking, then add the oil. Stir-fry the ginger and garlic for 30 seconds. Add the green onions and cook for a further 30 seconds. Add the asparagus and cook, stirring frequently, for another 3 to 4 minutes.

Add the snow peas and cook for 2 to 3 minutes, until the vegetables are still crunchy but beginning to soften. Finally, add the bean sprouts and toss in the hot oil for 1 to 2 minutes before pouring in the soy sauce and removing from the heat.

Serve immediately with steamed rice and extra soy sauce, if desired.

For stir-fried vegetable omelettes, for each omelette, beat together 3 eggs with 2 tbsp (30 ml) water and salt and pepper. Cook in a frying pan until lightly set. Top with a quarter of the cooked vegetables and fold in half. Set aside to keep warm and make 3 more.

RÖSTI WITH TOMATO & THREE CHEESES

Serves 2
Preparation time 20 minutes
Cooking time 25 minutes

13 oz (400 g) Yukon gold or red potatoes
½ small onion, grated
1 tsp (5 ml) dried oregano
Salt and pepper
2 tbsp (30 ml) butter
1 tbsp (15 ml) olive oil
3 small tomatoes, sliced
2 oz (60 g) Gruyère cheese, grated
3 oz (75 g) mozzarella cheese, sliced
2 tbsp (30 ml) freshly grated Parmesan cheese
Handful of pitted black olives
Small fresh basil leaves, to garnish

Coarsely grate the potatoes and pat dry between paper towels. Mix in a bowl with the onion, oregano and plenty of salt and pepper.

Melt the butter with the oil in a medium-sized, heavy-bottomed frying pan. Tip in the rösti mixture and spread it out in an even layer, pressing down gently to compact it. Cook over very low heat for about 10 minutes or until the underside has turned golden. Test by lifting at the edge. To turn the rösti, invert it onto a plate and then slide it back into the pan to cook for a further 5 to 10 minutes, until crisp and golden.

Arrange the tomato slices on top, seasoning with a little pepper. Sprinkle the Gruyère over the tomatoes and arrange the mozzarella slices on top. Sprinkle with the Parmesan and scatter with the olives. Cook under a preheated moderate broiler for about 5 minutes, until the cheese bubbles and begins to color. Garnish with basil leaves and serve with a green salad.

For rösti with mushrooms and sour cream, grate 12 oz (375 g) Yukon Gold or red potatoes and pat dry. Combine with 1 sliced onion, 1 tbsp (15 ml) chopped fresh dill, ½ tsp (2 ml) salt and 1½ tbsp (22 ml) all-purpose flour, then add 1 beaten egg. Heat a little oil in a nonstick pan, divide the rösti mixture into 8 and fry for 3 to 4 minutes on each side. Keep warm. For the sauce, melt 2 tbsp (30 ml) butter and fry 2 chopped shallots and 1 crushed clove garlic for 5 minutes, then stir-fry 12 oz (375 g) button mushrooms for 5 to 6 minutes. Stir in 2 tbsp (30 ml) chopped dill, 6 tbsp (90 ml) sour cream and 2 tsp (10 ml) horseradish sauce, season and serve with the rösti.

BAKED EGGPLANT & MOZZARELLA

Serves 4
Preparation time 10 minutes
Cooking time about 25 minutes

2 eggplants, sliced in half lengthwise
3 tbsp (45 ml) olive oil, divided
1 onion, chopped
1 clove garlic, crushed
8 oz (250 g) can chopped tomatoes
1 tbsp (15 ml) tomato purée
10 oz (300 g) mozzarella cheese, cut into thin slices
Salt and pepper
Fresh basil, to garnish

Brush the eggplant with 2 tbsp (30 ml) of the oil and arrange, cut side up, on a baking sheet. Roast in a preheated 400°F (200°C) oven for 20 minutes.

Meanwhile, heat the remaining oil in a frying pan; add the onion and garlic and cook until the onion is soft and starting to brown. Add the tomatoes and tomato purée and simmer for 5 minutes or until the sauce has thickened.

Remove the eggplant from the oven and cover each half with some sauce and 2 of the mozzarella slices. Season to taste with salt and pepper and return to the oven for 4 to 5 minutes to melt the cheese. Serve immediately, scattered with basil leaves.

For roasted garlic bread to serve as an accompaniment, separate 2 garlic bulbs into separate cloves. Put on a square of foil and drizzle generously with olive oil. Bring up the sides of the foil and twist together at the top. Bake in the oven alongside the eggplant, then unwrap and allow to cool slightly before squeezing the flesh from the skins and spreading onto slices of hot French bread. Serve with the baked eggplant.

BEET RISOTTO

Serves 4
Preparation time 5–10 minutes
Cooking time 30 minutes

1 tbsp (15 ml) olive oil
1 tbsp (15 ml) butter
1 tsp (5 ml) crushed or coarsely ground coriander
    seeds
4 green onions, thinly sliced
13 oz (400 g) freshly cooked beets, cut into ½-inch
    (1 cm) dice
2 cups (500 g) risotto rice
6 cups (1.5 L) hot vegetable stock
7 oz (200 g) cream cheese
¼ cup (60 ml) finely chopped fresh dill
Salt and pepper

To garnish
Fresh dill sprigs (optional)
Crème fraîche (optional)

Heat the oil and butter in a large saucepan. Add the crushed or ground coriander seeds and green onions and stir-fry briskly for 1 minute.

Add the beets and the rice. Cook, stirring, for 2 to 3 minutes to coat all the grains with oil and butter. Gradually pour in the hot stock a ladleful at a time, stirring frequently until each ladleful is absorbed before adding the next. This should take about 25 minutes, by which time the rice should be tender but retaining a little bite.

Stir in the cream cheese and dill and season with salt and pepper to taste. Serve immediately, garnished with dill sprigs and a little crème fraîche, if using.

For spinach and lemon risotto, heat the oil and butter and cook 2 finely chopped shallots and 2 crushed cloves garlic for 3 minutes. Stir in 1¼ cups (300 ml) risotto rice and gradually add 4 cups (1 L) vegetable stock as above. Before you add the last of the stock, stir in 1 lb (500 g) chopped spinach and the grated zest and juice of 1 lemon and season. Increase the heat and stir, then add the remaining stock and ¼ cup (60 ml) butter and cook for a few minutes. Stir in ¼ cup (60 ml) grated Parmesan. Garnish with more Parmesan, and grated lemon zest, if you like, before serving.

240

VEGGIE SAUSAGE HOTPOT

Serves 4
Preparation time 10 minutes
Cooking time 40 minutes

3 tbsp (45 ml) butter, softened, divided
1 tbsp (15 ml) olive oil
8 vegetarian sausages
3½ oz (100 g) cremini mushrooms, sliced
1 red onion, sliced
1 cup (250 ml) Puy lentils, rinsed
2 cups (500 ml) vegetable stock
2 tbsp (30 ml) chopped fresh oregano
2 tbsp (30 ml) sun-dried tomato paste
10 oz (300 g) cherry tomatoes, halved
Salt and pepper
1 clove garlic, crushed
2 tbsp (30 ml) chopped fresh parsley
8 small or 4 large slices ciabatta bread

Melt half the butter with the oil in a sauté pan or flameproof casserole and fry the sausages with the mushrooms and onion until lightly browned.

Add the lentils, stock, oregano and tomato paste and mix the ingredients together. Bring to a boil and cover with a lid, then reduce the heat and cook very gently for about 20 minutes, until the lentils are tender and the stock is nearly absorbed.

Stir in the tomatoes and check the seasoning. Cook for a further 5 minutes.

Meanwhile, mix the garlic and parsley with the remaining butter and spread thinly over the ciabatta slices. Arrange over the hotpot and cook under a preheated moderate broiler for about 5 minutes, until the bread is lightly toasted.

For spicy veggie burgers, heat 1 tbsp (15 ml) oil and fry ½ red onion, 1 clove garlic and 1 tsp (5 ml) each grated ginger, ground cumin and coriander and cayenne pepper for 10 minutes. Cool slightly, then blend with a 14-oz (398 ml) can red kidney beans, 1 cup (250 ml) fresh breadcrumbs, 2 tbsp (30 ml) each fresh coriander and soy sauce and salt and pepper. With wet hands, form the mixture into 8 small burgers and fry for 2 to 3 minutes on each side. Use the veggie burgers instead of the vegetarian sausages in the hotpot or serve them with a fresh tomato sauce.

CURRIED CAULIFLOWER WITH CHICKPEAS

Serves 4
Preparation time 10 minutes
Cooking time 20 minutes

2 tbsp (30 ml) olive oil
1 onion, chopped
2 cloves garlic, crushed
¼ cup (60 ml) medium curry paste
1 small cauliflower, divided into florets
1½ cups (375 ml) vegetable stock, made with
   1 vegetable stock cube and boiling water
4 tomatoes, roughly chopped
13 oz (400 g) canned chickpeas, drained and rinsed
2 tbsp (30 ml) mango chutney
Salt and pepper
¼ cup (60 ml) chopped fresh coriander, to garnish
Whisked plain yogurt, to serve (optional)

Heat the oil in a saucepan; add the onion and garlic and cook until the onion is soft and starting to brown. Stir in the curry paste; add the cauliflower and stock and bring to a boil. Reduce the heat, cover tightly and simmer for 10 minutes.

Add the tomatoes, chickpeas and chutney and continue to cook, uncovered, for 10 minutes. Season to taste with salt and pepper. Serve garnished with coriander and drizzled with a little whisked yogurt, if desired.

For homemade mango chutney, put the peeled, pitted and sliced flesh of 6 ripe mangoes in a large saucepan with 1¼ cups (300 ml) white wine vinegar and cook over low heat for 10 minutes. Add 1 cup (250 ml) soft dark brown sugar, 2 oz (60 g) fresh ginger, peeled and finely chopped, 2 crushed cloves garlic, 2 tsp (10 ml) chili powder and 1 tsp (5 ml) salt and bring to a boil, stirring constantly. Reduce the heat and simmer for 30 minutes, stirring occasionally. Ladle into a sterilized screw-top jar and replace the lid. Store in the refrigerator and use within 1 month.

CALDO VERDE

Serves 4
Preparation time 15 minutes
Cooking time 35 minutes

¼ small head dark green cabbage, e.g., Cavolo Nero
¼ cup (60 ml) olive oil
1 large onion, chopped
1½ lb (625 g) baking or russet potatoes, cut into small
   chunks
2 cloves garlic, chopped
4 cups (1 L) vegetable stock
14-oz (398 ml) can cannellini beans, drained
¾ cup (175 ml) fresh coriander, roughly chopped
Salt and pepper

Discard any tough stalk ends from the cabbage and roll the leaves up tightly. Using a large knife, shred the cabbage as finely as possible.

Heat the oil in a large saucepan and gently fry the onion for 5 minutes. Add the potatoes and cook, stirring occasionally, for 10 minutes. Stir in the garlic and cook for a further 1 minute.

Add the stock and bring to a boil. Reduce the heat and simmer gently, covered, for about 10 minutes, until the potatoes are tender. Use a potato masher to lightly mash the potatoes into the soup so that they are broken up but not completely puréed.

Stir in the beans, shredded cabbage and coriander and cook gently for a further 10 minutes. Season to taste with salt and pepper.

For colcannon, boil 500 g (I lb) unpeeled potatoes until tender. Drain and add ⅔ cup (150 ml) milk. Meanwhile, boil 1 small head finely shredded green cabbage for 10 minutes or until the cabbage is tender. Drain and add 6 finely chopped green onions. When cool enough to handle, peel and mash the potatoes in a bowl, then beat in the cabbage and green onions. Season and beat in ¼ cup (60 ml) butter.

GOAT'S CHEESE & BABY BEAN TORTILLA

Serves 4
Preparation time 15 minutes
Cooking time 40 minutes

⅓ cup (75 ml) olive oil

1 onion, chopped

1¼ lb (625 g) medium-sized Yukon Gold or red potatoes, sliced

Salt

6 eggs

2 tsp (10 ml) green peppercorns in brine, rinsed, drained and lightly crushed

7 oz (200 g) goat's cheese, e.g. chèvre blanc, roughly crumbled

4 oz (125 g) frozen baby broad, lima or fava beans

Heat the oil in a 9½ to 10 inch (24 to 25 cm) sturdy frying pan. Add the onion and potatoes and sprinkle with salt. Gently fry on the lowest setting for about 15 to 20 minutes, turning frequently, until softened. If a lot of oil is left in the pan once the potatoes are softened, drain it off but leave a little to finish cooking.

Beat the eggs in a bowl with the green peppercorns and a little extra salt.

Toss the cheese and beans with the potato mixture until evenly combined. Spread the mixture in a thin layer and pour the eggs over the top. Keep the heat at its lowest setting and cook gently for 10 to 15 minutes, until almost set. Finish by cooking under a preheated moderate broiler for 5 minutes, until lightly browned. Serve warm or cold with a mixed salad.

For a green bean and pepper tortilla, omit the peppercorns, goat's cheese and beans and add 2 sliced red bell peppers, or 1 red and 1 green, and some sliced green beans with the onion and potatoes. Pour over the eggs and cook as above.

BROILED POLENTA & CHEESE BAKE

Serves 4
Preparation time 8 minutes
Cooking time 25–30 minutes

7 oz (200 g) roasted red peppers in olive oil

2 lb (1 kg) ready-made firm polenta, cut into ¼-inch (5 mm) slices

5 oz (150 g) fontina cheese, grated

5 oz (150 g) pecorino cheese, grated

1 clove garlic, chopped

1½ cups (375 ml) tomato sauce or passata

1 tsp (5 ml) finely grated lemon zest

Pinch of granulated or fruit sugar

Small bunch of fresh basil, shredded, plus extra whole leaves to garnish

Salt and pepper

Drain and slice the red peppers, reserving 3 tbsp (45 ml) of the oil.

Arrange half the polenta slices in a lightly buttered ovenproof dish and scatter half the sliced peppers and cheeses, overtop.

Repeat the layers and cook in a preheated 475°F (240°C) oven for 15 minutes.

Meanwhile, heat the oil from the peppers in a pan and fry the garlic over medium heat until soft and beginning to turn golden. Stir in the remaining ingredients, season to taste and bring to a boil, then reduce the heat and leave to bubble gently for 15 to 20 minutes.

Put the polenta bake under a preheated hot broiler for 5 minutes to brown the top. Garnish with basil leaves and serve immediately with the tomato sauce.

For semolina gnocchi, add 1½ cups (375 ml) semolina to 3⅔ cups (900 ml) boiling milk, reduce the heat and simmer for 5 minutes, stirring the mixture constantly with a whisk until thick. Add a little butter, then pour into a large loaf tin. Cook in a preheated 350°F (180°C) oven until firm, and slice. Layer and broil as above.

VEGETABLE & CHEESE WRAP

Serves 4
Preparation time 10 minutes
Cooking time 6–8 minutes

7 oz (200 g) soft, mild goat's cheese
8 medium-sized soft tortilla wraps
16 fresh basil leaves
5 oz (150 g) grilled artichokes in oil, drained
5 oz (150 g) grilled eggplant in oil, drained
5 oz (150 g) grilled peppers in oil, drained
8 sun-dried tomatoes
2 oz (60 g) pine nuts, lightly toasted
3 oz (75 g) baby arugula
¼ cup (60 ml) Parmesan cheese shavings (optional)

Spread the cheese over the tortillas and arrange the basil leaves lengthwise in the center of each wrap. Top with the vegetables and finish with the pine nuts, arugula and Parmesan shavings, if using.

Roll up each tortilla by bringing in the sides and then rolling the wrap so that the sides are closed and the filling is concealed.

Heat a large, dry grill pan or frying pan over medium heat. Cook the wraps for about 6 to 8 minutes, turning frequently. Remove from the heat, cut each one diagonally and serve immediately.

For cheese & tomato wraps with peppers, replace the goat's cheese with a soft cheese with herbs and garlic. Omit the artichokes and eggplant and replace the sun-dried tomatoes with 13 oz (400 g) fresh cherry tomatoes, which you should halve.

VEGETARIAN

STUFFED SWEET POTATO MELT

Serves 4
Preparation time 10 minutes
Cooking time 50 minutes

4 sweet potatoes
11½ oz (350 g) Taleggio or fontina cheese, sliced
½ tsp (2 ml) dried thyme
Sprigs of fresh parsley, to garnish

Caramelized onions
⅓ cup (75 ml) vegetable oil
6 large onions, sliced
¼ cup (60 ml) white wine
3 tbsp (45 ml) white wine vinegar
1 tbsp (15 ml) brown sugar
1 tsp (5 ml) dried thyme
Salt and pepper

Prick the sweet potatoes with a sharp knife and put them in a preheated 425°F (220°C) oven for about 45 minutes or until the flesh is soft when tested with a knife.

Meanwhile, make the caramelized onions. Heat the oil in a large frying pan over low heat and add all the remaining ingredients. Cook slowly, stirring occasionally, for about 30 minutes, until the onions are brown and soft.

Remove the sweet potatoes from the oven and put them on a baking sheet. Carefully slice the potatoes in half and pile on the caramelized onions. Top with the sliced Taleggio and a sprinkling of thyme and cook under a preheated hot broiler for 4 to 5 minutes, until bubbling and beginning to brown.

Garnish with sprigs of parsley and serve immediately with a crisp green salad and a dollop of sour cream, if desired.

For polenta with caramelized onions & goat's cheese rounds, cut 2 packages, 1 lb (500 g) each, of ready-made polenta into 8 slices and cut 2 goat's cheeses, 3½ oz (100 g) each, into 4 slices each. Broil the polenta slices on one side. Turn them over and top each one with some caramelized onions, prepared as above, and 1 slice of goat's cheese. Return to the broiler for about 5 minutes, until the cheese is brown on top and soft.

POTATO GRATIN WITH BELGIAN ENDIVE

Serves 4
Preparation time 10 minutes
Cooking time 43–45 minutes

3 lb (1.5 kg) baking or russet potatoes, peeled and cut
   into about ¼-inch (3 to 4 mm) slices
¼ cup (60 ml) butter
1 tbsp (15 ml) olive oil
1 onion, sliced
3 cloves garlic, chopped
7 oz (200 g) Cheddar cheese, grated
1⅔ cups (400 ml) whipping (35%) cream or full-fat
   crème fraîche
12 oz (375 g) Reblochon or Brie cheese, sliced
Salt and pepper

To serve
3 to 4 heads Belgian endive, separated into leaves
Ready-made French dressing

Cook the potatoes in lightly salted boiling water for 10 minutes, then drain.

Melt the butter with the oil in a medium saucepan and cook the onion for about 5 minutes or until soft and golden. Add the garlic and cook for a further 2 minutes.

Add the grated cheese and cream or crème fraîche. Stir until the mixture is hot and the cheese has melted. Season to taste.

Arrange half the potatoes in a lightly buttered shallow ovenproof dish. Place half the cheese slices over the potatoes and pour in half the cheese sauce. Cover with the remaining potato slices and the rest of the cheese sauce and top with the remaining cheese slices.

Cook in a preheated 425°F (220°C) oven for 30 to 35 minutes, until bubbling and golden brown. Serve immediately with the endive and dressing.

For Italian-style gratin, use 5 oz (150 g) grated pecorino and 13 oz (400 g) fontina for the hard and soft cheeses. Sprinkle over 1 tsp (5 ml) dried Italian herbs and add 1 tsp (5 ml) finely chopped fresh rosemary before baking.

246

PEA & LEEK OMELET

Serves 4
Preparation time 5–6 minutes
Cooking time 19–22 minutes

8 oz (250 g) baby new potatoes
⅓ cup (75 ml) butter
1 tbsp (15 ml) olive oil
1 large leek, trimmed, cleaned and cut into ½-inch
   (1 cm) slices
1½ cups (375 ml) frozen or fresh peas
6 eggs
⅔ cup (150 ml) milk
2 tbsp (30 ml) chopped fresh chives
Salt and pepper
4 oz (125 g) soft garlic-and-chive cheese

To serve
4 oz (125 g) salad leaves
¼ cup (60 ml) ready-made salad dressing

Cook the potatoes in boiling water for about 10 minutes or until cooked but still firm.

Meanwhile, melt the butter with the oil in a large frying pan; add the leek, cover and cook, stirring frequently, for 8 to 10 minutes or until soft. Stir in the peas.

Drain the potatoes, cut them into quarters and add to the frying pan. Continue cooking for 2 to 3 minutes.

Whisk the eggs with the milk and chives, season well with salt and pepper and pour into the frying pan. Move around with a spatula so that the vegetables are well coated and the egg begins to cook. Crumble the cheese on top and leave over medium heat for 2 to 3 minutes, until the egg becomes firm.

Place under a preheated hot broiler for 3 to 4 minutes, until the omelet is completely set and the top is golden brown. Serve in thick slices with a prepared salad and ready-made dressing.

For quick herb salad dressing, whisk together 6 tbsp (90 ml) olive oil, 2 tbsp (30 ml) wine vinegar, 3 tbsp (45 ml) chopped fresh parsley, ½ grated small onion, ½ tsp (2 ml) mustard, ¼ tsp (1 ml) granulated or fruit sugar and a little ground coriander. Season to taste.

SQUASH, LEEK & POTATO BAKE

Serves 4
Preparation time 30 minutes
Cooking time 2 hours

¼ cup (60 ml) hot horseradish sauce
1 tbsp (15 ml) chopped fresh thyme
1¼ cups (300 ml) whipping (35%) cream, divided
1 large leek, finely shredded
¾ cup (75 ml) walnuts, roughly chopped, divided
1 lb (500 g) butternut squash
1½ lb (750 g) baking potatoes, thinly sliced
Salt
⅔ cup (150 ml) vegetable stock
½ cup (125 ml) dry breadcrumbs
¼ cup (60 ml) butter, melted
2 tbsp (30 ml) pumpkin seeds

Mix the horseradish sauce in a large bowl with the thyme and half the cream. Add the leek and all but 2 tbsp (30 ml) of the walnuts and mix well.

Cut the squash into chunks, discarding the skin and seeds. Thinly slice the chunks.

Scatter half the potatoes in an 8-cup (2 L) shallow ovenproof dish, seasoning lightly with salt, and cover with half the squash chunks. Spoon the leek mixture on top, spreading in an even layer. Arrange the remaining squash slices on top and then the remaining potato slices. Sprinkle with salt.

Mix the remaining cream with the stock and pour over the potatoes. Mix the breadcrumbs with the butter and sprinkle over the top. Scatter with the pumpkin seeds and remaining nuts. Cover with foil and bake in a preheated 350°F (180°C) oven for 1 hour. Remove the foil and bake for a further 45 to 60 minutes, until golden and the vegetables feel tender when pierced with a knife.

For spicy squash and potato bake, use a finely chopped chile or 4-inch (10 cm) piece grated fresh ginger instead of the horseradish. Replace the leek with 1 large bunch green onions, finely chopped. Bake as above until the vegetables are tender.

GNOCCHI WITH SPINACH & GORGONZOLA

Serves 3–4
Preparation time 5 minutes
Cooking time 10 minutes

8 oz (250 g) baby spinach
1¼ cups (300 ml) vegetable stock
1 lb (500 g) potato gnocchi
5 oz (150 g) Gorgonzola cheese, cut into small pieces
3 tbsp (45 ml) whipping (35%) cream
Plenty of freshly grated nutmeg
Pepper

Wash the spinach leaves thoroughly, if necessary. Pat them dry with paper towels.

Bring the stock to a boil in a large saucepan. Tip in the gnocchi and return to a boil. Cook for 2 to 3 minutes or until plumped up and tender.

Stir in the cheese, cream and nutmeg and heat until the cheese melts to make a creamy sauce.

Add the spinach to the pan and cook gently for 1 to 2 minutes, turning the spinach with the gnocchi and sauce until wilted. Pile onto serving plates and season with plenty of black pepper.

For homemade vegetable stock, heat 2 tbsp (30 ml) olive oil in a large saucepan. Add 1 large chopped onion, 2 chopped carrots, 1 chopped turnip or parsnip, 3 sliced celery stalks and ½ to 1 cup (125 to 250 ml) sliced mushrooms and fry gently for 5 minutes. Add 2 bay leaves, several thyme and parsley sprigs, 2 chopped tomatoes, 2 tsp (10 ml) black peppercorns and the onion skin and cover with 12 cups (1.8 L) water. Bring to a boil, then partially cover and simmer gently for 1 hour. Cool, then strain. Refrigerate for up to 2 days or freeze.

SPINACH & SWEET POTATO CAKES

Serves 4
Preparation time 35 minutes, plus infusing
Cooking time about 40 minutes

1 lb (500 g) sweet potatoes, peeled and cut
    into chunks
4 oz (125 g) spinach leaves
4 to 5 green onions, finely sliced
Salt and pepper
Olive oil, for deep-frying
3 tbsp (45 ml) sesame seeds
¼ cup (60 ml) all-purpose flour

Red chile & coconut dip
¾ cup + 2 tbsp (200 ml) coconut cream
2 red chiles, seeded and finely chopped
1 stalk lemongrass, thinly sliced
3 kaffir lime leaves, shredded
Small bunch of fresh coriander, chopped
2 tbsp (30 ml) toasted sesame oil

To garnish
Lime wedges
Green onions, shredded

Cook the sweet potatoes in lightly salted boiling water for about 20 minutes or until tender. Drain, then return them to the pan and place over low heat for 1 minute, stirring constantly, so the excess moisture evaporates. Lightly mash the potatoes with a fork.

Meanwhile, put the spinach in a colander and pour on a kettle of boiling water. Refresh the spinach in cold water and squeeze dry. Stir the spinach into the sweet potatoes. Add the green onions, season with salt and pepper and set aside.

Make the dip. Gently warm the coconut cream in a pan with the chiles, lemongrass and lime leaves for about 10 minutes. Don't let it boil. Set aside to infuse.

In a large pan or deep-fat fryer, heat the oil to 350°F (180°C) or until a cube of bread browns in 20 seconds. Use your hands to form the sweet potato mixture into 12 cakes. Mix together the sesame seeds and flour and sprinkle over the cakes, then carefully lower them into the oil and fry, in batches for about 3 minutes, until they are golden and crispy. Drain on paper towels and keep warm while you cook the rest.

Stir the coriander and sesame oil into the dip and pour it into 4 individual dishes. Serve immediately with the potato cakes.

For sage-seasoned spinach & sweet potato cakes, shred 6 large fresh sage leaves and add to the potato cakes. Cook 2 peeled, cored apples and beat to a purée with ¼ cup (60 ml) sugar. Add 2 tbsp (30 ml) melted butter and the zest of 1 lemon. Serve the hot cakes with the applesauce.

ASPARAGUS WITH TARRAGON DRESSING

Serves 4
Preparation time 20 minutes
Cooking time about 5 minutes

3 tbsp (45 ml) olive oil (optional)
1 lb (500 g) asparagus
Salt and pepper
1½ lbs (750 g) arugula or other salad leaves
2 green onions, finely sliced
4 radishes, thinly sliced

Tarragon & lemon dressing
Finely grated zest of 2 lemons
¼ cup (60 ml) tarragon vinegar
2 tbsp (30 ml) chopped fresh tarragon
½ tsp (2 ml) Dijon mustard
Pinch of granulated or fruit sugar
Salt and pepper
⅔ cup (150 ml) olive oil

To garnish
Roughly chopped fresh herbs, such as tarragon, fresh
    parsley, chervil or dill
Thin strips of lemon zest

Make the dressing. Combine the lemon zest, vinegar, tarragon, mustard and sugar in a small bowl and season to taste. Stir to mix, then gradually whisk in the oil. Alternatively, place all the ingredients in a screw-top jar and shake well to combine. Set aside.

Heat the oil (if using) in a large frying pan. Add the asparagus in a single layer and cook for about 5 minutes, turning occasionally. The asparagus should be tender when pierced with the tip of a sharp knife and lightly patched with brown.

Transfer the asparagus to a shallow dish and sprinkle with salt and pepper. Cover with the dressing, toss gently and leave to stand for 5 minutes.

Arrange the salad leaves in a serving dish, sprinkle on the onions and radishes and pile the asparagus in the center of the leaves. Garnish with chopped herbs and thin strips of lemon zest. Serve on its own with bread or as an accompaniment to a main dish.

For garlic & mustard dressing as an alternative to tarragon and lemon, place in a screw-top jar 1 finely chopped small clove garlic, 1 finely chopped small shallot, 2 tbsp (30 ml) whole-grain mustard, a pinch each of salt, pepper and sugar, ½ cup (125 ml) olive oil and 2 to 3 tbsp (30 to 45 ml) shallot or red wine vinegar. Place the lid on the jar and shake until the ingredients are well combined. Serve drizzled over the asparagus.

QUICK & EASY MISO SOUP

Serves 4
Preparation time 10 minutes
Cooking time 10 minutes

4 cups (1 L) vegetable stock
2 tbsp (30 ml) miso paste
4 oz (125 g) shiitake mushrooms, sliced
7 oz (200 g) firm tofu, cubed

Put the stock in a saucepan and heat until simmering.

Add the miso paste, shiitake mushrooms and tofu to the stock and simmer gently for 5 minutes. Serve immediately with rice.

For sticky rice, to serve as an accompaniment, wash 1¼ cups (300 ml) glutinous rice in several changes of water and drain. Put in a large mixing bowl, cover with cold water and leave to soak for about 1 hour. Drain the rice and wash it again. Put in a saucepan with 1¼ cups (300 ml) water and bring to a simmer. Cover and cook very gently for 20 minutes or until the water is absorbed and the rice is tender. Add a little more water if the pan dries out before the rice is cooked.

BEAN & TOMATO SOUP

Serves 4
Preparation time 10 minutes
Cooking time 20 minutes

3 tbsp (45 ml) olive oil
1 onion, finely chopped
2 stalks celery, thinly sliced
2 cloves garlic, thinly sliced
2 cans (14 oz/398 ml each) butter, lima or fava beans, rinsed and drained
¼ cup (60 ml) sun-dried tomato paste
3⅔ cups (900 ml) vegetable stock
1 tbsp (15 ml) chopped fresh rosemary or thyme
Salt and pepper
Parmesan cheese shavings, to serve

Heat the oil in a saucepan. Add the onion and fry for 3 minutes, until softened. Add the celery and garlic and fry for 2 minutes.

Add the beans, sun-dried tomato paste, stock, rosemary or thyme and a little salt and pepper. Bring to a boil, then reduce the heat, cover and simmer gently for 15 minutes. Serve sprinkled with the Parmesan shavings. This soup makes a light main course served with bread and plenty of Parmesan.

For spiced carrot and lentil soup, in a saucepan, heat 2 tbsp (30 ml) oil and fry 1 chopped onion, 2 crushed cloves garlic and 2½ cups (625 ml) chopped carrots for 10 minutes. Add a 14-oz (398 ml) can lentils, drained, 2 tsp (10 ml) ground coriander, 1 tsp (5 ml) ground cumin and 1 tbsp (15 ml) chopped thyme and fry for 1 minute. Stir in 4 cups (1 L) vegetable stock, a 14-oz (398 ml) can chopped tomatoes and 2 tsp (10 ml) lemon juice and bring to a boil. Cover and simmer gently for 20 minutes. Blend until smooth, then warm through.

FENNEL & LEMON SOUP

Serves 4
Preparation time 20 minutes, plus chilling
Cooking time 25 minutes

3 tbsp (45 ml) olive oil
3 fat green onions, chopped
1 bulb fennel, about 8 oz (250 g), trimmed, cored and
   thinly sliced
1 potato, diced
Finely grated zest and juice of 1 lemon
About 12 cups (1.8 L) hot vegetable stock
Pepper

Gremolata
1 small clove garlic, finely chopped
Finely grated zest of 1 lemon
¼ cup (60 ml) chopped fresh parsley
16 black olives, pitted and chopped

Heat the oil in a large saucepan; add the green onions and cook for 5 minutes or until beginning to soften. Add the fennel, potato and lemon zest and cook for 5 minutes, until the fennel begins to soften. Pour in the stock and bring to a boil. Reduce the heat, cover and simmer for about 15 minutes or until the ingredients are tender.

Meanwhile, make the gremolata. Mix together the garlic, lemon zest and parsley, then stir the chopped olives into the mixture. Cover and chill.

Purée the soup in a food processor or blender and pass it through a sieve. The soup should not be too thick, so add more stock if necessary. Return it to the rinsed pan and warm through. Taste and season with pepper and plenty of lemon juice. Pour into warm bowls and sprinkle each serving with gremolata, to be stirred in before eating. Serve with slices of toasted crusty bread, if desired.

For bean & fennel soup, heat 3²/₃ cups (900 ml) vegetable stock with 2 trimmed, cored and sliced fennel bulbs, 1 sliced onion, 1 sliced carrot, 1 sliced zucchini and 2 crushed cloves garlic. Boil gently for 20 minutes, then add 2 cans (14 oz/398 ml each) butter, lima or fava beans and a 14-oz (398 ml) can chopped tomatoes. Heat, stir in 2 tbsp (30 ml) chopped fresh sage, process to blend and serve.

SPICED PUMPKIN & SPINACH SOUP

Serves 4
Preparation time 10 minutes
Cooking time 30–32 minutes

¼ cup (60 ml) butter
2 tbsp (30 ml) olive oil
1 onion, roughly chopped
2 cloves garlic, peeled
3 lb (1.5 kg) pumpkin, peeled and roughly chopped
1 tsp (5 ml) ground coriander
½ tsp (2 ml) cayenne pepper
½ tsp (2 ml) ground cinnamon
¼ tsp (1 ml) ground allspice
3 cups (750 ml) hot vegetable stock
5 oz (150 g) frozen spinach
Salt and pepper

To serve
2 tbsp (30 ml) pumpkin seeds, lightly toasted
4 tsp (20 ml) pumpkin seed oil

Heat the butter and oil in a large, heatproof casserole or Dutch oven and add the onion and garlic. Cook over medium heat for 5 to 6 minutes, until soft and golden.

Add the pumpkin and continue cooking for a further 8 minutes, stirring frequently, until beginning to soften and turn golden. Add the spices and cook for 2 to 3 minutes, making sure that the pumpkin is well coated.

Pour in the hot stock and bring to a boil, then reduce the heat, cover and leave to bubble gently for about 15 minutes, until the pumpkin is soft.

Use a handheld blender to purée the pumpkin until smooth, then stir in the spinach. Reheat for about 5 minutes, until the spinach has wilted and the soup is hot. Season to taste.

Spoon the soup into bowls, scatter on top the lightly toasted pumpkin seeds and a drizzle of pumpkin oil and serve immediately.

For butternut, spinach & coconut soup, use 1 lb (500 g) butternut squash, peeled, seeded and cubed, instead of the pumpkin and cook as above. Stir in ³/₄ cup + 2 tbsp (200 ml) coconut milk before serving.

GREEN BEAN, MISO & NOODLE SOUP

Serves 2
Preparation time 10 minutes
Cooking time 10 minutes

3 tbsp (45 ml) brown miso paste
4 cups (1 L) vegetable stock
2-inch (5 cm) piece fresh ginger, grated
2 cloves garlic, thinly sliced
1 small hot red chile, seeded and thinly sliced
3½ oz (100 g) soba, whole wheat or plain noodles
1 bunch green onions, finely shredded
½ cup (125 ml) fresh or frozen peas
1 cup (250 ml) large flat green beans, trimmed and shredded
3 tbsp (45 ml) mirin
1 tbsp (15 ml) granulated sugar
1 tbsp (15 ml) rice wine vinegar

Blend the miso paste with a dash of the stock in a saucepan to make a thick, smooth paste. Add a little more stock to thin the paste and then pour in the remainder. Add the ginger, garlic and chile and bring almost to a boil.

Reduce the heat to a gentle simmer and stir in the noodles, stirring until they have softened into the stock – about 5 minutes.

Add the green onions, peas, beans, mirin, sugar and vinegar and stir well.

Cook gently for 1 to 2 minutes, until the vegetables have softened slightly. Ladle into bowls and serve immediately.

For miso soup with tofu, make dashi stock by boiling ½ oz (15 g) kombu seaweed in 12 cups (1.8 L) water, skimming any scum. Add 1½ tbsp (22 ml) dried bonito flakes and simmer, uncovered, for 20 minutes. Off the heat, stir in ½ tbsp (7 ml) dried bonito flakes and set aside for 5 minutes. Strain and return to the pan. Mix 2 tbsp (30 ml) red or white miso with a little dashi stock, then add 1 tbsp (15 ml) at a time to the stock, stirring until dissolved. Cut 1 small leek into fine julienne strips and 4 oz (125 g) firm tofu into small squares and add to the warm soup with 1 tbsp (15 ml) wakame seaweed. Garnish with chopped chives.

VEGETARIAN

RED PEPPER SOUP

Serves 4
Preparation time 15 minutes
Cooking time 35 minutes

2 onions, finely chopped
2 tbsp (30 ml) olive oil
1 clove garlic, crushed
3 red bell peppers, seeded and roughly chopped
2 zucchini, finely chopped, divided
3⅔ cups (900 ml) vegetable stock or water
Salt and pepper

To garnish
Plain yogurt or whipping (35%) cream
Chopped fresh chives

Put the onions in a large saucepan with the oil and gently fry for 5 minutes or until softened and golden brown. Add the garlic and cook gently for 1 minute.

Add the red peppers and half the zucchini and fry for 5 to 8 minutes or until softened and brown.

Add the stock or water to the pan with salt and pepper and bring to a boil. Reduce the heat, cover the pan and simmer gently for 20 minutes.

When the vegetables are tender, blend the mixture, in batches, to a smooth soup and return to the pan. Season to taste, reheat and serve topped with the remaining chopped zucchini and garnished with yogurt or a swirl of cream and chopped chives. This vibrant and warming soup is ideal for any meal and tastes just as good warm or cold.

For Provençal peppers, heat 1 tbsp (15 ml) oil and fry 2 sliced onions until soft. Add 4 sliced red bell peppers and 1 crushed clove garlic and cook for 5 minutes. Stir in a 14-oz (398 ml) can tomatoes and 2 tbsp (30 ml) chopped fresh herbs and season with salt and pepper. Bring to a boil, then reduce the heat and simmer, uncovered, for 15 minutes. Serve hot or cold.

TABBOULEH WITH FRUIT & NUTS

Serves 4
Preparation time 10 minutes, plus soaking

1 cup (250 ml) bulgur wheat
⅔ cup (150 ml) unsalted, shelled pistachio nuts
1 small red onion, finely chopped
3 cloves garlic, crushed
¾ cup (175 ml) flat-leaf (Italian) parsley, chopped
⅓ cup (75 ml) fresh mint, chopped
Finely grated zest and juice of 1 lemon or lime
1 cup (250 ml) ready-to-eat prunes, sliced
¼ cup (60 ml) olive oil
Salt and pepper

Put the bulgur wheat in a bowl, cover with plenty of boiling water and leave to soak for 15 minutes.

Meanwhile, put the nuts in a separate bowl and cover with boiling water. Leave to stand for 1 minute, then drain. Rub the nuts between several thicknesses of paper towel to remove most of the skins, then peel away any remaining skins with your fingers.

Mix the nuts with the onion, garlic, parsley, mint, lemon or lime zest and juice and prunes in a large bowl.

Drain the bulgur wheat thoroughly in a sieve, pressing out as much moisture as possible with the back of a spoon. Add to the other ingredients with the oil and toss together. Season to taste with salt and pepper and chill until ready to serve.

For classic tabbouleh, omit the nuts and prunes and add 6 chopped tomatoes and 2 oz (60 g) chopped black olives. Use only 2 cloves garlic and be sure to use a lemon, not a lime.

ZESTY QUINOA SALAD

Serves 4
Preparation time 15 minutes
Cooking time 15–20 minutes

1 cup (250 ml) quinoa, rinsed
1 small yellow bell pepper, cored, seeded and diced
1 small red bell pepper, cored, seeded and diced
4 green onions, sliced
⅓ cucumber, seeded and diced
½ bulb fennel, finely diced
2 tbsp (30 ml) finely chopped fresh curly parsley
2 tbsp (30 ml) finely chopped fresh mint
2 tbsp (30 ml) finely chopped fresh coriander
2 tbsp (30 ml) sunflower seeds, divided
Juice and finely grated zest of 2 limes
8 physalis, or cape gooseberries, quartered

Dressing
4 tsp (20 ml) harissa
Juice and finely grated zest of 2 limes
8 tbsp (120 ml) sunflower oil
Salt and pepper

Put the quinoa in a pan of cold water, bring to a boil and cook for 15 to 20 minutes or until the quinoa is translucent and just cooked. Drain and rinse thoroughly in cold water.

Meanwhile, make the dressing by mixing together the harissa paste, lime juice and zest and oil. Season to taste and set aside.

Mix the cooked quinoa with the prepared vegetables and herbs, 1 tbsp (15 ml) of the sunflower seeds and the lime juice and zest.

Scatter the physalis and the remaining sunflower seeds on top and serve with the dressing.

For baked potatoes with quinoa salad, coat 4 large potatoes, about 14 oz (400 g) each, with olive oil and salt, prick all over with a fork and bake in a preheated 425°F (220°C) oven for about an hour, until the skins are crisp and a skewer slides in easily. Make the salad as above, omitting the sunflower seeds, limes and physalis. Mix ¾ cup (200 ml) sour cream with 2 tbsp (30 ml) chopped fresh chives and a little nutmeg. Fill the potatoes with the salad and top with the sour cream instead of the dressing.

SPICY FRIED RICE WITH SPINACH SALAD

Serves 3–4
Preparation time 10 minutes
Cooking time 10 minutes

4 eggs
2 tbsp (30 ml) sherry
2 tbsp (30 ml) light soy sauce, divided
1 bunch green onions, divided
¼ cup (60 ml) stir-fry or wok oil, divided
½ cup (125 ml) unsalted cashew nuts
1 green bell pepper, seeded and finely chopped
½ tsp (2 ml) Chinese five-spice powder
1½ to 2 cups (375 to 500 ml) ready-cooked long-grain rice
5 oz (150 g) baby spinach
3½ oz (100 g) sprouted mung beans or 2 oz (60 g) pea shoots
Salt and pepper
Sweet chili sauce, to serve

Beat the eggs with the sherry and 1 tbsp (15 ml) of the soy sauce in a small bowl. Cut 2 of the green onions into 3-inch (7 cm) lengths, then cut lengthwise into fine shreds. Leave in a bowl of very cold water to curl up slightly. Finely chop the remaining green onions, keeping the white and green parts separate.

Heat half the oil in a large frying pan or wok and fry the cashew nuts and green parts of the green onions, turning in the oil, until the cashew nuts are lightly browned. Drain with a slotted spoon.

Add the white parts of the green onions to the pan and stir-fry for 1 minute. Add the beaten eggs and cook, stirring constantly, until the egg starts to scramble into small pieces rather than one omelet.

Stir in the green bell pepper and five-spice powder with the remaining oil and cook for 1 minute, then tip in the cooked rice and spinach with the remaining soy sauce, mixing the ingredients together well until thoroughly combined and the spinach has wilted.

Return the cashew nuts and green onions to the pan with the mung beans or pea shoots and season to taste. Pile onto serving plates, scatter with the drained green onion curls and serve with sweet chili sauce.

For spicy fried rice with baby corn, replace the spinach with ½ small Chinese cabbage, shredded, and 7 oz (200 g) baby corn, sliced, and add to the pan in the fourth step with the green bell pepper.

BABY BEAN SALAD

Serves 4
Preparation time 10 minutes
Cooking time 20 minutes

2 eggplants, thinly sliced into rounds
2 yellow summer squash, thinly sliced lengthwise
4 to 6 tbsp (60 to 90 ml) olive oil, divided
10 oz (300 g) frozen baby broad, lima or fava beans
1 tbsp (15 ml) chopped fresh dill
1 tbsp (15 ml) chopped fresh mint
Salt and pepper
1 small bulb fennel, thinly sliced
7 oz (200 g) feta cheese, crumbled
Fresh mint leaves, to garnish
1 lemon, cut into wedges, to serve

Brush the eggplant and summer squash with oil and cook in a grill pan for 2 to 3 minutes on each side, until soft and golden. You will have to do this in several batches.

Cook the baby beans in boiling water until tender. Drain and toss with 1 tbsp (15 ml) of the oil, the herbs and plenty of salt and pepper.

Leave the beans, eggplant and squash to cool before assembling or serve them as a warm salad. Arrange the eggplant and squash on serving plates. Scatter the beans and sliced fennel and then the feta overtop. Sprinkle on a few mint leaves and serve with lemon wedges.

For bean & celeriac salad, replace the squash with 2 thinly sliced red bell peppers and the fennel with 8 oz (250 g) coarsely grated celeriac.

WILD RICE & GOAT'S CHEESE SALAD

Serves 4
Preparation time 10 minutes
Cooking time about 15 minutes

1 cup (250 ml) mixed long-grain and wild rice
¾ cup (175 ml) fine green beans
¼ cup (60 ml) olive oil
3 red onions, thinly sliced
⅔ cup (150 ml) balsamic vinegar
1 tsp (5 ml) chopped fresh thyme
Salt and pepper
4 oz (125 g) goat's cheese, sliced
8 baby plum tomatoes, halved
Small bunch fresh basil

Cook the rice in lightly salted boiling water for about 15 minutes, until tender, or according to the instructions on the package. Add the green beans for the final 2 minutes of cooking. Drain and set aside.

Meanwhile, heat the oil in a large frying pan and cook the onions gently for about 12 minutes or until soft and golden. Add the balsamic vinegar and thyme, season with salt and pepper and allow to bubble gently for 2 to 3 minutes, until the mixture thickens slightly.

Stir the onions into the rice and beans and leave to cool. Once cool, scatter on the cheese, tomatoes and basil leaves and serve.

For pearl barley salad with smoked cheese, replace the rice with the same quantity of pearl barley and cook in boiling water for 25 to 35 minutes, until tender, then drain. Substitute the goat's cheese with diced smoked cheese.

BEET & SQUASH SPAGHETTI

Serves 4
Preparation time 8 minutes
Cooking time 10 minutes

10 oz (300 g) dried spaghetti or fusilli
1¼ cups (300 ml) fine green beans
1 lb (500 g) butternut squash, peeled, seeded and cut
   into ½-inch (1 cm) dice
¼ cup (60 ml) olive oil
1 lb (500 g) raw beets, cut into ½-inch (1 cm) dice
½ cup (125 ml) walnuts, crushed
5 oz (150 g) goat's cheese, diced
2 tbsp (30 ml) lemon juice
Freshly grated Parmesan cheese (optional)

Cook the pasta in lightly salted boiling water for 10 minutes or until just cooked. Add the beans and squash for the final 2 minutes of cooking time.

Meanwhile, heat the oil in a large frying pan; add the beets and cook, stirring occasionally, for 10 minutes, until cooked but still firm.

Toss the drained pasta mixture with the beets, walnuts and goat's cheese. Squeeze in the lemon juice and serve immediately with a bowl of Parmesan, if desired.

For baby carrot & squash spaghetti, replace the beets with the same quantity of baby carrots, cooked in boiling water for about 5 minutes, until tender. Roast the butternut squash with 4 cloves garlic and the oil in a preheated 475°F (240°C) oven for about 40 minutes or until softened. Replace the goat's cheese with havarti or dolcelatte.

RICOTTA-BAKED LARGE PASTA SHELLS

Serves 4
Preparation time 20 minutes
Cooking time 30 minutes

8 oz (250 g) dried conchiglie rigate
13 oz (400 g) ricotta cheese
1 small clove garlic, crushed
4 oz (125 g) Parmesan cheese, freshly grated, divided
½ cup (125 ml) fresh basil, finely chopped
4 oz (125 g) baby spinach, roughly chopped
2⅓ cups (575 ml) tomato sauce
5 oz (150 g) mozzarella cheese, cut into cubes
Salt and pepper

Cook the pasta in a large saucepan of salted boiling water according to the package instructions, until al dente. Drain, refresh in cold water, then drain again thoroughly.

Meanwhile, make the filling. Put the ricotta in a large bowl and break up with a fork. Stir in the garlic, half the Parmesan, the basil and spinach. Season generously with salt and pepper and use this mixture to stuff the pasta shells.

Spoon one-quarter of the tomato sauce over the bottom of an ovenproof dish and arrange the pasta shells, open side uppermost, on top. Pour the remaining sauce evenly over, then scatter on the mozzarella and the remaining Parmesan.

Bake in a preheated 425°F (220°C) oven for 20 minutes, until golden brown.

For watercress & chickpea shells with béchamel, use the béchamel sauce from the Spring Cannelloni recipe below instead of the tomato sauce. Finely chop 5 oz (150 g) watercress and combine with 2 chopped green onions and a 14-oz (398 ml) can chickpeas, drained and chopped. Mix with the ricotta, Parmesan and basil as above, omitting the garlic and spinach. Layer the béchamel and filled pasta shells, then top with cheese as above.

VEGETARIAN

SPRING CANNELLONI

Serves 4
Preparation time 30 minutes
Cooking time 30–40 minutes

2 cups (500 ml) milk
1 bay leaf
1 small onion, quartered
⅔ cup (150 ml) shelled broad or fava beans, fresh or frozen
⅔ cup (150 ml) shelled peas, fresh or frozen
½ cup (125 ml) fresh mint, chopped
½ cup (125 ml) fresh basil, chopped
1 clove garlic, crushed
10 oz (300 g) ricotta cheese
3 oz (75 g) Parmesan cheese, plus extra for sprinkling
3 tbsp (45 ml) butter
3 tbsp (45 ml) all-purpose flour
⅓ cup (75 ml) dry white wine
Salt and pepper
5 oz (150 g) dried lasagna sheets

Bring the milk with the bay leaf and onion to a simmer in a saucepan. Infuse off the heat for 20 minutes. Strain.

Meanwhile, cook the beans and peas in boiling water until tender: 6 to 8 minutes for fresh or 2 minutes for frozen. Drain and refresh in cold water. Process half in a food processor with the herbs and garlic to a rough purée. Combine with the ricotta, Parmesan and remaining vegetables. Season with salt and pepper.

Melt the butter in a saucepan over very low heat. Add the flour and cook, stirring, for 2 minutes, until a light golden color. Remove from the heat and slowly add the infused milk, stirring away any lumps as you go. Return to the heat, bring to a simmer, stirring, and pour in the wine. Simmer for 5 to 6 minutes, until thick. Season with salt and pepper.

Cook the pasta in a large saucepan of salted boiling water according to the package instructions, until just al dente. Drain, refresh in cold water, then cut into 16 pieces, 3¼ x 3½ inches (8 x 9 cm).

Spread 1½ tbsp (30 ml) of filling onto each pasta piece and roll up. Spread half the sauce in an ovenproof dish and top with the rolls in a single layer. Spoon the remaining sauce over. Sprinkle with Parmesan. Bake in a preheated 400°F (200°C) oven for 15 minutes, until golden brown.

For spinach cannelloni, chop and wilt 8 oz (250 g) spinach in a little butter in a covered pan and use instead of the beans and peas. Cook as above, replacing the mint and basil with grated nutmeg.

BLUE CHEESE & SPINACH GNOCCHI

Serves 4
Preparation time 5 minutes
Cooking time 20 minutes

1 lb (500 g) store-bought gnocchi
1 tbsp (15 ml) unsalted butter
4 oz (125 g) baby spinach
Large pinch freshly grated nutmeg
Salt and pepper
6 oz (175 g) dolcelatte or other creamy blue cheese, cut
  into cubes
½ cup (125 ml) whipping (35%) cream
3 tbsp (45 ml) freshly grated Parmesan cheese

Cook the gnocchi in a large saucepan of salted boiling water until they rise to the surface: according to the package instructions for store-bought gnocchi or for 3 to 4 minutes if using homemade. Drain thoroughly.

Meanwhile, melt the butter in a saucepan over high heat, and when it starts to sizzle, add the spinach and cook, stirring, for 1 minute or until just wilted. Remove from the heat and season with nutmeg and salt and pepper, then stir in the dolcelatte, cream and gnocchi.

Transfer to an ovenproof dish and scatter on the Parmesan. Bake in a preheated 425°F (220°C) oven for 12 to 15 minutes, until the sauce is bubbling and golden.

For blue cheese, kale & leek gnocchi, replace the spinach with 8 oz (250 g) finely shredded kale and 1 finely sliced leek, cooked in butter for 3 to 4 minutes. Omit the nutmeg. Season with salt and pepper and combine with the blue cheese, cream and gnocchi. Bake as above.

EGGPLANT & RIGATONI BAKE

Serves 4–6
Preparation time 30 minutes, plus standing
Cooking time 40 minutes

Olive oil, for frying
3 large eggplants, cut into ¼-inch (5 mm) slices
1½ tbsp (22 ml) dried oregano
Salt and pepper
12 oz (375 g) dried penne or rigatoni
2 cups (500 ml) tomato sauce
2 mozzarella balls, about 5 oz (150 g) each, roughly
  chopped
3 oz (75 g) Parmesan cheese, freshly grated
2 tbsp (30 ml) fresh white breadcrumbs

Heat ½ inch (1 cm) oil in a large frying pan over high heat until the surface of the oil seems to shimmer slightly. Add the eggplant, in batches, and fry until golden on both sides. Remove with a slotted spoon and drain on a dish lined with paper towels. Scatter with the oregano and season lightly with salt.

Cook the pasta in a large saucepan of salted boiling water according to the package instructions, until almost al dente. Drain, then stir in a bowl with the tomato sauce, mozzarella and Parmesan. Season with salt and pepper.

Meanwhile, line the bottom and sides of a 7-inch (18 cm) springform pan with the eggplant slices. Overlap the slices slightly, to ensure that there are no gaps, then fill the pan with the pasta mixture. Press down so that the pasta is tightly packed, then cover with the remaining egg-plant slices.

Scatter the breadcrumbs over the top of the pasta cake and bake on a baking sheet in a preheated 400°F (200°C) oven for 15 minutes, until golden brown. Leave the cake to stand for 15 minutes before unclipping and removing the ring to serve. Don't attempt to remove the cake from its base, as it will most probably break in the process.

For zucchini & rigatoni bake, use 6 to 7 large zucchini instead of the eggplant and cut them into long slices before frying.

TOMATO, PINE NUT & ARUGULA PESTO

Serves 4–6
Preparation time 10 minutes
Cooking time 10–12 minutes

13 oz to 1 lb 2 oz (400 to 600 g) dried pasta twists,
   such as fusilli
3 ripe tomatoes
4 cloves garlic, peeled
2 oz (60 g) arugula leaves, plus extra to garnish
3½ oz (100 g) pine nuts
⅔ cup (150 ml) olive oil
Salt and pepper

Cook the pasta in a large saucepan of salted boiling water according to the package instructions, until al dente.

Meanwhile, finely chop the tomatoes, garlic, arugula and pine nuts by hand, then stir in the oil. Season with salt and pepper. Transfer to a bowl.

Drain the pasta; add to the bowl with the pesto and toss to combine. Serve immediately, garnished with a few fresh basil leaves.

For tomato, parsley & almond pesto, put 4 ripe tomatoes, 2 cloves garlic, 1½ cups (375 ml) fresh parsley, ⅔ cup (150 ml) almonds and ⅔ cup (150 ml) olive oil in a food processor and process until smooth.

CLASSIC BASIL PESTO

Serves 4
Preparation time 2 minutes
Cooking time 10–12 minutes

13 oz (400 g) dried trofie pasta
2 cups (500 ml) fresh basil leaves
2 oz (60 g) pine nuts
2 cloves garlic
2 oz (60 g) Parmesan cheese, freshly grated, plus extra
   to serve
⅓ cup + 2 tbsp (100 ml) olive oil
Salt and pepper
Fresh basil leaves, to garnish

Cook the pasta in a large saucepan of salted boiling water according to the package instructions, until al dente.

Meanwhile, put the basil, pine nuts and garlic in a food processor and process until well blended. Transfer to a bowl and stir in the Parmesan and oil. Season with salt and pepper.

Drain the pasta, reserving a ladleful of the cooking water, and return to the pan. Stir in the pesto, adding enough of the reserved pasta cooking water to loosen the mixture. Serve immediately with a scattering of grated Parmesan and garnished with fresh basil leaves.

For potato & bean pesto pasta, the classic Genovese way of serving pesto, start by cooking 8 oz (250 g) peeled and sliced potatoes in a large saucepan of salted boiling water for 5 minutes, then add the pasta and cook according to the package instructions, until al dente. When there are 5 minutes of the cooking time remaining, add 1 cup (250 ml) trimmed, sliced green beans to the pan. After draining the pasta, stir in the pesto as above. A long pasta shape such as linguine suits this variation better.

ROASTED TOMATO & RICOTTA PASTA

Serves 4
Preparation time 10 minutes
Cooking time 15–20 minutes

1 lb (500 g) cherry tomatoes, halved
¼ cup (60 ml) extra virgin olive oil
2 tsp (10 ml) chopped fresh thyme leaves
4 cloves garlic, sliced
Pinch hot pepper flakes
Salt and pepper
13 oz (400 g) dried pasta
1 bunch fresh basil leaves, torn, divided
4 oz (125 g) ricotta cheese, crumbled

Put the tomatoes in a roasting pan with the oil, thyme, garlic and hot pepper flakes and season with salt and pepper. Roast in a preheated 400°F (200°C) oven for 15 to 20 minutes, until the tomatoes have softened and released their juices.

Meanwhile, cook the pasta in a large saucepan of salted boiling water according to the package instructions, until al dente. Drain and return to the pan.

Stir the tomatoes with all their pan juices and most of the basil leaves into the pasta and toss gently until combined. Season with salt and pepper and spoon into serving bowls.

Chop the remaining basil, mix into the ricotta and season with salt and pepper. Spoon into a small dish for guests to spoon onto the pasta.

For roasted tomato & goat's cheese sauce, replace the ricotta with 4 oz (125 g) crumbly goat's cheese. This piquant, herb-scented dish goes well with pasta verde, spinach-flavored pasta shapes.

VEGGIE CARBONARA

Serves 4
Preparation time 5 minutes
Cooling time 15 minutes

2 tbsp (30 ml) olive oil
2 cloves garlic, finely chopped
3 zucchini, thinly sliced
6 green onions, cut into ½-inch (1 cm) lengths
13 oz (400 g) dried penne
4 egg yolks
Salt and pepper
⅓ cup + 2 tbsp (100 ml) crème fraîche
3 oz (75 g) freshly grated Parmesan cheese, plus extra
   to serve

Heat the oil in a heavy-bottomed frying pan over medium-high heat. Add the garlic, zucchini and green onions and cook, stirring, for 4 to 5 minutes, until the zucchini are tender. Set aside.

Cook the pasta in a large saucepan of salted boiling water according to the package instructions, until al dente.

Meanwhile, put the egg yolks in a bowl and season with salt and a generous grinding of pepper. Mix together with a fork.

Just before the pasta is ready, return the pan with the zucchini mixture to the heat. Stir in the crème fraîche and bring to a boil.

Drain the pasta thoroughly, return it to the pan and immediately stir in the egg mixture, Parmesan and the creamy zucchini mixture. Stir vigorously and serve immediately with a scattering of grated Parmesan.

For asparagus carbonara, replace the zucchini with 8 oz (250 g) asparagus spears. Cut the spears into 1-inch (2.5 cm) lengths and cook in exactly the same way as the zucchini.

WILD MUSHROOM PAPPARDELLE

Serves 4
Preparation time 15 minutes
Cooking time 12–25 minutes

12 oz (375 g) mixed wild mushrooms, cleaned
6 tbsp (90 ml) olive oil
1 clove garlic, thinly sliced
1 fresh red chile, seeded and finely chopped
Juice of ½ lemon
3 tbsp (45 ml) roughly chopped flat-leaf (Italian) parsley
¼ cup (60 ml) unsalted butter, cut into cubes
Salt and pepper
13 oz (400 g) dried pappardelle or homemade pappardelle
Fresh Parmesan cheese shavings, to serve

Trim the mushrooms, slicing porcini mushrooms (if you can find some fresh) and tearing large delicate mushrooms such as chanterelles or oyster mushrooms.

Heat the oil in a large, heavy-bottomed frying pan over low heat. Add the garlic and chile and leave the flavors to infuse for 5 minutes. If the garlic begins to color, simply remove the pan from the heat and leave to infuse in the heat of the pan.

Increase the heat to high; add the mushrooms and cook, stirring, for 3 to 4 minutes, until they are tender and golden. Remove from the heat and stir in the lemon juice, parsley and butter. Season with salt and pepper.

Cook the pasta in a large saucepan of salted boiling water until it is al dente: according to the package instructions for dried pasta or for 2 to 3 minutes for fresh pasta. Drain thoroughly, reserving a ladleful of the cooking water.

Return the pan with the mushroom mixture to medium heat and stir in the pasta. Toss until well combined, then pour in the reserved pasta cooking water and continue stirring until the pasta is well coated. Serve immediately with Parmesan shavings.

For creamy mushroom pappardelle, omit the chile, halve the quantity of oil and stir ¾ cup (175 ml) crème fraîche into the mushrooms with the butter. Bring to a boil before removing from the heat, then continue with the recipe as above. Drizzle with 2 tsp (10 ml) truffle oil before serving.

VEGETARIAN

CHILE POLENTA WITH CHERRY TOMATOES

Serves 4
Preparation time 10 minutes
Cooking time 30 minutes

3 tbsp (45 ml) chile-infused olive oil, divided
1 clove garlic, crushed
1 oz (30 g) Parmesan cheese, freshly grated
⅓ cup (75 ml) sun-dried tomato pesto
1 lb (500 g) ready-made polenta
8 oz (250 g) cherry tomatoes, halved
½ small red onion, thinly sliced
⅓ cup (75 ml) chopped fresh parsley
⅓ cup (75 ml) chopped fresh chives
2 oz (60 g) black olives, sliced
2 oz (60 g) pine nuts
Salt
2 tbsp (30 ml) balsamic glaze

Mix 1 tbsp (15 ml) of the oil with the garlic, Parmesan and pesto. Slice the polenta horizontally into 2 thin slabs, then cut each in half to make 4 chunky slices. Cut each of the slices in half horizontally and use to sandwich the filling, making 4 sandwiches.

Arrange, slightly apart, in a shallow ovenproof dish and bake in a preheated 375°F (190°C) oven for 15 minutes.

Meanwhile, mix the tomatoes in a bowl with the red onion, parsley, chives, olives, pine nuts and a little salt. Pile on top of the polenta and return to the oven for a further 15 minutes.

Beat the remaining oil with the balsamic glaze. Transfer the polenta stacks to serving plates and drizzle with the dressing. Serve with an arugula salad.

For homemade sun-dried tomato pesto, drain 4 oz (125 g) sun-dried tomatoes in oil and chop finely. Grind or process with 2 oz (60 g) pine nuts, 2 cloves garlic and 6 tbsp (90 ml) grated Parmesan. Blend to a thick paste with ½ cup (125 ml) olive oil, then season. This sauce can be kept, covered and chilled, for up to 5 days.

GOAT'S CHEESE & PEPPER LASAGNA

Serves 4

Preparation time 20 minutes, plus standing

Cooking time 50 minutes–1 hour

11-oz (325 g) can or jar of pimientos

6 tomatoes, peeled and roughly chopped

1 yellow bell pepper, seeded and finely chopped

2 zucchini, thinly sliced

3 oz (75 g) sun-dried tomatoes, thinly sliced

⅓ cup (75 ml) sun-dried tomato pesto

¾ cup (175 ml) fresh basil

¼ cup (60 ml) olive oil

Salt and pepper

5 oz (150 g) soft fresh goat's cheese

2⅓ cups (600 ml) store-bought or homemade cheese
   sauce

5 oz (150 g) dried egg lasagna sheets

6 tbsp (90 ml) grated Parmesan cheese

Drain the pimientos and roughly chop. Mix in a bowl with the tomatoes, yellow pepper, zucchini, sun-dried tomatoes and pesto. Tear the basil leaves and add to the bowl with the oil and a little salt and pepper. Mix the ingredients together thoroughly.

Spoon a quarter of the ingredients into a 7-cup (1.8 L) shallow oven-proof dish and dot with a quarter of the goat's cheese and ¼ cup (60 ml) of the cheese sauce. Cover with a third of the lasagna sheets in a layer, breaking them to fit where necessary. Repeat the layering, finishing with a layer of the tomato mixture and goat's cheese.

Spoon the remaining cheese sauce on top and sprinkle with the Parmesan. Bake in a preheated 375°F (190°C) oven for 50 to 60 minutes, until deep golden. Leave to stand for 10 minutes before serving with a leafy salad.

For homemade cheese sauce, put 2 cups (500 ml) milk in a saucepan with 1 small onion and 1 bay leaf. Heat until just boiling, then remove from the heat and leave to infuse for 20 minutes. Strain the milk into a jug. Melt ¼ cup (60 ml) butter, then tip in 6 tbsp (90 ml) all-purpose flour and stir in quickly. Cook, stirring, for 1 to 2 minutes, then, off the heat, gradually whisk in the milk until blended. Bring gently to a boil, stirring, and cook for 2 minutes. Off the heat, stir in 1 cup (250 ml) shredded Cheddar or Gruyère.

266

VEGETARIAN

ORECCHIETTE WITH WALNUT SAUCE

Serves 4

Preparation time 5 minutes

Cooking time 10–12 minutes

12 oz (375 g) dried orecchiette

¼ cup (60 ml) butter

15 fresh sage leaves, roughly chopped

2 cloves garlic, finely chopped

1⅓ cups (325 ml) walnuts, finely chopped

⅔ cup (150 ml) table (18%) or half-and-half 10% cream

2½ oz (65 g) Parmesan cheese, freshly grated

Salt and pepper

Cook the pasta in a large saucepan of salted boiling water according to the package instructions, until al dente.

Meanwhile, melt the butter in a frying pan over medium heat. When it begins to foam and sizzle, stir in the sage and garlic and cook, stirring, for 1 to 2 minutes, until golden. Remove from the heat and stir in the walnuts, cream and Parmesan.

Drain the pasta and stir it thoroughly into the sauce. Season with salt and pepper and serve immediately.

For spinach, green onion & avocado salad to serve with the pasta, use 5 oz (150 g) baby spinach leaves, 4 finely sliced green onions and 2 peeled, pitted and sliced avocados. Toss together and spoon into separate side dishes.

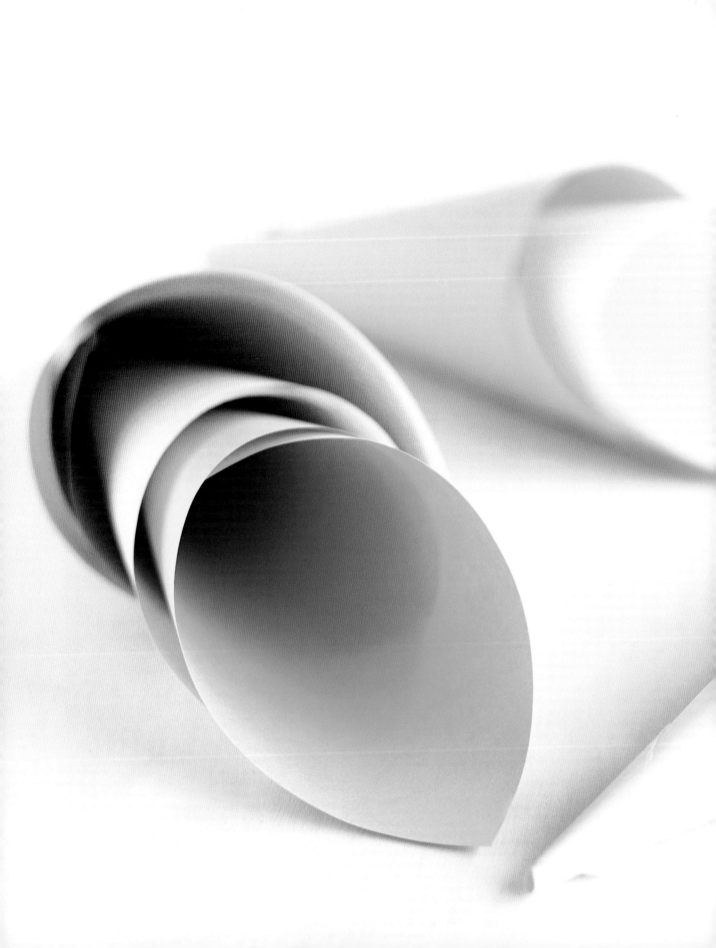

FUN RECIPES
FOR KIDS

HERBY BEANS & BACON

Serves 4
Preparation time 10 minutes
Cooking time 15 minutes

1 tbsp (15 ml) olive oil
6 slices bacon, roughly chopped
1 small carrot, finely grated
14-oz (398 ml) can chopped tomatoes
3 tbsp (45 ml) tomato paste
2 tbsp (30 ml) liquid honey
14-oz (398 ml) can borlotti or romano beans, drained
  and rinsed
3 tbsp (45 ml) chopped flat-leaf (Italian) parsley
  (optional)
4 thick slices whole wheat or multigrain bread
2½ tbsp (37 ml) freshly grated Parmesan cheese
  (optional)

Heat the oil in a large heavy-bottomed frying pan, then cook the bacon over medium heat for 2 to 3 minutes, until beginning to turn pale golden. Add the carrot and cook for 1 minute more.

Add the tomatoes, tomato paste and honey and heat until the tomato juice is bubbling. Add the beans, then reduce the heat and simmer for 4 minutes, uncovered, until the tomato juice has reduced and thickened slightly. Stir in the parsley, if using, and set aside.

Lightly toast the bread until golden and just crisp. Place on warmed serving plates and pile the herby beans and bacon on top. Sprinkle with the Parmesan, if desired.

For sausage & beans, cook 4 good-quality sausages in the oil for 5 to 6 minutes, turning, until golden. Remove from the pan and slice, then return to the pan with 3½ oz (100 g) thinly sliced chorizo sausage and cook for 2 minutes, stirring occasionally, until the sausages are golden. Continue as above and serve scattered with Parmesan, if desired.

BREAKFAST CRUMBLE

Serves 8
Preparation time 30 minutes
Cooking time 45–50 minutes

1 lb (500 g) apples, peeled, cored and roughly
  chopped
8 oz (250 g) pears, peeled, cored and roughly chopped
Finely grated zest and juice of 1 orange
¼ cup (60 ml) liquid honey
½ tsp (2 ml) ground ginger
6 oz (175 g) strawberries, hulled and quartered

Crumble
½ cup (125 ml) all-purpose flour
3 tbsp (45 ml) ground flaxseed
¼ cup (60 ml) butter, cubed
½ cup (125 ml) rolled oats
⅓ cup (75 ml) mixed seeds (such as pumpkin,
  sunflower, sesame and hemp)
¼ cup (60 ml) demerara sugar

Place the apples and pears in a medium heavy-bottomed saucepan with the orange zest and juice, honey and ginger. Bring to a gentle simmer, stirring occasionally, then cover and simmer for 10 minutes, until soft and slightly pulpy. Add the strawberries and cook for a further 2 to 3 minutes, until soft yet still retaining their shape. Remove the pan from the heat and transfer the mixture to an ovenproof gratin dish. Set aside while making the crumble.

Put the flour in a bowl and stir in the flaxseed. Add the butter and rub into the mixture until it resembles chunky breadcrumbs. Add the oats and again rub the butter into the mixture, using your fingertips to distribute it well. Stir in the seeds and sugar, then sprinkle over the fruit.

Bake the crumble in a preheated 400°F (200°C) oven for 30 to 35 minutes, until the topping is golden. Serve the crumble warm.

For amber crumble, omit the apples, pears and strawberries, roughly chop 4 ripe peaches and 6 ripe apricots and segment 4 oranges, then toss with ¼ cup (60 ml) liquid honey and 1 tsp (5 ml) ground cinnamon. Place the uncooked fruit in the gratin dish, sprinkle with the crumble and bake as above.

TOFFEE-APPLE PORRIDGE

Serves 4
Preparation time 10 minutes
Cooking time 15 minutes

1 lb (500 g) apples, peeled, cored and roughly
  chopped
½ tsp (2 ml) pumpkin pie spice
½ tsp (2 ml) ground ginger
5 tbsp (75 ml) brown sugar, divided
8 tbsp (120 ml) water
2⅓ cups (600 ml) milk
1¼ cups (300 ml) rolled oats
Maple syrup, to serve

Place the apples in a medium heavy-bottomed saucepan with the spices, 3 tbsp (45 ml) of the sugar and the water. Bring to a boil, then reduce the heat to a simmer. Cover and simmer over very low heat for 4 to 5 minutes, stirring occasionally, until the apples are soft yet still retain some of their shape. Set aside with a lid to keep warm while making the porridge.

Bring the milk and remaining sugar to a boil, stirring occasionally. Remove from the heat and add the rolled oats. Stir well, then return to low heat, stirring continuously, for 4 to 5 minutes, until the porridge has thickened.

Stir half the apple mixture through the porridge until well mixed, then ladle into 4 warmed serving bowls. Spoon on the remaining apple mixture and drizzle with maple syrup to serve, if desired.

For hot-pink swirled porridge, mash 8 oz (250 g) fresh raspberries with 1 tsp (5 ml) light brown sugar. Make up the porridge following the method above, then remove from the heat and spoon in the mashed raspberries. Using 1 to 2 stirs only, swirl the raspberries into the porridge, then ladle the swirled porridge into warmed bowls and serve with spoonfuls of Greek yogurt on top, if desired.

HUMMUS PITA POCKETS

Serves 6
Preparation time 15 minutes
Cooking time 3 minutes

14-oz (398 ml) can chickpeas, drained and rinsed
3 tbsp (45 ml) tahini paste
Finely grated zest and juice of ½ lemon
1 tbsp (15 ml) olive oil
3 tbsp (45 ml) chopped fresh chives (optional)
¼ cup (60 ml) water
2 medium carrots, grated
½ cucumber, chopped
Handful of freshly cut cress or alfalfa sprouts
4 whole wheat or white pita breads

Place the chickpeas in a food processor with the tahini paste and mix until thick. Add the lemon zest and juice, olive oil, chives and water. Mix again until smooth and creamy.

Toss the carrots, cucumber and cress in a bowl.

Lightly toast the pita breads for 1 minute, until warm and slightly "puffed." Halve each pita and fill, while warm, with the hummus and salad. Serve immediately.

For pockets with beet hummus, place 6 oz (175 g) cooked, drained beets (not in vinegar) into a food processor with 2 tbsp (30 ml) tahini paste, the juice of ½ lemon and 1 tsp (5 ml) horseradish sauce. Mix until smooth and creamy. Use to fill the pita pockets as above along with the salad.

TUNA MELTS

Serves 2
Preparation time 10 minutes
Cooking time 11–13 minutes

6½-oz (150 ml) can tuna, in oil or brine, drained
½ cup (125 ml) frozen corn
3 tbsp (45 ml) mayonnaise
2 panini buns, cut in half horizontally
3 oz (75 g) Gruyère or Emmenthal cheese, thinly sliced

Flake the tuna into a bowl. Put the corn in a small saucepan and pour boiling water over to just cover it. Cook for 3 minutes and drain through a sieve. Rinse the corn under cold water and add it to the tuna. Stir in the mayonnaise until well mixed.

Spread the tuna mixture over the two panini bases. Arrange the cheese on top of the tuna. Press the panini tops down firmly on the filling.

Heat a heavy-bottomed frying pan or ridged broiler pan for 2 minutes. Add the buns and cook on low heat for 3 to 4 minutes on each side, turning them carefully with a spatula or tongs. Wrap the tuna melts in parchment or wax paper and chill in the refrigerator until ready to serve.

For warm haloumi & vegetable melts, heat 1 tbsp (15 ml) olive oil in a frying pan and cook 1 small, thinly sliced zucchini and 1 thinly sliced red bell pepper for 3 to 4 minutes, until softened. Fill the paninis with the vegetables and top with 4 oz (125 g) thinly sliced haloumi cheese. Cook as above, then transfer to serving plates and serve.

BEAN, COCONUT & SPINACH SOUP

Serves 4
Preparation time 5 minutes
Cooking time about 20 minutes

1 tbsp (15 ml) olive oil
1 onion, chopped
2 large cloves garlic, crushed
1 tsp (5 ml) ground coriander
2 cans (14 oz/398 ml each) mixed beans, drained
14-oz (400 ml) can coconut milk
⅔ cup (150 ml) vegetable stock
8 oz (250 g) fresh spinach

Heat the oil in a large heavy-bottomed saucepan and cook the onion and garlic over medium heat for 3 to 4 minutes, until softened. Add the coriander and beans and cook for 1 minute, then add the coconut milk and stock. Bring to a boil, then reduce the heat, cover and simmer for 10 minutes.

Add the spinach to the pan. Stir well and cook for a further 5 minutes.

Mix the soup in a food processor in 2 batches until smooth, then ladle into warmed serving bowls and serve immediately.

For red lentil & bacon soup, heat 1 tbsp (15 ml) olive oil and cook 1 chopped onion, 3½ oz (100 g) roughly chopped bacon, 2 large carrots, cut into large chunks, and 1 crushed clove garlic for 3 to 4 minutes. Add 1 cup (250 ml) red lentils, ½ tsp (2 ml) ground nutmeg and 3⅔ cups (900 ml) chicken stock and bring to a boil. Reduce the heat, cover and simmer for 40 minutes, until the lentils are soft and cooked. Mix the soup in a food processor in 2 batches until smooth.

TRAFFIC-LIGHT SCRAMBLED EGGS

Serves 4
Preparation time 10 minutes
Cooking time 10 minutes

3 tbsp (45 ml) olive oil
1 small onion, finely chopped
½ green bell pepper, cored, seeded and roughly chopped
½ red bell pepper, cored, seeded and roughly chopped
½ yellow bell pepper, cored, seeded and roughly chopped
1 clove garlic, crushed
3 tbsp (45 ml) water
6 eggs, beaten
⅓ cup + 2 tbsp (100 ml) table (18%) or half-and-half (10%) cream
4 thick slices whole wheat bread, to serve

Heat the oil in a large nonstick frying pan and cook the onion and peppers over medium heat for about 4 to 5 minutes, until softened. Add the garlic and cook for a further 1 minute, then add the water. Cover the pan and simmer for 2 minutes.

Beat together the eggs and cream. Remove the lid from the pan, pour in the eggs and stir over low heat with a wooden spoon until the eggs are creamy and cooked.

Meanwhile, lightly toast the bread slices. Serve the eggs spooned over the warm toast.

For cheesy eggs & cress, beat together the eggs, cream and ½ cup (125 ml) grated Cheddar cheese. Heat 1 tbsp (15 ml) butter in a large nonstick frying pan and add the egg mixture. Stir over low heat with a wooden spoon until creamy and cooked. Serve on warm whole wheat toast with freshly cut cress or alfalfa sprouts sprinkled over.

JEWELED COUSCOUS

Serves 2–3
Preparation time 20 minutes
Cooking time 2 minutes

¾ cup (175 ml) couscous
¾ cup (175 ml) hot vegetable stock
¼ cup (60 ml) green beans, trimmed and cut into ½-inch (1 cm) lengths
1 small orange
2 tbsp (30 ml) olive oil
1 tbsp (15 ml) liquid honey
1 pomegranate
½ small pineapple, chopped into small pieces
1 small red bell pepper, cored, seeded and finely diced

Put the couscous in a heatproof bowl and add the stock. Cover and leave to stand for 20 minutes.

Meanwhile, bring a small pan of water to a boil and add the beans. Cook for 2 minutes. Drain the beans through a colander and rinse in cold water.

Finely grate half the zest of the orange and mix it in a small bowl with 3 tbsp (45 ml) of the orange juice, the oil and the honey. Whisk lightly with a fork.

Cut the pomegranate in half. Pull the fruit apart with your hands and ease out the clusters of seeds. Separate the seeds, discarding any white parts of the fruit, which are bitter. Add the pomegranate seeds, beans, pineapple and red pepper to the couscous along with the orange-and-honey dressing. Mix well and chill in the refrigerator until ready to serve.

For chicken, pea & mint couscous, make the couscous as above and leave to stand. Replace all the above vegetables with 6 oz (175 g) cooked chicken, ⅔ cup (150 ml) cooked peas and 3 tbsp (45 ml) fresh chopped mint. Mix the zest and juice of half a lemon into a ¾-cup (175 ml) container of crème fraîche and serve spooned over the couscous.

PEKING WRAPS

Serves 2
Preparation time 10 minutes
Cooking time about 10 minutes

1 duck breast, about 6 oz (175 g), with skin, cut across
  into very thin slices
½ tsp (2 ml) Chinese five-spice powder
1 tbsp (15 ml) vegetable oil
2 large soft flour tortillas
2 tbsp (30 ml) hoisin sauce
2 iceberg lettuce leaves, thinly shredded
2-inch (5 cm) piece cucumber, sliced into matchsticks
2 green onions, thinly sliced diagonally

Put the slices of duck on a plate and sprinkle with the five-spice powder.
Turn the slices in the spice until coated all over. Heat the oil in a small
frying pan for 1 minute. Add the duck and fry gently for 5 minutes,
turning the pieces with a long metal spatula. Using the spatula, transfer
the duck to a plate and leave to cool while you prepare the filling.

Heat the tortillas one at a time in the microwave on full power for
8 seconds. Alternatively, warm them under a hot broiler or in a frying
pan for approximately 10 seconds.

Spread the hoisin sauce over one side of each tortilla. Scatter a line
of lettuce, then the cucumber, green onions and duck down the center
of each tortilla, keeping the ingredients away from the ends.

Fold 2 sides of each tortilla over the ends of the filling, then roll them up
tightly from an unfolded side so that the filling is completely enclosed.
Cut the wraps in half, wrap in parchment or wax paper and chill in the
refrigerator until ready to go.

For crispy lamb & lettuce Peking wraps, toss 6 oz (175 g) lean lamb
strips in the five-spice powder and cook as above. Use shredded
lettuce, green onion and cucumber as before, as well as strips of finely
sliced carrot.

CHINESE-STYLE TURKEY WRAPS

Serves 2
Preparation time 10 minutes
Cooking time 1–2 minutes

½ tsp (2 ml) vegetable oil
3½ oz (100 g) turkey breast, thinly sliced
1 tbsp (15 ml) liquid honey
2 tbsp (30 ml) soy sauce
1 tbsp (15 ml) toasted sesame oil
2 soft flour tortillas
2 oz (60 g) bean sprouts
¼ red bell pepper, cored, seeded and thinly sliced
¼ onion, thinly sliced
1 oz (30 g) snow peas, sliced
2 cobs baby corn, canned or thawed frozen, thinly
  sliced

Heat the oil in a frying pan over medium heat and add the turkey to the
pan. Stir for 1 to 2 minutes, until cooked through. Reduce the heat and
stir in the honey, soy sauce and toasted sesame oil, making sure that
the turkey is well coated. Set aside to cool.

Assemble a wrap by placing half the turkey mixture down the center of
a tortilla. Add half the bean sprouts and red pepper, onion, snow peas
and baby corn. Repeat with the other tortilla. (Alternatively, retain the
remaining tortilla and mixture for use another day; the mixture will keep
for up to 24 hours in the refrigerator.)

Roll up the tortilla securely and wrap in parchment or wax paper (plastic
wrap can make the wrap rather soggy).

For Chinese-style pork & bok choy wraps, replace the turkey with 4 oz
(125 g) pork tenderloin strips tossed with ½ tsp (2 ml) Chinese five-
spice powder and cook as above for 3 to 4 minutes. Add 1 small head
bok choy, shredded, with the honey, soy sauce and sesame oil and
cook for a further 2 minutes. Assemble as above with 4 oz (125 g)
bean sprouts, omitting the snow peas, onion and corn.

SPICY CHORIZO WRAP

Serves 2
Preparation time 15 minutes
Cooking time 5–7 minutes

4 eggs
½ tsp (2 ml) mild chili powder
2 oz (60 g) sliced chorizo sausage, cut into
  thin shreds
2 tbsp (30 ml) olive oil
1 container mustard and cress or alfalfa sprouts
2 large soft flour tortillas
2 tbsp (30 ml) sun-dried tomato pesto

Break the eggs into a bowl and add the chili powder. Whisk well until the eggs are completely broken up. Stir in the chorizo. Heat the oil in a small frying pan for 1 minute. Tip the egg mixture into the pan. When the eggs start to set around the edges, use a fork to push the cooked parts into the center of the pan so the uncooked egg flows into the space. Keep doing this until the eggs are no longer runny, then let the omelet cook until just set (3 to 5 minutes). Slide the omelet onto a plate and leave to cool.

Put the mustard and cress or alfalfa sprouts in a sieve. Rinse under cold water and leave to drain.

Prepare the tortillas by heating in the microwave on full power for 10 seconds. Alternatively, warm them under a hot broiler or heat in the frying pan for approximately 10 seconds (wipe out the pan with a paper towel first, taking care, as it might still be hot).

Spread one side of each of the tortillas with the pesto and lay the omelet on top. Sprinkle with the mustard and cress or sprouts. Roll up tightly so the filling is completely enclosed. Cut the wraps in half, wrap in parchment or wax paper and chill in the refrigerator until ready to serve.

For pesto chicken wraps, replace the chorizo with 3 oz (75 g) cooked and tornup chicken pieces and 2 oz (60 g) black olives, sliced. Spread the tortilla with 1 tbsp (15 ml) green pesto and top with the omelet. Omit the cress, roll up and serve warm.

CORN FRITTERS & TOMATO DIP

Makes 20
Preparation time 15 minutes
Cooking time 20–30 minutes

⅔ cup (150 ml) all-purpose flour
½ tsp (2 ml) paprika
⅔ cup (150 ml) milk
1 egg, beaten
9-oz (275 g) can corn niblets, drained
3 tbsp (45 ml) chopped fresh parsley
2 green onions, finely chopped
½ red bell pepper, finely chopped
¼ cup (60 ml) vegetable oil

Tomato dip
1 tbsp (15 ml) olive oil
6 ripe tomatoes, roughly chopped
1 tbsp (15 ml) brown sugar
½ tsp (2 ml) paprika
1 tbsp (15 ml) red wine vinegar

Sift the flour and paprika into a bowl, then add the milk and egg and whisk together to form a thick batter. Add the corn, parsley, green onions and red pepper and mix well. If the mixture is too thick, add 1 tbsp (15 ml) water to loosen. Set aside while making the tomato dip.

Heat the oil in a medium heavy-bottomed pan, add the tomatoes and cook over medium heat for 5 minutes, stirring occasionally. Add the sugar, paprika and vinegar, reduce the heat, cover and simmer over very low heat for 10 to 15 minutes, stirring occasionally, until the tomatoes are thick and pulpy. Remove from the heat and transfer to a bowl to cool.

Heat the vegetable oil in a large nonstick frying pan and spoon tablespoons of the corn mixture into the pan, well spaced apart, and cook for 1 to 2 minutes on each side, in batches, until golden and firm. Remove the fritters from the pan using a metal spatula and drain on paper towels.

Serve the corn fritters with a pot of the sauce to dip, or wrap in foil to keep warm for transport.

For minted zucchini fritters, replace the corn with 1 finely chopped large zucchini. Heat 1 tsp (5 ml) of oil in a large frying pan and cook the zucchini over medium heat for 3 to 4 minutes, stirring occasionally, until pale golden. Add to the batter with 2 tbsp (30 ml) chopped fresh mint.

CHICKPEA & HERB SALAD

Serves 4
Preparation time 10 minutes
Cooking time 5 minutes (optional)

⅔ cup (150 ml) bulgur wheat
¼ cup (60 ml) olive oil
1 tbsp (15 ml) lemon juice
2 tbsp (30 ml) chopped flat-leaf (Italian) parsley
1 tbsp (15 ml) chopped fresh mint
14-oz (398 ml) can chickpeas, drained and rinsed
4 oz (125 g) cherry tomatoes, halved
1 tbsp (15 ml) chopped mild onion
⅔ cup (150 ml) diced cucumber
5 oz (150 g) feta cheese, diced

Put the bulgur wheat in a heatproof bowl and pour over sufficient boiling water just to cover. Set aside until the water has been absorbed. (If you want to give a fluffier finish to the bulgur wheat, transfer it to a steamer and steam for 5 minutes. Spread out on a plate to cool.)

Mix together the oil, lemon juice, parsley and mint in a large bowl. Add the chickpeas, tomatoes, onion, cucumber and bulgur wheat. Mix well and add the feta, stirring lightly to avoid breaking up the cheese.

Serve immediately or pack into an airtight container to transport.

For tuna, bean & black olive salad, replace the chickpeas, tomatoes, onion and cucumber with a 6½-oz (150 ml) can tuna, drained and flaked, a 14-oz (398 ml) can mixed beans, drained and rinsed, 4 oz (125 g) black olives and ¼ cup (60 ml) lemon juice. Toss well before serving.

CHICKEN FAJITAS & NO-CHILE SALSA

Serves 4
Preparation time 20 minutes
Cooking time about 5 minutes

½ tsp (2 ml) ground coriander
½ tsp (2 ml) ground cumin
½ tsp (2 ml) paprika
1 clove garlic, crushed
3 tbsp (45 ml) chopped fresh coriander
12 oz (375 g) boneless skinless chicken breasts, cut into bite-size strips
1 tbsp (15 ml) olive oil
4 soft flour tortillas
Sour cream (optional)

Salsa
3 large ripe tomatoes, finely chopped
3 tbsp (45 ml) chopped fresh coriander
⅛ cucumber, finely chopped
1 tbsp (15 ml) olive oil

Guacamole
1 large avocado, roughly chopped
Grated zest and juice of ½ lime
2 tsp (10 ml) sweet chili sauce (optional)

Place all the ground spices, garlic and coriander in a mixing bowl. Toss the chicken in the oil, then add to the spices and toss to coat lightly in the spice mixture.

Make the salsa. Mix the tomatoes, coriander and cucumber in a bowl and drizzle the oil over. Transfer to a serving bowl.

Make the guacamole. Mash the avocado with the lime zest and juice and sweet chili sauce, if using, until soft and rough-textured. Transfer to a serving bowl.

Heat a grill pan or heavy-bottomed frying pan and cook the chicken for 3 to 4 minutes, turning occasionally, until golden and cooked through. Fill the tortillas with the hot chicken slices, guacamole and salsa, and fold into quarters. Spoon on a little sour cream, if desired.

For beef fajitas, replace the chicken with rump or sirloin steak, cut into bite-size strips. For a slightly "warmer" version, replace the paprika with mild chili powder.

VEGETABLE BURGERS

Serves 8
Preparation time 20 minutes, plus chilling
Cooking time 12–15 minutes

8 oz (250 g) spinach, washed and patted dry
1 tbsp (15 ml) olive oil
1 small red bell pepper, cored, seeded and very finely
    chopped
4 green onions, finely sliced
14-oz (398 ml) can chickpeas, drained and rinsed
4 oz (125 g) ricotta cheese
1 egg yolk
½ tsp (2 ml) ground coriander
½ cup (125 ml) all-purpose flour
1 egg, beaten
1½ cups (375 ml) dry whole-grain breadcrumbs
¼ cup (60 ml) vegetable oil

To serve
8 mini burger buns
Ketchup
Cherry tomatoes (optional)

Put the moist spinach in a pan over medium heat for 2 to 3 minutes, stirring continuously, until wilted. Remove from the heat, drain well and set aside.

Heat the olive oil in a frying pan and cook the pepper and green onions over medium heat for 4 to 5 minutes, until soft. Set aside.

Place the chickpeas in a food processor with the ricotta and blend until smooth. Add the spinach, egg yolk and coriander and blend again to mix well. Transfer to a mixing bowl and fold in the pepper-and-green-onion mixture. Shape the mixture into 8 patties, toss them lightly in the flour, then roll first in the beaten egg and then in the breadcrumbs, to coat. Chill for 30 minutes.

Heat the vegetable oil in a large heavy-bottomed frying pan and cook the burgers over medium heat for 6 to 7 minutes, turning once, until golden and crisp. Serve in the buns with ketchup and cherry tomatoes, if desired.

For sausage & pepper burgers, cook the spinach, pepper and onions as above. Chop the spinach roughly. Place 12 oz (375 g) good-quality sausage meat in a bowl and add 1 tbsp (15 ml) tomato chutney or chili sauce and 1 tsp (5 ml) Dijon mustard. Mix well, then stir in the spinach, pepper and onions and mix well. Do not coat, but simply heat the oil and cook for 2 to 3 minutes on each side, until golden. Serve as above.

MINI SCONE PIZZAS

Serves 4
Preparation time 25 minutes
Cooking time 15–20 minutes

2 cups (500 ml) self-raising whole wheat flour
¼ cup (60 ml) butter, cubed
⅔ cup (150 ml) milk
⅔ cup (150 ml) tomato sauce or passata
3 tbsp (45 ml) tomato paste
2 tbsp (30 ml) chopped fresh basil
4 thick slices good-quality ham, shredded
4 oz (125 g) pitted black olives, halved
5 oz (150 g) mozzarella cheese, grated
Oil for drizzling

Sift the flour into a bowl and rub in the butter until the mixture resembles fine breadcrumbs. Make a well in the center and stir in enough of the milk to give a fairly soft dough. Turn it out on to a lightly floured surface and knead gently. Cut into 4 pieces, then knead again to shape each into a rough round. Roll out 4 rough circles, each about 6 inches (15 cm), and place on a baking sheet.

Mix together the tomato sauce, tomato paste and basil. Divide between the scone bases and spread to within ½ inch (1 cm) of the edges. Pile each with the ham and olives, then sprinkle with the mozzarella.

Drizzle with a little oil and bake in a preheated 400°F (200°C) oven for 15 to 20 minutes, until the bases are risen and the cheese is golden. Wrap in foil and serve warm or cold.

For egg & bacon scone pizzas, form each pizza base into a slight bowl shape with a ridge around the edge. Spread with the tomato sauce. Heat 1 tbsp (15 ml) olive oil and cook 6 roughly chopped back bacon slices for 2 minutes, until golden. Drain on paper towels. Sprinkle the pizzas with the bacon pieces, then crack an egg over the top of each. Bake in the oven as above, without the cheese. Remove from the oven and, while still warm, sprinkle each with 1 tbsp (15 ml) grated mozzarella and some chopped parsley.

SPAGHETTI BOLOGNESE

Serves 6
Preparation time 30 minutes
Cooking time 35 minutes

2 tbsp (30 ml) olive oil, divided
1 onion, finely chopped
2 carrots, grated
1 zucchini, grated
1 lb (500 g) lean ground beef
2 tbsp (30 ml) all-purpose flour
2 tbsp (30 ml) tomato paste
2⅓ cups (600 ml) rich beef stock
7-oz (200 g) can chopped tomatoes
8 oz (250 g) spaghetti or linguine
Freshly grated Parmesan cheese, to serve

Heat 1 tbsp (15 ml) of the oil in a large heavy-bottomed saucepan and cook the onion, carrots and zucchini over medium heat for 5 to 6 minutes, stirring occasionally, until soft. Remove the vegetables from the pan and set aside.

Add the ground beef to the pan and cook over high heat for 4 to 5 minutes, stirring frequently, until browned all over. Return the vegetables to the pan, add the flour and stir well to coat lightly. Add the tomato paste to the beef stock and stir well, then add the stock to the meat along with the chopped tomatoes. Bring to a boil, then reduce the heat, cover with a lid and simmer for 20 minutes.

Meanwhile, cook the pasta for 8 to 10 minutes or according to package instructions, until tender. Drain and toss with the remaining oil. Arrange the pasta in warmed serving bowls and pile the bolognese sauce on top. Sprinkle with the Parmesan.

For bolognese pasta bake, cook 8 oz (250 g) macaroni until just tender. Drain and toss with 1 tbsp (15 ml) olive oil. Make up the bolognese sauce as above and mix with the macaroni. Transfer to a large gratin dish. Mix ¾ cup + 2 tbsp (200 ml) crème fraîche with 3 tbsp (45 ml) freshly grated Parmesan cheese and 2 tbsp (30 ml) chopped fresh parsley, and spoon over the top of the macaroni. Bake in a preheated 400°F (200°C) oven for 20 to 25 minutes, until the topping is golden and bubbling.

CHICKEN RICE SALAD

Serves 4
Preparation time 10 minutes, plus cooling
Cooking time about 15 minutes

4 chicken thighs, skinned and boned
¾ cup (175 ml) long-grain rice
2 tsp (10 ml) lemon juice
2 tbsp (30 ml) peanut butter (optional)
2 tbsp (30 ml) olive oil
2 pineapple rings, chopped
1 red bell pepper, cored, seeded and chopped
2½ oz (75 g) sugar snap peas, sliced
¼ cup (60 ml) peanuts (optional)

Place the chicken thighs in a steamer set over boiling water and cook for 10 to 12 minutes, until cooked through. Alternatively, simmer them in shallow water in a frying pan for 10 minutes. Remove from the steamer or pan and set aside to cool.

Meanwhile, cook the rice according to the package instructions. Drain and rinse under cold water to cool the rice completely, then tip it into a large bowl.

Make the dressing. Mix together the lemon juice and peanut butter, if using, until well combined, then whisk in the oil.

Dice the chicken thighs into bite-size pieces and stir into the rice. Add the pineapple, red pepper, sugar snap peas and peanuts, if using. Pour the dressing over the chicken rice salad and serve.

For shrimp rice salad, make up the peanut dressing as above. Replace the chicken with 5 oz (150 g) shrimp tossed with 2 tbsp (30 ml) toasted sesame seeds. Cut ¼ cucumber into thin sticks and toss with the rice, peanut sauce, shrimp and seeds.

BAKED SWEET POTATOES & SHRIMP

Serves 4
Preparation time 10 minutes
Cooking time 25–30 minutes

1 tbsp (15 ml) olive oil
4 large sweet potatoes, skin on, scrubbed, patted dry
8 oz (250 g) medium shrimp, defrosted if frozen
1 ripe avocado, cut into small chunks
2 tbsp (30 ml) mayonnaise
2 tbsp (30 ml) milk or water
3 tbsp (45 ml) crème fraîche
1 tbsp (15 ml) tomato paste

To serve
Paprika
1 container alfalfa sprouts or other small sprouts

Drizzle a little of the oil over each sweet potato, then rub it all over the skin. Put the potatoes on a baking sheet. Bake in a preheated 400°F (200°C) oven for 25 to 30 minutes, until tender and cooked through.

Meanwhile, place the shrimp and avocado in a bowl and toss together. Mix the mayonnaise with the milk or water until smooth, then add the crème fraîche and tomato paste and mix until well blended. Add the shrimp and avocado and toss well to coat lightly.

Remove the sweet potatoes from the oven. Split the hot potatoes and fill them with the shrimp mixture. Serve garnished with a pinch of paprika and some fresh sprouts.

For baked sweet potatoes & creamy mushrooms, bake the sweet potatoes as above. Heat 1 tbsp (15 ml) olive oil in a heavy-bottomed frying pan and cook 8 oz (250 g) quartered cremini mushrooms over high heat for 3 to 4 minutes, until golden and softened. Remove from the heat, add ¾ cup + 2 tbsp (200 ml) crème fraîche and 1 tsp (5 ml) Dijon mustard and stir well for a few seconds, until piping hot. Spoon into the sweet potatoes as above.

SWEET POTATO–TOPPED FISH PIE

Serves 4
Preparation time 45 minutes
Cooking time 45 minutes

12 oz (375 g) cod fillet
1¼ cups (300 ml) water
8 oz (250 g) shrimp, thawed if frozen, drained
1 large carrot, roughly chopped
½ bunch broccoli, cut into small florets
2 tbsp (30 ml) butter
¼ cup (60 ml) all-purpose flour
1¼ cups (300 ml) milk
2 oz (60 g) Cheddar cheese, grated

Potato topping
1¼ lb (625 g) sweet potatoes, peeled and chopped
¼ cup (60 ml) butter
3 tbsp (45 ml) chopped fresh parsley
1 oz (30 g) Cheddar cheese, finely grated

Place the cod fillet in a heavy-bottomed frying pan and pour in the water. Bring to a boil, reduce the heat, cover and simmer for 3 minutes, until the fish is opaque and cooked through. Drain and reserve the fish stock. Flake the fish into chunks and gently toss with the shrimp.

Cook the carrot and broccoli in boiling water for 5 minutes, drain and set aside. Melt the butter in a pan, remove from the heat and add the flour. Stir over low heat for 30 seconds. Remove from the heat and gradually add the milk a little at a time, stirring well after each addition, then add the reserved fish stock and stir well.

Return the pan to the heat and bring to a boil, stirring continuously until thickened. Remove from the heat and add the Cheddar. Pour over the fish, add the vegetables and very gently fold together. Transfer to a large gratin dish and set aside.

Meanwhile, cook the sweet potatoes for 8 to 10 minutes, until tender. Drain, add the butter and mash well. Stir in the parsley, spoon over the top of the fish and sauce and sprinkle with the Cheddar. Bake in a preheated 400°F (200°C) oven for 30 minutes, until a golden crust forms.

For cheesy tuna & shrimp pie, replace the cod with 2 cans (6½ oz/150 ml each) tuna in brine, drained and flaked. Cook 1½ lb (750 g) white potatoes and mash with the butter, an extra 2 oz (60 g) Cheddar and 6 tbsp (90 ml) milk. Fold in the parsley and spoon over the pie, sprinkle with the remaining cheese and bake as above.

POTATO & CHEESE RÖSTIS

Makes 4
Preparation time 10 minutes
Cooking time 25 minutes

1 lb (500 g) red or Yukon Gold potatoes, unpeeled
2 oz (60 g) mild Cheddar cheese, grated
1 red onion, finely chopped
3 tbsp (45 ml) vegetable oil
Ketchup (see page 12), to serve

Put the potatoes in a large pan of water and bring to a boil. Boil for about 20 minutes, until the potatoes are just cooked but firm. Drain and cool.

Peel the potatoes and grate them into a bowl. Stir in the grated Cheddar and onion. With wet hands, shape into 4 rounds, then press down with 2 fingers to form into röstis. Tidy up the edges.

Brush lightly with oil on both sides and broil or grill on a foil-lined broiler rack at medium heat for 2 to 3 minutes on each side, until golden brown.

Serve the röstis warm with the ketchup. (Any that are not needed straight away may be stored in an airtight container in the refrigerator for up to 3 days.)

For potato, bacon & tomato röstis, make the potato mixture as above, omitting the onion. Add 1 finely chopped large tomato and 2 slices finely chopped cooked bacon to the mixture along with 2 tbsp (30 ml) ketchup. Shape into 4 patties and cook as above. Use to fill warm toasted whole wheat pita breads, with watercress and extra ketchup.

GREEN CHEESE PASTA

Serves 4
Preparation time 10 minutes
Cooking time 10 minutes

8 oz (250 g) pasta shapes
10 oz (300 g) fresh spinach
1 tsp (5 ml) ground nutmeg
¼ cup (60 ml) butter
½ cup (125 ml) all-purpose flour
2⅓ cups (600 ml) milk
4 oz (100 g) Cheddar cheese, grated

Cook the pasta shapes for 8 to 10 minutes or according to package instructions, until just tender. Drain and set aside.

Meanwhile, place the spinach in a pan of boiling water and cook, stirring continuously, over medium heat for 2 minutes, until wilted. Remove from the heat and drain well, then return to the pan and toss with the nutmeg. Set aside.

Melt the butter in a medium heavy-bottomed saucepan. Remove from the heat, add the flour and stir to form a thick paste. Return to the heat and cook gently for a few seconds, stirring continuously. Remove from the heat and gradually add the milk, stirring well after each addition. Return to the heat and bring to a boil, stirring continuously, until the sauce has boiled and thickened.

Remove from the heat and add the spinach and cheese. Stir, then transfer to a food processor and mix until smooth. Return to the pan and add the pasta. Stir well to coat, then divide between 4 warmed serving bowls.

For zucchini & garlic pasta, replace the spinach with 3 large zucchini, trimmed and grated. Heat 1 tbsp (15 ml) olive oil in a nonstick frying pan and cook the zucchini and 1 crushed clove garlic over medium heat for 4 to 5 minutes, until soft and tender. Add 3 tbsp (45 ml) chopped fresh chives, then add to the sauce in place of the spinach and mix until smooth before tossing with the pasta.

SALMON PASTA BAKE

Serves 6
Preparation time 20 minutes
Cooking time 30 minutes

8 oz (250 g) pasta shapes
2 tbsp (30 ml) butter
¼ cup (60 ml) all-purpose flour
1¼ cups (300 ml) milk
¾ cup (175 ml) crème fraîche
3½ oz (100 g) freshly grated Parmesan cheese, divided
3 tbsp (45 ml) chopped fresh herbs such as chives or dill
2 cans (7 oz/200 g each) red salmon, drained and flaked
⅔ cup (150 ml) frozen peas

Cook the pasta for 8 to 10 minutes or according to package instructions, until tender. Drain and set aside.

Heat the butter in a nonstick pan until melted. Remove from the heat, add the flour and stir well to form a thick paste. Return the pan to the heat and cook, stirring continuously, for 1 minute. Remove from the heat and gradually add the milk, a little at a time, stirring well, until all the milk is used.

Return the pan to the heat and bring to a boil, stirring continuously, until boiled and thickened. Add the crème fraîche and half the Parmesan and stir well. Add the drained pasta, herbs, flaked salmon and peas and toss gently to mix, taking care not to break up the fish. Transfer to 6 individual gratin dishes and sprinkle over the remaining Parmesan.

Bake in a preheated 350°F (180°C) oven for 20 minutes, until golden and bubbling. Serve with warm bread and a simple salad.

For tuna pasta bake with corn, replace the salmon with 2 cans (6½ oz/ 150 ml each) tuna in brine, drained and flaked, and replace the peas with ⅔ cup (150 ml) corn. Add 1 tbsp (15 ml) whole-grain mustard and mix well. Cut a garlic baguette into slices and place on top of the pasta. Sprinkle with the remaining Parmesan and bake as above until the bread is crisp and golden and the sauce is bubbling.

ASIAN NOODLES WITH SHRIMP

Serves 2
Preparation time 20 minutes
Cooking time 10 minutes

3 tbsp (45 ml) plum sauce
2 tbsp (30 ml) seasoned rice vinegar
2 tbsp (30 ml) soy sauce
3½ oz (100 g) fine or medium egg noodles
1 tbsp (15 ml) vegetable oil
2 green onions, sliced diagonally into chunky pieces
½ mild red chile, cored, seeded and finely chopped
5 oz (150 g) bok choy or cabbage, thinly sliced
3½ oz (100 g) baby corn, cut in half diagonally
7 oz (200 g) peeled shrimp, thawed if frozen, drained

Mix the plum sauce with the rice vinegar and soy sauce in a small bowl and set aside.

Pour plenty of freshly boiled water into a medium saucepan and bring back to a boil. Add the noodles and cook for 3 minutes. Drain in a colander.

Heat the oil in a large frying pan or wok for 1 minute. Add the green onions and chile and fry for 1 minute, stirring with a wooden spoon. Add the bok choy or cabbage and the corn and fry for a further 2 to 3 minutes, until the vegetables are softened.

Tip the noodles, shrimp and sauce into the pan and cook, stirring gently, over low heat until the ingredients are mixed together and hot. Serve immediately.

For Asian noodles with beef & coconut, replace the red chile and bok choy with 1 cup (250 ml) blanched broccoli florets. Add to the wok with the green onions and cook for 1 minute. Add 6 oz (175 g) round steak, cut into thin strips, and cook in the pan for a further 2 to 3 minutes, until golden. Add a 14-oz (400 ml) can coconut milk with 2 tbsp (30 ml) soy sauce to replace the plum sauce and toss with the noodles. Heat for 1 minute, until hot.

KORMA-STYLE CURRIED SHRIMP

Serves 4
Preparation time 5 minutes
Cooking time about 25 minutes

1 tbsp (15 ml) vegetable oil
1 onion, roughly chopped
½-inch (1 cm) piece ginger, peeled and finely grated
1 tsp (5 ml) ground coriander
½ tsp (2 ml) ground cumin
½ tsp (2 ml) curry powder
14-oz (398 ml) can chopped tomatoes
1 tbsp (15 ml) brown sugar
14-oz (400 ml) can coconut milk
8 oz (250 g) shrimp, thawed if frozen
⅔ cup (150 ml) frozen peas
3 tbsp (45 ml) chopped fresh coriander
Rice or naan, to serve

Heat the oil in a large nonstick frying pan and cook the onion and ginger over low heat for 3 to 4 minutes, stirring regularly, until soft but not golden. Add the spices and cook for a further 1 minute. Add the chopped tomatoes and sugar and increase the heat slightly, continuing to cook for a further 5 minutes, stirring occasionally, until the tomatoes have reduced slightly and thickened.

Pour in the coconut milk and bring to a boil. Reduce the heat and simmer, uncovered, for 10 minutes, until the sauce has reduced and thickened. Drain the shrimp well, then add to the sauce with the peas and coriander and cook for a further 2 to 3 minutes, until piping hot.

Serve the mild curry in warmed serving bowls, with either rice or naan breads to mop up the juices.

For mild chicken & squash curry, omit the ginger and replace the shrimp with 8 oz (250 g) roughly chopped chicken breast and the peas with 1 cup (250 ml) peeled and cubed butternut squash. Cook both the chicken and the squash with the onion as above, then add the spices and continue to follow the recipe as above.

NO-MESS CHEESY PEPPERONI CALZONES

Serves 8
Preparation time 30–40 minutes
Cooking time 25–30 minutes

10 oz (300 g) pizza dough mix
Flour, for dusting
1 tbsp (15 ml) olive oil
1 small red bell pepper, cored, seeded and roughly chopped
1 small yellow bell pepper, cored, seeded and roughly chopped
6 oz (175 g) chorizo sausage, sliced
1 large tomato, roughly chopped
½ tsp (2 ml) dried Italian herbs
5-oz (150 g) package mozzarella cheese, drained and cubed

Make up the pizza dough according to package instructions and turn out onto a lightly floured surface. Divide the dough into 8 pieces. Knead each lightly to produce smooth rounds, then roll each into an 8-inch (20 cm) circle. Loosely cover with plastic wrap.

Heat the oil in a large nonstick frying pan and cook the peppers over medium heat for 5 minutes, stirring occasionally. Add the chorizo slices and cook for 2 minutes before adding the tomato. Cook for a further 3 to 4 minutes, stirring occasionally, until the tomato has softened. Remove from the heat and stir in the herbs and mozzarella.

Allow to cool slightly before dividing the filling between the 8 dough circles. Lightly brush the edges with a little water, then fold the circles in half to enclose the filling and press to seal. Place on a baking sheet and bake in a preheated 425°F (220°C) oven for 15 to 20 minutes. Serve warm.

For butternut squash & feta cheese calzones, heat 1 tbsp (15 ml) olive oil in a pan and cook 1 cup (250 ml) cubed butternut squash over medium heat for 5 to 6 minutes, until beginning to soften. Add 5 tbsp (75 ml) water, cover and cook over low heat for 3 minutes. Remove from the heat and allow to cool. Add 2 tbsp (30 ml) chopped fresh parsley and 1 cup (250 ml) crumbled feta. Use the filling as above.

BAKED CABBAGE WITH NUTS & CHEESE

Serves 4
Preparation time 15 minutes
Cooking time 30 minutes

4 to 5 cups (1 L) shredded white cabbage
1½ to 2 cups (375 to 500 ml) shredded green or
  Savoy cabbage
1 tsp (5 ml) ground nutmeg
4 oz (125 g) roasted unsalted peanuts, toasted
2 tbsp (30 ml) butter
¼ cup (60 ml) all-purpose flour
1¾ cups (425 ml) milk
4 oz (125 g) strong Cheddar cheese, grated, divided
1 tsp (5 ml) Dijon mustard
2 tbsp (30 ml) chopped fresh parsley
¼ cup (60 ml) whole wheat breadcrumbs

Cook the two types of cabbage in boiling water for 5 minutes, until just tender. Drain and place in a large mixing bowl and toss with the nutmeg and peanuts.

Heat the butter in a nonstick saucepan until melted. Remove from the heat, add the flour and mix to a paste. Return to the heat and cook for a few seconds. Remove from the heat and add the milk a little at a time, stirring well between each addition. Return to the heat and bring to a boil, stirring continuously until boiled and thickened.

Remove the pan from the heat and add 3 oz (75 g) of the grated Cheddar and the mustard. Mix well, then pour over the cabbage and mix it in.

Transfer the mixture to a gratin dish or 4 individual gratin dishes. Toss the remaining cheese with the parsley and breadcrumbs, then sprinkle over the top and bake in a preheated 400°F (200°C) oven for 20 minutes, until golden and bubbling.

For root vegetable bake with nuts & cheese, replace the cabbage with 1½ cups (375 ml) sliced butternut squash and 1 cup (250 ml) sliced parsnips. Cook in boiling water for 5 minutes and drain. Mix with the peanuts and cheese sauce, sprinkle with the cheesy breadcrumbs and bake as above.

SPANISH TORTILLA

Serves 8
Preparation time 10 minutes
Cooking time 20–25 minutes

2 tbsp (30 ml) olive oil, divided
2 onions, sliced
1 clove garlic, crushed
1 lb (500 g) cooked red or Yukon Gold potatoes, sliced
6 eggs
¼ cup (60 ml) milk

Heat 1 tbsp (15 ml) of the olive oil in a medium ovenproof frying pan over low heat; add the onions and garlic. Cook for 5 minutes, until golden, then add the cooked potatoes and heat through.

Meanwhile, in a large bowl, beat together the eggs and milk. Add the potatoes, onions and garlic to the egg mixture and stir well.

Return the pan to the heat, and heat the remaining oil. Tip the potato-and-egg mixture into the pan and cook over low heat for 7 to 8 minutes, until beginning to set. Preheat the broiler and cook the tortilla in its pan under medium heat for 3 to 5 minutes, until the top is golden and set.

Turn the tortilla out onto a plate and allow to cool. Cut into slices and serve warm or cold. (You can wrap any unused tortilla securely and refrigerate it – eat within 3 days.)

For meaty chorizo Spanish tortilla, layer the potatoes with a 3-oz (75 g) package sliced chorizo and 2 tbsp (30 ml) chopped fresh parsley and cook as above. Serve either warm or cold with cherry tomatoes.

CRUMB-TOPPED MACARONI & CHEESE

Serves 4
Preparation time 15 minutes
Cooking time about 25 minutes

7 oz (200 g) macaroni
⅔ cup (150 ml) fresh or frozen peas
⅔ cup (60 ml) butter, divided
5 tbsp (75 ml) all-purpose flour
2 cups (500 ml) milk
1 tsp (5 ml) Dijon mustard
5 oz (150 g) Cheddar cheese, coarsely grated
3½ oz (100 g) ham, chopped into small pieces
1 cup (250 ml) fresh breadcrumbs

Cook the macaroni for about 10 minutes or according to the package instructions, until just tender. Add the peas to the pan and cook for a further 2 minutes. Drain and put to one side.

Melt 3 tbsp (45 ml) of the butter in the rinsed and dried saucepan. Add the flour and stir it in with a wooden spoon. Cook over low heat, stirring, for 1 minute. Remove the pan from the heat and gradually pour in the milk, whisking well. Return the pan to the heat and cook over low heat, stirring continuously, until the sauce is thickened and smooth.

Add the mustard, Cheddar and ham and stir until the cheese has melted. Tip in the macaroni and peas and stir until coated in the sauce, then pour into a shallow heatproof dish.

Melt the remaining butter in a small saucepan and stir in the breadcrumbs until they are coated. Sprinkle the breadcrumbs over the macaroni and cook under a moderate broiler for about 5 minutes or until golden, watching closely, as the breadcrumbs will brown quickly. Use oven mitts to remove the dish from under the broiler, and serve.

For crumb-topped eggplant, macaroni & cheese, omit the peas and ham and replace with ½ roughly chopped eggplant cooked in 2 tbsp (30 ml) olive oil until soft, and 3 roughly chopped tomatoes. Top with the crumbs and bake as above.

SALMON RÖSTI CAKES

Serves 6
Preparation time 30 minutes
Cooking time 25–30 minutes

1 lb (500 g) white potatoes, peeled but left whole
2 tbsp (30 ml) butter
8 oz (250 g) salmon fillets
2 tbsp (30 ml) sunflower oil
¾ cup (175 ml) crème fraîche
3 green onions, finely sliced
2 tbsp (30 ml) chopped fresh chives
Lemon wedges, to serve

Bring a large pan of lightly salted water to a boil. Cook the potatoes for 10 minutes, until beginning to soften. Drain and set aside to cool.

Heat the butter in a small frying pan and add the salmon. Cover with a tight-fitting lid and reduce the heat to very low. Cook for 8 to 10 minutes, until the salmon is just cooked. Remove from the heat and set aside until the salmon is cool enough to handle. Flake the salmon and place in a bowl with the pan juices.

Grate the cooled potatoes, add to the bowl with the salmon and toss together to mix. Divide the mixture into 6 portions and form into flattened patty shapes. Heat the oil in a large nonstick frying pan and cook the rösti over medium heat for 2 to 3 minutes on each side, until golden and cooked through, turning with a metal spatula.

Meanwhile, place the crème fraîche in a bowl with the green onions and chives and mix well. Drain the rösti on paper towels, then spoon over the crème fraîche and serve with lemon wedges.

For rösti with bacon & eggs, follow the recipe above, omitting the salmon and adding 1 tbsp (15 ml) chopped fresh parsley before shaping. Serve the crisp rösti each with 2 lightly fried bacon slices and a poached egg on top, and homemade ketchup (see page 12).

BUTTERNUT SQUASH RISOTTO

Serves 4
Preparation time 15 minutes
Cooking time about 25 minutes

2 tbsp (30 ml) olive oil
1 onion, finely chopped
1 lb (500 g) butternut squash, peeled, seeded and
  roughly chopped
1 cup (250 ml) Arborio rice
3⅔ cups (900 ml) rich chicken stock
½ cup (125 ml) freshly grated Parmesan cheese, plus
  extra to serve
¼ cup (60 ml) pine nuts, toasted
8 oz (250 g) fresh spinach leaves

Heat the oil in a large heavy-bottomed frying pan and cook the onion and squash over low to medium heat for 10 minutes, until softened. Add the rice and cook for 1 minute, then add half the stock. Bring to a boil, then reduce the heat and simmer gently for 5 minutes, until almost all the stock has been absorbed, stirring occasionally.

Continue to add the stock ⅔ cup (150 ml) at a time and cook over low heat until almost all the stock has been absorbed before adding more. Once the rice is tender, remove the pan from the heat, add the Parmesan, pine nuts and spinach and stir well to combine and wilt the spinach, returning to the heat for 1 minute if necessary.

Serve in warmed serving bowls with extra freshly grated Parmesan.

For chicken & pea risotto, replace the butternut squash with 3 chicken breasts, 5 oz (150 g) each, chopped, cooked with the onion. Cook in the same way as above, adding 1 cup (250 ml) frozen peas and also adding the spinach if desired. Serve with extra Parmesan sprinkled over.

MINI QUICHES

Makes 18
Preparation time 45 minutes
Cooking time 20 minutes

Vegetable oil, for greasing
All-purpose flour, for dusting
12 oz (375 g) ready-rolled shortcrust pastry, thawed if
  frozen and taken out of the refrigerator 15 minutes
  before use
2 eggs
¾ cup (175 ml) milk
4 slices ham, diced
2 green onions, chopped
5 cherry tomatoes, chopped
2 oz (60 g) Cheddar cheese, grated

Smear some oil all around the cups of 2 muffin or bun tins. Sprinkle some flour onto a work surface and unroll the pastry. Flatten it with the heels of your hands. Stamp circles out of the pastry with a cutter and place each circle in a cup of the pan, gently pressing it down with your fingertips.

Place the eggs and milk in a measuring cup and beat with a fork.

Put the ham, green onions and cherry tomatoes in a bowl and mix together. Put a generous tablespoon (15 ml) of the mixture into each pastry cup.

Pour some of the egg-and-milk mixture into each cup. Sprinkle some Cheddar over the top. Bake the quiches in a preheated 425°F (220°C) oven for 20 minutes or until set and golden. Serve the quiches hot or cold.

For red pepper, garlic & Parmesan quiches, replace the ham, green onions and cherry tomatoes with the following – heat 1 tbsp (15 ml) olive oil in a small pan and cook 1 roughly chopped red bell pepper and 1 crushed clove garlic for 2 to 3 minutes, until soft. Place in the pastry shells with ⅓ cup (75 ml) freshly grated Parmesan cheese and pour over the egg and milk as above. Omit the Cheddar and bake as above.

CHICKEN SATAY SKEWERS

Serves 4
Preparation time 20 minutes, plus marinating
Cooking time 8–10 minutes

6 tbsp (90 ml) dark soy sauce
2 tbsp (30 ml) toasted sesame oil
1 tsp (5 ml) Chinese five-spice powder
12 oz (375 g) boneless skinless chicken breasts, cut
   into long, thin strips

Sauce
¼ cup (60 ml) peanut butter
1 tbsp (15 ml) dark soy sauce
½ tsp (2 ml) ground coriander
½ tsp (2 ml) ground cumin
Pinch of paprika or chili powder
8 tbsp (120 ml) water
Cucumber, cut into strips, to serve

Place the soy sauce, toasted sesame oil and five-spice powder into a bowl and mix. Add the chicken and toss together to coat in the marinade. Cover and set aside for 1 hour, stirring occasionally.

Thread the chicken, zigzag fashion, onto 10 soaked bamboo skewers (soaking them in warm water for 30 minutes will prevent the sticks burning while cooking), and place the chicken under a hot broiler or on a hot grill for 8 to 10 minutes, turning once, until golden and cooked through.

Meanwhile, put all the sauce ingredients in a small pan and heat, stirring, until warm and well mixed. Transfer to a small serving bowl.

Place the bowl of sauce on a serving plate with the cucumber on one side and the hot chicken skewers around it.

For pork satay skewers, replace the chicken with 12 oz (375 g) pork tenderloin, cut into long strips along its length. Complete and cook as above. For children who can handle a hotter sauce, fry ½ small red chile, finely chopped, in 1 tsp (5 ml) cooking oil and add to the peanut sauce.

CHICKEN & BACON WRAPS

Serves 2
Preparation time 15 minutes
Cooking time 5 minutes

1 tbsp (15 ml) olive oil
2 boneless skinless chicken breasts, 5 oz (150 g) each
2 slices unsmoked back bacon
2 soft flour tortillas
¼ cup (60 ml) mayonnaise
2 handfuls spinach

Lightly oil 2 sheets of plastic wrap with the oil. Place the 2 chicken breasts, well spaced apart, between the 2 sheets and bash with a rolling pin until the chicken is ¼ inch (5 mm) thick.

Heat a grill or heavy-bottomed frying pan and cook the chicken for 5 minutes, turning once, until golden and cooked through, adding the bacon to the pan for the final 2 minutes.

Spread each of the tortillas with 2 tbsp (30 ml) mayonnaise. Place the chicken breast over the top, then lay 2 bacon slices on top of the chicken. Sprinkle with the spinach, then roll up tightly, securing with cocktail sticks. Cut in half and serve immediately, or wrap tightly in wax paper and secure with string to transport.

For tuna & coleslaw wraps, drain a 6½-oz (150 ml) can of tuna in brine and mix with 2 roughly chopped tomatoes and 1 tbsp (15 ml) chopped fresh chives. Mix ⅛ cabbage, finely shredded, with 1 large grated carrot and 1 tsp (5 ml) poppy seeds and set aside. Mix ¼ cup (60 ml) mayonnaise with 2 tbsp (30 ml) water until well blended, then pour over the cabbage and carrot and toss to mix. Spread the tuna mixture over 4 flour tortillas, then spoon over the coleslaw. Roll tightly and secure with cocktail sticks as above.

ROASTED VEGETABLE COUSCOUS

Serves 6
Preparation time 15 minutes, plus soaking
Cooking time 30–35 minutes

1 cup (250 ml) couscous
1 chicken stock cube
1¾ cups (450 ml) hot water
2 zucchini, cut into chunks
1 red bell pepper, cored, seeded and cut into chunks
1 yellow bell pepper, cored, seeded and cut into chunks
12 oz (375 g) butternut squash, peeled, seeded and cut into chunks
1 red onion, chopped
5 tbsp (75 ml) olive oil, divided
3 tbsp (45 ml) chopped fresh parsley or basil
5 tbsp (75 ml) pine nuts, toasted

Place the couscous in a bowl, crumble in the stock cube and stir well. Add the water, stir, then cover and set aside while preparing and cooking the vegetables.

Put all the prepared vegetables into a large roasting pan, drizzle with 3 tbsp (45 ml) of the oil and toss to coat lightly. Roast in a preheated 400°F (200°C) oven for 30 to 35 minutes, until the vegetables are soft and lightly charred.

Lightly fork the soaked couscous to fluff it up, then drizzle on the remaining oil and toss well. Add the warm vegetables, parsley or basil and pine nuts and toss well before serving.

For roasted vegetable quinoa with toasted cashews, replace the couscous with quinoa. Wash 1 cup (250 ml) quinoa in a sieve, then drain. Place in a large, heavy-bottomed nonstick frying pan and lightly toast over medium heat for 2 to 3 minutes, until the grain turns a shade darker. Add 1¾ cups (450 ml) water and 1 chicken stock cube and cook over medium heat for 8 to 10 minutes, until the grain is tender and cooked. Drain and set aside. Add the roasted vegetables and parsley as above and replace the pine nuts with 1 cup (250 ml) roughly chopped toasted cashews.

SUNSET WEDGES & SOUR CREAM

Serves 6
Preparation time 20 minutes
Cooking time 30–35 minutes

3 sweet potatoes, skins on
2 large baking potatoes, skins on
3 tbsp (45 ml) olive oil
1 tsp (5 ml) Cajun spices
2 tbsp (30 ml) chopped fresh parsley

Dip
⅔ cup (150 ml) Greek yogurt
¼ cup (60 ml) sour cream
¼ cup (60 ml) chopped fresh chives
2 tbsp (30 ml) freshly grated Parmesan cheese

Cut the sweet potatoes in half, then cut each half into 4 wedges and place in a large mixing bowl. Cut the baking potatoes in half, then cut each half into 6 thick wedges and place in the bowl. Drizzle with olive oil, then toss well to coat all the potato wedges.

Transfer the potatoes to a large baking sheet or oven tray in a single layer. Sprinkle on the Cajun spices. Roast in a preheated 400°F (200°C) oven for 30 to 35 minutes, until golden and cooked through. Turn onto a serving platter and sprinkle with the parsley.

Mix the yogurt, sour cream, chives and Parmesan in a small mixing bowl. Serve the dip with the warm potato wedges.

For creamy cucumber & garlic dip to serve as an alternative accompaniment, replace the chives and Parmesan with ¼ grated cucumber and 1 crushed clove garlic. Stir in 2 tbsp (30 ml) freshly chopped mint and mix well. Serve the dip with the warm potato wedges.

TOMATO-GARLIC BREAD WITH HAM

Serves 2
Preparation time 10 minutes

1 clove garlic, halved
4 slices soft white bread
2 tomatoes, 1 halved and 1 thinly sliced
5 oz (150 g) ham, finely sliced
2½ oz (75 g) Manchego cheese, sliced

Rub the cut faces of the garlic all over the bread, concentrating particularly on the crusts. Repeat with the tomato halves.

Sandwich the bread with the ham, cheese and sliced tomato. Halve and wrap securely. The sandwiches can be kept in the refrigerator for 1 day.

For tomato-garlic bread with salami & mozzarella, flavor the bread with the garlic and tomato as above and fill with 5 oz (150 g) finely sliced salami and 2½ oz (75 g) mozzarella. Add 1 sliced tomato. Warm on a baking sheet in a preheated 400°F (200°C) oven for 10 minutes before serving warm, cut into triangles.

SUPPER IN A HURRY

Serves 4
Preparation time 25 minutes
Cooking time 20 minutes

1 ciabatta bread
Small handful of fresh chives
½ cup (125 ml) garlic butter, softened
5 tbsp (75 ml) olive oil, divided
4 boneless skinless chicken breasts, cut in half
  horizontally
4 tomatoes, sliced
5 oz (150 g) mozzarella cheese, sliced
1 tbsp (15 ml) white wine vinegar
1 tbsp (15 ml) whole-grain mustard
1 tsp (5 ml) granulated or fruit sugar

Cut the bread at ¾-inch (2 cm) intervals, leaving the slices only just attached at the base.

Snip the chives with scissors and mix half in a bowl with the garlic butter. Roughly spread a dot of butter into each cut of the bread. Lay the loaf on a piece of foil and bring the edges up over the top, scrunching them together. Bake in a preheated 425°F (220°C) oven for 10 minutes.

Meanwhile, heat 1 tbsp (15 ml) of the oil in a large frying pan. Add the chicken and fry gently for 5 minutes, until golden on the underside (check by lifting a piece with a spatula). Turn the pieces over and fry for a further 5 minutes.

Using oven mitts, carefully open out the foil on the garlic bread and bake for a further 10 minutes.

Scatter the tomato and mozzarella slices in a shallow dish.

Make a dressing by whisking together the remaining oil with the vinegar, mustard and sugar in a bowl. Scatter the remaining chives over the salad and drizzle with the dressing. Using oven mitts, remove the garlic bread from the oven and serve with the salad and chicken.

For speedy breaded pork cutlets, toss 4 pork cutlets in a little flour, dip in 4 beaten eggs, then coat in 1½ cups (375 ml) dry breadcrumbs tossed with 2 pinches smoked paprika. Heat 2 tbsp (30 ml) oil in a nonstick frying pan and cook the cutlets for 2 to 3 minutes on each side, until golden. Serve with the tomato and mozzarella salad as above.

ASPARAGUS IN BLANKETS

Serves 4
Preparation time 10 minutes
Cooking time 15 minutes

2 bunches thick asparagus spears, trimmed to about
   6 inches (15 cm) long
1 tbsp (15 ml) olive oil
2 tbsp (30 ml) butter, softened
16 slices Parma, prosciutto or serrano ham
¼ cup (60 ml) freshly grated Parmesan cheese

Bring a large pan of water to a boil. Cook the asparagus for 5 minutes in the boiling water, then remove with a slotted spoon and place in a bowl. Toss with the olive oil.

Grease a gratin dish with the butter. Wrap each of the asparagus spears in a piece of ham and place them in the greased dish side by side. Sprinkle with the Parmesan and bake in a preheated 400°F (200°C) oven for 10 minutes, until the cheese is golden and melted.

Serve the asparagus in blankets with chunks of warm fresh bread and homemade Tomato Ketchup (see page 12).

For cheesy pizza-style asparagus, replace the Parma, prosciutto or serrano ham with thin slices of honey-roast ham and place the wrapped asparagus in the gratin dish. Sprinkle with 2 oz (60 g) chopped black olives and 3½ oz (100 g) grated mozzarella instead of the Parmesan, and bake as above. Serve the pizza-style asparagus with garlic bread.

BEANFEAST

Serves 4
Preparation time 10 minutes
Cooking time about 15 minutes

2 small or 1 large tomato
1 tbsp (15 ml) vegetable oil
½ small onion, chopped into small pieces
1 stalk celery, chopped into small pieces
19-oz (540 ml) can navy, great Northern or cannellini
   beans, drained and rinsed
2 tsp (10 ml) whole-grain mustard
2 tbsp (30 ml) molasses
3 tbsp (45 ml) ketchup
1 tbsp (15 ml) Worcestershire sauce
4 slices toast or 4 baked potatoes, to serve

Put the tomatoes into a heatproof bowl and just cover with freshly boiled water. Leave to stand for 1 to 2 minutes, until the skins start to split. Carefully pour off the hot water and peel away the skins. Roughly chop the tomatoes on a chopping board.

Heat the oil in a medium heavy-bottomed saucepan for 1 minute. Add the onion and celery and fry gently for 5 minutes, stirring until just beginning to color.

Tip in the beans, tomatoes, mustard, molasses, ketchup and Worcestershire sauce and stir the ingredients together. Heat until the liquid starts to bubble around the edges. Reduce the heat to its lowest setting and cover the pan with a lid. Cook gently for about 10 minutes, until the tomatoes have softened to make a sauce.

Serve with toast or on baked potatoes.

For lentil & paneer feast, replace the can of beans with a 14-oz (398 ml) can Puy lentils, drained and rinsed, and add to the pan with the tomatoes. Cook for 10 minutes, adding 8 oz (250 g) cubed paneer, feta or dry cottage cheese for the final 2 to 3 minutes.

HAM & FRESH PINEAPPLE PIZZA

Serves 4

Preparation time 25 minutes, plus rising

Cooking time about 20 minutes

2 cups (500 ml) whole wheat all-purpose flour

½ tsp (2 ml) salt

1 tsp (5 ml) fast-acting dried yeast

⅔ cup (150 ml) warm water

1 tbsp (15 ml) olive oil, plus extra for oiling

Topping

2 tbsp (30 ml) olive oil, divided

1 small onion, finely chopped

⅔ cup (150 ml) tomato sauce or passata

3 tbsp (45 ml) tomato paste

3 thick slices good-quality ham, cut into strips

2 thick rings fresh pineapple, cut into chunks

5 oz (150 g) mozzarella cheese, thinly sliced

Fresh thyme leaves (optional)

Sift the flour and salt into a bowl, add the yeast and mix well. Make a well in the center and add the water and oil. Stir until it forms a wet dough, then beat for 2 minutes. Turn the dough out onto a well-floured surface and knead for about 2 minutes, until it becomes smooth and elastic. Roll out to a 12-inch (30 cm) circle and place on a lightly oiled baking sheet. Cover with lightly oiled plastic wrap and leave in a warm place while making the topping.

Heat 1 tbsp (15 ml) of the oil in a small frying pan and cook the onion over medium heat for 2 to 3 minutes. Remove from the heat and add the tomato sauce and paste. Spread over the pizza base to within 1 inch (2.5 cm) of the edges and scatter the ham overtop.

Toss the pineapple with the remaining oil. Scatter it over the ham, then top with the mozzarella. Bake in a preheated 425°F (220°C) oven for 15 to 18 minutes, until golden. Scatter with thyme leaves, if desired.

For chicken & chorizo pizza, replace the ham and pineapple with 2 boneless skinless chicken breasts, 5 oz (150 g) each, and 3½ oz (100 g) chorizo sausage, both thinly sliced. Heat 1 tbsp (15 ml) olive oil in a frying pan and cook the chicken over medium heat for 3 to 4 minutes, until golden. Add the chorizo and fry for a further 1 minute. Toss with 3 tbsp (45 ml) fresh basil and pile onto the pizza base, then top with the mozzarella. Omit the thyme.

MINI STEAK BURGERS

Makes 8
Preparation time 10 minutes, plus chilling
Cooking time 12–15 minutes

12 oz (375 g) finely ground steak
2 tbsp (30 ml) ketchup
1 tbsp (15 ml) whole-grain mustard
3 tbsp (45 ml) chopped fresh chives
1 tbsp (15 ml) olive oil
3½ oz (100 g) cremini mushrooms, sliced
8 thin slices Gruyère cheese

To serve
4 mini burger buns, cut in half
Ketchup or sauces

Place the ground steak in a bowl with the ketchup, mustard and chives. Mix really well together, working the mixture with a fork to grind and blend the ingredients. Shape into 8 patties and place on a plate. Cover with plastic wrap and chill for 30 minutes to firm.

Heat the oil in a large frying or grill pan and cook the mushrooms over high heat for 3 to 4 minutes, until golden and soft. Remove from the pan using a slotted spoon. Add the burgers and cook over medium heat for 4 to 5 minutes on each side, until golden and cooked through. Sit a Gruyère slice on top of each of the burgers and cover with a baking sheet for 1 minute to allow the cheese to soften.

Top the base of each bun with a burger, then spoon over the mushrooms and spread the top half of each bun with ketchup or a sauce of the child's choice. Place the lids on and serve.

For pork & apple burgers, replace the steak with 12 oz (375 g) good-quality ground pork. Core 1 apple and grate with the skin on. Add to the ground pork with the mustard and chives and blend well together using a fork. Form into 8 patties and cook as above.

NO-SUGAR BROWNIES WITH BERRIES

Serves 12
Preparation time 20 minutes
Cooking time 30 minutes

8 oz (250 g) plain dark chocolate (70% cocoa solids)
½ cup (125 ml) unsalted butter
4 eggs
1¼ cups (300 ml) all-purpose flour
½ cup (125 ml) ground almonds
½ cup (125 ml) plain dark chocolate chips
⅓ cup (75 ml) pecans, roughly chopped (optional)

To serve
Fresh blueberries, raspberries and strawberries
Ice cream or crème fraîche

Lightly grease an 11 x 7 inch (28 x 18 cm) baking pan and line the base with parchment paper.

Melt the chocolate together with the butter. Remove from the heat and allow to cool for 2 minutes. Whisk the eggs in a separate bowl until frothy (about 3 minutes), then stir in the cooled chocolate mixture.

Fold in the flour, ground almonds, chocolate chips and pecans, if using. Transfer to the prepared baking pan and bake in a preheated 350°F (180°C) oven for 25 to 30 minutes, until just firm to the touch.

Leave the brownies to cool in the pan for 20 minutes before cutting into 12 squares and serving with the fresh berries and ice cream or crème fraîche.

For white chocolate & strawberry brownies (containing sugar in the chocolate), replace the plain dark chocolate with white chocolate, and the chocolate chips and pecans with ½ cup (125 ml) finely chopped strawberries. This brownie will be soft and will only keep in the refrigerator for 3 days.

STICKY FIG & BANANA SNACKING CAKE

Serves 6
Preparation time 10 minutes
Cooking time 20 minutes

½ cup (125 ml) margarine or butter, softened
½ cup (125 ml) packed brown sugar
1 tsp (5 ml) ground ginger
2 eggs
1 cup (250 ml) all-purpose flour
3 figs, quartered
1 large banana, cut into chunks
2 tbsp (30 ml) maple syrup
Ice cream or vanilla custard, to serve

Beat the margarine or butter and sugar until smooth and creamy. Add the ginger, eggs and flour and beat again until a smooth mixture is formed. Lightly grease a 9-inch (23 cm) square baking pan or ovenproof dish, then spoon in the mixture and level with the back of a spoon.

Toss the figs and banana with the maple syrup and arrange over the top of the cake, pressing the fruit into the cake in places. Bake in a preheated 350°F (180°C) oven for 20 minutes, until the cake is well risen and golden and the fruit is soft.

Serve the cake in squares with either scoops of ice cream or vanilla custard (see below).

For vanilla custard to serve as an accompaniment, heat 1¼ cups (300 ml) milk, with the seeds of ½ vanilla pod scraped into it, in a nonstick pan until boiling. Meanwhile, blend 2 egg yolks with 1 tsp (5 ml) cornstarch and 2 tbsp (30 ml) granulated or fruit sugar. Pour the milk over the egg mixture once boiled and whisk well to blend. Return to the heat, stirring continuously, until just beginning to boil and thicken. It will coat the back of a spoon.

CHOCOLATE SCRIBBLE CAKE

Makes 9 squares
Preparation time 15 minutes
Cooking time 20 minutes

2 oz (60 g) plain dark chocolate, broken into small
   pieces
¼ cup (60 ml) butter or margarine
2 eggs
¾ cup (175 ml) packed brown sugar
⅓ cup + 2 tbsp (100 ml) self-raising flour
Icing pens (optional)

Melt the chocolate together with the butter.

Break the eggs into a mixing bowl, then add the sugar and sift in the flour. Stir them together vigorously.

Stir the melted chocolate and butter and carefully pour them into the mixing bowl. Stir the mixture until it is smooth, then pour into a shallow cake pan, 8 inches (20 cm) square, lined with parchment paper, using the spatula to scrape every last bit from the bowl. Place on the top shelf of a preheated 350°F (180°C) oven for 20 minutes or until just firm when you touch it very gently in the middle.

Allow the cake to cool in the pan, then cut it into 9 pieces in the pan. Using the icing pens, decorate the squares with icing scribbles, if desired.

For pink coconut cake, make an all-in-one cake mix of 1 cup (250 ml) self-raising flour, ½ cup (125 ml) soft margarine, ½ cup (125 ml) granulated or fruit sugar and 2 eggs; beat together until smooth and creamy and then transfer to an 8-inch (20 cm) square greased and parchment paper–lined pan. Bake in the preheated oven as above for 20 minutes, until golden and a skewer inserted comes out clean. Transfer to a wire rack to cool. Mix ⅔ cup (150 ml) sifted icing sugar with 1 to 2 tsp (5 to10 ml) beet juice until smooth and blended. Spread thinly over the cake and scatter with 1 tbsp (15 ml) shredded coconut. Cut into squares to serve.

BREAD MONSTERS

Makes 8
Preparation time 30 minutes, plus rising
Cooking time 15–20 minutes

2⅓ cups (575 ml) white bread flour, plus extra for
   dusting
1 tsp (5 ml) salt
1¼ tbsp (19 ml) fast-acting dried yeast
1 tbsp (15 ml) vegetable oil
¾ cup (175 ml) warm water
12 dried currants, cut in half, for the eyes and mouths
1 egg, beaten

Sift the flour and salt together in a mixing bowl and add the yeast, oil and water. Mix everything together with a wooden spoon, then use your hands to draw the mixture together into a firm dough. If the mixture is too dry to come together, add a little more water. If the mixture sticks to your hands, add some more flour.

Turn the dough out onto a well-floured surface and knead thoroughly for at least 5 minutes, then divide it into 8 equal pieces and knead into balls. Make a pointy snout at one end of each ball and place on a baking sheet lined with parchment paper. Leave plenty of space between the rolls, as they will double in size. Make prickles on the monsters by snipping into the dough with the tips of scissors. Press the currant halves into the dough to make the eyes and mouths.

Cover the rolls with a clean dish towel, then leave in a warm place for 1 hour or until they have doubled in size.

Brush the rolls with the beaten egg and bake in a preheated 450°F (230°C) oven for 15 to 20 minutes. If the rolls are cooked, they will sound hollow when tapped on the bottom (remember to pick them up with oven mitts, as they will be hot). Transfer to a wire rack to cool.

For sweet bread-roll snacks, add 8 oz (250 g) mixed dried fruit to the dry ingredients with 2 tsp (10 ml) ground cinnamon and 3 tbsp (45 ml) granulated or fruit sugar. Continue as above, shaping into 8 round balls and baking as above. Cool and serve either warm or cold, split and spread thinly with a little unsalted butter.

STRAWBERRY & VANILLA MILKSHAKE

Serves 2
Preparation time 5–6 minutes, plus cooling
Cooking time 5–6 minutes

1¼ cups (300 ml) milk
1¼ cups (300 ml) table (18%) or half-and-half (10%)
  cream
½ vanilla pod
8 oz (250 g) strawberries, hulled

Put the milk and cream in a pan. Remove the vanilla seeds from the pod using the back of a spoon and place the pod and seeds in the pan with the milk and cream. Bring to a boil, stirring. Once the boiling point has been reached, remove from the heat and allow to cool completely.

Place the strawberries in a food processor and mix until smooth. Add the cooled vanilla milk and mix again until pink. Pour into chilled glasses and serve with straws.

For strawberry & vanilla ice cream milkshake, put the milk and strawberries in a food processor with 5 scoops good-quality vanilla ice cream and mix until smooth and blended. Add some ice and mix again. Pour into chilled glasses and serve.

MANGO, MELON & ORANGE JUICE

Makes about 1⅔ cups (400 ml)
Preparation time 5–6 minutes

1 ripe mango, roughly chopped
½ Galia melon, seeded and roughly chopped
¾ cup (75 ml) orange juice
2 ice cubes

Place the mango and melon in a blender and mix until smooth.

Add the orange juice and ice cubes, then purée until smooth. Serve immediately.

For coconut & pineapple juice, place 1 can (14 oz/400 ml) coconut milk in a food processor with ½ small pineapple, peeled, cored and roughly chopped. Mix until smooth, then serve poured over ice and decorated with fresh cherries or strawberries for color.

WATERMELON & RASPBERRY JUICE

Makes about ¾ cup (175 ml)
Preparation time 5–6 minutes

10 oz (300 g) watermelon (¼ an average fruit), seeded
  and chopped
4 oz (125 g) raspberries
Ice cubes, crushed (optional)

Put the watermelon and raspberries in a blender and mix until smooth. Press the juice through a sieve to remove any raspberry seeds.

Pour the juice into glasses over some crushed ice cubes, if desired.

For melon & apple juice, place half a small seeded and chopped green melon into a food processor with 1 green apple, cored and cut into wedges (keep the skin on). Add 1 tbsp (15 ml) lemon juice and mix until smooth. Pour over crushed ice if desired.

FRESH LEMONADE

Makes 7 cups (1.8 L)
Preparation time 4–5 minutes, plus cooling
Cooking time 4–5 minutes

⅓ cup (75 ml) superfine sugar
7 cups (1.8 L) water, divided
4 lemons, sliced, plus extra slices to serve
Ice cubes

Place the sugar in a pan with 2⅓ cups (600 ml) of the water and all the sliced lemons. Bring to a boil, stirring well until all the sugar has dissolved.

Remove from the heat and add all the remaining water. Stir, then set aside to cool completely.

Once cold, roughly crush the lemons to release all the juice. Strain through a sieve, add the ice cubes and serve in glasses decorated with slices of lemon.

For fresh limeade, simply use 6 limes instead of 4 lemons, or use a mixture of the two. Try chopping some fresh mint and adding while the limeade cools, for a mint flavor. Strain as above.

FAIRY CRUMBLE

Serves 6
Preparation time 20 minutes
Cooking time 30 minutes

1 lb (500 g) strawberries, hulled and halved
8 oz (250 g) raspberries
1 orange, peeled and segmented
¼ cup (60 ml) granulated or fruit sugar
½ tsp (2 ml) ground cinnamon

Topping
2 cups (500 ml) all-purpose flour
½ cup (125 ml) butter, chilled and cubed
⅓ cup (75 ml) packed brown sugar
⅓ cup (75 ml) toasted hazelnuts, roughly chopped, or
    flaked almonds (optional)

Custard
2 egg yolks
2 tbsp (30 ml) cornstarch
3 tbsp (45 ml) granulated or fruit sugar
1½ cups (375 ml) milk
2 tbsp (30 ml) beet juice (from store-bought cooked
    beets) or a drop of cochineal or red food coloring

Place the strawberries, raspberries, orange segments (plus any juice), sugar and cinnamon in a bowl and toss together gently to coat the fruit lightly in the sugar, taking care not to break up the raspberries. Transfer the fruit to a gratin dish and set aside while making the crumble topping.

Place the flour into a bowl and, using your fingertips, rub the butter into it until the mixture resembles fine breadcrumbs. Stir in the sugar and nuts, if using, then spoon the crumble over the top of the fruit. Bake in a preheated 400°F (200°C) oven for 25 to 30 minutes, until the topping is golden and crisp in places.

Make the pink custard. Place the egg yolks, cornstarch and sugar in a bowl and blend together well. Put the milk in a heavy-bottomed nonstick saucepan and bring to a boil. Pour the milk over the egg mixture, add the beet juice and whisk together well. Return to the heat and cook gently, stirring continuously, until thickened.

Serve the crumble in bowls with the pink custard to spoon over.

For Caribbean-style crumble, replace the red berries with 1 large mango, cut into chunks, and 6 thick slices fresh pineapple, cut into chunks. Toss with the orange and ½ cup (125 ml) raisins. Replace the nuts with ¼ cup (60 ml) shredded coconut in the crumble. Serve with ice cream rather than custard.

FUN RECIPES FOR KIDS

UPSIDE-DOWN TARTS

Serves 4
Preparation time 10 minutes
Cooking time 15–18 minutes

2 tbsp (30 ml) unsalted butter
2 tbsp (30 ml) light muscovado sugar
2 oz (60 g) red currants
2 ripe pears, peeled, cored and cut into chunky pieces
½ package (10 oz/375 g) ready-rolled puff pastry,
  thawed if frozen and removed from the refrigerator

Thinly slice the butter and divide it among 4 small heatproof ramekins. Sprinkle with the sugar. If the red currants are still attached to their stalks, reserve 4 clusters for decoration and remove the rest from the stalks (the easiest way to do this is to run the currants between the prongs of a fork). Scatter several red currants into each dish, then add the pears.

Unroll the pastry and cut out rounds using a 4-inch (10 cm) cookie cutter. Lay the pastry rounds over the pears, tucking the edges down inside the dishes.

Place the dishes on a baking sheet and bake in a preheated 425°F (220°C) oven for 15 to 18 minutes or until the pastry is well risen and pale golden. Using oven mitts, remove the baking sheet from the oven and put it on a heatproof surface. Leave to cool slightly.

Loosen the edges of the pastry with a knife. Hold a ramekin with oven mitts and invert a small serving plate on top. Carefully flip over the dish and plate so that the plate is the right way up. Lift off the dish to reveal the tart with its fruity topping. Repeat with the remaining tarts. Serve decorated with the remaining red currants.

For banana & maple syrup upside-down tarts, replace the red currants and pears with 2 thinly sliced bananas, placing them in the bottoms of each of the buttered ramekins and drizzling each with 1 tbsp (15 ml) maple syrup. Top with the pastry and bake as above.

NECTARINE & RASPBERRY YOGURT ICE

Serves 2
Preparation time 5 minutes

3 ripe nectarines, halved and pitted
6 oz (175 g) raspberries
⅔ cup (150 ml) plain yogurt
Handful of ice cubes

Put the nectarines and raspberries in a food processor and mix until really smooth. Add the yogurt and mix again, then add the ice and mix until very crushed and the shake thickens.

Pour into chilled glasses. Decorate with cocktail umbrellas and anything else to make the drink look fun!

For banana & mango coconut ice, replace the nectarines and raspberries with 1 large ripe banana and 1 mango, cut into chunks, and mix until smooth. Add ⅔ cup (150 ml) coconut milk and mix again. Add the ice and mix until the shake thickens. Pour into chilled glasses to serve.

TRAFFIC-LIGHT SMOOTHIE

Makes 1⅔ cups (400 ml)
Preparation time 9–10 minutes

3 kiwifruit, roughly chopped
⅔ cup (150 ml) tangy-flavored yogurt (such as lemon or orange)
1 small mango, roughly chopped
2 tbsp (30 ml) orange or apple juice
5 oz (150 g) raspberries
1 to 2 tsp (5 to 10 ml) liquid honey

Mix the kiwifruits in a blender until smooth and spoon the mixture into 2 tall glasses. Top each with a spoonful of yogurt, spreading the yogurt to the sides of the glasses.

Blend the mango to a purée with the orange or apple juice and spoon into the glasses. Top with another layer of yogurt.

Mix the raspberries and push through a sieve over a bowl to extract the seeds. Check their sweetness (you might need to stir in a little honey if they are very sharp). Spoon the raspberry purée into the glasses to serve.

For zebra-layered blackberry smoothie, place 6 oz (175 g) blackberries into a food processor with 2 tbsp (30 ml) liquid honey and mix until smooth. Layer alternately with the yogurt to replace the kiwi, mango and orange juice.

PEACH, APPLE & STRAWBERRY POPSICLES

Makes 4
Preparation time 7–8 minutes, plus freezing

2 peaches, peeled, pitted and cut into chunks
1¼ cups (300 ml) water, divided
1 red apple, peeled
4 oz (125 g) strawberries, hulled

Place the peaches in a blender and mix until smooth. Add one-third of the water and divide evenly between 4 popsicle moulds. Freeze until just set.

Chop the apples into even-sized chunks and juice them. Add one-third of the water and pour on top of the frozen peach mixture, then freeze until just set.

Hull the strawberries and juice them. Add the remainder of the water and pour on top of the frozen apple mixture, then freeze until set.

For chocolate & orange popsicles, place 1 can (10 oz/300 g) mandarin orange segments in a food processor and mix until smooth. Place in a pan with 4 oz (125 g) organic plain 70% cocoa solids chocolate and gently heat until the chocolate has melted. Stir well with the orange pureé and pour into 4 popsicle moulds. Freeze for 2 hours until firm.

PUMPKIN SEED & FRUIT BARS

Makes 8
Preparation time 15 minutes, plus chilling
Cooking time 5 minutes

⅓ cup (75 ml) pumpkin seeds
½ cup (125 ml) dried soybeans
½ cup (125 ml) raisins
½ cup (125 ml) ready-to-eat dried apricots, roughly chopped
½ cup (125 ml) dried cranberries
10 oz (300 g) plain dark chocolate, broken into pieces

Lightly grease an 11 x 7 inch (28 x 18 cm) baking pan and line with parchment paper. Put the seeds, soybeans and all the fruit into a bowl.

Melt the chocolate. Remove from the heat, pour over the seed and fruit mixture and stir well to coat completely.

Transfer the mixture to the prepared pan and level with the back of a spoon to fill the pan evenly. Chill in the refrigerator for 1 hour, until set and firm. Cut into 8 bars and keep refrigerated in an airtight container until ready to use.

For yogurt-coated bars, replace the plain dark chocolate with 7 oz (200 g) white chocolate melted over simmering water. When melted, remove from the heat and add 2 tbsp (30 ml) plain yogurt and ½ tsp (2 ml) vanilla extract. Stir well, then add to the dry ingredients and stir to coat. Transfer to the pan and chill as above.

BAKED

DATE CHOCOLATE TORTE

Serves 4
Preparation time 10 minutes, plus cooling
Cooking time 30 minutes

⅞ cup (100 g) flaked almonds
1 cup (250 ml) plain dark chocolate, roughly chopped
1 cup (150 ml) dried ready-to-eat dates, pitted
3 egg whites
½ cup (125 ml) granulated or fruit sugar, plus 2 tbsp
  (30 ml) for the topping
½ cup (125 ml) whipping (35%) cream
Unsweetened cocoa powder, to sprinkle

Grease a 9-inch (23 cm) springform pan and line with parchment paper. Put the almonds and chocolate in a food processor and pulse until finely chopped. Finely chop the dates with a knife.

Whisk the egg whites in a large, perfectly clean bowl until soft peaks form. Slowly add the ½ cup (125 ml) sugar and continue whisking until it has dissolved. Fold in the almond-and-chocolate mixture, then the dates. Spoon the mixture into the prepared pan and level the surface.

Bake in a preheated 350°F (180°C) oven for 30 minutes or until set and starting to come away from the side. Leave to cool in the pan before carefully turning out onto a serving plate.

Whip the cream and the remaining 2 tbsp (30 ml) sugar in a small bowl until soft peaks form. Using a spatula, spread the cream evenly over the top of the torte. Serve cut into thin slices and dusted with cocoa.

For iced date chocolate muffins, spoon the chocolate mixture into 12 large, deep muffin tins lined with paper muffin cups and bake in a preheated 350°F (180°C) oven for 20 to 25 minutes or until set. Transfer to a wire rack to cool. Melt 2½ oz (75 g) chopped plain dark chocolate with 3 tbsp (45 ml) butter in a heatproof bowl set over a saucepan of gently simmering water. Meanwhile, toast ¼ cup (60 ml) flaked almonds in a dry frying pan, stirring constantly, until golden brown. Stir the chocolate mixture, then spoon over the muffins and sprinkle with the toasted almonds. Leave until set.

TIPSY BERRY WAFFLES

Serves 4
Preparation time 5 minutes
Cooking time 1–2 minutes

1 tbsp (15 ml) butter
8 oz (250 g) mixed berries, such as blueberries,
  blackberries and raspberries
1 tbsp (15 ml) granulated or fruit sugar
2 tbsp (30 ml) kirsch
4 waffles
¼ cup (60 ml) crème fraîche

Melt the butter in a nonstick frying pan; add the berries, sugar and kirsch and cook over high heat, stirring gently, for 1 to 2 minutes.

Meanwhile, toast or reheat the waffles according to the package instructions. Put a waffle on each serving plate, spoon the berries over the waffles and top each portion with 1 tbsp (15 ml) crème fraîche. Serve immediately.

For homemade waffles, sift 1 cup (250 ml) all-purpose flour, 1 tsp (5 ml) baking powder and a pinch of salt into a bowl. Make a well in the center and gradually beat in 2 eggs and ⅔ cup (150 ml) milk until the batter is thick and smooth. Just before cooking, beat in 3 tbsp (45 ml) cooled melted butter. Heat a waffle iron and oil if necessary. Spoon in enough batter to give a good coating, close and cook for about 1 minute on each side. Lift the lid and remove the waffle. Repeat with the remaining batter.

HOT BERRY SOUFFLÉS

Serves 4
Preparation time 10 minutes
Cooking time 15 minutes

1 tbsp (15 ml) butter
½ cup (125 ml) granulated or fruit sugar, divided
2 oz (60 g) blackberries
7 oz (200 g) raspberries
4 large egg whites
Icing sugar (optional)

Use the butter to grease 4 ramekins, ¾ cup (175 ml) each, and then coat evenly with a little of the sugar, tipping out the excess sugar. Set the ramekins on a baking sheet.

Purée the blackberries and raspberries in a food processor or blender, reserving a few of the berries to decorate, then pour the purée into a bowl. Alternatively, the berries can be rubbed through a fine sieve to make a smooth purée.

Whisk the egg whites until stiff but not dry in a large, perfectly clean bowl. Gradually sprinkle in the remaining sugar, whisking continuously, and continue whisking until the whites are stiff and shiny.

Gently fold the egg whites into the berry purée, then spoon the mixture into the prepared ramekins. Bake immediately in a preheated 375°F (190°C) oven for 15 minutes or until risen and golden.

Dust the soufflés with icing sugar and decorate with the reserved berries. Serve immediately, with custard or ice cream, if desired.

For homemade custard to serve as an accompaniment, gently heat 1¼ cups (300 ml) milk in a saucepan without boiling. Meanwhile, beat 2 egg yolks in a bowl with 1 tbsp (15 ml) sugar and a few drops of vanilla extract, then pour the milk into the bowl, stirring constantly. Return the mixture to the pan and heat over low heat, stirring constantly, until the custard thickens enough to coat the back of the spoon. Serve immediately with the soufflés.

316

BAKED

WALNUT & WHITE CHOCOLATE COOKIES

Makes about 25
Preparation time 15 minutes, plus cooling
Cooking time 12–15 minutes

1 egg
⅔ cup (150 ml) light brown sugar
2 tbsp (30 ml) granulated or fruit sugar
1 tsp (5 ml) vanilla extract
½ cup (125 ml) vegetable oil
½ cup (125 ml) all-purpose flour
3 tbsp (45 ml) self-raising flour
¼ tsp (1 ml) ground cinnamon
½ cup (125 ml) shredded coconut
1¼ cup (300 ml) walnuts, toasted and chopped
⅔ cup (150 ml) white chocolate chips

Grease 2 baking sheets and line with parchment paper. In a bowl, beat the egg and sugars together until light and creamy. Stir in the vanilla extract and oil. Sift in the flours and cinnamon, then add the coconut, walnuts and white chocolate chips and mix well with a wooden spoon.

Form rounded tablespoonfuls of the mixture into balls and place on the prepared baking sheets, pressing the mixture together with your fingertips if it is crumbly. Bake in a preheated 350°F (180°C) oven for 12 to 15 minutes or until golden. Leave to cool slightly on the sheets, then transfer to a wire rack to cool completely.

For hazelnut & chocolate chip cookies, follow the recipe above but use ½ tsp (2 ml) ground ginger in place of the cinnamon, toasted and chopped hazelnuts instead of the walnuts and plain dark chocolate chips in place of the white.

RHUBARB SLUMPS

Serves 4
Preparation time 10 minutes
Cooking time 20–25 minutes

13 oz (400 g) rhubarb, cut into chunks
6 tbsp (90 ml) light brown sugar
Grated zest and juice of 1 orange, divided
1¼ cups (300 ml) rolled oats
6 tbsp (90 ml) whipping (35%) cream
2 tbsp (30 ml) dark muscovado sugar

Mix together the rhubarb, light brown sugar and orange zest and half the juice in a bowl. Spoon the mixture into 4 individual ramekins.

Put the oats, cream, dark muscovado sugar and remaining orange juice in the bowl and mix together. Drop spoonfuls of the oat mixture all over the surface of the rhubarb mixture.

Set the ramekins on a baking sheet and bake in a preheated 350°F (180°C) oven for 20 to 25 minutes, until the topping is browned. Serve hot.

For apple and blackberry crumbles, peel, core and chop 2 apples, then mix with 3½ oz (100 g) blackberries, 6 tbsp (90 ml) light brown sugar and 1 tbsp (15 ml) apple juice. Spoon into the ramekins as above. Sift 1 cup (250 ml) all-purpose flour into a bowl; add ¼ cup (60 ml) diced butter and rub in with the fingertips until the mixture resembles coarse breadcrumbs. Stir in ¼ cup (60 ml) dark muscovado sugar, ½ cup (125 ml) wheat bran and ⅓ cup (75 ml) chopped mixed nuts. Spoon the mixture over the fruit and flatten slightly with the back of a spoon. Bake as above until the topping is lightly golden.

APRICOT TARTLETS

Serves 4
Preparation time 15 minutes
Cooking time 20–25 minutes

12 oz (375 g) ready-rolled puff pastry, defrosted
   if frozen
3½ oz (100 g) marzipan
12 canned apricot halves, drained
Light muscovado sugar, for sprinkling
Apricot jam, for glazing

Using a saucer as a template, cut 4 rounds from the pastry, each approximately 3½ inches (8 cm) in diameter. Score a line about ½ inch (1 cm) from the edge of each round with a sharp knife.

Roll out the marzipan to ⅛-inch (2.5 mm) thick and cut out 4 rounds to fit inside the scored circles. Lay the pastry rounds on a baking sheet, place a circle of marzipan in the center of each and arrange 3 apricot halves, cut side up, on top. Sprinkle a little sugar into each apricot.

Put the baking sheet on top of a second preheated baking sheet (this helps to crisp the bottom of the pastry) and bake in a preheated 400°F (200°C) oven for 20 to 25 minutes, until the pastry is puffed and browned and the apricots are slightly caramelized around the edges. While still hot, brush the tops with apricot jam to glaze. Serve immediately.

For banana tartlets with rum mascarpone, follow the recipe above but use 2 thickly sliced bananas in place of the apricots. While the tartlets are baking, in a bowl, mix together ¼ cup (60 ml) mascarpone cheese, 2 tbsp (30 ml) rum and 2 tbsp (30 ml) light muscovado sugar. Spoon on top of the hot tartlets and serve immediately.

CHOCOLATE SOUFFLÉS

Serves 4
Preparation time 12 minutes
Cooking time about 15 minutes

7 oz (200 g) plain dark chocolate, chopped
^{2}/$_3$ cup (150 ml) butter, diced and softened
6 eggs
1 cup (250 ml) superfine sugar
1 cup (250 ml) all-purpose flour
Icing sugar, to dust

Butter 4 ramekins, ^{3}/$_4$ cup (175 ml) each. Melt the chocolate with the butter in a heatproof bowl set over a saucepan of gently simmering water.

Beat the eggs and sugar together in a bowl until very light and creamy. Sift the flour, then fold into the egg mixture. Fold in the chocolate mixture.

Divide the soufflé mixture between the prepared ramekins. Bake in a preheated 350°F (180°C) oven for 8 to 12 minutes. The soufflés should rise and form a firm crust, but you want them still to be slightly runny in the center. Serve immediately, dusted with icing sugar, with ice cream or cream.

For homemade vanilla ice cream to serve with the soufflés, in a heatproof bowl, mix together 1 whole egg, 1 egg yolk and 3 tbsp (45 ml) superfine sugar. Bring 1 cup (250 ml) table (18%) or half-and-half (10%) cream gently to boiling point in a saucepan and pour onto the egg mixture, stirring vigorously. Strain, then stir in 1 to 2 drops vanilla extract. Leave to cool, then fold in ^{2}/$_3$ cup (150 ml) whipped cream. Pour into a rigid freezerproof container. Cover, seal and freeze for 1 hour. Remove and stir well, then refreeze until firm. Transfer to the refrigerator for 20 minutes to soften before serving.

318

BAKED

BANANA & CHOC WHOLE WHEAT MUFFINS

Makes 12
Preparation time 15 minutes
Cooking time 20–25 minutes

1^1/$_4$ cups (300 ml) self-raising whole wheat flour
1 cup (250 ml) all-purpose flour
1 tsp (5 ml) baking powder
1 tsp (5 ml) baking soda
^{1}/$_2$ tsp (2 ml) salt
^{2}/$_3$ cup (150 ml) light brown sugar
3 large ripe bananas, mashed
1 egg, beaten
^{1}/$_3$ cup (75 ml) water
^{1}/$_3$ cup (75 ml) vegetable oil
2^1/$_2$ oz (75 g) carob or plain dark chocolate, roughly
  chopped

Sift the flours, baking powder, baking soda and salt into a large bowl, then add the wheat bran left in the sieve. Stir in the sugar. Mix together the bananas, egg, water and oil, then pour into the dry ingredients and gently mix until just combined. Fold in the carob or chocolate.

Line a 12-cup muffin pan with 12 paper muffin cups and three-quarters fill each with the mixture.

Bake in a preheated 350°F (180°C) oven for 20 to 25 minutes, until they are well risen and spring back when you press them. Place on a wire rack to cool.

For fresh cherry & vanilla muffins, omit the bananas, mix 2 tsp (10 ml) vanilla extract into the egg, water and oil mixture, and fold in 8 oz (250 g) fresh pitted cherries instead of the chocolate. Bake as above.

LEMON COOKIES

Makes 18–20
Preparation time 15 minutes, plus cooling
Cooking time 15–20 minutes

½ cup (125 ml) unsalted butter, diced and softened
½ cup (125 ml) granulated or fruit sugar
2 egg yolks
2 tsp (10 ml) grated lemon zest
1¼ cups (300 ml) all-purpose flour
¾ cup (175 ml) coarse cornmeal
Saffron (optional)
Icing sugar, for dusting

Line a baking sheet with parchment paper. In a bowl, beat the butter and sugar together until light and fluffy. Mix in the egg yolks, lemon zest, flour and cornmeal until a soft dough forms.

Roll out the dough on a lightly floured surface to ½ inch (1 cm) thick. Using a 2½-inch (6 cm) round cutter, cut out rounds from the dough, rerolling the trimmings. Transfer to the prepared baking sheet, then sprinkle with saffron, if desired, and bake in a preheated 325°F (160°C) oven for 15 to 20 minutes or until lightly golden. Transfer to a wire rack to cool, then dust with icing sugar.

For no-cook lemon cheesecakes, roughly crush 10 of the above cookies and place them in the bottom of 4 dessert bowls or glasses. Whisk together 10 oz (300 g) cream cheese with the finely grated zest and juice of 1 lemon, ⅔ cup (150 ml) superfine sugar and ⅔ cup (150 ml) whipping (35%) cream. Spoon this mixture into the prepared glasses and chill for 1 to 2 hours before serving.

DEVONSHIRE SPLITS

Makes 12 splits

Time 1½–2½ hours, depending on bread machine, plus
  shaping, proofing and baking

Dough

1¼ cups (300 ml) cold water
2 tbsp (30 ml) butter, at room temperature
½ tsp (2 ml) salt
2 tbsp (30 ml) milk powder
3½ cups (875 ml) white bread flour
2 tsp (10 ml) granulated or fruit sugar
1¼ tsp (6 ml) fast-acting dried yeast

To finish
Beaten egg, to glaze
⅔ cup (150 ml) strawberry jam
1 cup (250 ml) clotted cream
Icing sugar, for dusting

Lift the bread pan out of the machine and fit the blade. Put the dough ingredients in the pan, following the order specified in the manual.

Fit the pan into the machine and close the lid. Set to the dough program.

At the end of the program, turn the dough out onto a floured surface and cut it into 12 pieces. Shape each piece into a ball. Put them on large, greased baking sheets, leaving a little space around each one. Cover loosely with oiled plastic wrap and leave to rise in a warm place for 20 to 30 minutes.

Brush the rolls with beaten egg. Bake in a preheated 400°F (200°C) oven for 10 minutes, until golden and the bottoms sound hollow when tapped with the fingertips. Transfer to a wire rack to cool.

When ready to serve, cut a diagonal slice down through the rolls almost but not quite through to the bottom. Spoon the jam into the slit, then add spoonfuls of clotted cream. Transfer to serving plates and dust with icing sugar.

For lemon splits, make and bake the dough as above, adding the finely grated zest of 2 lemons to the dough. To finish, slice the rolls as above and fill with lightly whipped cream and lemon curd.

PEACH & RASPBERRY TARTLETS

Serves 4
Preparation time 15 minutes
Cooking time 8–10 minutes, plus cooling

1 tbsp (15 ml) butter, melted
4 sheets phyllo pastry, each about 10 inches
    (25 cm) square
½ cup (125 ml) whipping (35%) cream
1 tbsp (15 ml) light brown sugar
2 peaches, peeled, halved, pitted and diced
2 oz (60 g) raspberries
Icing sugar, for dusting

Brush 4 deep muffin cups or molds with the melted butter. Cut a sheet of phyllo pastry in half, then across, into 4 equal-sized squares. Use these phyllo squares to line 1 muffin cup, arranging at slightly different angles, pressing down well and tucking the pastry into the pan neatly. Repeat with the remaining pastry to line the other muffin cups.

Bake the phyllo pastry tartlets in a preheated 375°F (190°C) oven for 8 to 10 minutes or until golden. Carefully remove the tartlet shells from the tins and leave to cool on a wire rack.

Whip the cream and brown sugar lightly in a bowl until it holds its shape. Spoon into the tartlet shells and top with the peaches and raspberries. Dust with icing sugar. Serve immediately.

For strawberry and blueberry tartlets, grease 4 deep muffin cups as above. From ready-rolled shortcrust pastry (defrosted if frozen), cut out 4 rounds large enough to line the muffin cups. Prick the bottoms all over with a fork. Bake in a preheated 375°F (190°C) oven for 15 minutes or until golden brown. Carefully remove from the molds and leave to cool on a wire rack. Lightly whip the cream with 1 tbsp (15 ml) icing sugar, then spoon into the tartlet shells. Top with 2 oz (60 g) sliced strawberries and 2 oz (60 g) blueberries. Dust with icing sugar and serve immediately.

MADELEINES

Makes 14
Preparation time 15 minutes, plus cooling
Cooking time 12 minutes

3 eggs
⅓ cup + 2 tbsp (100 ml) superfine sugar
1¼ cups (300 ml) all-purpose flour
7 tbsp (105 ml) unsalted butter, melted
Grated zest of 1 lemon
Grated zest of 1 orange

Brush a tray of madeleine molds with melted butter and coat with all-purpose flour, then tap the tray to remove the excess flour.

Whisk the eggs and sugar in a bowl until thick and pale and the whisk leaves a trail when lifted. Sift the flour, then gently fold into the egg mixture. Fold in the melted butter and lemon and orange zest. Spoon into the molds, leaving a little room for rising.

Bake in a preheated 400°F (200°C) oven for 12 minutes or until golden and springy to the touch. Remove the madeleines from the tray and leave to cool on a wire rack.

For quick sherry trifle, line the bottom of a dessert or trifle bowl with the madeleines and sprinkle on 2 to 3 tbsp (30 to 45 ml) sweet sherry. Top with 10 oz (300 g) defrosted frozen mixed berries and top that with ¾ cup + 2 tbsp (200 ml) custard. Whip ¾ cup + 2 tbsp (200 ml) whipping (35%) cream until soft peaks form and pipe or spoon over the top. Cover and chill in the refrigerator for 2 to 3 hours before serving.

STICKY CHELSEA BUNS

Makes 12 buns
Time 1½–2½ hours, depending on bread machine, plus
   shaping, proofing and baking

Dough
1 egg, beaten
1 cup (250 ml) milk
¼ cup (60 ml) unsalted butter, softened
½ tsp (2 ml) salt
Finely grated zest of 1 lemon
3½ cups (875 ml) white bread flour
⅓ cup (75 ml) superfine sugar
1½ tsp (7 ml) fast-acting dried yeast

To finish
¼ cup (60 ml) unsalted butter, softened
¼ cup (60 ml) light muscovado sugar
1 tsp (5 ml) pumpkin pie spice
7 oz (200 g) luxury mixed dried fruit
2-inch (5 cm) piece fresh ginger, grated
¼ cup (60 ml) granulated or fruit sugar

Lift the bread pan out of the machine and fit the blade. Put the dough ingredients in the pan, following the order specified in the manual. Fit the pan into the machine and close the lid. Set to the dough program.

Mix together the butter and muscovado sugar to make a paste. Toss the pumpkin pie spice with the fruit and ginger in a bowl.

At the end of the program, turn the dough out onto a floured surface and roll it out into a rectangle, about 18 x 10 inches (45 x 25 cm). Spread to the edges with the butter-and-sugar paste and scatter on the fruit mixture. Roll up the dough, starting from a long side. Use a sharp knife to cut the log into 12 equal slices.

Grease a shallow 11 x 7 inch (28 x 18 cm) baking dish. Arrange the slices in the dish with the cut sides up. Cover loosely with oiled plastic wrap and leave to rise in a warm place for about 45 minutes or until doubled in size.

Bake the buns in a preheated 400°F (200°C) oven for 25 to 35 minutes, until risen and golden.

Meanwhile, put the superfine sugar in a pan with ⅓ cup + 2 tbsp (100 ml) water and heat gently until the sugar dissolves. Bring to a boil and boil for 1 minute. Transfer the buns to a wire rack and brush them with the syrup. Leave to cool.

For chocolate, fruit & nut buns, substitute the lemon zest with orange. Replace the butter paste and fruit mixture with 7 oz (200 g) chopped chocolate, 1 tsp (5 ml) ground ginger, ⅔ cup (150 ml) raisins and ½ cup (125 ml) chopped hazelnuts. Drizzle with melted chocolate.

A VERY HAPPY BIRTHDAY CAKE

Serves 12
Preparation time 25 minutes
Cooking time 35–40 minutes

¾ cup (175 ml) soft margarine, plus extra for greasing
¾ cup (175 ml) granulated or fruit sugar
2 tsp (10 ml) vanilla extract
2½ cups (625 ml) self-raising flour
2 tsp (10 ml) baking powder
3 eggs
⅓ cup (75 ml) ground rice
⅔ cup (150 ml) low-fat plain yogurt
6 oz (175 g) strawberries, finely chopped
1¼ cups (300 ml) whipping (35%) cream
3 tbsp (45 ml) reduced-sugar strawberry jam

Lightly grease two 8-inch (20 cm) round cake pans with removable bottoms and line the bases of the pans with parchment paper. Cream the margarine and sugar in a food processor with the vanilla until smooth.

Sift the flour and baking powder over the creamed mixture; add the eggs, ground rice and yogurt and mix together until creamy. Fold the strawberries into the mixture.

Divide the mixture between the prepared tins and bake in a preheated 350°F (180°C) oven for 35 to 40 minutes, until risen, golden and springy to the touch. Allow to cool in the pans for 10 minutes before removing to a wire rack to cool completely. Remove the baking paper.

Whisk the cream until soft peaks form. Cut the top off one of the cakes to level it, then spread with the jam and then half the cream to the edges. Scatter with two-thirds of the strawberries. Place the other cake on top and spread with the remaining cream. Scatter with the remaining strawberries or form them into your child's initials. Add candles.

For chocolate birthday cake, replace ¼ cup (60 ml) of the flour with unsweetened cocoa powder and bake as above. Omit the jam and simply fill with the cream. Replace the strawberries with 7 oz (200 g) chocolate-coated honeycomb balls, lightly crushed, used to fill and decorate the cake.

CHERRY, BRAN & RAISIN MUFFINS

Makes 12
Preparation time 15 minutes
Cooking time 20–25 minutes

1 cup (250 ml) oat bran
2 cups (500 ml) self-raising flour
1 tsp (5 ml) baking powder
1 tsp (5 ml) baking soda
1 tsp (5 ml) ground cinnamon
½ tsp (2 ml) ground ginger
½ cup (125 ml) lightly packed brown sugar
1 egg
⅓ cup (75 ml) vegetable oil
⅓ cup + 2 tbsp (100 ml) milk
8 oz (250 g) cherries, pitted and halved
⅔ cup (150 ml) raisins

Topping
8 oz (250 g) mascarpone cheese
2 tbsp (30 ml) icing sugar

To decorate
12 cherries
Pinch of ground cinnamon (optional)

Place the oat bran in a bowl. Sift the flour, baking powder, baking soda, cinnamon and ginger over top and mix together. Add the sugar and stir well.

Mix together in a measuring cup the egg, oil and milk, then pour into the dry ingredients along with the cherries and raisins and stir until just mixed. Line a 12-cup muffin pan with 12 paper muffin cups and divide the mixture between them. Bake in a preheated 350°F (180°C) oven for 20 to 25 minutes, until well risen and golden. Remove the muffins from the pan and place on a wire rack to cool.

Beat the mascarpone and icing sugar in a bowl, then spoon and swirl on top of each cooled muffin. Decorate each with a cherry and a sprinkling of cinnamon, if desired.

For carrot cake muffins, omit the oat bran and increase the flour to 2¼ cups (550 ml). Add 1 tsp (5 ml) pumpkin pie spice. Replace the cherries with 2 grated carrots and add ½ cup (125 ml) roughly chopped walnuts or pecans. Bake as above, then decorate with the same topping and a walnut half instead of a cherry.

CHOCOLATE & PECAN SPIRAL

Makes 1 extra-large loaf
Time 1½–2½ hours, depending on bread machine, plus shaping, proofing and baking

Dough
2 eggs, beaten
¾ cup (175 ml) milk
3 tbsp (45 ml) unsalted butter, softened
½ tsp (2 ml) salt
3½ cups (875 ml) white bread flour
¼ cup (60 ml) granulated or fruit sugar
1½ tsp (7 ml) fast-acting dried yeast

To finish
½ cup (125 ml) plain dark chocolate, finely chopped, divided
½ cup (125 ml) pecans, roughly chopped, divided
2 tbsp (30 ml) granulated or fruit sugar
1 egg yolk, to glaze

Lift the bread pan out of the machine and fit the blade. Put the dough ingredients in the pan, following the order specified in the manual.

Fit the pan into the machine and close the lid. Set to the dough program.

At the end of the program, turn the dough out onto a floured surface and roll it into an 11-inch (28 cm) square. Sprinkle on three-quarters of the chocolate and the nuts and all of the sugar. Roll up the dough, then put it into a greased 11 x 7 inch (28 x 18 cm) loaf pan. Cover loosely with oiled plastic wrap and leave in a warm place for 30 minutes or until the dough reaches just above the top of the pan.

Mix the egg yolk with 1 tbsp (15 ml) water and brush it over the dough. Sprinkle on the remaining chocolate and pecans and bake in a preheated 400°F (200°C) oven for 35 to 40 minutes, until the bread is well risen and deep brown and sounds hollow when tapped with the fingertips. Cover with foil after 10 minutes to prevent the nuts from overbrowning.

For brandied prune & chocolate slice, roughly chop 7 oz (200 g) soft pitted prunes and put them in a bowl with 2 tbsp (30 ml) brandy and steep for 2 hours. Make the dough as above. Turn the dough out onto a floured surface and work in the prunes and 3½ oz (100 g) each of plain and white chocolate. Shape into a log and drop into a greased 11 x 7 inch (28 x 18 cm) loaf pan. Cover loosely with oiled plastic wrap and leave in a warm place until almost doubled in size. Bake as above. After baking, dust with a mixture of unsweetened cocoa powder and icing sugar.

RUDOLPH'S SANTA SNACKS

Makes about 14
Preparation time 15 minutes
Cooking time 15 minutes

1 cup (250 ml) cornflakes cereal
7 tbsp (105 ml) butter or margarine, softened
⅓ cup (75 ml) granulated or fruit sugar
1 egg yolk
Few drops vanilla extract
1 cup (250 ml) self-raising flour
¼ cup (60 ml) cornstarch
7 glacé cherries, sliced in half, to decorate

Place the cornflakes in a plastic bag. Crush them with your hands or bash them with a rolling pin, then tip onto a plate and set aside.

Put the butter and sugar into a mixing bowl and cream them together with a wooden spoon until pale and fluffy. Add the egg yolk and vanilla and stir in. Sift in the flour and cornstarch and stir them into the mix.

Take walnut-sized amounts of the mixture to make about 14 balls. Roll the balls in the crushed cornflakes until covered, then place them on a baking sheet lined with parchment paper, leaving plenty of space between them, and decorate the top of each one with half a glacé cherry.

Bake the cookies in a preheated 375°F (190°C) oven for 15 minutes or until a light golden brown, then remove from the oven and allow to cool a little before transferring to a wire cooling rack.

For Santa's chocolate snowy snacks, add 2 oz (60 g) plain chocolate chips to the mixture with the flour and cornstarch, then add 1 tbsp (15 ml) unsweetened cocoa powder. Stir and then cook as above. Once cooked, dust with a little icing sugar to resemble snow.

326

BAKED

GRANOLA SQUARES

Makes 12
Preparation time 15 minutes, plus chilling
Cooking time 20 minutes

¾ cup (175 ml) butter, plus extra for greasing
⅔ cup (150 ml) liquid honey
2 tbsp (30 ml) maple syrup
1 tsp (5 ml) ground cinnamon
½ cup (125 ml) ready-to-eat dried apricots, roughly chopped
½ cup (125 ml) ready-to-eat dried papaya or mango, roughly chopped
½ cup (125 ml) raisins
¼ cup (60 ml) pumpkin seeds
2 tbsp (30 ml) sesame seeds
3 tbsp (45 ml) sunflower seeds
3 oz (75 g) pecans, roughly chopped
3 cups (750 ml) rolled oats

Grease an 11 x 7 inch (28 x 18 cm) baking dish with butter and line the bottom with parchment paper.

Place the butter, honey and maple syrup in a medium saucepan and heat, stirring continually, until the butter has melted. Add the cinnamon, dried fruit, seeds and nuts, stir the mixture and heat for 1 minute. Remove from the heat and add the oats, stirring until they are well coated in the syrup.

Transfer the mixture to the prepared pan and smooth down with the back of a spoon to compact into the pan and level. Bake in a preheated 350°F (180°C) oven for 15 minutes, until the top is just beginning to brown. Remove from the oven and allow to cool in the pan, then chill in the refrigerator for 30 to 60 minutes.

Turn out the chilled granola mixture, upside down, on a chopping board, then carefully flip it back over to its correct side. Using a long, sharp knife (preferably longer than the granola slab itself), cut into 12 squares.

For fruity white chocolate granola squares, leave out the pecans and seeds and replace with 3 oz (75 g) roughly chopped ready-to-eat dried apples. Once cooled, drizzle 2 oz (60 g) melted white chocolate over the top. Allow to set in the refrigerator for 10 minutes before cutting into squares.

327

BLUEBERRY & SOFT CHEESE BARS

Serves 12
Preparation time 20 minutes
Cooking time 20 minutes

¾ cup (175 ml) butter, softened, divided
⅓ cup (75 ml) brown sugar
12 oz (375 g) soft cheese, divided
2 tsp (10 ml) vanilla extract
3 eggs
1½ cups (375 ml) all-purpose flour
1½ cups (375 ml) whole wheat flour
6 oz (175 g) blueberries
½ cup (125 ml) icing sugar, sifted
½ tsp (2 ml) ground cinnamon, divided (optional)

Grease an 11 x 7 inch (28 x 18 cm) baking dish lightly with butter and line the bottom with parchment paper.

Place ⅔ cup (150 ml) of the butter into a bowl and beat well until smooth with a wooden spoon. Add the sugar, 5 oz (150 g) of the soft cheese and the vanilla extract and beat again. Add the eggs and sift in the flours. Mix together to combine well.

Fold the blueberries into the cake mixture, then transfer to the prepared pan and level. Bake in a preheated 350°F (180°C) oven for 20 minutes, until golden and firm to the touch. Allow to cool for 10 minutes in the pan before turning the cake out onto a wire rack to cool completely.

Beat together the remaining soft cheese and remaining butter with the icing sugar and half of the cinnamon, if using, and spread over the surface of the cake. Cut into 12 squares, then sprinkle with the remaining cinnamon, if desired.

For raspberry & orange bars, add the grated zest of ½ orange to the creamed butter, sugar and soft cheese mixture, then replace the blueberries with ½ cup (125 ml) raspberries, folding in very carefully so as not to break up the fruit. Bake as above, then make up the same topping, replacing the cinnamon with the remaining orange zest, and spread over the top.

BAKED

CHOC-PEANUT CAKE

Makes a 2-lb (1 kg) loaf cake
Preparation time 15 minutes
Cooking time about 1 hour

1 cup (250 ml) all-purpose flour
⅓ cup + 1 tbsp (90 ml) whole wheat flour
1 tsp (5 ml) baking powder
3 tbsp (45 ml) light brown sugar
⅓ cup (75 ml) smooth peanut butter
½ cup (125 ml) butter, softened
3 eggs, lightly beaten
1 tsp (5 ml) vanilla extract
¼ cup (60 ml) apple juice
3½ oz (100 g) plain chocolate chips or plain dark
   chocolate, chopped
1 large apple, peeled, cored and chopped

Line a 2-lb (1 kg) loaf pan with parchment paper. Sift the flours and baking powder into a large bowl. Mix in the sugar, peanut butter, butter, eggs, vanilla extract and apple juice. Stir through the chocolate chips and apple.

Spoon the mixture into the prepared pan and bake in a preheated 350°F (180°C) oven for 1 hour. To see if it is cooked, insert a skewer in the center of the loaf – if it comes out clean it is done, but if cake batter is attached to the skewer it will need another 10 minutes.

Remove the cake from the oven and turn out onto a wire rack. Peel off the baking paper and leave to cool. Serve cut into slices.

For honey cake, replace the peanut butter with ⅓ cup (75 ml) thick honey and omit the chocolate chips. Drizzle with 2 tbsp (30 ml) liquid honey before serving.

BANANA & CHOCOLATE LOAF CAKE

Serves 8–10
Preparation time 15 minutes
Cooking time 55–60 minutes

1 cup (250 ml) butter, softened, plus extra for greasing
⅔ cup (150 ml) granulated or fruit sugar
1 tsp (5 ml) vanilla extract
3 eggs, beaten
2½ cups (625 ml) self-raising flour
1 tsp (5 ml) baking powder
3 ripe bananas, mashed
2 tbsp (30 ml) milk
6 oz (175 g) plain dark chocolate, roughly chopped, or chocolate chips

Grease a 2-lb (1 kg) loaf pan lightly with butter and line the bottom with parchment paper. Beat the butter, sugar and vanilla extract together in a bowl until smooth and creamy. Add the eggs and sift in the flour and baking powder. Beat together until smooth and creamy.

Add the bananas, milk and chopped chocolate and fold together until well mixed. Transfer the mixture to the prepared pan and bake in a preheated 350°F (180°C) oven for 55 to 60 minutes, until the cake is well risen and golden.

Cool the cake in the pan for 10 minutes before turning out onto a wire rack to cool completely. Serve cut into slices.

For double-chocolate no-wheat banana loaf, replace the flour with 1¾ cup + 2 tbsp (450 ml) rice flour and add ¼ cup (60 ml) unsweetened cocoa powder when sifting into the bowl.

VANILLA FLOWERS

Makes 30
Preparation time 30 minutes
Cooking time 10–15 minutes

¾ cup + 2 tbsp (200 ml) butter, softened
Few drops vanilla extract
⅓ cup (75 ml) icing sugar
1½ cups (375 ml) all-purpose flour
½ cup (125 ml) cornstarch
Cake decorations, to decorate

Place the butter and vanilla extract in a mixing bowl and sift in the icing sugar. Cream the ingredients together with a wooden spoon. Sift in the flour and the cornstarch a little at a time and fold in with a metal spoon.

Spoon the mixture into a piping bag and pipe the mixture onto a baking sheet lined with parchment paper, making little flower shapes. To finish a flower, push the nozzle down into the piped flower as you stop squeezing. Press a decoration into the center of each one.

Bake the cookies in a preheated 375°F (190°C) oven for 10 to 15 minutes or until they are a pale golden color. Remove from the oven and allow to cool for a few minutes on the baking sheet before transferring to a cooling rack.

For ginger flowers, mix 1 tsp (5 ml) ground allspice or pumpkin pie spice in with the cornstarch. Decorate the center of each with ¼ piece preserved ginger in syrup or candied ginger before baking as above

END-OF-SUMMER CUSTARD PIE

Serves 6–8
Preparation time 20 minutes, plus chilling
Cooking time 25 minutes

1¼ cups (300 ml) all-purpose flour, plus extra for
  dusting
3 tbsp (45 ml) custard powder
2 tbsp (30 ml) icing sugar
⅓ cup (75 ml) butter, chilled and cut into cubes
2 to 3 tbsp (30 to 45 ml) cold water
1 lb (500 g) blackberries
2 apples, peeled, cored and roughly chopped
¼ cup (60 ml) granulated or fruit sugar
1 tbsp (15 ml) liquid honey
Beaten egg
Vanilla ice cream or crème fraîche (optional)

Sift the flour, custard powder and icing sugar into a bowl. Rub the butter, using your fingertips, into the flour until the mixture resembles fine breadcrumbs. Sprinkle on the water, then, using a round-bladed knife, begin to work the mixture into a smooth, firm dough. Wrap and chill for 15 minutes.

Toss the blackberries and apples with the sugar and honey and place in an 8-inch (20 cm) round pie dish or ovenproof dish.

Roll out the pastry, on a well-floured surface, to a round slightly larger than the pie dish. Place the dish on the pastry and cut around it, using a sharp knife, to produce a circle the correct size for the top. Using the pastry trimmings, make a border strip about ½ inch (1 cm) wide. Dampen the edges of the pie dish and fit the strips of pastry around the edge, pressing firmly. Dampen this pastry too before placing the circle on top and pressing again firmly to hold in place. Using any remaining trimmings, decorate the pie with leaves, flowers, birds or other shapes.

Brush with beaten egg to glaze, and bake in a preheated 400°F (200°C) oven for 20 to 25 minutes, until golden and crisp. Serve with vanilla ice cream or crème fraîche, if desired.

For cinnamon & peach custard pie, drain 2 cans (13 oz/400 g each) of peaches in natural juice and toss with the apples, 1 tbsp (15 ml) brown sugar and 1 tsp (5 ml) ground cinnamon. Use instead of the blackberries with the custard pastry as above.

CHOCOLATE ORANGE BROWNIES

Makes 16
Preparation time 15–20 minutes
Cooking time 30–35 minutes

8 oz (250 g) orange-flavored chocolate, or plain dark
  chocolate with 1 tsp (5 ml) orange extract
1 cup (250 ml) unsalted butter
⅔ cup (150 ml) granulated or fruit sugar
4 eggs
Finely grated zest of 1 orange
1½ cups (375 ml) all-purpose flour
Pinch of salt
1 tsp (5 ml) baking powder
5 oz (150 g) milk chocolate, roughly chopped
3 oz (75 g) macadamia nuts, roughly chopped

Put the chocolate and butter in a heavy-bottomed saucepan over very low heat and stir until both ingredients are just melted. Remove from the heat, stir in the sugar and set aside to cool a little.

Pour the chocolate mixture into a large bowl and beat in the eggs, orange zest and orange extract (if using).

Sift the flour, salt and baking powder into the bowl and fold in, together with the chocolate chunks and macadamia nuts.

Pour the mixture into a greased and lined cake pan, about 8 x 12 x 2 inches (20 x 30 x 5 cm).

Cook in a preheated 350°F (180°C) oven for 25 to 30 minutes or until set but not too firm. Leave the brownies to cool in the pan, then cut into squares and serve.

For ginger chocolate brownies, use plain dark chocolate (not orange-flavored chocolate) and omit the orange zest. Instead, add 1 tbsp (15 ml) ground ginger to the flour and ¼ cup (60 ml) chopped candied ginger to the chocolate.

BANANA & RAISIN SQUARES

Makes 12
Preparation time 10 minutes
Cooking time 10 minutes

⅔ cup (150 ml) butter
⅔ cup (150 ml) maple syrup
⅔ cup (150 ml) raisins
2 large bananas, well mashed
4 cups (1 L) rolled oats

Place the butter in a medium pan with the maple syrup and melt over low heat. Stir in the raisins. Remove from the heat and add the bananas, stirring well. Add the oats and stir well until all the oats have been coated.

Spoon the mixture into an 11 x 7 inch (28 x 18 cm) nonstick pan and level the surface using a potato masher for ease. Bake in a preheated 375°F (190°C) oven for 10 minutes, until the top is just beginning to turn a pale golden. The mixture will still seem somewhat soft.

Allow to cool for 10 minutes in the pan before cutting into 12 squares. Remove from the pan and allow to cool completely.

For ginger squares, add 1 tsp (5 ml) ground ginger to the melted butter and maple syrup and replace the bananas with 3 oz (75 g) finely chopped preserved ginger. Stir through with the raisins and spoon into the prepared pan and level. Bake and cut into squares as above.

RHUBARB & RASPBERRY CRUMBLE

Serves 4
Preparation time 10 minutes
Cooking time 25 minutes

1¾ cups (425 ml) all-purpose flour
Pinch of salt
⅔ cup (150 ml) unsalted butter
1 cup (250 ml) lightly packed brown sugar, divided
1 lb (500 g) fresh or frozen rhubarb (thawed if frozen), sliced
½ cup (125 ml) fresh or frozen raspberries
3 tbsp (45 ml) orange juice
Raspberry ripple ice cream (optional)

Put the flour and salt in a bowl; add the butter and rub in with the fingertips until the mixture resembles breadcrumbs. Stir in ¾ cup (175 ml) of the sugar.

Mix together the fruits, the remaining sugar and orange juice and tip into a buttered dish. Sprinkle on the topping and cook in a preheated 400°F (200°C) oven for about 25 minutes or until golden brown and bubbling.

Remove and serve hot with raspberry ripple ice cream, if desired.

For apple & blackberry crumble, substitute the rhubarb and raspberries with 14½ oz (450 g) apples, peeled and chopped, and 14½ oz (450 g) blackberries. You could also use 14½ oz (450 g) plums, pitted and quartered, and 4 peeled and thinly sliced ripe pears.

MINT CHOC CHIP CHEESECAKE

Serves 4–6
Preparation time 12 minutes, plus setting

7 oz (200 g) chocolate wafers
3½ oz (100 g) mint-flavored dark chocolate, chopped
¼ cup (60 ml) butter, melted
7 oz (200 g) cream cheese
7 oz (200 g) mascarpone cheese
¼ cup (60 ml) superfine sugar
1 tbsp (15 ml) crème de menthe or peppermint extract
2 drops green food coloring
⅓ cup (75 ml) plain dark chocolate chips, divided

Put the wafers and chocolate in a food processor or blender and process to make fine crumbs. Mix with the melted butter and press the mixture gently over the base of an 8-inch (20 cm) round springform cake pan. Place in the freezer to set while making the cream cheese mixture.

Beat together the cream cheese, mascarpone, sugar, mint liqueur or extract and food coloring in a large bowl. Stir in ¼ cup (60 ml) of the chocolate chips and spoon the mixture over the wafer base, smoothing with the back of a spoon.

Place in the refrigerator to chill for about 1 hour.

Loosen the edge with a knife, then remove the cheesecake from the pan carefully. Scatter on the remaining chocolate chips, roughly chopped.

For individual ginger cake cheesecakes, use four 3-inch (7.5 cm) fluted tartlet pans. Make a base for each cheesecake by pressing a slice of ginger cake inside each pan. Replace the mint liqueur with ginger wine.

UPSIDE-DOWN GRAPEFRUIT CAKES

Serves 6
Preparation time 15 minutes
Cooking time about 40 minutes

1 grapefruit, peeled and cut into 6 thin slices
6 tbsp (90 ml) corn syrup
¾ cup (175 ml) unsalted butter, at room temperature
1¼ cups (300 ml) lightly packed brown sugar
2 eggs
1½ cups (375 ml) self-raising flour
Pinch of salt
Finely grated zest of 1 lime
2 tbsp (30 ml) grapefruit juice
2 to 3 tbsp (30 to 45 ml) milk

Push a slice of grapefruit into the bottom of each of 6 buttered oven-proof custard cups or ramekins and drizzle each with 1 tbsp (15 ml) corn syrup. Set aside.

Cream together the butter and sugar until light and fluffy. Add the eggs, one at a time, beating well until incorporated. Gently fold in the flour, salt and lime zest, then fold in the grapefruit juice and milk so that the mixture has a good dropping consistency.

Spoon the mixture into the custard cups or ramekins and smooth down.

Put the cups in a large roasting pan half-filled with boiling water and cook in a preheated 350°F (180°C) oven for about 40 minutes or until risen and golden.

Remove the cakes from the oven, lift them out of the hot water and leave to cool for 5 minutes. Loosen the sides of the cakes by running a knife around the inside of the molds and then turn them out into serving bowls. Serve immediately with cream.

For crème anglaise to serve as an accompaniment for a special occasion, heat 2 cups (500 ml) milk with a split vanilla pod to boiling point. Remove from the heat. Beat together 6 egg yolks and ⅔ cup (150 ml) superfine sugar, then slowly beat in the hot milk. Return to the heat and stir continuously until the custard thickens. Remove the vanilla pod and serve.

CHRISTMAS GARLANDS

Makes 6
Preparation time 30 minutes
Cooking time about 15 minutes

¼ cup (60 ml) butter
1¼ cups (300 ml) all-purpose flour
¼ cup (60 ml) granulated or fruit sugar, plus a little for sprinkling
Finely grated zest of 1 small lemon
1 egg, beaten, divided
Pieces of candied angelica and glacé cherries, to decorate

Put the butter in a bowl, sift in the flour and rub together until the mixture resembles fine breadcrumbs. Add the sugar and lemon zest and stir everything together with a wooden spoon. Add most of the egg and stir again until the mixture comes together, then use your hands to draw the dough together into a ball.

Pick off small pieces of dough and roll them into balls, each about the size of a cherry. Press 8 balls of cookie dough together into a circle, then repeat to make a further 5 garlands. Place small pieces of glacé cherry or angelica between the balls.

Place the garlands on a baking sheet lined with parchment paper and bake in a preheated 375°F (190°C) oven for about 15 minutes or until pale golden. Just before the end of the cooking time, brush with the remainder of the egg and sprinkle with granulated or fruit sugar, then return to the oven to finish cooking.

Remove from the oven and allow to cool a little before transferring to a cooling rack. Thread onto ribbons and use as decorations.

For Christmas trees, using 10 small balls of dough per tree, create Christmas tree shapes by starting with 1 as a top row, followed by 2, 3, then 4 on the bottom row. This will create a classic triangular Christmas tree shape. Decorate the trees with angelica and glacé cherries and bake as above.

LEMON DRIZZLE CAKE

Serves 8
Preparation time 20 minutes
Cooking time 22–28 minutes

5 eggs
½ cup (125 ml) granulated or fruit sugar
Pinch of salt
1 cup (250 ml) all-purpose flour
1 tsp (5 ml) baking powder
Finely grated zest of 1 lemon
1 tbsp (15 ml) lemon juice
7 tbsp (105 ml) butter, melted and cooled
Crème fraîche or sour cream, to serve

Syrup
2 cups (500 ml) icing sugar
½ cup (125 ml) lemon juice
Finely grated zest of 1 lemon
Seeds scraped from 1 vanilla pod

Put the eggs, sugar and salt in a large heatproof bowl set over a pan of barely simmering water. Beat the mixture with a handheld electric mixer for 2 to 3 minutes or until it triples in volume and thickens to the consistency of lightly whipped cream. Remove from the heat.

Sift in the flour and baking powder; add the lemon zest and juice and drizzle the butter down the sides of the bowl. Fold in gently, then pour into a greased and lined 8½-inch (22 cm) square cake pan and cook in a preheated 350°F (180°C) oven for 20 to 25 minutes or until risen, golden and coming away from the sides of the pan.

Meanwhile, put all the ingredients for the syrup in a small pan and heat gently until the sugar has dissolved. Increase the heat and boil rapidly for 4 to 5 minutes. Set aside to cool a little.

Remove the cake from the oven, leave it to rest for 5 minutes, then make holes over the surface with a skewer. Drizzle two-thirds of the warm syrup over the cake. Leave the cake to cool and absorb the syrup.

Remove the cake from the pan and peel away the lining paper. Place the cake on a dish and serve in squares or slices with a heaped spoonful of crème fraîche or sour cream and an extra drizzle of syrup.

For citrus drizzle cake with sorbet, use orange zest and juice instead of lemon and serve topped with lemon sorbet.

LARDY CAKE

Makes 10 thick slices

Time 1½–2½ hours, depending on bread machine, plus shaping, proofing and baking

Dough

1¼ cups (300 ml) water

2 tbsp (30 ml) lard, softened

¼ tsp (1 ml) salt

2 tbsp (30 ml) milk powder

1 tsp (5 ml) pumpkin pie spice

3⅓ cups (825 ml) white bread flour

2 tbsp (30 ml) light brown sugar

1¼ tsp (6 ml) fast-acting dried yeast

To finish

⅓ cup + 2 tbsp (100 ml) lard, softened

2 tbsp (30 ml) unsalted butter, softened

8 oz (250 g) mixed dried fruit

2 oz (60 g) chopped candied peel

½ cup (125 ml) granulated sugar, plus extra for sprinkling

Milk, to brush

Lift the bread pan out of the machine and fit the blade. Put the dough ingredients into the pan, following the order specified in the manual.

Fit the pan into the machine and close the lid. Set to the dough program.

At the end of the program, turn the dough out onto a floured surface and roll it out into a rectangle, about 16 x 9 inches (40 x 23 cm), with a short end facing you. Using a knife, dot the lard over the dough, then dot on smaller pieces of butter.

Mix together the dried fruit, peel and sugar and scatter over the dough. Press down gently with your hand. Fold the bottom third of the dough over and press down gently, then fold the top third of the dough over to form a rectangle of 3 layers. Turn the dough through 45 degrees and reroll to a similar-sized rectangle. Fold the ends in as before and reroll to a rectangle slightly smaller than the size of a shallow, greased 11 x 7 inch (28 x 18 cm) baking pan. Lift the dough into the pan, cover loosely with oiled plastic wrap and leave to rise in a warm place until risen by about half again.

Brush with a little milk and sprinkle with extra sugar. Bake in a preheated 400°F (200°C) oven for about 45 minutes, until risen and golden. Leave in the pan for 10 minutes, then transfer to a wire rack to cool. Serve warm, cut into chunky slices.

For lardy cake with ginger, grate a 2½-inch (6 cm) piece fresh ginger and add to the pan with the water when making the dough. Chop ¼ cup (60 ml) preserved ginger and mix with the dried fruit and sugar. Finish as above.

GOOEY CHOCOLATE NUT BREAD

Makes 8–10 slices

Time 1½–2½ hours, depending on bread machine, plus shaping, proofing and baking

Dough

1 large egg, beaten

⅔ cup (150 ml) milk

2 tsp (10 ml) vanilla bean paste

⅓ cup (75 ml) unsalted butter, softened

¼ tsp (1 ml) salt

3 cups (750 ml) white bread flour

½ cup (125 ml) ground hazelnuts

¼ cup (60 ml) granulated or fruit sugar

1¼ tsp (6 ml) fast-acting dried yeast

To finish

7 oz (200 g) chocolate hazelnut spread, divided

3½ oz (100 g) hazelnuts, roughly chopped, divided, plus 1 oz (25 g) to decorate

Beaten egg, to glaze

2 oz (60 g) plain dark chocolate, chopped

Unsweetened cocoa powder and icing sugar, for dusting

Lift the bread pan out of the machine and fit the blade. Put the dough ingredients in the pan, following the order specified in the manual and adding the ground hazelnuts with the flour. Fit the pan into the machine and close the lid. Set to the dough program. Grease an 8-inch (20 cm) round cake pan with a removable bottom.

At the end of the program, turn the dough out onto a floured surface. Roll one-third of the dough into a 10½-inch (26 cm) round. Place it in the pan so it comes about 1¼ inches (3 cm) up the sides to make a shell.

Dot one-third of the chocolate spread over the base and scatter with one-third of the nuts. Divide the remaining dough into 3 pieces and roll each into an 8-inch (20 cm) round. Place one layer in the pan and dot with another third of the chocolate spread and nuts. Continue layering, finishing with a layer of dough.

Brush the dough with beaten egg. Press the chopped chocolate and reserved nuts into the dough. Cover loosely with oiled plastic wrap and leave to rise in a warm place for 45 to 60 minutes or until about half the size again.

Bake in a preheated 400°F (200°C) oven for 50 minutes. Cover it with foil if the top starts to overbrown. Transfer to a wire rack to cool. Serve dusted with unsweetened cocoa powder and icing sugar.

For white chocolate & pecan bread, instead of the chocolate spread, melt together 7 oz (200 g) white chocolate, 2 tbsp (30 ml) unsalted butter, 1 tbsp (15 ml) corn syrup and 2 tbsp (30 ml) milk. Substitute pecans for the hazelnuts and white chocolate for plain chocolate.

CARAMELIZED BANANA PUFF TART

Serves 4
Preparation time 10 minutes
Cooking time 15–20 minutes

3 bananas, sliced
12 oz (375 g) ready-made puff pastry, defrosted
  if frozen
1 egg, beaten
3 tbsp (45 ml) unrefined demerara sugar
1¼ cups (300 ml) whipping (35%) cream (optional)

Slice the bananas in half horizontally. Roll the pastry into an 8-inch (20 cm) square and cut the pastry into equal quarters. Place on a baking sheet and score a ½-inch (1 cm) border around the edge of each pastry square. Arrange the bananas, cut side up, on the pastry inside the border, then brush the border with the beaten egg. Sprinkle the top of the bananas with the sugar.

Bake in a preheated 400°F (200°C) oven for 15 to 20 minutes or until the pastry is puffed and golden and the bananas are caramelized. Serve the tarts hot with cream, if desired.

For cinnamon coffee liqueur cream as an alternative accompaniment to the tarts, in a bowl whip ¾ cup + 2 tbsp (200 ml) whipping (35%) cream until soft peaks form, then stir in 2 tsp (10 ml) ground cinnamon and 2 tbsp (30 ml) Baileys Irish Cream or any other creamy coffee liqueur.

BAKED

STOLLEN

Makes 1 small loaf (about 10 thick slices)
Time 1½–2½ hours, depending on bread machine, plus
    shaping, proofing and baking

Dough
¾ cup + 2 tbsp (200 ml) milk
Finely grated zest of 1 lemon
¼ cup (60 ml) unsalted butter, softened
½ tsp (2 ml) salt
½ tsp (2 ml) pumpkin pie spice
3 cups (750 ml) white bread flour
¼ cup (60 ml) light brown sugar
1¼ tsp (6 ml) fast-acting dried yeast
½ cup (125 ml) sultanas
½ cup (125 ml) blanched hazelnuts, chopped
⅓ cup (75 ml) candied peel, chopped

To finish
8 oz (250 g) hazelnut marzipan (see right)
    or almond marzipan
Icing sugar, for dusting

Lift the bread pan out of the machine and fit the blade. Put the dough ingredients, except the sultanas, nuts and peel, in the pan, following the order specified in the manual.

Fit the pan into the machine and close the lid. Set to the dough program, adding the sultanas, hazelnuts and peel when the machine beeps.

Roll the marzipan into a thick log about 10 inches (25 cm) long.

At the end of the program, turn the dough out onto a floured surface and roll it out into an oval, about 12 x 7 inches (30 x 18 cm). Lay the log of marzipan over the dough slightly to one side of the center. Brush a long edge with a little water and fold the wider piece of dough over the filling, pressing it down gently.

Transfer the stollen to a large, greased baking sheet and cover loosely with oiled plastic wrap. Leave to rise in a warm place until almost doubled in size. Bake in a preheated 400°F (200°C) oven for about 25 minutes, until risen and golden. Transfer to a wire rack to cool. Dust generously with icing sugar before serving.

For homemade hazelnut marzipan, grind 5 oz (150 g) whole blanched hazelnuts in a food processor. Add ¼ cup (60 ml) granulated or fruit sugar and ⅓ cup (75 ml) icing sugar to the processor and blend briefly to mix. Add 1 small egg white and blend until the mixture comes together to make a paste. Gather into a ball, wrap in plastic wrap and keep in a cool place until ready to use.

BLUEBERRY & VANILLA BRAID

Makes 1 large braid (about 10 thick slices)
Time 1½–2½ hours, depending on bread machine, plus
  shaping, proofing and baking

Dough
⅔ cup (150 ml) water
2 tsp (10 ml) vanilla bean paste
1 large egg, beaten
⅓ cup (75 ml) unsalted butter, softened
¼ tsp (1 ml) salt
3 cups (750 ml) white bread flour
½ cup (125 ml) ground almonds
¼ cup (60 ml) granulated or fruit sugar
1¼ tsp (6 ml) fast-acting dried yeast

To finish
4 oz (125 g) ricotta cheese
8 oz (250 g) blueberries, divided
3 tbsp (45 ml) granulated or fruit sugar
Beaten egg, to glaze
Vanilla sugar, for sprinkling

Lift the bread pan out of the machine and fit the blade. Put the dough ingredients in the pan, following the order specified in the manual. The vanilla bean paste should be added with the liquids and the ground almonds with the flour. Fit the pan into the machine and close the lid. Set to the dough program.

At the end of the program, turn the dough out onto a floured surface and divide it into 3 equal pieces. Roll each piece into a strip about 14 x 5 inches (35 x 12 cm). Spread ricotta over each strip to about ¾ inch (2 cm) from the edges. Scatter with 7 oz (200 g) of the blueberries and sprinkle 1 tbsp (15 ml) sugar over each strip. Bring up the edges over the filling, pinching them together firmly to make 3 thick ropes. Roll them over so the joins are underneath. Braid the ropes together, tucking the ends underneath, and carefully lift onto a large, greased baking sheet. Cover loosely with oiled plastic wrap and leave to rise in a warm place for 40 minutes or until nearly doubled in size.

Brush with beaten egg. Scatter with the remaining blueberries and sprinkle with vanilla sugar. Bake in a preheated 400°F (200°C) oven for 30 minutes or until risen and golden. Cool on a wire rack.

For red fruit & vanilla loaf, make and shape the dough as above. Use cream cheese instead of the ricotta and 7 oz (200 g) mixed dried red fruit (such as cranberries, sour cherries and strawberries) instead of the blueberries. Before cooking, scatter with an extra 2 oz (60 g) chopped red fruits and sprinkle with vanilla sugar.

340

SPICY APPLE PARKIN

Makes 8 slices
Time about 1 hour, depending on bread machine, plus
  cooking

4 tart apples, such as Granny Smith
5 tbsp (75 ml) apple juice
¼ tsp (1 ml) ground cloves
½ cup (125 ml) molasses
⅓ cup + 2 tbsp (100 ml) corn syrup
⅓ cup (75 ml) unsalted butter, softened
¾ cup (175 ml) self-raising whole wheat flour
¾ cup (175 ml) self-raising white flour
1 tsp (5 ml) baking soda
2 tsp (10 ml) ground ginger
2 cups (500 ml) quick-cooking rolled oats

Peel, core and slice the apples and put the slices in a small saucepan with the apple juice and ground cloves. Bring to a boil, reduce the heat and cook gently, uncovered, for about 5 minutes or until the apples have softened slightly. Drain and leave to cool.

Lift the bread pan out of the machine and fit the blade. Add the molasses, syrup, butter, flour, baking soda, ginger and oats to the pan.

Fit the pan into the machine and close the lid. Set to the cake program. After about 5 minutes, use a plastic spatula to scrape the mixture down from the sides and from the corners of the pan. Stir in the apples.

Test the cake after 1 hour by inserting a skewer into the center. If it comes out clean, the cake is ready. If not, cook a little longer or complete the program. Transfer the cake to a wire rack to cool.

For brandied prune parkin, roughly chop 7 oz (200 g) prunes. Make the cake mixture as above, omitting the first step and adding the prunes, 2 tbsp (30 ml) brandy and the grated zest of 1 orange with the rest of the ingredients.

CHOCOLATE FUDGE SLICE

Makes 10 slices
Time about 1 hour, depending on bread machine

Cake
¾ cup (175 ml) unsweetened cocoa powder
3 oz (75 g) plain dark chocolate, chopped
⅔ cup (150 ml) unsalted butter, softened
1 cup + 1 tbsp (265 ml) light muscovado sugar
2 large eggs, beaten
1¾ cups (425 ml) self-raising flour
½ tsp (2 ml) baking powder

Icing
7 oz (200 g) plain dark chocolate
1¼ cups (300 ml) icing sugar
⅔ cup (150 ml) unsalted butter, softened

Whisk the cocoa powder in a bowl with 1 cup (250 ml) boiling water until smooth. Stir in the chopped chocolate and leave to cool, stirring occasionally, until the chocolate has melted.

Lift the bread pan out of the machine and fit the blade. Put the cake ingredients in the pan.

Fit the pan into the machine and close the lid. Set to the cake program. After about 5 minutes, use a plastic spatula to scrape the mixture down from the sides and from the corners of the pan.

Test the cake after 1 hour by inserting a skewer into the center. If it comes out clean, the cake is ready. If not, cook a little longer or complete the program. Transfer the cake to a wire rack to cool.

Make the icing. Melt the chocolate in a small bowl and leave to cool slightly. Beat together the icing sugar and butter, then beat in the chocolate. Split the cake in half and sandwich with one-quarter of the icing. Transfer to a serving plate and use a palette knife to spread the remaining icing over the top and sides.

For double chocolate fudge slice, make the cake as above, then measure 1 cup (250 ml) whipping (35%) cream and pour half into a small saucepan. Heat gently until it bubbles around the edges, then remove from the heat and tip in 8 oz (250 g) chopped white chocolate. Leave to stand for a few minutes, until the chocolate has melted, then stir lightly and turn into a bowl. Leave until cool. Add the remaining cream and whisk with a handheld electric mixer until the mixture just starts to hold its shape. Use to cover the cake.

CHERRY & ALMOND MADEIRA CAKE

Makes 8 slices
Time about 1¼ hours, depending on bread machine, plus cooking

3 oz (75 g) dried black cherries
⅓ cup (75 ml) apple juice
¾ cup (175 ml) unsalted butter, softened
¾ cup (175 ml) granulated or fruit sugar, plus extra for dusting
3 large eggs, beaten
1¾ cups + 2 tbsp (455 ml) self-raising flour
½ tsp (2 ml) baking powder
1 cup (250 ml) ground almonds
1 tsp (5 ml) almond extract

Put the cherries and apple juice in a small saucepan and heat gently, uncovered, for about 5 minutes, until the cherries have plumped up slightly and the juice has been absorbed. Leave to cool.

Lift the bread pan out of the machine and fit the blade. Put the ingredients, except the cherries, in the pan, following the order specified in the manual.

Fit the pan into the machine and close the lid. Set to the cake program. After about 5 minutes, use a plastic spatula to scrape the mixture down from the sides and from the corners of the pan. Scatter the cherries into the pan once the cake is evenly mixed.

Test the cake after 1¼ hours by inserting a skewer into the center. If it comes out clean the cake is ready. If not, cook a little longer or complete the program.

Transfer the cake to a wire rack to cool. Serve dusted with extra sugar.

For coffee & walnut Madeira cake, omit the cherries, juice and almond extract. Dissolve 1 tbsp (15 ml) espresso coffee powder in 2 tbsp (30 ml) boiling water and add to the pan with the remaining ingredients. Make as above, adding 1 cup (250 ml) roughly chopped walnuts to the pan once the cake is evenly mixed. Finish as above.

SUMMER FRUIT CHEESECAKE SLICES

Makes 8 slices

Time 1½–2½ hours, depending on bread machine, plus shaping, proofing and baking

Dough

1 egg, beaten

⅔ cup (150 ml) milk

1 tbsp (15 ml) vanilla bean paste or vanilla extract

2 tbsp (30 ml) unsalted butter, softened

1 tbsp (15 ml) milk powder

2⅓ cups (575 ml) white bread flour, plus 1 tbsp (15 ml)

¼ cup (60 ml) granulated or fruit sugar

¾ tsp (3 ml) fast-acting dried yeast

To finish

7 oz (200 g) cream cheese

¼ cup (60 ml) granulated or fruit sugar, plus 1 tbsp (15 ml) for sprinkling

1 tsp (5 ml) vanilla bean paste or vanilla extract

1 egg

5 oz (150 g) raspberries, divided

5 oz (150 g) strawberries, hulled and halved, divided

Icing sugar, for dusting

Lift the bread pan out of the machine and fit the blade. Put the dough ingredients in the pan, following the order specified in the manual. Fit the pan into the machine and close the lid. Set to the dough program.

Beat the cream cheese to soften, then beat in the sugar, vanilla paste or extract and egg until smooth.

At the end of the program, turn the dough out onto a floured surface and cut off one-quarter. Roll out the remainder into a round about 11 inches (28 cm) in diameter. Grease a 9-inch (23 cm) springform cake pan. Press the dough into the pan so that it comes about 1¼ inches (3 cm) up the sides, making a shell.

Divide the remaining dough into 10 equal pieces and scatter them into the shell. Dot the cream cheese mixture between the dough pieces, then scatter with half the berries. Cover loosely with oiled plastic wrap and leave to rise in a warm place until slightly risen.

Bake in a preheated 400°F (200°C) oven for about 45 minutes, until the bread is risen and golden. Make sure the center of the dough is cooked by piercing it with a skewer. Transfer to a wire rack to cool. Scatter with the remaining fruits and dust with icing sugar.

For spiced peach & red currant slice, add 1 tsp (5 ml) ground cinnamon instead of the vanilla paste or vanilla. Chop 4 ripe peaches into small chunks and use instead of the berries. After baking, drizzle the cake with melted red currant jelly and scatter with clusters of red currants.

WHITE CHOCOLATE & BANANA LOAF

Makes 1 large loaf
Time 1–2 hours, depending on bread machine

1 cup (250 ml) mashed banana (about 2 medium
  bananas)
²⁄₃ cup (150 ml) warm milk
¼ cup (60 ml) unsalted butter, softened
½ tsp (2 ml) salt
3⅓ cups (825 ml) white bread flour
¼ cup (60 ml) granulated or fruit sugar
2½ tsp (12 ml) fast-acting dried yeast
7 oz (200 g) white chocolate, chopped
1 cup (250 ml) pecans, roughly chopped
Icing sugar, for dusting

Lift the bread pan out of the machine and fit the blade. Put the ingredients, except the chocolate and nuts, in the pan, following the order specified in the manual. Add the mashed banana with the milk.

Fit the pan into the machine and close the lid. Set to a 1½-lb (750 g) loaf size on the fast/rapid bake program. Add the white chocolate and pecans when the machine beeps.

At the end of the program, lift the pan out of the machine and shake the bread out onto a wire rack to cool. Serve dusted with icing sugar.

For dark chocolate & ginger rolls, put the ingredients in the bread machine as above, replacing ¼ cup (60 ml) of the flour with ¼ cup (60 ml) unsweetened cocoa powder. Reduce the yeast to 1½ tsp (7 ml) and add 3 pieces of preserved ginger from a jar, finely chopped. Use chopped plain dark chocolate instead of the white. Set to the dough program, adding the chocolate and nuts when the machine beeps. At the end of the program, turn out the dough and shape into 8 small balls. Space well apart on a greased baking sheet and cover loosely with oiled plastic wrap. Leave in a warm place to rise until almost doubled in size. Bake in a preheated 425°F (220°C) oven for about 15 minutes, until risen and lightly browned. Transfer to a wire rack to cool and serve dusted with icing sugar.

CINNAMON DOUGHNUTS

Makes 10 doughnuts

Time 1½–2½ hours, depending on bread machine, plus shaping, proofing and cooking

Dough

1 large egg, beaten

1 cup (250 ml) milk

2 tsp (10 ml) vanilla extract

2 tbsp (30 ml) unsalted butter, softened

½ tsp (2 ml) salt

3½ cups (875 ml) white bread flour

¼ cup (60 ml) granulated or fruit sugar

1¼ tsp (6 ml) fast-acting dried yeast

To finish

½ cup (125 ml) granulated or fruit sugar

1 tsp (5 ml) ground cinnamon

Oil, for deep frying

Lift the bread pan out of the machine and fit the blade. Put the dough ingredients in the pan, following the order specified in the manual.

Fit the pan into the machine and close the lid. Set to the dough program.

At the end of the program, turn the dough out onto a floured surface and cut it into 10 equal pieces. Shape each into a ball and space them, well apart, on a large, greased baking sheet. Cover loosely with oiled plastic wrap and leave to rise in a warm place for 30 to 40 minutes or until almost doubled in size.

Mix together the sugar and cinnamon on a plate. Put 3 inches (8 cm) oil in a large saucepan and heat it until a small piece of bread sizzles on the surface and turns pale golden in about 30 seconds.

Fry the doughnuts, 3 to 4 at a time, for about 3 minutes, turning them once, until golden on both sides. Drain with a slotted spoon onto several paper towels. Cook the remainder. Roll the doughnuts in the cinnamon sugar while still warm.

For doughnuts with chocolate sauce, make the dough and leave to rise as above. Place 3½ oz (100 g) chopped plain chocolate in a heatproof bowl with 1 tbsp (15 ml) butter, ¼ cup (60 ml) icing sugar and 2 tbsp (30 ml) milk. Rest the bowl over a pan of gently simmering water and leave until melted, stirring frequently until smooth. Fry the doughnuts as above, draining them and rolling in the spiced sugar. Serve with little pots of the chocolate sauce.

344

BAKED

TROPICAL FRUIT DRIZZLE CAKE

Makes 8–10 slices

Time about 1¼ hours, depending on bread machine

4 oz (125 g) semi-dried tropical fruits such as mango, papaya and pineapple, divided

3½ oz (100 g) creamed coconut

⅔ cup (150 ml) unsalted butter, softened

¾ cup (175 ml) light brown sugar

3 eggs, beaten

Finely grated zest of 3 limes, plus ¼ cup (60 ml) juice

1¾ cups (425 ml) self-raising flour

1 tsp (5 ml) baking powder

¼ cup (60 ml) granulated or fruit sugar, for sprinkling

Roughly chop the tropical fruit mix if it is in large pieces. If the creamed coconut is in a solid block, microwave on medium power for 2 to 3 minutes to make a soft paste.

Lift the bread pan out of the machine and fit the blade. Add half the chopped fruits, the creamed coconut, butter, light brown sugar, eggs, lime zest, flour and baking powder to the pan.

Fit the pan into the machine and close the lid. Set to the cake program. After about 5 minutes, use a plastic spatula to scrape the mixture down from the sides and from the corners of the pan. Scatter in the remaining tropical fruit mixture.

Test the cake after 1¼ hours by inserting a skewer into the center. If it comes out clean, the cake is ready. If not, cook a little longer or complete the program. Transfer the cake to a wire rack to cool.

While the cake is still warm, drizzle over the lime juice and then sprinkle over the ¼ cup (60 ml) sugar. Leave to cool.

For lemon & coconut drizzle cake, omit the tropical fruits and use the zest of 3 lemons instead of limes, and use superfine or fruit sugar instead of brown sugar. While the cake is cooking, blend ¼ cup (60 ml) lemon juice with ¼ cup (60 ml) granulated or fruit sugar. Transfer the cake to a wire rack and drizzle the lemon syrup overtop.

CHOCOLATE & RASPBERRY SOUFFLÉS

Serves 4
Preparation time 10 minutes
Cooking time 13–18 minutes

3½ oz (100 g) plain dark chocolate
3 eggs, separated
⅓ cup + 1 tbsp (90 ml) self-raising flour, sifted
2½ tbsp (37 ml) granulated or fruit sugar
5 oz (150 g) raspberries, plus extra to serve (optional)
Icing sugar, sifted, to decorate

Break the chocolate into squares and put them in a large heatproof bowl over a saucepan of simmering water. Leave until melted, then remove from the heat and allow to cool a little. Whisk in the egg yolks and fold in the flour.

Whisk the egg whites and sugar in a medium bowl until they form soft peaks. Beat a spoonful of the egg whites into the chocolate mixture to loosen it before gently folding in the rest.

Put the raspberries into 4 lightly greased ramekins, pour over the chocolate mixture and cook in a preheated 375°F (190°C) oven for 12 to 15 minutes, until the soufflés have risen.

Sprinkle the soufflés with icing sugar and serve with extra raspberries, if desired.

For white chocolate & mango soufflés, substitute the plain dark chocolate with white chocolate and the raspberries with 1 mango, peeled, pitted, diced and divided among the ramekins.

CHOCOLATE CHIP COOKIES

Makes 16
Preparation time 10 minutes, plus cooling
Cooking time 15 minutes

½ cup (125 ml) unsalted butter, diced and softened
¾ cup (175 ml) packed light brown sugar
1 tsp (5 ml) vanilla extract
1 egg, lightly beaten
1 tbsp (15 ml) milk
1¾ cups (425 ml) all-purpose flour
1 tsp (5 ml) baking powder
1⅓ cups (325 ml) plain dark chocolate chips

Line a large baking sheet with parchment paper. In a large bowl, beat the butter and sugar together until light and fluffy. Mix in the vanilla extract, then gradually beat in the egg, beating well after each addition. Stir in the milk.

Sift the flour and baking powder into a separate large bowl, then fold into the butter-and-egg mixture. Stir in the chocolate chips.

Drop level tablespoonfuls (15 ml) of the cookie mixture onto the prepared baking sheet, leaving about 1½ inches (3.5 cm) between each cookie, then lightly press with a floured fork. Bake in a preheated 350°F (180°C) oven for 15 minutes or until lightly golden. Transfer to a wire rack to cool.

For chocolate & mandarin log, drain a 10-oz (300 g) can mandarin orange segments and finely chop, reserving a few whole segments for decoration. In a bowl, whip 1¼ cups (300 ml) whipping (35%) cream with ¼ cup (60 ml) icing sugar until thick, then fold in the chopped mandarins. Sandwich the cooked chocolate chip cookies one on top of the other with half the mandarin cream, then carefully set the log on its side and wrap in foil. Chill in the refrigerator for at least 2 to 3 hours or overnight. Just before serving, put the log on a serving plate, cover with the remaining mandarin cream and decorate with the reserved mandarins. Serve in slices, cut on the diagonal.

OLIVE & TOMATO BREAD

Makes 1 large loaf
Time 1½–2½ hours, depending on bread machine, plus
shaping, proofing and baking

Dough
1 cup + 2 tbsp (275 ml) water
2 tbsp (30 ml) olive oil
1 tsp (5 ml) salt
3¾ cups (925 ml) white bread flour
1 tsp (5 ml) granulated or fruit sugar
1¼ tsp (6 ml) fast-acting dried yeast

To finish
4 oz (125 g) pitted or stuffed green olives, roughly
chopped
1½ oz (40 g) sun-dried tomatoes (not in oil), roughly
chopped
Coarse sea salt and paprika, for sprinkling

Lift the bread pan out of the machine and fit the blade. Put the dough ingredients in the pan, following the order specified in the manual.

Fit the pan into the machine and close the lid. Set to the dough program.

At the end of the program, lift the pan out of the machine and turn the dough out onto a floured surface. Gradually work in the chopped olives and tomatoes. Pat the dough into a circle about 8 inches (20 cm) across and use a floured knife to mark it into 8 wedges. Do not cut right through to the base.

Sprinkle the salt and paprika over the dough, transfer to a large, lightly greased baking sheet, cover loosely with oiled plastic wrap and leave to rise in a warm place for 30 minutes, until it is half as big again.

Bake in a preheated 400°F (200°C) oven for 30 minutes. Check after 15 minutes and cover with foil if overbrowning. Transfer to a wire rack to cool.

For pancetta & Parmesan bread, finely chop 3½ oz (100 g) pancetta. Heat 1 tbsp (15 ml) olive oil in a small frying pan and fry the pancetta with 1 chopped shallot for 5 minutes, until it is beginning to color. Leave to cool. Make the bread as above, adding the pancetta and shallot and ⅓ cup (75 ml) grated Parmesan cheese to the dough instead of the olives and tomatoes. Finish as above.

SPEEDY SESAME BREAD

Makes 1 large loaf
Time 1–2 hours, depending on bread machine

1 cup + 2 tbsp (275 ml) warm water
2 tbsp (30 ml) sunflower oil
1 tsp (5 ml) salt
2 tbsp (30 ml) milk powder
2 tbsp (30 ml) sesame seeds
3¾ cups (925 ml) white bread flour
1 tbsp (15 ml) granulated or fruit sugar
2½ tsp (12 ml) fast-acting dried yeast

To finish
Melted butter, to brush
Sesame seeds, for sprinkling

Lift the bread pan out of the machine and fit the blade. Put the dough ingredients in the pan, following the order specified in the manual.

Fit the pan into the machine and close the lid. Set to a 1½-lb (750 g) loaf size on the fast/rapid bake program.

At the end of the program, lift the pan out of the machine and shake the bread out onto a wire rack. Brush the top of the loaf with the butter and sprinkle with a few extra sesame seeds. Brown under the broiler, if desired.

For speedy three-grain bread, omit the milk powder and sesame seeds from the above recipe and reduce the sugar to 1½ tsp (7 ml). Replace 1½ cups (375 ml) of the white flour with malted bread flour and a further ⅓ cup (75 ml) with wheat flakes cereal. Just before baking begins, lightly brush the top of the dough with milk and scatter with extra wheat flakes. Close the lid gently and complete the program.

OLIVE OIL, ROSEMARY & RAISIN BREAD

Makes 1 large loaf

Time 1½–2½ hours, depending on bread machine, plus
  shaping, proofing and baking

1⅓ cups (325 ml) water

⅓ cup + 2 tbsp (100 ml) extra virgin olive oil

2 tsp (10 ml) sea salt, plus extra for sprinkling

2 tbsp (30 ml) milk powder

2 tsp (10 ml) fennel seeds, lightly crushed

1 tbsp (15 ml) chopped fresh rosemary

4¾ cups (1.1 L) white bread flour

1 tbsp (15 ml) granulated or fruit sugar

2 tsp (10 ml) fast-acting dried yeast

½ cup (125 ml) raisins

Fresh rosemary sprigs, to garnish

Lift the bread pan out of the machine and fit the blade. Put the ingredients, except the raisins, in the pan, following the order specified in the manual. Add the seeds and chopped rosemary with the flour.

Fit the pan into the machine and close the lid. Set to the dough program, adding the raisins when the machine beeps.

At the end of the program, turn the dough out onto a floured surface and shape it into a round. Make a hole through the center of the loaf with your fingertips, then enlarge it with your hand until the dough is ring-shaped, with a hole 4 inches (10 cm) in diameter in the middle. Put the dough on a large, greased baking sheet, cover loosely with oiled plastic wrap and leave to rise in a warm place for about 45 minutes or until it has almost doubled in size.

Score the dough at intervals with a floured knife and scatter with rosemary sprigs and sea salt. Bake in a preheated 425°F (220°C) oven for 40 minutes, until risen and golden. Cover the bread with foil and replace the rosemary sprigs if they start to overbrown.

For Mediterranean herb bread, make the dough as above, using 2 tsp (10 ml) dried oregano instead of the rosemary and omitting the fennel seeds. Add ¾ cup (175 ml) torn basil leaves and 3 tbsp (45 ml) capers, drained and dried, when the machine beeps. Finish as above, without the rosemary sprigs.

BRIOCHE

Makes 1 loaf

Time 1½–2½ hours, depending on bread machine, plus
  shaping, proofing and baking

3 eggs, beaten

⅓ cup (75 ml) unsalted butter, softened

¼ tsp (1 ml) salt

2 cups (500 ml) white bread flour

1½ tbsp (22 ml) granulated or fruit sugar

1 tsp (5 ml) fast-acting dried yeast

Egg yolk, to glaze

Lift the bread pan out of the machine and fit the blade. Put the ingredients in the pan, following the order specified in the manual.

Fit the pan into the machine and close the lid. Set to the dough program. Thoroughly butter a 3-cup (750 ml) brioche mold or a 2-lb (1 kg) loaf pan.

At the end of the program, turn the dough out onto a floured surface and cut off one-quarter. Shape the larger piece into a ball and drop it into the brioche pan. Push a deep, wide hole into the dough with your fingers. Shape the remaining dough into a ball and press it gently into the indented top. (If you are using a loaf pan, shape the dough into an oval and drop it into the pan.) Cover loosely with oiled plastic wrap and leave to rise in a warm place for 50 to 60 minutes or until almost doubled in size.

Mix the egg yolk with 1 tbsp (15 ml) water and gently brush over the dough. Bake in a preheated 425°F (220°C) oven for 20 to 25 minutes or until deep golden and firm. (Cover the loaf with foil if the crust starts to overbrown.)

After baking, leave the bread in the pan for a few minutes, then shake out onto a wire rack to cool.

For baby chocolate brioche buns, make the dough as above and divide it into 8 pieces. Push ½ oz (15 g) plain dark chocolate into the center of each piece and seal the dough around the chocolate. Space the buns well apart on a greased baking sheet. Cover loosely with oiled plastic wrap and leave to rise in a warm place until almost doubled in size. Glaze and bake as above, reducing the cooking time to about 15 minutes.

BREAKFAST MUESLI BREAD

Makes 1 extra-large loaf
Time 3–4 hours, depending on bread machine

1¼ cups (300 ml) apple juice
1 large egg, beaten
2 tbsp (30 ml) unsalted butter, softened
1½ tsp (7 ml) salt
2 tbsp (30 ml) milk powder
1 tsp (5 ml) pumpkin pie spice
1 cup (250 ml) fruit muesli, plus extra for sprinkling
3⅓ cups (825 ml) white bread flour
¼ cup (60 ml) light muscovado sugar
1¼ tsp (6 ml) fast-acting dried yeast
⅓ cup (75 ml) raisins
Milk, to brush

Lift the bread pan out of the machine and fit the blade. Put the ingredients, except the raisins, in the pan following the order specified in the manual.

Fit the pan into the machine and close the lid. Set to a 2-lb (1 kg) loaf size on the basic white program. Select your preferred crust setting. Add the raisins when the machine beeps.

Just before baking begins, brush the top of the dough lightly with milk and sprinkle with a little muesli. Close the lid gently.

At the end of the program, lift the pan out of the machine, loosen the bread with a spatula if necessary and shake it out onto a wire rack to cool.

For fresh blueberry conserve to accompany the bread, blend 1 tsp (5 ml) cornstarch with 1 tbsp (15 ml) water in a small saucepan. Add ⅓ cup + 2 tbsp (100 ml) apple or orange juice, 3 tbsp (45 ml) granulated or fruit sugar and ½ tsp (2 ml) vanilla extract. Heat gently, stirring, until slightly thickened. Tip in 7 oz (200 g) fresh or frozen blueberries and cook gently for 1 to 2 minutes, until the blueberries soften and start to burst. Serve warm or cold, spooned over the bread and topped with Greek yogurt.

RICH FRUIT TEA BREAD

Makes 1 extra-large loaf

Time 1½–2½ hours, depending on bread machine, plus
   shaping, proofing and baking

¾ cup (175 ml) strong black tea, cooled

1 egg, beaten

¼ cup (60 ml) unsalted butter, softened

½ tsp (2 ml) salt

Finely grated zest of 1 orange

1 tbsp (15 ml) pumpkin pie spice

3 cups (750 ml) white bread flour

⅓ cup (75 ml) dark muscovado sugar

1½ tsp (7 ml) fast-acting dried yeast

7 oz (200 g) luxury mixed dried fruit

3½ oz (100 g) ready-to-eat dried apricots, roughly
   chopped

3½ oz (100 g) Brazil nuts, chopped

Demerara sugar, for sprinkling

Lift the bread pan out of the machine and fit the blade. Put the ingredients, except the dried fruit and nuts, in the pan, following the order specified in the manual. Add the spice with the flour.

Fit the pan in the machine and close the lid. Set to the dough program, adding the dried fruits and nuts when the machine beeps.

At the end of the program, turn the dough out onto a floured surface and shape it into an oval. Grease a 2-lb (1 kg) loaf pan and drop the dough into the pan. Cover loosely with oiled plastic wrap and leave to rise in a warm place for 50 to 60 minutes or until almost doubled in size.

Sprinkle generously with demerara sugar and bake in a preheated 425°F (220°C) oven for 35 to 40 minutes, until risen and golden. Cover the top with foil if the surface starts to overbrown. Turn out of the pan and tap the base: it should sound hollow. If necessary, return to the oven (out of the pan) for a little longer.

For chunky fruit & nut loaf, put 1 egg, ¾ cup (175 ml) milk, ¼ cup (60 ml) very soft butter, 1 tbsp (15 ml) molasses, ½ tsp (2 ml) salt, 3 cups (750 ml) white bread flour, 1 tbsp (15 ml) pumpkin pie spice, ¼ cup (60 ml) dark muscovado sugar and 1¼ tsp (6 ml) fast-acting dried yeast in the bread pan, following the order specified in the manual. Set to the sweet program. Add 5 oz (150 g) luxury mixed dried fruit and 3 oz (75 g) roughly chopped almonds when the machine beeps. At the end of the program, shake the bread out onto a wire rack to cool.

WARM SEEDY ROLLS

Makes 12
Preparation time 1 hour 40 minutes, including resting time
Cooking time 15–20 minutes

2¼ tsp (11 ml) active dried yeast
1¼ cups (300 ml) warm water (not hot)
4 cups (1 L) all-purpose flour, plus extra for dusting
1 tsp (5 ml) salt, plus a pinch
2 tbsp (30 ml) butter, cut into cubes, plus extra for
    greasing
¼ cup (60 ml) sunflower seeds
2 tbsp (30 ml) poppy seeds
2 tbsp (30 ml) pumpkin seeds
1 egg yolk
1 tbsp (15 ml) water

Sprinkle the yeast over the warm water, stir well and set aside for 10 minutes, until it goes frothy. Sift the flour and salt into a large bowl and add the butter. Rub the butter into the flour until the mixture resembles fine breadcrumbs. Add all the seeds and stir. Make a well in the center and add the yeast mixture. Stir well with a wooden spoon, then use your hands to mix to a firm dough.

Knead for 5 minutes, until the dough feels firm, elastic and no longer sticky. Return to the bowl, cover with plastic wrap and set aside in a warm place for 30 minutes, until the dough has doubled in size.

Turn out the dough and knead again to knock out the air, then divide into 12 pieces. Knead each piece briefly, then form into a roll shape, or roll each piece into a long sausage shape and form into a loose knot. Place the rolls on a lightly greased baking sheet, cover with a clean tea towel and set aside in a warm place for 30 minutes, until almost doubled in size.

Mix the egg yolk in a small bowl with a pinch of salt and the water and brush over the rolls to glaze. Bake in a preheated 400°F (200°C) oven for 15 to 20 minutes, until golden and sounding hollow when tapped lightly on the bottom. Remove from the oven and allow to cool a little. Serve warm with soup.

For cheesy onion rolls, replace the seeds with 5 green onions, finely chopped and lightly cooked for just 1 minute in 1 tbsp (15 ml) olive oil. Once glazed, sprinkle with 3 tbsp (45 ml) freshly grated Parmesan cheese.

BAKED

WALNUT & HONEY BREAD

Makes 1 large loaf
Time 3½–5 hours, depending on bread machine

⅔ cup (150 ml) walnut pieces
1½ cups (350 ml) water
3 tbsp (45 ml) liquid honey, plus extra to drizzle
3 tbsp (45 ml) unsalted butter, softened
1½ tsp (7 ml) salt
2¾ cups (675 ml) whole wheat bread flour
1¼ cups (300 ml) white bread flour
1¼ tsp (6 ml) fast-acting dried yeast

Lightly toast the walnuts either in a frying pan over low heat or under the broiler.

Lift the bread pan out of the machine and fit the blade. Put the ingredients, except the walnuts, in the pan, following the order specified in the manual.

Fit the pan into the machine and close the lid. Set to a 1½-lb (750 g) loaf size on the whole wheat program. Select your preferred crust setting. Add the walnuts when the machine beeps.

At the end of the program, lift the pan out of the machine and shake the bread out onto a wire rack to cool. Serve drizzled with extra honey.

For mini pecan & maple loaves, lightly toast ⅔ cup (150 ml) roughly chopped pecan. Make the bread as above, using the pecans instead of the walnuts and replacing the honey with 3 tbsp (45 ml) maple syrup. Use the dough program, cut the dough into 8 pieces and press into 8 greased ¾-cup (175 ml) individual loaf tins. Cover loosely with oiled plastic wrap and leave to rise in a warm place for 30 minutes. Brush with a little maple syrup and bake in a preheated 425°F (220°C) oven for about 20 minutes, until well risen and golden. Serve drizzled with extra maple syrup.

GRANDMA'S ZUCCHINI LOAF

Serves 8–10
Preparation time 30 minutes
Cooking time about 1 hour 15 minutes

2¼ cups (550 ml) self-raising flour
1 tsp (5 ml) baking powder
2 tsp (10 ml) pumpkin pie spice
2 zucchini, grated
⅔ cup (150 ml) lightly packed brown sugar
1 egg
⅓ cup (75 ml) milk
⅓ cup (75 ml) butter, plus extra for greasing
½ cup (125 ml) raisins
½ cup (125 ml) chopped walnuts

Topping
¼ cup (60 ml) all-purpose flour
2 tbsp (30 ml) soft brown sugar
½ tsp (2 ml) pumpkin pie spice
¼ cup (60 ml) chilled butter, cut into cubes
⅓ cup (60 g) finely chopped walnuts

Grease a 2-lb (1 kg) loaf pan lightly with butter and line the bottom with parchment paper. Sift the flour, baking powder and pumpkin pie spice into a large bowl and add the zucchini and sugar. Stir well.

Beat the egg and milk together in a measuring cup. Melt the butter in a small pan, then add the raisins and stir well over low heat for a few seconds to help plump them up. Pour the melted butter and milk-and-egg mixture into the dry ingredients and stir until well combined. Add the walnuts and stir again. Transfer to the prepared pan and level.

Make the streusel topping. Mix the flour with the sugar and pumpkin pie spice, then rub the butter into the dry ingredients until the mixture resembles fine breadcrumbs. Stir in the walnuts, then scatter over the cake.

Bake the loaf in a preheated 350°F (180°C) oven for 1 hour to 1 hour 10 minutes, until well risen and firm to the touch and a skewer inserted comes out clean. Allow it to cool for 10 minutes in the pan before turning out onto a wire rack to cool completely.

For moist mango loaf, replace the zucchini, raisins and walnuts with ³/₄ cup + 2 tbsp (200 ml) mango purée, 1 tsp (5 ml) vanilla extract and ¹/₂ mango, roughly chopped, all folded into the wet mixture. Use the same streusel topping as above, but bake for 40 to 45 minutes, until firm and well risen.

COFFEE & WALNUT BREAD

Makes 1 large loaf
Time 2¾–3½ hours, depending on bread machine

2 tbsp (30 ml) espresso coffee powder
1 large egg, beaten
¼ cup (60 ml) unsalted butter, melted
¼ tsp (1 ml) salt
2¾ cups (675 ml) white bread flour
¼ cup (60 ml) light muscovado sugar
1¼ tsp (6 ml) fast-acting dried yeast
⅔ cup (150 ml) walnut pieces, lightly toasted

Blend the coffee with ²/₃ cup (150 ml) boiling water and leave to cool. Lift the bread pan out of the machine and fit the blade. Put the ingredients, except the walnuts, in the pan, following the order specified in the manual.

Fit the pan into the machine and close the lid. Set to a 1½-lb (750 g) loaf size on the sweet program (or basic if the machine doesn't have a sweet setting). Add the walnuts to the pan when the machine beeps.

At the end of the program, lift the pan out of the machine and shake the bread out onto a wire rack to cool.

For maple butter to spread over the freshly baked bread, whisk together 7 tbsp (105 ml) soft unsalted butter, ¹/₄ cup (60 ml) icing sugar and 1 tsp (5 ml) vanilla bean paste or vanilla extract until completely smooth. Beat in 5 tbsp (75 ml) maple syrup until combined. Turn into a small serving dish and chill until ready to serve.

ASIAN-STYLE FLATBREADS

Makes 8 breads

Time 1½–2½ hours, depending on bread machine,
   plus shaping, proofing and cooking

⅓ cup (75 ml) sesame seeds

1 cup (250 ml) water

1 clove garlic, chopped

2-inch (1.5 cm) piece fresh ginger, grated

¾ cup (175 ml) roughly chopped fresh coriander

2 tbsp (30 ml) toasted sesame oil

2 tsp (10 ml) salt

3½ cups (875 ml) white bread flour

1 tbsp (15 ml) granulated or fruit sugar

1¼ tsp (6 ml) fast-acting dried yeast

Put the sesame seeds in a food processor and grind until broken up. (The seeds won't grind to a powder.)

Lift the bread pan out of the machine and fit the blade. Put the ingredients in the pan, following the order specified in the manual. Add the seeds, garlic, ginger and coriander with the water.

Fit the pan into the machine and close the lid. Set to the dough program.

At the end of the program, turn the dough out onto a floured surface and divide it into 8 equal pieces. Roll out each piece into a circle 8 inches (20 cm) across. Leave the rounds on the floured surface, covered with a clean, dry dish towel, for 15 minutes.

Heat a large frying pan or grill pan, then reduce to the lowest setting. Place a piece of dough in the pan and cook for 3 to 4 minutes, turning once, until golden brown in places. Slide the bread onto a plate and cover with a clean, damp dish towel while you cook the rest.

For spicy chicken wraps, diagonally slice 1 bunch green onions. Thinly slice 2 celery stalks. Heat 3 tbsp (45 ml) vegetable oil in a large frying pan and fry the onions and celery for 2 minutes. Drain to a plate. Add 3 thinly sliced chicken breasts or chicken tenders to the pan and fry quickly, stirring, for about 5 minutes or until cooked through. Add ¼ cup (60 ml) sweet chili sauce and 2 tsp (10 ml) rice wine vinegar. Return the onions and celery to the pan and stir to mix. Spoon the filling across 4 of the wraps (the remainder can be chilled or frozen for another time) and scatter with pea shoots or soybean sprouts. Roll up and serve warm.

BAKED

TOMATO FOCACCIA

Makes 2 loaves

Time 1½–2½ hours, depending on bread machine, plus shaping, proofing and baking

Dough

1⅓ cups (325 ml) white bread flour

1 tsp (5 ml) granulated or fruit sugar

1 tsp (5 ml) salt

1½ tsp (7 ml) fast-acting dried yeast

3 tbsp (45 ml) olive oil

1 cup + 2 tbsp (275 ml) water

To finish

7 oz (200 g) cherry tomatoes

A few fresh rosemary sprigs

A few black olives

1 tsp (5 ml) salt flakes

3 tbsp (45 ml) olive oil, divided

Lift the bread pan out of the machine and fit the blade. Put the dough ingredients in the pan, following the order specified in the manual.

Fit the pan into the machine and close the lid. Set to the dough program.

At the end of the program, turn the dough out onto a floured surface and cut it in half. Press each into a rough oval a little larger than your hand.

Transfer the loaves to 2 greased baking sheets and use the end of a wooden spoon to make indentations over the surface. Press the tomatoes into some of the indentations; add small sprigs of rosemary and olives to some of the others. Sprinkle with salt flakes and leave, uncovered, for 20 minutes.

Drizzle the loaves with a little of the oil and bake in a preheated 400°F (200°C) oven for 15 minutes. Swap the shelf positions during cooking so that both loaves brown evenly. Drizzle with the remaining oil and serve warm or cold, torn into pieces.

For onion, sage & gorgonzola focaccia, make the dough as above, adding 1 tbsp (15 ml) chopped fresh sage with the flour. After shaping and making indentations, scatter the loaves with ½ small red onion, very finely sliced, and ½ cup (125 ml) crumbled Gorgonzola cheese. Drizzle with olive oil as above and scatter with small sage leaves halfway through baking.

CLASSIC
DESSERTS

RAINBOW TART

Serves 8
Preparation time 25 minutes
Cooking time 30 minutes

12-oz (375 g) package sweet pastry
2 egg yolks
3 tbsp (45 ml) cornstarch
3 tbsp (45 ml) granulated or fruit sugar
1¼ cups (300 ml) milk
1 tsp (5 ml) vanilla extract
1 large orange, segmented
6 oz (175 g) strawberries, halved
4 oz (125 g) blueberries
2 thick fresh pineapple rings, cut into bite-size chunks
2 kiwifruit, sliced
Icing sugar, to dust
Crème fraîche or plain yogurt, to serve

Line a 9-inch (23 cm) fluted flan pan with the pastry. Trim the edges, then press the pastry firmly into the grooves so the rim sits a little higher than the edges of the pan. Fill with scrunched-up parchment paper and baking beans, then bake in a preheated 350°F (180°C) oven for 15 minutes. Remove the paper and beans and bake for a further 5 minutes. Set aside to cool.

Mix the egg yolks, cornstarch and sugar in a bowl. Put the milk in a heavy-bottomed nonstick pan and bring to a boil. Pour over the egg mixture and blend well, using a balloon whisk. Add the vanilla extract, then return to the rinsed-out pan and bring to a boil, whisking continuously until boiled and thickened. Transfer to a bowl to cool, stirring occasionally. Cover with plastic wrap to prevent a skin forming.

Place the cooled pastry shell on a serving plate and fill with the custard, using a metal spoon to swirl up to the rim. Put the fruit in a bowl and toss to mix, then loosely arrange over the top of the custard. Dust with icing sugar and serve in wedges with spoonfuls of crème fraîche or yogurt.

For sunshine tart, mix 2 segmented oranges, 3 thick slices fresh pineapple, cut into chunks, 2 bananas, cut into chunks and tossed in 2 tbsp (30 ml) lemon or lime juice, and 1 small mango, cut into chunks. Toss together and use to fill as above.

FIG & HONEY POTS

Serves 4
Preparation time 10 minutes, plus chilling

6 ripe fresh figs, thinly sliced, plus 2 extra, cut into wedges, to decorate (optional)
1¾ cups (425 ml) Greek yogurt
¼ cup (60 ml) liquid honey
2 tbsp (30 ml) chopped pistachio nuts

Arrange the fig slices snugly in the bottom of 4 glasses or glass bowls. Spoon the yogurt over the figs and chill in the refrigerator for 10 to 15 minutes.

Just before serving, drizzle 1 tbsp (15 ml) honey over each dessert and sprinkle the pistachio nuts on top. Decorate with the wedges of fig, if desired.

For hot figs with honey, heat a grill pan, add 8 whole ripe fresh figs and cook for 8 minutes, turning occasionally, until charred on the outside. Alternatively, cook under a preheated broiler. Remove and cut in half. Divide between 4 plates, top each with a tablespoonful (15 ml) of Greek yogurt and drizzle with a little liquid honey.

CHOCOLATE, DATE & ALMOND PANINI

Serves 4
Preparation time 10 minutes, plus cooling
Cooking time 26–28 minutes

1 oz (25 g) whole blanched almonds
2 tbsp (30 ml) icing sugar
2½ oz (75 g) white chocolate, finely grated
8 soft dates, pitted and chopped
1 oz (25 g) flaked almonds, lightly toasted
8 slices brioche, buttered on both sides
¼ cup (60 ml) whipping (35%) cream, whipped

Put the blanched almonds in a colander and sprinkle with a little cold water. Shake off any excess water and place the almonds on a nonstick baking sheet. Sift the icing sugar over the top and bake in a preheated 350°F (180°C) oven for about 20 minutes, until they have crystallized.

Remove the almonds from the oven and set aside to cool, then put them in a freezer bag and tap lightly with a rolling pin until they are crushed but not powdery.

Mix together the grated white chocolate, dates and flaked almonds. Spoon the mixture onto 4 slices of the buttered brioche and top with the remaining slices to make 4 sandwiches.

Heat a grill pan or panini press over medium heat and cook the brioche sandwiches for 3 to 4 minutes. Turn them over and cook the other side for another 3 to 4 minutes to make a panini.

Cut the panini in half diagonally and serve immediately with whipped cream and sprinkled with the crushed almonds.

For eggy bread, substitute the brioche with sweet French toasts. Dip each French toast in a mixture of 2 eggs lightly beaten with ¼ cup (60 ml) milk. Fry in butter, turning, until golden on both sides. Omit the nuts and cream and serve with honey or syrup.

CLASSIC DESSERTS

FIGS WITH YOGURT & HONEY

Serves 4
Preparation time 5 minutes
Cooking time 10 minutes

8 ripe figs
¼ cup (60 ml) plain yogurt
2 tbsp (30 ml) liquid honey

Slice the figs in half and place on a hot grill pan, skin side down. Sear for 10 minutes, until the skins begin to blacken, then remove.

Arrange the figs on 4 plates and serve with a spoonful of yogurt and some honey spooned over the top.

For brioche French toasts with figs, yogurt & honey, brush 4 slices brioche with a mixture of ¼ cup (60 ml) melted butter and ¼ cup (60 ml) table (18%) or half-and-half (10%) cream and toast under a broiler. Top with figs, as above.

STRAWBERRY JELLIES

Serves 6
Preparation time 10 minutes, plus standing and chilling
Cooking time 5 minutes

14½ oz (450 g) strawberries, hulled, divided
½ cup (125 ml) granulated or fruit sugar
2 cups (500 ml) white grape juice, divided
2 packages (⅓ oz/10 g each) of powdered gelatin or 6
  gelatin leaves
⅓ cup (75 ml) crème de cassis (optional)

Roughly chop three-quarters of the strawberries and put them in a food processor or blender with 1¼ cups (300 ml) boiling water and the sugar. Blend until smooth, then pour the mixture into a sieve set over a bowl and stir to allow the liquid to drip through.

Pour ¾ cup + 2 tbsp (200 ml) of the grape juice into a heatproof bowl, sprinkle on the gelatin and allow to stand for 10 minutes. Place the bowl over a saucepan of simmering water and stir until the gelatin has dissolved. Leave to cool, then stir in the cassis (if using), strawberry liquid and the remaining grape juice.

Arrange the remaining strawberries in 6 large wineglasses, pour in the liquid and chill until the jelly has set.

For raspberry champagne jellies, substitute the strawberries with raspberries and omit the cassis. Dissolve the gelatin in only ⅓ cup + 2 tbsp (100 ml) grape juice and, when cool, stir in 1½ cups (400 ml) sparkling white wine. Finish as above.

MELON & PINEAPPLE SALAD

Serves 4
Preparation time 10 minutes

½ cantaloupe, peeled, seeded and diced
½ small pineapple, peeled, cored and diced
Finely grated zest of 1 lime
2 tsp (10 ml) granulated fructose
Quarter-slices of lime, to decorate

Put the melon and pineapple in a bowl or plastic storage box.

Mix together the lime zest and fructose until well combined. Sprinkle over the fruit and mix together well – in 1 hour or so, the fructose will have dissolved.

Decorate with the lime slices and serve.

For watermelon, pear & strawberry salad, cut ½ small watermelon into cubes and place in a plastic storage box. Toss with 2 peeled, cored and sliced pears and 6 oz (175 g) hulled and halved small strawberries. Mix with 3 tbsp (45 ml) orange juice and decorate with orange or clementine slices.

MULTICOLORED FRESH FRUIT POPSICLES

Serves 8
Preparation time 20 minutes, plus freezing
Cooking time 15 minutes

10 oz (300 g) fresh raspberries
1½ tsp (7 ml) granulated or fruit sugar
⅔ cup (150 ml) water, plus ¼ cup (60 ml)
14-oz (398 ml) can peaches in natural juice

Place the raspberries and sugar in a small pan with ¼ cup (60 ml) of the water and bring to a boil, stirring well until the sugar dissolves. Add the remaining water.

Put the raspberry liquid through a sieve, pressing down well with a metal spoon to make as much of the pulp go through as possible, only discarding the seeds.

Pour the mixture into 8 popsicle molds, filling just the bottom of each. (Try using 8 rinsed yogurt pots placed in a roasting pan. Cover with foil and push popsicle sticks through the foil into the center of each pot. The foil will help secure the stick in the center.) Freeze for 1 to 2 hours, until firm.

Meanwhile, put the peaches and juice into a food processor and mix until smooth. Once the raspberry base is firm, pour the peach liquid over the top of the raspberry mixture and freeze for a further 1 to 2 hours or overnight, until firm.

For yogurt peach melba popsicles, omit the sugar and water and mix together the raspberries, peaches and ⅔ cup (150 ml) raspberry-flavored drinking yogurt in a food processor. Divide between 8 popsicle molds and freeze for 4 to 5 hours, until firm.

PEACH & BLUEBERRY CRUNCH

Serves 4
Preparation time 8 minutes
Cooking time 8–10 minutes

¼ cup (60 ml) ground hazelnuts
¼ cup (60 ml) ground almonds
1½ tsp (7 ml) granulated or fruit sugar
¼ cup (60 ml) breadcrumbs
14-oz (398 ml) can peaches in natural juice
4 oz (125 g) blueberries
⅔ cup (150 ml) whipping (35%) cream
Seeds from 1 vanilla pod
1 tbsp (15 ml) icing sugar, sifted

Gently cook the ground nuts in a large frying pan with the sugar and breadcrumbs, stirring constantly until golden. Remove from the heat and leave to cool.

Put the peaches in a food processor or blender and blend with enough of the peach juice to make a thick, smooth purée.

Fold the blueberries gently into the purée and spoon into 4 glasses or individual serving dishes. Set aside some of the blueberries to decorate.

Whip the cream with the vanilla seeds and icing sugar until thick but not stiff and spoon evenly over the peach purée. When the crunchy topping is cool, sprinkle it overtop, top with the remaining blueberries and serve.

For apple & blackberry wafer crunch, peel 14½ oz (450 g) tart apples and cook with 2 to 3 tbsp (30 to 45 ml) sugar and 2 tbsp (30 ml) water. Purée apple mixture in a food processor or blender. Fold 4 oz (125 g) blackberries into the apple purée and continue as above, but instead of breadcrumbs, use crushed graham wafers. Use the same amount and toast in the same way, but reduce the sugar to 1 tbsp (15 ml).

MANGO & PASSION FRUIT FOOL

Serves 4
Preparation time 15 minutes, plus chilling

2 ripe mangoes, peeled and pitted
1 tbsp (15 ml) chopped fresh mint
Juice of ½ lime
1 cup (250 ml) whipping (35%) cream
1 cup (250 ml) Greek yogurt
2 passion fruit

Dice 1 mango and combine with the mint. Divide almost half the mango mixture between 4 small bowls, reserving a little for the topping.

Purée the remaining mango with the lime juice in a food processor or blender.

Beat the cream in a bowl until just holding soft peaks, then stir in the yogurt. Fold the cream mixture into the mango purée and swirl to marble.

Divide the mango-cream mixture between the bowls and top with the reserved diced mango. Halve the passion fruit, then scoop the seeds of each half over each fool. Chill in the refrigerator until ready to serve.

For peach & amaretti fool, use a 14-oz (398 ml) can peach halves, drained and diced, in place of the mango, mix with 2 tbsp (30 ml) toasted flaked almonds and divide between 4 small bowls. Follow the recipe as above until the final stage. Then omit the passion fruit and instead top each dessert with a roughly crushed amaretti cookie.

STRAWBERRY CHEESECAKE POTS

Serves 4
Preparation time 15 minutes, plus cooling and chilling
Cooking time 5 minutes

2 tbsp (30 ml) butter
5 graham wafers
6 oz (175 g) strawberries
2 tbsp (30 ml) superfine (fruit) sugar
8 oz (250 g) mascarpone cheese
¼ cup (60 ml) whipping (35%) cream
¼ cup (60 ml) icing sugar
Grated zest and juice of 1 lemon

Melt the butter in a small saucepan, then transfer to a food processor with the graham wafers and process to fine crumbs. Divide the mixture between 4 glasses and press into the bottom of each. Chill in the refrigerator.

Meanwhile, put the strawberries and superfine sugar in a saucepan and cook, stirring, for 2 to 3 minutes, then leave to cool. In a bowl, mix together the mascarpone, cream, icing sugar and lemon zest and juice.

Fill the glasses with the mascarpone mixture and top each with the strawberries. Chill for 2 to 3 hours before serving.

For ginger raspberry cheesecake pots, follow the recipe above, but use gingersnap cookies in place of the graham wafers, raspberries instead of strawberries and Greek yogurt in place of the mascarpone. Sprinkle the top of each dessert with 1 tsp (5 ml) chopped preserved ginger.

PINEAPPLE WITH LIME & CHILE SYRUP

Serves 4
Preparation time 10 minutes, plus cooling
Cooking time 10 minutes

½ cup (125 ml) granulated or fruit sugar
⅓ cup + 2 tbsp (100 ml) water
3 red chiles, finely chopped
Grated zest and juice of 1 lime
1 baby pineapple, halved or quartered, cored and cut
    into wafer-thin slices
Ice cream (optional)

Put the sugar in a saucepan with the water. Heat slowly until the sugar has dissolved, then add the chiles, bring to a boil and boil rapidly until the liquid becomes syrupy. Leave to cool.

Stir the lime zest and juice into the cooled syrup. Lay the pineapple slices on a plate and drizzle the syrup over. Serve chilled with a dollop of ice cream, if desired.

For pears with cinnamon syrup, peel 4 ripe pears, cut into quarters and remove the cores. Put in a saucepan, pour in water to cover and add the sugar as above, together with the grated zest and juice of 1 lemon, 1 cinnamon stick and 6 cloves. Simmer, turning occasionally, for 10 minutes or until tender. Remove the pears with a slotted spoon and set aside. Bring the liquid to a boil and boil rapidly until the liquid becomes syrupy. Leave to cool, then pour over the pears.

CLASSIC DESSERTS

HOT PEACH & CINNAMON PANCAKES

Makes 8
Preparation time 10 minutes
Cooking time 20 minutes

3 small ripe peaches
1 tsp (5 ml) ground cinnamon, divided
6 tbsp (90 ml) maple syrup
½ cup (125 ml) self-raising flour
2 tbsp (30 ml) light brown sugar
1 egg
⅔ cup (150 ml) milk
A little oil, for greasing

Halve and pit the peaches. Roughly chop 1 of them and set it aside, then cut the remaining 2 into wedges and toss with a small pinch of the ground cinnamon and all the maple syrup in a small bowl and set aside.

Sift the flour and remaining cinnamon into a bowl and add the sugar. Make a well in the center and set aside. Beat the egg and milk together well, then pour into the center of the flour mixture. Mix quickly and as lightly as possible to make a batter the consistency of thick cream. Stir in the chopped peach.

Lightly oil a heavy-bottomed frying pan or flat grill pan. Drop a heaped tbsp (15 ml) of the batter onto the pan surface and cook over a steady medium heat for 1 to 2 minutes, until bubbles rise to the surface and burst. Turn the pancake over and cook for a further 1 to 2 minutes. Remove from the pan and keep warm while making the remaining pancakes.

Serve the pancakes warm, with a large spoonful of the peach-and-maple-syrup mixture over the top of each.

For creamy banana pancakes, make the batter as above, replacing the chopped peach with 1 small banana, roughly chopped. Cook for 1 minute on each side, until golden, and serve with 1 thinly sliced banana tossed with 2 tbsp (30 ml) maple syrup over the top.

LEMON & ORANGE MOUSSE

Serves 4
Preparation time 15 minutes, plus chilling

1¼ cups (300 ml) whipping (35%) cream
Grated zest and juice of 1 lemon, plus extra finely pared
  strips of zest to decorate
Grated zest and juice of ½ orange, plus extra finely
  pared strips of zest to decorate
⅓ cup (75 ml) granulated or fruit sugar
2 egg whites

Whip together the cream, grated lemon and orange zest and sugar in a large bowl until the mixture starts to thicken. Add the lemon and orange juices and whisk again until the mixture thickens.

Whip, in a separate large, perfectly clean bowl, the egg whites until soft peaks form, then fold into the citrus mixture. Spoon the mousse into 4 glasses and chill in the refrigerator. Decorate with lemon and orange zest strips.

For raspberry mousse, purée 7 oz (200 g) raspberries in a food processor or blender, then pass through a fine sieve. In a large bowl, whip together the cream and sugar as above until the mixture starts to thicken, then add the sieved raspberry purée and whip again until thickened. Continue with the recipe as above, but decorate with whole raspberries and plain dark chocolate shavings, shaved from a bar using a swivel-bladed vegetable peeler.

CLASSIC DESSERTS

SOFT-COOKED BANANAS & YOGURT ICE

Serves 4
Preparation time 20 minutes, plus freezing
Cooking time 10 minutes

3 tbsp (45 ml) granulated or fruit sugar
⅔ cup (150 ml) water
4 cups (1 L) plain yogurt
1 tbsp (15 ml) vanilla extract
1 tbsp (15 ml) butter, softened
4 ripe bananas
½ tsp (2 ml) ground cinnamon or nutmeg (optional)

To serve
¼ cup (60 ml) maple syrup
⅓ cup (75 ml) broken pecans

Place the sugar and water in a heavy-bottomed saucepan and bring to a boil. Continue to boil for 3 to 5 minutes, until the syrup has reduced by half. Remove from the heat and stir in the yogurt and vanilla. Transfer to a freezerproof container and freeze for 3 hours.

Remove the ice from the freezer and beat with a wooden spoon until slushy. Freeze for a further 4 hours or overnight, until firm.

Heat the butter in a large nonstick frying pan. Halve the bananas lengthwise, then cut each of the halves in half again across its width. Sprinkle the bananas, cut side up, with the spice, if using, and cook in the hot butter for 30 to 60 seconds on each side, until golden. Remove from the pan using a slotted spoon.

Pile the bananas onto serving plates in a lattice pattern, then drizzle with the maple syrup and scatter with the pecans. Serve with scoops of the vanilla yogurt ice on top.

For strawberry yogurt ice to serve as an alternative accompaniment, make as above, replacing the plain yogurt with a strawberry yogurt. Cook 12 oz (375 g) halved strawberries with ½ tsp (2 ml) freshly grated orange zest and 1 tbsp (15 ml) maple syrup in the butter for 2 to 3 minutes, until soft yet retaining their shape. Serve the warm strawberries with the strawberry yogurt ice.

COCONUT SYLLABUB & ALMOND BRITTLE

Serves 4
Preparation time 15 minutes, plus cooling and chilling
Cooking time about 10 minutes

½ cup (125 ml) superfine sugar
½ cup (125 ml) flaked almonds, toasted

For the syllabub
¾ cup + 2 tbsp (200 ml) coconut cream
1¼ cups (300 ml) whipping (35%) cream
15 cardamom seeds, lightly crushed
2 tbsp (30 ml) granulated or fruit sugar

To make the brittle, put the granulated sugar and almonds in a saucepan over a low heat. While the sugar melts, lightly oil a baking sheet. When the sugar has melted and turned golden, pour the mixture onto the baking sheet and leave to cool.

To make the syllabub, pour the coconut cream and whipping cream into a large bowl. Add the crushed cardamom seeds and 2 tbsp (30 ml) superfine sugar, then lightly whip until just holding soft peaks.

Spoon the syllabub into 4 glasses and chill in the refrigerator. Meanwhile, lightly crack the brittle into irregular shards. When ready to serve, top the syllabub with some of the brittle and serve the remainder separately on the side.

For lemon syllabub, put the grated zest and juice of 1 lemon in a bowl with ½ cup (125 ml) white wine and 2½ tbsp (37 ml) superfine sugar. Cover and leave to soak for about 1 hour. Whip 1¼ cups (300 ml) whipping cream until it forms soft peaks, then gradually add the wine mixture and continue whipping until it holds its shape. In a separate, perfectly clean bowl, whisk 1 egg white until stiff, then whisk in 2½ tbsp (37 ml) superfine sugar. Carefully fold into the cream mixture and spoon into 4 glasses. Chill in the refrigerator before serving.

SPIDER'S WEB PANCAKES

Serves 8
Preparation time 15 minutes
Cooking time 15–20 minutes

2 eggs
1¼ cups (300 ml) all-purpose flour
1 tsp (5 ml) granulated or fruit sugar
1¼ cups (300 ml) milk
1 tbsp (15 ml) butter, melted
1¼ cups (300 ml) whipping (35%) cream
1 tbsp (15 ml) liquid honey
8 oz (250 g) raspberries
Vegetable oil, for frying
Icing sugar, to dust

Whisk the eggs, flour and sugar in a bowl until well combined, then whisk in the milk until you have a smooth batter. Whisk in the melted butter, then set the batter aside.

Whip the cream very lightly until just beginning to peak, then fold in the honey and raspberries and chill while making the pancakes.

Heat a few drops of oil in a small nonstick frying pan. Transfer the batter to a jug with a narrow spout and pour a very thin stream of the batter, starting in the center of the pan and continuing in continuous circles around, then across the pan, to form a small web pattern about 6 inches (15 cm) in diameter. Cook for about 1 minute, until set, then, using a metal spatula, flip the pancake over and cook the other side for 30 seconds. Repeat to make 8 pancakes, stacking them between sheets of wax or parchment paper to keep warm.

Serve the warm pancakes filled with a little raspberry cream and dusted with icing sugar.

For apple & cinnamon spider's web pancakes, place 2 large peeled, cored and roughly chopped tart apples in a pan with 3 tbsp (45 ml) sultanas, 3 tbsp (45 ml) water, ½ tsp (2 ml) ground cinnamon and 2 tbsp (30 ml) brown sugar. Cook over low heat for 3 to 5 minutes, stirring continuously, until soft and pulpy. Remove from the heat and allow to cool. Serve folded into the cream as above, replacing the raspberries, or fill the pancakes with the apple mixture alone and serve with yogurt.

QUICK WHITE CHOCOLATE MOUSSE

Serves 4
Preparation time 5 minutes, plus chilling
Cooking time 10 minutes

½ cup (125 ml) granulated or fruit sugar
⅓ to ½ cup (75 to 125 ml) shelled pistachios
7 oz (200 g) white chocolate, chopped
1 cup + 2 tbsp (280 ml) whipping (35%) cream

Dissolve the sugar with ¼ cup (60 ml) water in a small pan over low heat. Increase the heat and boil until it begins to caramelize. Tip in the pistachios and stir, then pour the mixture onto some wax paper on a baking sheet and leave to set.

Put the white chocolate in a heatproof bowl. Heat the cream in a pan until it reaches boiling point, then remove from the heat and pour directly over the chocolate, stirring constantly until it has melted. Refrigerate until cold, then beat with a handheld electric beater until thick.

Spoon the cold white chocolate mixture into serving dishes, decorate with broken shards of the pistachio praline and serve.

For dark chocolate & orange mousse, substitute the white chocolate with plain dark chocolate, add ¼ tsp (1 ml) orange extract to the melted chocolate and use chopped walnuts instead of pistachios in the praline.

STAR-OF-THE-DAY DESSERT

Serves 6
Preparation time 20 minutes, plus chilling
Cooking time 3 minutes

4 oz (125 g) ready-to-eat prunes, roughly chopped
⅔ cup (150 ml) water
4 oz (125 g) plain dark chocolate (70% cocoa solids),
  broken into pieces
2 cups (500 ml) plain yogurt
1 oz (25 g) milk or plain dark chocolate, made into
  shavings, to decorate

Place the prunes in a pan with the water and bring to a boil. Immediately remove from the heat, transfer to a food processor and mix until completely smooth.

Return the prune purée to the pan with the chocolate pieces and heat over very low heat, stirring continuously, until the chocolate has melted. Remove from the heat and beat in the yogurt. Allow to cool.

Divide the dessert between 4 serving glasses and decorate with the chocolate shavings. Chill for about 30 minutes and serve.

For minted chocolate star-of-the-day dessert, use a mint-flavored chocolate (70% cocoa solids), dust the tops with a little organic cocoa powder and serve with mint-chocolate sticks for a real treat.

BLUEBERRY & PEACH CLAFOUTI

Serves 4
Preparation time 20 minutes
Cooking time 40 minutes

3 eggs
1¼ cups (300 ml) all-purpose flour
1 cup (250 ml) icing sugar, plus extra to dust
1¼ cups (300 ml) milk
1 tsp (5 ml) vanilla extract
1 tbsp (15 ml) butter, softened
2 peaches, halved, pitted and cut into wedges
4 oz (125 g) blueberries
Finely grated zest of 1 lemon

Beat the eggs, flour, sugar, milk and vanilla extract in a bowl until thick and creamy. Heavily grease an 8-inch (20 cm) round tin or ovenproof dish with the butter and arrange the peaches and blueberries inside. Sprinkle the lemon zest over.

Pour the batter over the fruit and bake in a preheated 375°F (190°C) oven for 35 minutes, until the batter is firm.

Dust with icing sugar and serve warm in wedges.

For strawberry, banana & cherry clafouti, replace the peaches and blueberries with 1 large banana, sliced into chunks, 6 oz (175 g) strawberries and 4 oz (125 g) pitted fresh cherries. Try adding 1 tsp (5 ml) ground cinnamon to the fruit and toss, if desired.

CLASSIC DESSERTS

BERRIED TREASURES

Serves 4
Preparation time 15 minutes
Cooking time 2 minutes

4 oz (125 g) white chocolate, at room temperature,
  divided
2 tbsp (30 ml) milk
⅔ cup (150 ml) whipping (35%) cream
5 oz (150 g) blackberries
1 tbsp (15 ml) liquid honey
1 egg white

Break off a quarter of the white chocolate. Using a potato peeler, shave off some chocolate curls to decorate the desserts.

Place the remaining pieces of chocolate in a small heatproof bowl. Add the milk and microwave on full power for 2 minutes. Leave to stand for 1 minute, then stir. If lumps remain in the chocolate, microwave again for a further 30 seconds, until melted. (Alternatively, put the chocolate and milk in a small heatproof bowl and rest it over a small saucepan of gently simmering water.) Stir in the cream and pour into a cool bowl, allow to cool completely, then put in the freezer for 5 minutes.

Reserve 4 blackberries and blend the remainder in a food processor with the honey until puréed. Turn into a fine-meshed sieve over a bowl and press the purée through with the back of a large spoon to extract the seeds.

Whisk the egg white until it stands in soft peaks when the whisk is lifted from the bowl.

Remove the chocolate cream from the freezer and whisk until it starts to thicken. This might take a few minutes. Gently stir in the egg white.

Spoon half the chocolate mixture into 4 small serving dishes or cups and spoon on the fruit purée. Top with the remaining chocolate mixture and give each a light stir with the handle end of a small spoon so you can see a swirl of the blackberry purée. Decorate with the reserved berries and chocolate curls and chill until ready to serve.

TOFFEE PEACHES

Serves 4
Preparation time 10 minutes
Cooking time 15 minutes

4 peaches, halved and pitted
½ cup (125 ml) ground almonds

Sauce
⅔ cup (150 ml) lightly packed brown sugar
5 tbsp (75 ml) maple syrup
2 tbsp (30 ml) butter
⅔ cup (150 ml) table (18%) or half-and-half (10%)
  cream

Cut four 8-inch (20 cm) square pieces of foil and place 2 peach halves on each. Sprinkle on the ground almonds. Scrunch up the foil to form 4 parcels and place under a preheated medium broiler for 5 to 8 minutes, turning once or twice during cooking, until the peaches are soft.

Meanwhile, make the sauce. Place the sugar, maple syrup and butter in a nonstick saucepan over medium-low heat until the sugar dissolves. Stir continuously until the sauce boils and thickens, which should take about 3 minutes. Add the cream and return to a boil, then immediately remove from the heat.

Drizzle the sauce over the peaches and serve.

For toffee apples, place 4 halved apples in sheets of foil and divide 1 tbsp (15 ml) butter between them in cubes, dotting over the top. Sprinkle with a little ground cinnamon and broil for 10 to 12 minutes, until the apples have softened, yet still retain their shape. Serve with the sauce as above.

374

DRUNKEN ORANGE SLICES

Serves 4
Preparation time 10 minutes
Cooking time 12 minutes

4 large sweet oranges
¼ cup (60 ml) brown sugar
3 tbsp (45 ml) Cointreau, divided
2 tbsp (30 ml) whisky
Juice of 1 small orange
1 vanilla pod, split
1 cinnamon stick
4 cloves
2 to 3 blades of mace (optional)
Ginger ice cream, to serve

Cut off the base and the top of each orange. Cut down around the curve of the orange to remove all the skin and pith, leaving just the orange flesh. Cut the flesh horizontally into ½-inch (1 cm) slices and set aside.

Heat ¼ cup (60 ml) water gently with the sugar, 2 tbsp (30 ml) of the Cointreau, the whisky, orange juice, vanilla pod, cinnamon stick, cloves and mace (if using) until the sugar has dissolved. Increase the heat and boil rapidly for 5 minutes. Allow to cool slightly but keep warm.

Heat a grill pan over high heat and quickly cook the orange slices for about 1 minute on each side, until caramelized. Top with the remaining Cointreau and set alight. Once the flames have died down, arrange the orange slices on serving dishes and drizzle with the orange syrup.

Serve the orange slices immediately with some ginger ice cream.

For non-alcoholic orange slices, slice 6 oranges as above and arrange them in a dish. Cut away the pith from the skin and finely slice the zest. Put it in a saucepan with just enough water to cover. Bring to a boil, then immediately refresh in cold water. Place the zest in a clean pan, cover with water and simmer for 25 minutes. Dissolve ¾ cup (175 ml) granulated or fruit sugar in ⅔ cup (150 ml) water, boil for a few minutes and stir in 2 tbsp (30 ml) lemon juice. Add the drained zest and pour over the sliced oranges. Chill, then serve with ice cream.

SUGARED FRUIT PANCAKES

Makes 20–24
Preparation time 15 minutes
Cooking time 10 minutes

2 eggs
2 tbsp (30 ml) unsalted butter
⅓ cup + 2 tbsp (100 ml) milk
¾ cup (175 ml) all-purpose flour
1 tsp (5 ml) baking powder
2 tbsp (30 ml) vanilla or superfine sugar, divided
4 oz (125 g) blueberries
Cooking oil, for frying

Separate the eggs into 2 bowls, egg yolks in one and egg whites in another. Put the butter in a heatproof bowl and heat in the microwave for 30 seconds, until melted. Add the milk and pour the mixture over the egg yolks, stirring well.

Put the flour, baking powder and 1 tbsp (15 ml) of the sugar in a large bowl. Add the milk mixture and whisk well to make a smooth batter. Stir in the blueberries.

Whisk the egg whites until they form firm peaks. Using a large metal spoon, gently fold the whites into the batter until well mixed.

Heat a little oil in a large frying pan for 1 minute. Add a large spoonful of the batter to one side of the pan so it spreads to make a little cake. Add 2 to 3 more spoonfuls, depending on the size of the pan, so the pancakes can cook without touching. When the pancakes are golden on the underside (check by lifting with a palette knife or metal spatula), flip them over and cook again until golden. Remove the pancakes from the pan and transfer to a serving plate, then keep them warm while you cook the remainder.

Sprinkle with the remaining sugar and serve.

For vanilla & fig pancakes, add 1 tsp (5 ml) vanilla extract to the milk in the pancakes, omit the blueberries and make as above. Cut 3 small figs into wedges and place in a pan with 1 tbsp (15 ml) unsalted butter and 3 tbsp (45 ml) maple syrup and heat for 2 minutes, stirring until soft. Spoon over the warm pancakes and serve with yogurt.

PAPAYA & LIME SALAD

Serves 4
Preparation time 15 minutes
Cooking time 3–5 minutes

3 firm, ripe papayas
2 limes
2 tsp (10 ml) light brown sugar
½ cup (125 ml) blanched almonds, toasted
Lime wedges, to garnish

Cut the papayas in half; scoop out the seeds and discard. Peel the halves, roughly dice the flesh and place in a bowl.

Finely grate the zest of both limes, then squeeze one of the limes and reserve the juice. Cut the pith off the second lime and segment the flesh over the bowl of diced papaya to catch the juice. Add the lime segments and grated zest to the papaya.

Pour the reserved lime juice into a small saucepan with the sugar and heat gently until the sugar has dissolved. Remove from the heat and leave to cool.

Pour the cooled lime juice over the fruit and toss thoroughly. Add the toasted almonds and serve with lime wedges.

For papaya & lime yogurt, use 1 papaya and 1 lime. Prepare the papaya as above, omitting the lime segments and syrup. Chop the almonds. Mix with 1⅔ cup (400 ml) thick Greek yogurt and serve for breakfast with muesli or as a simple dessert, topped with granola. It is also very good as a topping for waffles.

ICED CHOCOLATE MOUSSES

Serves 6
Preparation time 30 minutes, plus cooling and freezing
Cooking time 10 minutes

8 oz (250 g) plain dark chocolate
1 tbsp (15 ml) unsalted butter
2 tbsp (30 ml) liquid glucose
3 tbsp (45 ml) fresh orange juice
3 eggs, separated
¾ cup + 2 tbsp (200 ml) whipping (35%) cream

Make chocolate curls by paring the underside of the block of chocolate with a swivel-bladed vegetable peeler. If the curls are very small, microwave the chocolate in 10-second bursts on full power (or place in a warm oven) until the chocolate is soft enough to shape. When you have enough curls to decorate 6 mousses, break the remainder into pieces – you should have 7 oz (200 g) – and melt.

Stir the butter and glucose into the chocolate, then mix in the orange juice. Stir the egg yolks one by one into the mixture, until smooth. Take off the heat and leave to cool.

Whisk the egg whites until softly peaking. Whip the cream until it forms soft swirls. Fold the cream, then the egg whites, into the chocolate mix. Pour the mixture into 6 coffee cups or ramekin dishes.

Freeze for 4 hours or overnight, until firm. Decorate the tops with chocolate curls.

For chilled chocolate & coffee mousses, omit the chocolate curls and instead melt 7 oz (200 g) plain dark chocolate, then add 1 tbsp (15 ml) butter (omit the liquid glucose), 3 tbsp (45 ml) strong black coffee and 3 egg yolks. Fold in 3 whisked egg whites, then pour the mixture into 4 small dishes or glasses and chill in the refrigerator for 4 hours, until set. Whip ½ cup (125 ml) whipping (35%) cream until it forms soft swirls, then fold in 2 tbsp (30 ml) coffee cream liqueur, if desired. Spoon onto the tops of the mousses and decorate with a little sifted cocoa powder.

BAKED LEMON CUSTARDS

Serves 4
Preparation time 10 minutes, plus infusing
Cooking time about 1 hour

12 bay leaves, bruised
2 tbsp (30 ml) finely grated lemon zest
⅓ cup + 2 tbsp (100 ml) whipping (35%) cream
4 eggs, plus 1 egg yolk
⅔ cup (150 ml) granulated or fruit sugar
⅓ cup + 2 tbsp (100 ml) lemon juice

Put the bay leaves, lemon zest and cream in a small saucepan and heat gently until it reaches boiling point. Remove immediately from the heat and set aside for 2 hours to infuse.

Whisk together the eggs, egg yolk and sugar until the mixture is pale and creamy, then whisk in the lemon juice. Strain the cream mixture through a fine sieve into the egg mixture and stir until combined. Set aside 4 bay leaves for decoration.

Pour the custard into 4 individual ramekins and place on a baking sheet. Cook in a preheated 250°F (120°C) oven for 50 minutes or until the custards are almost set in the middle. Leave to stand until cold, then chill until required. Allow to return to room temperature before serving, decorated with the reserved bay leaves.

For plain baked custard, mix 1 tbsp (15 ml) granulated or fruit sugar with 1 egg, ⅔ cup (150 ml) warm milk and a pinch of salt. Use the mixture to fill 1 flan shell or 12 small pastry shells made from 8 oz (250 g) short-crust pastry, pricked and baked blind in a preheated 400°F (200°C) oven for 20 to 25 minutes. Sprinkle on grated nutmeg and bake in a pre-heated 400°F (200°C) oven for about 20 minutes.

CHOCOLATE OVERLOAD

Serves 4
Preparation time 8 minutes

8 chocolate cream sandwich cookies, crushed
2 tbsp (30 ml) butter, melted
2 cups (500 ml) softened chocolate cookie ice cream
2 tbsp (30 ml) runny caramel or dulce de leche
   (optional)
White chocolate shavings, to decorate
Milk chocolate shavings, to decorate

Mix the crushed cookies with the melted butter and press firmly into the bottom of 4 dessert dishes.

Scoop the ice cream over top of the base. Drizzle with the caramel or spoon over the dulce de leche (if using) and decorate with white and milk chocolate shavings. Serve immediately.

For chocolate sundaes with raspberries, replace the cookies with 20 mini meringues and omit the butter. Layer the ice cream, meringues and 7 oz (200 g) raspberries in glasses. Drizzle with table (18%) or half-and-half (10%) cream and top with grated chocolate.

HOT CARIBBEAN FRUIT SALAD

Serves 4
Preparation time 15 minutes
Cooking time 6–7 minutes

¼ cup (60 ml) unsalted butter
¼ cup (60 ml) light muscovado sugar
1 large papaya, halved, seeded, peeled and sliced
1 large mango, pitted, peeled and sliced
½ pineapple, cored, peeled and cut into chunks
14-oz (400 ml) can full-fat coconut milk
Grated zest and juice of 1 lime

Heat the butter in a large frying pan, add the sugar and heat gently until just dissolved. Add all the fruit and cook for 2 minutes, then pour in the coconut milk, half the lime zest and all the juice.

Heat gently for 4 to 5 minutes, then serve warm in shallow bowls, sprinkled with the remaining lime zest.

For flamed Caribbean fruit salad, omit the coconut milk and add 3 tbsp (45 ml) dark or white rum. When the rum is bubbling, light with a long match and stand well back. When the flames have subsided, add the lime zest and juice and serve with scoops of vanilla ice cream.

CROISSANTS WITH CHESTNUT CREAM

Serves 4
Preparation time 15 minutes
Cooking time 2–3 minutes

⅓ cup (75 ml) unsalted butter, melted
4 day-old croissants, split in half horizontally
4 tsp (20 ml) muscovado sugar
½ cup (125 ml) sweetened chestnut purée
½ cup (125 ml) mascarpone cheese
2 tbsp (30 ml) plain yogurt
1 tbsp (15 ml) liquid honey, plus extra for drizzling

To serve
Chopped marrons glacés (optional)
Crushed chocolate-covered coffee beans (optional)

Brush the melted butter over the cut sides of the croissants, then sprinkle them with the sugar. Set aside.

Beat the chestnut purée with the mascarpone, yogurt and honey until smooth.

Heat a grill pan over low heat and cook the croissants gently, cut side down, for 2 to 3 minutes, until hot and golden.

Transfer the croissants to serving plates, top with some of the chestnut cream and drizzle with a little extra honey. Sprinkle with a few chopped marrons glacés or crushed chocolate-covered coffee beans, if desired, and serve immediately.

For chocolate cream to serve as an alternative to chestnut cream, substitute the chestnut purée with ¼ cup (60 ml) chocolate spread and mix with the mascarpone and yogurt. Omit the honey. After cooking the croissants, spread them with apricot conserve and then with the chocolate cream.

WHITE CHOC & RASPBERRY TIRAMISU

Serves 6
Preparation time 20 minutes

1 tbsp (15 ml) instant coffee
7 tbsp (105 ml) icing sugar, divided
1 cup (250 ml) boiling water
12 ladyfingers, about 3½ oz (100 g)
8 oz (250 g) mascarpone cheese
⅔ cup (150 ml) whipping (35%) cream
3 tbsp (45 ml) kirsch (optional)
8 oz (250 g) fresh raspberries, divided
3 oz (75 g) white chocolate, diced, divided

Put the coffee and ¼ cup (60 ml) of the icing sugar into a shallow dish, then pour on the boiling water and mix until dissolved. Dip 6 ladyfingers, one at a time, into the coffee mixture, then crumble into the bottom of 6 glass tumblers.

Put the mascarpone into a bowl with the remaining icing sugar, then gradually whisk in the cream until smooth. Stir in the kirsch, if using, then divide half the mixture between the glasses.

Break up half the raspberries over the top of the mascarpone in the glasses, then sprinkle with half the chocolate. Dip the remaining ladyfingers in the coffee mix, crumble and add to the glasses. Then add the rest of the mascarpone and the remaining raspberries, this time left whole, finishing with a sprinkling of white chocolate. Serve immediately or chill until required.

For classic tiramisu, omit the raspberries and white chocolate from the layers. Mix the mascarpone with the cream and 3 tbsp (45 ml) Kahlúa coffee liqueur or brandy, then layer in one large glass dish with the coffee-dipped ladyfingers and 3 oz (75 g) diced plain dark chocolate.

BLOOD ORANGE SORBET

Serves 4–6
Preparation time 25 minutes, plus chilling and freezing
Cooking time about 20 minutes

1 cup (250 ml) granulated or fruit sugar
Pared zest of 2 blood oranges
1¼ cups (300 ml) blood orange juice
Chilled Campari (optional)
Orange zest, to decorate

Heat the sugar over low heat in a small saucepan with 1 cup (250 ml) water, stirring occasionally, until completely dissolved.

Add the orange zest and increase the heat. Without stirring, boil the syrup for about 12 minutes and then set aside to cool completely.

When it is cold, strain the sugar syrup over the orange juice and stir together. Refrigerate for about 2 hours, until really cold.

Pour the chilled orange syrup into an ice cream machine and churn for about 10 minutes. When the sorbet is almost frozen, scrape it into a plastic container and put it in the freezer compartment for a further hour, until completely frozen. Alternatively, pour the chilled orange syrup into a shallow metal container and put it in the freezer for 2 hours. Remove and whisk with a handheld electric beater or balloon whisk, breaking up all the ice crystals. Return it to the freezer and repeat this process every hour or so until frozen.

Serve scoops of sorbet with a splash of chilled Campari, if desired, and decorate with thin strips of orange zest.

For papaya & lime sorbet, dissolve ½ cup (125 ml) superfine sugar in ⅔ cup (150 ml) water. Boil for 5 minutes, then set aside to cool. Seed, peel and dice the flesh of 1 ripe papaya. Process the papaya with the cooled sugar syrup. Stir in the grated zest and juice of 2 limes, chill and proceed as above.

SUMMER FRUIT CRUNCH

Serves 4–6
Preparation time 10 minutes
Cooking time 20 minutes

⅔ cup (150 ml) rolled oats
½ tsp (2 ml) ground cinnamon
½ tsp (2 ml) pumpkin pie spice
Pinch of ground ginger
1 tbsp (15 ml) butter, melted
1 tbsp (15 ml) liquid honey
2 tbsp (30 ml) sultanas
13 oz (400 g) mixed fresh or frozen summer fruits
6 tbsp (90 ml) icing sugar, plus extra to garnish
2 tbsp (30 ml) crème de cassis
½ tsp (2 ml) vanilla extract
1 tbsp (15 ml) flaked almonds, toasted, to garnish

Mix the oats and spices with the melted butter and honey until well combined.

Press onto a baking sheet and cook in a preheated 350°F (180°C) oven for 20 minutes, turning once. Remove and leave to cool before mixing in the sultanas.

Meanwhile, put the summer fruits in a pan with the icing sugar and 1 tbsp (15 ml) water. Warm over medium-low heat, stirring occasionally, until the fruit begins to collapse. Remove from the heat and stir in the crème de cassis and vanilla extract.

Spoon the fruit into dishes and sprinkle on the crunchy topping. Garnish with the toasted almonds and a sprinkling of icing sugar. Serve immediately.

For autumn plum crunch, pit and quarter 1 lb (500 g) plums and use instead of the summer fruits. Cook the plums in ⅓ cup + 2 tbsp (100 ml) apple juice until just tender. Substitute the crème de cassis with sloe gin. Spoon into dishes and finish as above.

MUFFIN TRIFLE WITH BOOZY BERRIES

Serves 4
Preparation time 15 minutes

13 oz (400 g) fresh mixed berries, such as
   strawberries, red currants and raspberries, plus extra
   to decorate
3 tbsp (45 ml) crème de cerises or cherry brandy
1 tbsp (15 ml) maple syrup
2 large blueberry muffins, sliced
⅔ cup (150 ml) whipping (35%) cream, whipped to
   soft peaks

Put the fruit in a bowl and use the back of a fork to crush it with the cherry liqueur or brandy and maple syrup until well combined.

Arrange the sliced muffins in the bottom of a glass dish. Spoon on the fruit and top with the whipped cream. Decorate with the extra berries and serve.

For Black Forest trifle, slice 1 chocolate Swiss roll and arrange in the bottom of a glass dish. Substitute the mixed berries with pitted black cherries. Scrape the seeds of a vanilla pod into the cream before whipping. Finish as above.

APPLE & SULTANA POT

Serves 4
Preparation time 15 minutes
Cooking time 15–23 minutes

2 lapsang souchong tea bags
1 tbsp (15 ml) liquid honey
3 tbsp (45 ml) sultanas
3 apples, peeled, cored and diced
½ tsp (2 ml) pumpkin pie spice
2 tbsp (30 ml) dark brown sugar
2 tbsp (30 ml) unsalted butter
⅔ cup (150 ml) whipping (35%) cream, whipped to
   soft peaks
Superfine sugar, as required
Gingersnaps, to serve

Make a strong infusion of tea using the tea bags in ⅓ cup + 2 tbsp (100 ml) boiling water. Stir in the honey and sultanas and set aside to infuse.

Put the apples in a saucepan with the pumpkin pie spice, brown sugar and butter. Remove the tea bags from the infusion and pour the liquid over the apples.

Cover and cook over medium-low heat, stirring frequently, for 15 to 20 minutes, until the apples start to collapse. Crush to a chunky purée.

Stir the cream into the apple purée until well combined, then spoon the mixture into 4 individual ovenproof dishes.

Sprinkle the surface generously with superfine sugar, then place the dishes under a hot broiler until the sugar begins to caramelize. Serve warm or cold with gingersnaps.

For raspberry & rose water pots with ground almonds, use the back of a fork to lightly crush 8 oz (250 g) fresh raspberries with 2 tbsp (30 ml) honey. Stir in 1 tbsp (15 ml) rose water and 3 tbsp (45 ml) ground almonds. Spoon into 4 ramekin dishes and top each one with a generous tbsp (15 ml) whipped cream before sprinkling with superfine sugar and caramelizing as above.

CHOCOLATE ICE CREAM

Serves 4
Preparation time 20 minutes, plus cooling and freezing
Cooking time 10 minutes

1¼ cups (300 ml) whipping (35%) cream
2 tbsp (30 ml) milk
6 tbsp (90 ml) icing sugar, sifted
½ tsp (2 ml) vanilla extract
4 oz (125 g) good-quality plain dark chocolate, broken
    into pieces
2 tbsp (30 ml) table (18%) or half-and-half (10%)
    cream

Chocolate sauce (optional)
⅔ cup (150 ml) water
3 tbsp (45 ml) granulated or fruit sugar
5 oz (150 g) plain dark chocolate, broken into pieces

Put the whipping cream and milk in a bowl and whisk until just stiff. Stir in the icing sugar and vanilla extract. Pour the mixture into a shallow freezer container and freeze for 30 minutes or until the ice cream begins to set around the edges. (This ice cream cannot be made in an ice cream machine.)

Melt the chocolate together with the table cream over a pan of gently simmering water. Stir until smooth, then set aside to cool.

Remove the ice cream from the freezer and spoon into a bowl. Add the melted chocolate and quickly stir it through the ice cream with a fork. Return the ice cream to the freezer container, cover and freeze until set. Transfer the ice cream to the refrigerator 30 minutes before serving, to soften slightly.

Heat all the ingredients for the chocolate sauce, if making, gently in a saucepan, stirring until melted. Serve immediately with scoops of the ice cream.

For chocolate double-mint ice cream, make the ice cream as above, adding 2 tbsp (30 ml) chopped fresh mint and ¾ oz (20 g) crushed peppermint candies to the whipped cream and milk. Freeze as above, then stir in the melted dark chocolate mix.

FRESH MELON SORBET

Serves 4–6
Preparation time 15 minutes, plus freezing

1 cantaloupe, weighing 2 lb (1 kg)
6 tbsp (90 ml) icing sugar
Juice of 1 lime or small lemon
1 egg white

Cut the melon in half and scoop out and discard the seeds. Scoop out the melon flesh with a spoon and discard the shells.

Place the flesh in a food processor or blender with the icing sugar and lime or lemon juice and process to a purée. (Alternatively, rub through a sieve.) Pour into a freezer container, cover and freeze for 2 to 3 hours. If using an ice cream machine, purée, then pour into the machine, churn and freeze until half-frozen.

Whisk the melon mixture to break up the ice crystals. Then whisk the egg white until stiff and whisk it into the half-frozen melon mixture. Return to the freezer until firm. Alternatively, add whisked egg white to the ice cream machine and churn until very thick.

Transfer the sorbet to the fridge 20 minutes before serving to soften slightly or scoop straight from the ice cream machine. Scoop the sorbet into glass dishes to serve. To make different-colored sorbets, make up 3 batches of sorbet using a cantaloupe in one and honeydew melon and watermelon in the others.

For gingered melon sorbet, peel and finely grate a 1-inch (2.5 cm) piece of fresh ginger, then stir into the melon purée. Scoop into small glasses and drizzle each glass with 1 tbsp (15 ml) ginger wine.

PISTACHIO & YOGURT SEMIFREDDO

Serves 6
Preparation time 40 minutes, plus cooling and freezing
Cooking time 10–15 minutes

4 eggs, separated
¾ cup (175 ml) granulated or fruit sugar, divided
Grated zest of 1 lemon
1½ tsp (7 ml) rose water (optional)
¾ cup + 2 tbsp (200 ml) Greek yogurt
½ fresh pineapple, sliced, halved and cored

Pistachio brittle
⅔ cup (150 ml) granulated sugar
6 tbsp (90 ml) water
⅔ cup (150 ml) roughly chopped pistachio nuts

Make the brittle. Heat the sugar and water in a frying pan until it dissolves, stirring gently from time to time. Add the nuts, then increase the heat and boil the syrup for 5 minutes, without stirring, until pale golden. Quickly tip the mixture onto a greased baking sheet and leave to cool. Break the brittle in half, then crush half in a plastic bag with a rolling pin.

Whisk the egg whites until very stiff, then gradually whisk in half the sugar until thick and glossy. Whisk the egg yolks in a second bowl with the remaining sugar until very thick and pale and the mixture leaves a trail. Fold in the lemon zest and rose water, if using, then the yogurt and crushed brittle, then the egg whites. Pour into a plastic box and freeze for 4 to 5 hours, until semi-frozen and firm enough to scoop.

Cook the pineapple slices on a hot barbecue or preheated grill pan for 6 to 8 minutes, turning once or twice, until browned. Divide between the serving plates, top with spoonfuls of semifreddo and decorate with broken pieces of the remaining brittle.

For rocky road ice cream, make the brittle with almonds, hazelnuts and pecans instead of pistachios. Whisk the egg whites, then the eggs and sugar, as for the semifreddo, then fold ½ cup (125 ml) ready-made custard and ⅔ cup (150 ml) whipped cream into the yolks with the crushed brittle. Fold in the egg whites as above, then freeze. Serve scooped into glasses with wafer cookies.

NUTTY CINNAMON RISOTTO

Serves 4
Preparation time 5 minutes
Cooking time 25 minutes

⅓ cup (75 ml) pecans
⅓ cup (75 ml) hazelnuts
¼ cup (60 ml) butter
½ cup (125 ml) risotto rice
5 tsp (25 ml) brown sugar,
1 tsp (5 ml) ground cinnamon
2⅓ cups (575 ml) hot milk

Heat a frying pan over medium heat and dry-fry the nuts until golden. Remove and set aside.

Melt the butter in a medium saucepan, add the rice and cook, stirring, for 1 minute.

Stir 4 tsp (20 ml) of the sugar and the cinnamon into the hot milk, then start adding the milk to the rice, adding a little more once each addition has been absorbed. This should take about 20 minutes, when the rice should be soft but still with a little bite.

Spoon the risotto into serving bowls.

Blitz the nuts in a food processor with the remaining 1 tsp (5 ml) sugar, then sprinkle the mix over top the risotto. Serve immediately.

For apricot, citrus & almond risotto, replace the pecans with ½ cup (125 ml) chopped ready-to-eat dried apricots, and the hazelnuts with ⅔ cup (150 ml) toasted almonds and 2 tbsp (30 ml) chopped Italian mixed peel.

HONEYED BANANA ICE CREAM

Serves 4–6
Preparation time 15 minutes, plus freezing and setting

1 lb (500 g) bananas, about 4 medium
2 tbsp (30 ml) lemon juice
3 tbsp (45 ml) thick honey
⅔ cup (150 ml) plain yogurt
⅔ cup (150 ml) chopped nuts
⅔ cup (150 ml) whipping (35%) cream
2 egg whites

Praline
¼ cup (60 ml) water
¾ cup (175 ml) granulated or fruit sugar
2 tbsp (30 ml) corn syrup
1¼ cups (300 ml) toasted almonds

Put the bananas in a bowl with the lemon juice and mash until smooth. Stir in the honey, followed by the yogurt and nuts, and beat well. Place the banana mix and the cream in an ice cream machine. Churn and freeze following the manufacturer's instructions until half-frozen. Alternatively, whisk the cream until it forms soft swirls, then fold into the banana mix and freeze in a plastic container for 3 to 4 hours, until partially frozen.

Whisk the egg whites lightly until they form soft peaks. Add to the ice cream machine and continue to churn and freeze until completely frozen. Alternatively, break up the ice cream in the plastic container with a fork, then fold in the whisked egg white and freeze until firm.

Make the praline. Pour the water into a heavy saucepan and add the sugar and syrup. Simmer gently until the sugar has dissolved, then cook to a caramel-colored syrup. Place the toasted almonds on a lightly greased piece of foil and pour the syrup over. Leave to set for 1 hour. Once set, break up into irregular pieces and serve with the ice cream.

For honeyed banana ice cream with sticky glazed bananas, make the ice cream as above. When ready to serve, heat 2 tbsp (30 ml) unsalted butter in a frying pan, add 3 thickly sliced bananas and fry until just beginning to soften. Sprinkle on 3 tbsp (45 ml) light muscovado sugar and cook until dissolved and the bananas are browning around the edges. Add the grated zest and juice of 1 lime, cook for 1 minute, then serve with the ice cream.

PINK GRAPEFRUIT PARFAIT

Serves 4
Preparation time 15 minutes

2 pink grapefruit
5 tbsp (75 ml) dark brown sugar, divided, plus extra for sprinkling
1 cup (250 ml) whipping (35%) cream
¾ cup (175 ml) Greek yogurt
3 tbsp (45 ml) elderflower cordial
½ tsp (2 ml) ground ginger
½ tsp (2 ml) ground cinnamon
Brandy snaps (optional)

Finely grate the zest of 1 grapefruit, making sure you don't get any of the bitter white pith. Cut the skin and the white membrane off both grapefruit and cut between the membranes to separate the segments. Put them in a large dish, sprinkle with 2 tbsp (30 ml) of the sugar and set aside.

Whisk together the cream and yogurt until thick but not stiff.

Fold in the elderflower cordial, spices, grapefruit zest and remaining sugar until smooth. Pour the mixture into attractive glasses, arranging the grapefruit segments between layers of cream mixture.

Sprinkle the top with sugar and serve immediately with brandy snaps, if desired.

For orange & black currant parfait, replace the grapefruit with segments from 3 oranges and the elderflower cordial with black currant cordial or crème de cassis. Omit the ground ginger and serve sprinkled with chocolate shavings.

CHERRY ALMOND ICE CREAM

Serves 6
Preparation time 20 minutes, plus cooling and freezing
Cooking time 20 minutes

⅔ cup (150 ml) milk
½ cup (125 ml) ground almonds
1 egg
1 egg yolk
⅓ cup (75 ml) granulated or fruit sugar
2 to 3 drops almond extract
1 lb (500 g) red cherries, pitted, or cherry compote
¼ cup (60 ml) slivered almonds
⅔ cup (150 ml) whipping (35%) cream

Pour the milk into a small saucepan and stir in the ground almonds. Bring to a boil, then set aside.

Put the egg and the yolk into a heatproof bowl with the sugar and beat until pale and thick. Pour in the milk-and-almond mixture. Place the bowl over a pan of gently simmering water and stir until thick. Stir in the almond extract and leave to cool.

Purée the cherries in a food processor or blender (or use cherry compote), then stir into the custard.

Toss the slivered almonds in a heavy pan over low heat to toast them. Leave to cool.

Whip the cream until it forms soft peaks. Fold the whipped cream into the cherry mixture.

Transfer the mixture to a freezer container, cover and freeze until firm, beating twice at hourly intervals. Stir the slivered almonds into the mixture at the last beating. (If using an ice cream machine, pour the cherry mixture into the machine, add the cream, churn and freeze. Once frozen, fold through the slivered almonds.) Serve the ice cream in individual glasses.

For strawberry & coconut ice cream, soak 1 cup (250 ml) shredded coconut in ⅔ cup (150 ml) hot milk. Mix egg and egg yolk with sugar and make into custard as above, omitting the almond extract. When cold, fold in 500 g (1 lb) puréed strawberries and ⅔ cup (150 ml) whipped cream. Freeze as above. Serve with extra strawberries.

SWEET CHESTNUT MESS

Serves 4
Preparation time 15 minutes

8 oz (250 g) fromage frais, low-fat cream cheese or ricotta
1 tbsp (15 ml) icing sugar, sifted
3½ oz (100 g) sweetened chestnut purée
3½ oz (100 g) meringues, crushed
Dark chocolate shards cut from a bar, to decorate

Beat the fromage frais with the icing sugar. Stir in half the chestnut purée and the crushed meringues.

Spoon the remaining chestnut purée into individual serving dishes and top with the meringue mess. Decorate with the dark chocolate shards and serve.

For sweet chestnut pancakes, stir the chestnut purée into the fromage frais. Heat 8 ready-made pancakes according to the instructions on the package and spread them with the chestnut purée mix. Roll them up and sprinkle with cocoa and icing sugar.

ORCHARD FRUIT CRUMBLE

Serves 6
Preparation time 20 minutes
Cooking time 30–35 minutes

2 apples
2 pears
13 oz (400 g) red plums, quartered and pitted
2 tbsp (30 ml) water
1/3 cup (75 ml) granulated or fruit sugar, divided
3/4 cup + 2 tbsp (200 ml) all-purpose flour
1/4 cup (60 ml) unsalted butter, diced
1 cup (250 ml) shredded coconut
1/3 cup (75 ml) milk chocolate chips

Quarter, core and peel the apples and pears. Slice the quarters and add the slices to a 4 1/2-cup (1.2 L) baking dish. Add the plums and the water, then sprinkle with 2 tbsp (30 ml) of the sugar. Cover the dish with foil and bake in a preheated 350°F (180°C) oven for 10 minutes.

Put the remaining sugar in a bowl with the flour and butter, then rub the butter in with your fingertips or an electric mixer until the mixture resembles fine crumbs. Stir in the coconut and chocolate chips.

Remove the foil from the fruit and spoon the crumble over the top. Bake for 20 to 25 minutes, until golden brown and the fruit is tender. Serve warm with custard or cream.

For plum & orange crumble, put 1 1/2 lb (750 g) plums, quartered and pitted, into a 4 1/2-cup (1.2 L) baking dish with 1/4 cup (60 ml) granulated or fruit sugar. Make the crumble as above, adding the grated zest of 1 small orange and 1/2 cup (125 ml) ground almonds instead of the coconut and chocolate chips. Bake as above.

PASSION FRUIT YOGURT FOOL

Serves 4
Preparation time 8 minutes

6 passion fruit, halved, flesh and seeds removed
1 1/4 cups (300 ml) Greek yogurt
1 tbsp (15 ml) liquid honey
3/4 cup + 2 tbsp (200 ml) whipping cream, whipped to soft peaks
4 pieces of shortbread, to serve

Stir the passion fruit flesh and seeds into the yogurt with the honey.

Fold the cream into the yogurt. Spoon into tall glasses and serve with the shortbread.

For mango & lime yogurt fool, omit the passion fruit, instead puréeing 1 large, ripe peeled and pitted mango with the zest of 1 lime and icing sugar to taste. Mix into the yogurt and fold in the cream. Omit the honey.

JAM ROLY-POLY

Serves 6
Preparation time 25 minutes
Cooking time 2 hours

2½ cups (625 ml) self-raising flour
1 tsp (5 ml) baking powder
1 cup (250 ml) shredded vegetable suet or vegetable
  shortening
⅓ cup (75 ml) granulated or fruit sugar
¾ cup (175 ml) fresh breadcrumbs
Finely grated zest of 1 lemon
Finely grated zest of 1 orange
1 egg, beaten
¾ cup (175 ml) milk
6 tbsp (90 ml) raspberry jam
5 oz (150 g) frozen raspberries, just defrosted

Put the flour, baking powder, suet and sugar in a bowl, then stir in the breadcrumbs and fruit zest. Add the egg, then gradually mix in enough milk to make a soft but not sticky dough.

Knead lightly, then roll out into a 12-inch (30 cm) square. Spread with the jam, leaving a 1-inch (2.5 cm) border, then sprinkle the raspberries on top. Brush the border with a little milk, then roll up the pastry. Wrap loosely in a large piece of wax or parchment paper, twisting the edges together and leaving a little space for the pudding to rise, then wrap loosely in foil.

Put on a roasting rack set over a large roasting pan, then pour boiling water into the pan but not up to the roasting rack. Cover the pan with foil and twist over the edges to seal well, then bake in a preheated 300°F (150°C) oven for 2 hours, until the pudding is well risen. Check once or twice during baking and top up the water level if needed.

Transfer the pudding to a chopping board using a dish towel. Unwrap, cut into thick slices and serve with hot custard sauce.

For spotted dick, warm 3 tbsp (45 ml) orange juice or rum in a small saucepan, add 1 cup (250 ml) raisins, 1 tsp (5 ml) ground ginger and ¼ tsp (1 ml) grated nutmeg and leave to soak for 1 hour or longer. Add to the flour mix just before adding the egg and milk. Shape into a long sausage, wrap in paper and foil and steam in the oven as above. Serve sliced with custard, flavored with a little extra rum, if desired.

SUMMER BERRY SPONGE

Serves 6–8
Preparation time 30 minutes, plus cooling
Cooking time 10–12 minutes

4 eggs
½ cup (125 ml) granulated or fruit sugar
¾ cup + 2 tbsp (200 ml) all-purpose flour
Finely grated zest and 2 tbsp (30 ml) juice of 1 lemon
⅔ cup (150 ml) whipping (35%) cream
½ cup (125 ml) fromage frais, low-fat cream cheese or
  ricotta
3 tbsp (45 ml) lemon curd
1 lb (500 g) small strawberries, halved
5 oz (150 g) blueberries
¼ cup (60 ml) red currant jelly
1 tbsp (15 ml) water (or lemon juice)

Whisk the eggs and sugar in a large bowl until very thick and the mixture leaves a trail when lifted. Sift the flour over the surface of the eggs, then fold in very gently. Add the lemon zest and juice and fold in until just mixed. Pour the mixture into a greased, floured 10-inch (25 cm) flan or tart pan, tilting the pan to ease into an even layer.

Bake in a preheated 350°F (180°C) oven for 10 to 12 minutes, until the top of the sponge is golden and the center springs back when lightly pressed. Cool the sponge in the pan for 5 to 10 minutes, then carefully turn it out onto a wire rack to cool.

Whip the cream until it forms soft swirls, then fold in the fromage frais and lemon curd. Transfer the sponge to a serving plate, spoon the cream into the center, spread into an even layer, then top with the strawberries and blueberries. Warm the red currant jelly in a small saucepan with the water (or lemon juice), then brush over the fruit.

For strawberry sponge with Pimm's, make the sponge as above, then fill with 1¼ cups (300 ml) whipped cream flavored with the grated zest of ½ orange. Top with 500 g (1 lb) sliced strawberries and 5 oz (150 g) raspberries that have been soaked in 3 tbsp (45 ml) undiluted Pimm's and 2 tbsp (30 ml) granulated or fruit sugar for 30 minutes.

CHOCO BREAD & BUTTER PUDDING

Serves 4
Preparation time 20 minutes, plus standing
Cooking time 25 minutes

4 chocolate croissants
¼ cup (60 ml) unsalted butter
3 tbsp (45 ml) granulated or fruit sugar
¼ tsp (1 ml) pumpkin pie spice
1¼ cups (300 ml) milk
4 eggs
1 tsp (5 ml) vanilla extract
Icing sugar, to decorate

Grease a 4½-cup (1.2 L) shallow, round ovenproof pie dish. Slice the croissants thickly and spread the butter over one side of each cut face of croissant. Stand the croissant slices upright and close together in the dish to completely fill it.

Mix the sugar and spice together, then spoon over the croissants and between the gaps. Stand the dish in a large roasting pan.

Beat the milk, eggs and vanilla extract together, then strain into the dish. Leave to stand for 15 minutes.

Pour hot water from the tap into the roasting pan to come halfway up the sides of the pie dish. Bake in a preheated 350°F (180°C) oven for about 25 minutes, until the pudding is golden and the custard just set.

Lift the dish out of the roasting pan, dust with sifted icing sugar and serve the pudding warm with a little cream.

For fruited bread & butter pudding, lightly butter 8 slices of white bread, cut into triangles and arrange in slightly overlapping layers in the dish, sprinkling with 3 oz (75 g) luxury dried fruit between the layers. Add the sugar as above, but omit the pumpkin pie spice. Mix the eggs, milk and vanilla, pour over the bread, then continue as above.

VANILLA CRÈME BRÛLÉE

Serves 6
Preparation time 20 minutes, plus standing and chilling
Cooking time 25–30 minutes

1 vanilla pod
2⅓ cups (575 ml) whipping (35%) cream
8 egg yolks
⅓ cup (75 ml) superfine sugar
3 tbsp (45 ml) icing sugar

Slit the vanilla pod lengthwise and place it in a saucepan. Pour the cream into the pan, then bring almost to a boil. Take off the heat and allow to stand for 15 minutes. Lift the pod out of the cream and, holding it against the side of the saucepan, scrape the black seeds into the cream. Discard the rest of the pod.

Use a fork to mix together the egg yolks and superfine sugar in a bowl. Reheat the cream, then gradually mix it into the eggs and sugar. Strain the mixture back into the saucepan.

Place 6 ovenproof ramekins in a roasting pan, then divide the custard between them. Pour warm water around the dishes to come halfway up the sides, then bake in a preheated 350°F (180°C) oven for 20 to 25 minutes, until the custard is just set with a slight softness at the center.

Leave the dishes to cool in the water, then lift them out and chill in the refrigerator for 3 to 4 hours. About 25 minutes before serving, sprinkle with the icing sugar and caramelize using a blowtorch (or under a hot broiler), then leave at room temperature.

For amaretto brûlée, omit the vanilla pod. Mix the egg yolks and sugar as above, bring the cream almost to a boil, then immediately mix into the egg yolks, adding ½ cup (125 ml) amaretto liqueur. Strain and continue as above. When chilled, sprinkle with 2 tbsp (30 ml) flaked almonds, then the sugar, and caramelize as above.

STICKY TOFFEE PUDDINGS

Makes 8
Preparation time 20 minutes
Cooking time 45–50 minutes

4 oz (125 g) pitted chopped dried dates
²⁄₃ cup (150 ml) water
½ cup (125 ml) unsalted butter, softened
½ cup (125 ml) granulated or fruit sugar
1 tsp (5 ml) vanilla extract
3 eggs
1⅓ cups (325 ml) self-raising flour
1 tsp (5 ml) baking powder

Toffee sauce
1¼ cups (300 ml) whipping (35%) cream, divided
²⁄₃ cup (150 ml) light brown sugar
¼ cup (60 ml) unsalted butter

Put the dates in a small pan with the water and simmer gently for 5 minutes, until the dates are soft and pulpy. Blend to a purée, then allow to cool.

Make the sauce. Heat half the cream in a small heavy-bottomed pan with the brown sugar and butter until the sugar dissolves. Bring to a boil, then let the sauce bubble for about 5 minutes, until a rich, dark caramel. Stir in the remaining cream and set aside.

Grease 8 metal ³⁄₄ cup + 2 tbsp (200 ml) pudding molds or custard cups and line the bottoms with parchment paper. Beat the butter, sugar, vanilla extract, eggs, flour and baking powder in a bowl for 1 to 2 minutes, until pale and creamy. Stir the date purée into the pudding mixture.

Divide the mixture among the molds. Level the tops and place in a roasting pan. Pour boiling water to a depth of ³⁄₄ inch (1.5 cm) in the pan and cover with foil. Bake in a preheated 350°F (180°C) oven for 35 to 40 minutes or until risen and firm to the touch.

Leave the puddings in the molds while you reheat the sauce, then loosen the edges and invert the puddings onto serving plates. Cover with sauce and serve with cream or ice cream, if desired.

For gingered figgy puddings, cook 4 oz (125 g) diced dried figs in the water in place of the dates. Make the sauce and puddings as above, adding 2 tbsp (30 ml) chopped candied ginger to the beaten pudding mix.

TUILE BASKETS & STRAWBERRY CREAM

Serves 6
Preparation time 40 minutes
Cooking time 15–18 minutes

2 egg whites
6 tbsp (90 ml) superfine sugar
¼ cup (60 ml) unsalted butter, melted
Few drops vanilla extract
¼ cup (60 ml) all-purpose flour
2 oranges, for shaping

Strawberry cream
1 cup (250 ml) whipping (35%) cream
¼ cup (60 ml) icing sugar, plus extra for dusting,
   divided
2 tbsp (30 ml) chopped fresh mint, plus extra leaves to
   decorate
8 oz (250 g) strawberries, halved or sliced, depending
   on size

Put the egg whites in a bowl and break up with a fork. Stir in the superfine sugar, then the butter and vanilla extract. Sift in the flour and mix until smooth.

Drop 1 heaped tbsp (15 ml) of the mixture onto a baking sheet lined with parchment paper. Drop a second spoonful well apart from the first, then spread each into a thin circle about 5 inches (13 cm) in diameter. Bake in a preheated 375°F (190°C) oven for 5 to 6 minutes, until just beginning to brown around the edges.

Add 2 more spoonfuls to a second paper-lined baking sheet and spread thinly. Remove the baked tuiles from the oven and put the second tray in. Allow the cooked tuiles to firm up for 5 to 10 seconds, then carefully lift them off the paper one at a time and drape each over an orange. Pinch the edges into pleats and leave to harden for 2 to 3 minutes, then carefully ease off the oranges. Repeat until 6 tuiles have been made.

Whip the cream lightly, then fold in half the icing sugar, the chopped mint and the strawberries, reserving 6 strawberry halves for decoration. Spoon into the tuiles, then top with the mint leaves and the strawberry halves. Dust with sifted icing sugar.

For fruit salad baskets, make the tuiles as above and fill with 7 oz (200 g) sliced strawberries, 5 oz (150 g) halved seedless ruby grapes, 2 kiwifruit, peeled, halved and sliced, and 2 small ripe peaches. Top with Greek yogurt and a drizzle of honey.

CRANBERRY EVE'S PUDDING

Serves 6
Preparation time 25 minutes
Cooking time 40–50 minutes

1½ lb (750 g) tart apples, quartered, cored, peeled and
   thickly sliced
4 oz (125 g) frozen cranberries
⅓ cup (75 ml) granulated or fruit sugar
1 tbsp (15 ml) water
Icing sugar, for dusting

Topping
½ cup (125 ml) unsalted butter, at room temperature,
   or soft margarine
½ cup (125 ml) granulated or fruit sugar
1 cup (250 ml) self-raising flour
2 eggs
Grated zest of 1 small orange, plus 2 tbsp (30 ml)
   of the juice

Put the apples and cranberries into a 6-cup (1.5 L), 2-inch (5 cm) deep ovenproof dish and sprinkle over the sugar and water. Cook, uncovered, in a preheated 350°F (180°C) oven for 10 minutes.

Put the butter, sugar, flour and eggs for the topping in a bowl and beat together until smooth. Stir in the orange zest and juice.

Spoon the mixture over the partially cooked fruit and spread into an even layer. Return to the oven and cook for 30 to 40 minutes, until the topping is golden and the center springs back when pressed with a fingertip. Dust with sifted icing sugar and serve warm with custard or cream.

For apple & blackberry pudding, omit the cranberries and add 4 oz (125 g) frozen blackberries. Make the topping as above, but add the grated zest of 1 lemon and 2 tbsp (30 ml) of the juice instead of the orange zest and juice.

GINGERED PINEAPPLE TRIFLE

Serves 4–5
Preparation time 20 minutes

7 oz (200 g) Jamaican ginger cake, diced
½ fresh pineapple, sliced, cored, peeled and diced
Grated zest, divided, and segmented flesh of 1 orange
2 kiwifruit, peeled, halved and sliced
3 tbsp (45 ml) rum
14-oz (425 g) can or carton custard
1¼ cups (300 ml) whipping (35%) cream
Grated zest of 1 lime, divided

Arrange the ginger cake in an even layer in the bottom of a 5-cup (1.2 L) glass serving dish. Spoon the pineapple, orange segments and kiwifruit on top and drizzle with the rum. Pour the custard over the fruit and spread into an even layer.

Whip the cream in a bowl until it forms soft swirls, then fold in half the orange zest and half the lime zest. Spoon the cream over the custard, then sprinkle with the remaining fruit zest. Chill until ready to serve.

For raspberry & peach trifle, dice 4 trifle sponges or slices of pound cake and arrange in the bottom of a glass dish instead of the ginger cake. Add 5 oz (150 g) fresh raspberries and the diced flesh of 2 ripe peaches. Drizzle with 3 tbsp (45 ml) dry sherry, then cover with custard as above. Whip the cream and flavor with the grated zest of 1 lemon, spoon it over the custard and sprinkle with 2 tbsp (30 ml) toasted flaked almonds.

DOUBLE CHOCOLATE PUDDINGS

Serves 6
Preparation time 25 minutes
Cooking time 18–20 minutes

½ cup (125 ml) unsalted butter, at room temperature,
  or soft margarine
⅔ cup (150 ml) light muscovado sugar
¾ cup (175 ml) self-raising flour
2 tbsp (30 ml) unsweetened cocoa powder
2 eggs
3 oz (75 g) plain dark chocolate
3½ oz (100 g) white chocolate, broken into pieces
⅔ cup (150 ml) whipping (35%) cream
¼ tsp (1 ml) vanilla extract

Put the butter or margarine, sugar, flour, cocoa and eggs into a mixing bowl or food processor and beat together until smooth. Divide the mixture between 6 greased sections of a deep muffin pan, then press squares of dark chocolate into each, covering with the pudding mixture.

Bake in a preheated 350°F (180°C) oven for 18 to 20 minutes, until well risen and slightly crusty around the edges and the center springs back when pressed with a fingertip.

Meanwhile, warm the white chocolate, cream and vanilla extract together in a small saucepan, stirring until the chocolate has completely melted.

Loosen the edges of the baked puddings with a round-bladed knife, then turn out and transfer to shallow serving bowls. Drizzle with the white chocolate cream and serve immediately.

For walnut & chocolate puddings, omit the cocoa powder from the puddings and mix the butter, sugar and eggs with 1 cup (250 ml) self-raising flour, ½ cup (125 ml) roughly chopped walnuts and 2 tsp (10 ml) instant coffee dissolved in 1 tbsp (15 ml) boiling water. Spoon into the muffin pan and press the chocolate squares into the center of each one as above. Bake as above and serve with table (10%) cream.

HOT BRIOCHE WITH CHOCOLATE SAUCE

Serves 4
Preparation time 5 minutes
Cooking time 12 minutes

3½ oz (100 g) plain dark chocolate
1 tbsp (15 ml) corn syrup
½ cup (125 ml) butter, divided
¼ cup (60 ml) whipping (35%) cream
4 thick slices brioche
½ cup (125 ml) demerara sugar
4 scoops vanilla or praline ice cream
2 tbsp (30 ml) flaked almonds, lightly toasted

Put the chocolate in a small saucepan with the syrup, 2 tbsp (30 ml) of the butter and the cream and heat, stirring occasionally, until shiny and melted.

Meanwhile, melt the remaining butter and brush it over the brioche slices. Sprinkle the sugar over.

Heat a large frying pan over low heat and cook the brioche slices in the pan for 3 to 4 minutes on each side, until golden and crispy.

Serve hot with a scoop of ice cream, the warm chocolate sauce and a scattering of nuts.

For quick ice cream brioche, serve 4 individual brioches cut in half and arranged on 4 dessert plates with a scoop of chocolate ice cream, whipped cream and a scattering of roughly chopped chocolate chips.

INDEX

INDEX

399

INDEX

ACKNOWLEDGMENTS

ACKNOWLEDGMENTS

Picture acknowledgments

Octopus Publishing Group/Stephen Conroy 2-3, 4-5, 23, 24, 25, 33, 35, 35, 37, 41, 43, 56, 61, 63, 67, 68, 75, 84, 93, 96-97, 109, 111, 129, 133, 135, 182-183, 185, 186, 195, 196, 197, 199, 200, 201, 203, 207, 208, 209, 213, 214, 215, 218, 219, 222, 223, 229, 230, 231, 235, 239, 244, 245, 256, 257, 315, 319, 320, 333, 338, 355, 356-357, 365, 366, 371, 383, 385; /Vanessa Davies 307, 326; /Gus Filgate 57, 60, 248; /Will Heap 312-313, 377, 384, 388, 393; /William Lingwood 40; /David Munns 17, 19, 85, 92, 115, 116, 117, 191; /Lis Parsons 1, 8-9, 11, 12, 18, 27, 28, 29, 52-53, 55, 64, 65, 69, 71, 79, 81, 88, 89, 99, 105, 106, 110, 121, 124, 125, 134, 139, 142-143, 145, 149, 154, 155, 157, 158, 159, 162, 163, 165, 166, 167, 171, 175, 179, 187, 226-227, 238, 243, 253, 259, 263, 264, 265, 267, 268-269, 271, 272, 273, 277, 278, 279, 283, 284, 285, 289, 290, 291, 295, 296, 297, 300, 301, 303, 308, 309, 325, 327, 331, 332, 359, 367, 372, 373; /Gareth Sambidge 13, 107, 249, 360, 361, 392; /William Shaw 48, 49, 337, 339, 342, 343, 345, 349, 350, 351, 354; /Ian Wallace 321.

Executive Editor Eleanor Maxfield
Managing Editor Clare Churly
Creative Director Tracy Killick
Design Janis Utton
Picture Library Manager Jennifer Veall
Senior Production Controller Carolin Stransky